World Crisis and Underdevelopment
A Critical Theory of Poverty, Agency, and Coercion

World Crisis and Underdevelopment examines the impact of poverty and other global crises in generating forms of structural coercion that cause agential and societal underdevelopment. It draws from discourse ethics and recognition theory in criticizing injustices and pathologies associated with underdevelopment. Its scope is comprehensive, encompassing discussions about development science, philosophical anthropology, global migration, global capitalism and economic markets, human rights, international legal institutions, democratic politics and legitimation, world religions and secularization, and moral philosophy in its many varieties.

David Ingram is Professor of Philosophy at Loyola University, Chicago. He received his Ph.D. from the University of California at San Diego in 1980, where he received his first exposure to critical theory. He is the author of several books. His book *Reason, History, and Politics* (1995) was awarded the Alpha Sigma Nu Prize in 1997. His life can be read from these pages as well: he has organized boycotts on behalf of the United Farm Workers Union, accompanied Loyola's students on their journey of awakening to Central America and the Caribbean, worked with Guatemalan refugees and community organizers in Chicago, and learned about the possibilities and limits of development while visiting the slums of Kibera with aid providers. He received Casa Guatemala's Human Rights Award in 1998 for sponsoring Guatemalan speakers to visit Loyola.

World Crisis and Underdevelopment

A Critical Theory of Poverty, Agency, and Coercion

DAVID INGRAM

Loyola University, Chicago

CAMBRIDGE
UNIVERSITY PRESS

CAMBRIDGE
UNIVERSITY PRESS

University Printing House, Cambridge CB2 8BS, United Kingdom

One Liberty Plaza, 20th Floor, New York, NY 10006, USA

477 Williamstown Road, Port Melbourne, VIC 3207, Australia

314–321, 3rd Floor, Plot 3, Splendor Forum, Jasola District Centre,
New Delhi –110025, India

79 Anson Road, #06–04/06, Singapore 079906

Cambridge University Press is part of the University of Cambridge.

It furthers the University's mission by disseminating knowledge in the pursuit of
education, learning, and research at the highest international levels of excellence.

www.cambridge.org
Information on this title: www.cambridge.org/9781108421812
DOI: 10.1017/9781108377874

First published 2018

Printed in the United States of America by Sheridan Books Inc.

A catalogue record for this publication is available from the British Library.

ISBN 978-1-108-42181-2 Hardback

Cambridge University Press has no responsibility for the persistence or accuracy of
URLs for external or third-party internet websites referred to in this publication
and does not guarantee that any content on such websites is, or will remain,
accurate or appropriate.

To my family: past, present, and future

"It is only for the sake of those without hope that hope is given us."

"Nur um der Hoffnungslosen willen ist uns die Hoffnung gegeben."

Walter Benjamin (concluding sentence of Benjamin's essay, Goethe's Elective Affinities, trans. Herbert Marcuse)

Contents

Preface   *page* xi

Acknowledgments   xix

Introduction   1
  Global Poverty and Inequality: How Deeply Should
    We Be Concerned?   1
  Unmet Duties   14
  Human Rights and Social Justice: Two Overlapping
    Approaches to Understanding Our Global Duties   16
  Controversial Claims   25
  A Critical Theory of Injustice and Underdevelopment   29

PART I AGENCY AND DEVELOPMENT

1   Recognition, Rational Accountability, and Agency   47
    Autonomy and Identity-Based Normative Agency   48
    Hegel on Recognition and Self-Certainty:
      Freedom and Identity as Conditions of Agency   51
    Rational Discourse and Autonomy Agency   58
    Pathologies of Abstract Individualism   61
    Honneth on Recognition as an Ethical Category   63
    Honneth's Theory of Recognition   65
    Recognition: Ascription or Perception?   69
    Recognition, Redistribution, and Participatory Parity:
      The Honneth-Fraser Debate   74
    Conflicted Agency and the Self-Subordination Social
      Recognition Paradox: Emancipating Women in Developing
      Countries through Micro-Finance   78

vii

2   Agency and Coercion: Empowering the Poor through Poverty
    Expertise and Development Policy   85
        The Culture of Poverty: The American Debate   87
        The Culture of Poverty: The Global Debate   90
        Poverty Expertise as Ideology: The American
            Experience   93
        Development Theory as Ideology: The Global
            Experience   95
        The Social Contractarian Foundations of Development
            Theory and the Limits of Rational Choice   101
        Coercive Environments as the Hidden Foundation
            of Injustice and Social Pathology   106
        Discourse Ethics and the Disclosure of Coercive
            Environments: Toward a Reform of Poverty
            Expertise   109
        Applying Discourse Ethics and Recognition
            Theory to Global Development Policy   114
        Concluding Remarks on the Structural Obstacles
            to Implementing Development Policy   120

                    PART II   GLOBAL CRISIS

3   Forced Migration: Toward a Discourse Theoretic
    Policy Governing Political and Economic Refugees   125
        Political Refugees: A Humanitarian Crisis   131
        The Evolving Definition of Refugee Status and the
            Discretionary Application of Humanitarian Law   137
        Refugees' Rights versus States' Rights   139
        Compromising Refugees' Rights on the Altar of State
            Sovereignty: The Evolving Role of the UNHCR   141
        Economic Refugees Reconsidered   144
        The Analogy between Hostile Work Environments
            and Poverty   147
        The Special Duty to Decriminalize and Protect
            Victims of Human Trafficking   148
        Cosmopolitanism and the Case for Open Borders   150
        Communitarianism and the Case for Restrictive
            Borders   154
        Parents Who Migrate: The Hidden Cost of Divided
            Agency   156
        Discourse Ethics and Border Policy   159
        Discourse Ethics and Immigration Policy   162
        Discourse Ethics and Immigration Courts   167

4   Imperial Power and Global Political Economy:
    Democracy and the Limits of Capitalism   171
      Imperial Power and International Relations: The Logic
        of Underdevelopment and Unsustainable Economies   173
      Contractarian Duties and the Moral Burdens of Empire   183
      Free versus Fair Trade   188
      Markets and Negative Externalities: Dependency,
        Environmental Degradation, and Global Warming   196
      Toward an Efficient and Just Reduction of Negative
        Externalities: Market Strategies versus Government
        Regulation   199
      The Limits of Capitalism   203
      Economic Democracy   212

            PART III HUMAN RIGHTS

5   Human Rights and Global Injustice: Institutionalizing
    the Moral Claims of Agency   221
      The Ambiguous Status of Human Rights   225
      Political Theories of Human Rights: Rawls on the Law
        of Peoples   232
      Legal Theories of Human Rights: Habermas on
        Constitutional Law   238
      Moral Approaches to Human Rights   243
      Understanding Human Rights Contextually: Pluralism
        Reconsidered   250
      Institutional and Interactional Human Rights: Do Global
        Economic Structures Violate Human Rights?   251
      Legitimating Human Rights: Discourse Theory and
        Democracy   258

6   Making Humanitarian Law Legitimate: The
    Constitutionalization of Global Governance   262
      Justifying the International Human Rights Regime   270
      Modern International Law and Constitutional
        Legitimacy: Preliminary Remarks   277
      The UN and Global Constitutional Order   282
      The UN Charter as Constitution of a Single Legal Order   292
      Toward a More Legitimate and Democratic International
        Order   298
      Subjecting the UNSC to Judicial Review: A Step Toward
        Democratic Constitutionalization   304
      Democratizing Global Constitutional Review in a
        Fragmented Legal Universe   306

7   Nationalism, Religion, and Deliberative Democracy:
     Networking Cosmopolitan Solidarity   313
         Solidarity: A Preliminary Analysis   316
         Mechanical and Organic Solidarity   318
         Civic Solidarity   320
         Civic Solidarity: An Incoherent Concept?   322
         Religion and Civic Solidarity   329
         From Religion to Cosmopolitan Solidarity   339
         Building Cosmopolitan Solidarity Out of Solidarity
             Networks   341

Bibliography   344
Index   361

Preface

The last thirty years have witnessed a momentous shift in our thinking about international justice. Since the end of the Cold War, humanitarian law has become a prominent tool in the struggle against genocide and other human rights violations. The decentering of international relations from state-centric concerns regarding the balance of power and maintenance of international peace brought in its wake a further departure from the old paradigm of *realpolitik*. Thanks to growing awareness of the impact of heightened economic globalization on the world's poor, underdevelopment has emerged alongside social justice and human rights as a pressing matter of deep concern. The study proposed here aims to develop a critical theory of underdevelopment that draws together these normative concerns within a critique of contemporary global capitalism.

Critical theory reflects on social crisis as the inextricable dilemma of our times. *World Crisis and Underdevelopment* extends this reflection to illuminate the injustices and social pathologies that specifically inform poverty remediation and social development within the current global order. My *institutional* analysis of that order draws from a wide range of thinkers within critical theory. Although its normative bearings chiefly derive from Habermas's theory of communicative action and Honneth's theory of recognition, it also appropriates much of the social contractarian tradition descending from Rawls and his followers along with insights developed by proponents of the capabilities approach.

Critical theory's chief advantage over these competing approaches lies in its linkage of theory and practice. In contrast to idealizing theory, it situates itself at the crossroads of historical reality and experience. How the disadvantaged experience deprivation and powerlessness as a modality of structural *coercion* guides its criticism.

In order to grasp the phenomenon of coercion as a function of structural and social incapacitation, I begin by discussing the concept of agency. Agency is the basic capability (or good) that human beings must have in order to acquire other capabilities. It forms the core of our freedom and thus constitutes one of the most central foci of human rights protection. It also constitutes the heart of social justice; for if agency implicates a distinctly social conception of freedom, as I think it must, freedom from social domination born of excessive social inequality must be one of its conditions.

Chapter 1 elaborates the concept of agency as social freedom. I begin this chapter by criticizing minimalist accounts of agency that neglect agency's social dimension. This dimension, I argue, is captured by Hegel's understanding of the importance of social recognition, in which what is done, as well as who is doing it, depends on critical confirmation from others. From this quasi-ontological characterization, which can be captured in terms of a model of communicative interaction of the sort developed by Habermas, Brandom, and Pippin, I then propose, following Honneth and Taylor, several richer schemes of social recognition. The *historical* (or *teleological*) scheme distinguishes between traditional and modern forms of social recognition, with the former based on the fulfillment of concrete role expectations within social hierarchies premised on honor and unquestioned (often inherited) authority, and the latter based on the fulfillment of abstract role expectations within egalitarian relationships of mutual accountability premised on mutual respect for the dignity and freedom of the other. The *societal* scheme distinguishes between familial, moral, and socio-ethical types of social recognition. These types of recognition foster (respectively) self-confidence (through loving relationships), self-respect (through moral relationships), and self-esteem (through forms of cooperative work and group membership).

Elaborating on this schema, I further differentiate social recognition and agency, noting that different types of agency and social recognition can be developed in opposition to each other. Here I endorse Nancy Fraser's criticism of Honneth's reduction of economic, political, and cultural injustices to experiences of misrecognition. Following her lead, I suggest that we view all injustices – if not all forms of social pathology – as violations of a principle of participatory parity in discussing not only cultural roles, economic distributions, and political systems of representation, but in questioning the basic frameworks in which such questions of justice are raised in the first place. In the final analysis, I propose a combination of Fraser's Habermas-inspired deontological theory of democratic justice and Honneth's teleological theory of recognitive development. Thus, using the example of microcredit in a social context still marked by traditional forms of recognition, I argue that the development of feminist agency, which may come at the expense of welfare agency, requires an expansive understanding of agency that entails participatory parity in all three dimensions of social interaction.

Chapter 2 exposes the underlying racism and ethnocentrism of modern development theory, specifically highlighting the failure of public policy and ethical theory to adequately conceptualize the relationship between poverty and coercion. I begin with a discussion of the debate over the causes of poverty in the United States and the importance of social recognition in establishing a notion of rational autonomy. I argue that the two dominant views embedded in public policy expertise – that poverty is caused by deficient cognitive and moral habits of the poor (the so-called "culture of poverty" view) and that poverty is caused by a lack of economic opportunities (the so-called "structural imposition of poverty" view) – are only partly correct. The moral and cognitive "habits" of the poor often reflect rational choices in the short term that are suboptimal in the long run; but these choices, free and rational as they may be, are not wholly unconstrained. They are "coerced" by situations characterized by lack of opportunity. In contrast to the abstract, individualistic understanding of free, rational choice (autonomy) found in liberal social contract theory, I defend a social-interactive view, which emphasizes the unreliability of our individual-centered knowledge of others as well as much of our second-hand expertise. Given the superficial picture of poverty provided by so-called experts, typically depicted as shortfalls in household income, and the susceptibility of such supposedly value-neutral data to multiple – conservative and progressive – interpretations, I argue that "poverty knowledge" should take its bearings from qualitative field research grounded in narrative interpretation of the sort that was pioneered by the Chicago Settlement movement. So construed, poverty knowledge would shed its deceptive appearance as a value-neutral, objective science and become a partisan advocate on behalf of enlightening, emancipating, and empowering the poor.

Using a combined discourse- and recognition-theoretic approach to reforming poverty expertise, I then turn to several models that have been proposed for implementing international development. Despite its checkered history as recounted in post-colonial literature, the right to development, I argue, can become an effective right once it is theoretically elaborated and practically implemented in dialogical collaboration between local communities and experts. The disadvantages of direct aid, even when it involves mediation of technical expertise and local knowledge, recommend alternative strategies of development that build on inclusive economic collaboration between cooperative worker-management experiments and foreign businesses. Fair trade relationships need to abide by discourse ethical norms of cooperation that respect the dignity and interests of all parties. However, as I point out, such negotiations will be constrained so long as power imbalances between providers and recipients of developmental assets persist.

Part II examines some of the most important global crises that threaten development today: coercive migration, poverty and global inequality, and environmental destruction. Chapter 3 discusses the ethical, political, and legal responsibilities associated with modern migration. Political refugees fleeing violence continue to suffer human rights violations and injustices at the hands of their would-be protectors, who have few qualms about treating them as criminals. The justification for this treatment is suspicion that self-identified political refugees are really economic opportunists. I argue that the distinction between political and economic migrants fails to apply when one scrutinizes today's global political economy, in which varying degrees of political abuse intersect a coercive and hostile economic environment. Economic refugees who engage the services of smugglers belie the stereotype of passive victims; being neither accomplice to nor victim of crime, the migrant who is compelled to violate the law out of desperation diminishes her own agency. I argue, however, that uprooting oneself from a community of social recognition out of economic necessity is agency diminishing even when undertaken legally. This diminishment is experienced by both migrants and the families (especially the children) they leave behind.

In my opinion, neither communitarian nor cosmopolitan moral theories adequately respond to the dilemmas faced by migrants who are forced to sacrifice some portion of their agency. Standing between cosmopolitanism and communitarianism, discourse ethics, I submit, responds more sensitively to this dilemma. Although discourse ethics provides a warrant for questioning border and immigration policy, its true value, I argue, resides in mandating an empathetic application of immigration law in a way that does justice to the uniquely coercive life circumstances of each claimant to asylum.

Chapter 4 examines the economic forces that drive migration. I begin by examining one political factor underlying these forces: the imperial hegemony exercised by the United States and its allies in imposing a neoliberal regime of finance and trade that perpetuates neocolonial dependency and inequality between developed and developing nations. After laying out the multiple social contractarian duties of repair and care that the United States and its allies have with respect to the global poor subject to their governance, I analyze the global economy from a less political social contractarian perspective. I ask whether an unregulated global trade regime of the sort defended by neoliberal apologists can be justified as mutually beneficial to all contracting parties. Crucial to my inquiry is an analysis of the principle of comparative advantage that economists invoke in touting the benefits of free trade in reducing poverty and advancing development.

In recommending models of poverty reduction and development that endorse fair trade principles permitting protectionist and import-substitution policies for developing nations, I defend more internationally engaged forms of economic cooperation that take account of the environmental and climatological effects of global production. Although I do not discount the advantages of combining market-based solutions to this problem with stronger forms of democratic regulation, I submit that any such model of green, sustainable development needs to be qualified by a sober analysis of the growth dynamics driving capitalism, which undermine efforts at government regulation. I therefore conclude that, given *this* contradiction between capitalism and democracy, any long-term solution to the chief economic and political crisis of our era will require infusing the economy with discourse ethical principles of the sort commensurate with market socialism and workplace democracy.

Special duties owed to conationals and foreigners who participate in, or find themselves subjected to, legal-political relationships of trade, finance, and imperial domination must be distinguished from the truly universal cosmopolitan duties owed to all human beings with whom we might have a lesser degree of contact. The question I address in Chapter 5 is whether such universal duties, specifically as they flow from human rights, provide a different set of reasons for condemning the economic injustices noted above. For example, ecological costs of doing business that endanger human rights might not be justifiable by appeal to overall greater benefits of doing business. If this is so, I argue, it is because human rights law imposes a duty on states to provide robust levels of social welfare to their subjects that should not be hindered by conditions of finance and trade imposed on states by the World Bank, the World Trade Organization, and other global economic multilaterals (GEMs).

It might be argued that such robust interpretation of human rights cannot be justified or practically implemented. Following an argument developed recently by Allen Buchanan, I argue that the problem of rights inflation, while real, is partly a figment of the philosophical fantasy that there is only one justification for human rights: their moral role in protecting individual agency. Once we drop this Mirroring View (as Buchanan refers to it) we are free to think of human rights as having multiple moral grounds, compatible with collectivist moralities, group rights, and the procurement of social welfare.

Having refuted one-sided political, constitutional, and ethical (agent-centered) theories of human rights, I argue that an institutional understanding of human rights must accompany an interactional understanding if we are to grasp the full range of justiciable human rights claims (both criminal and civil) that touch on poverty and resource deprivation. This explains why the official addressees of human rights should be expanded to include nonstate institutions. I conclude by defending a human right to democratic participation, which I argue must be respected at the level of global governance as well.

Chapter 6 examines the legitimation crisis facing the current human rights regime. Lack of accountability, both internal and external, has rendered this regime powerless to mitigate current humanitarian crises. Reforming that regime, I submit, requires infusing it with constitutional structure of the kind found in liberal democracy. This regime should incorporate institutions that function more like domestic legislative, judicial, and executive bodies without evolving into a full-fledged democratic government.

Buchanan's qualified justification of the current regime poses a serious challenge to my thesis insofar as he understands the regime's legitimacy as sufficiently established by its modular composition and dependence on sovereign democratic states. Although I agree that Buchanan's *ecological* understanding of the relationship between international human rights law and sovereign states is basically correct and allows for potential reform of the human rights system in ways that will increase its overall legitimacy, I submit that it does not go far enough in addressing concerns that Buchanan himself raises regarding human rights treaty law as an instrument for combatting global poverty and climate change.

To see how this might be done, I examine Habermas's much debated proposal for making the UN Security Council and the General Assembly more democratically accountable and less subject to manipulation by entrenched government interests. Habermas's intriguing proposal for integrating transnational negotiations regarding trade, development, and global environmental risks into human rights law as well as his suggestion that international human rights courts exercise some kind of review over executive decisions renders plausible a global institution that Habermas endorses at the domestic level: a constitutional court. Taking up this intriguing possibility, I examine the *Kadi* case in which judicial review has already been effectively exercised by the European Court of Justice with respect to the UN Security Council's unconstitutional listing of individuals suspected of terrorist activity.

The final chapter examines possibilities for achieving solidarity in fighting global poverty and environmental damage. Among the various types of solidarity, civic solidarity shows promise as an achievable cosmopolitan goal. However, its volatile combination of cosmopolitan and national loyalties raises obvious doubts on this score. One such doubt is skepticism about the human rights that compose its cosmopolitan core. Two skeptical challenges merit special consideration in this regard: the charge that human rights conflict with national obligations and the objection that they reflect a Western secular bias.

Responding to the first objection, I argue that the conflict between human rights and duties to the community, although internal to the humanitarian order, expresses a conflict that can occur between any human rights, in this instance between human rights ascribed to individuals and those ascribed to groups. Not only are group-ascribed human rights genuinely irreducible to individual-ascribed human rights, but both rights together capture the dual kinds of solidarity that should inform global democratic governance. A further concern that democratic deliberation erodes group solidarity likewise vindicates democracy's genuine potential to critically transform cultural identities without, however, undermining cultural attachments as such. Encouraging cultural groups to reflectively revise their self-understandings in dialogue with other groups further facilitates the convergence of group solidarities and cosmopolitan solidarity.

This fact informs my response to the second objection. This objection holds that human rights and secular democracy conflict with the core commitments of Islam and other world religions. I argue that this objection not only is unsubstantiated but also neglects the contribution of world religion as the most original cosmopolitan form of solidarity – and one, moreover, that has recently attained prominence in promoting human rights and secular democracy. This contribution depends on the capacity of believers and nonbelievers alike to avail themselves of the cultural values solidifying social justice struggles within civil dialogue qualified by the constraints of public reason.

The existence of sectarian fundamentalism reminds us of the formidable barriers to achieving solidarity. In this regard, global capitalism plays a contributing role. Not only does capitalism feed a self-centered consumer mentality that is hostile to communal forms of solidarity, but it exacerbates class conflict. Its pathological forgetfulness of any socially recognized community beyond that of economic status scarcely permits empathy for the world's poor and vulnerable.

I conclude that the possibility for achieving cosmopolitan civic solidarity depends on forging a different kind of cosmopolitan solidarity: network solidarity. Building upon the organic interdependence of groups struggling on behalf of different constituents, network solidarity opens lines of political communication that expand the internal identifications and attachments of regional and sectorial social justice movements to encompass a broader cosmopolitan horizon of solidarity. My analysis of the social factors engendering network solidarity – a preference for mutually beneficial cooperation, a consciousness of social dependency, and an awareness of luck's role in assigning us our place in life – compels a guardedly optimistic assessment of the prospects for achieving cosmopolitan civic solidarity.

I add this personal note as a final guidepost for the reader. This book is dedicated to Herbert Marcuse, who by his teaching and conduct inspired my interest in critical theory as a vehicle for political practice. Although I do not cite him, Chapter 4 honors his utopian vision. My life can be read from these pages as well: I organized boycotts on behalf of the United Farm Workers Union, accompanied Loyola's students on their journey of awakening to Central America and the Caribbean, worked with Guatemalan refugees and community organizers in Chicago, and learned about the possibilities and limits of development while visiting the slums of Kibera with aid providers. I hope this book vindicates in theory what our collective struggles have honored in practice.

Acknowledgments

I thank Robert Dreesen, Daniel George Brown, Sri Hari Kumar, the external readers, and the editorial staff at Cambridge University Press for their contributions toward publishing this book. I am especially indebted to Ndidi Nwaneri, Willy Moka-Mubelo, Asaf Bar-Tura, Drew Thompson, and Thomas Derdak for shaping its argument. Others who provided valuable feedback on parts of the manuscript include Jennifer Parks, Joy Gordon, David Schweickart, Johan Karlsson Schaffer, Cristina Lafont, George Mazur, Diana Meyers, Isaac Balbus, Albena Azmanova, Yiran Zhang, and Katherine Brichacek. I also thank the organizers of critical theory conferences held in Europe and North America for allowing me to present my research. Participation in workshops sponsored by Loyola on agency, poverty, and coercion and on Catholicism, democracy, and culture provided me with opportunities for generating new lines of research. Last but not least, I thank my students for being good research copartners. Needless to say, this book would not have been completed without the loving support of my family.

The author thanks Oxford University Press for reprinting excerpts of the chapter, "Poverty Knowledge, Coercion, and Social Rights," in D. Meyers (ed.), *Poverty, Agency, and Human Rights* (Oxford University Press, 2014), pp. 43–67.

Introduction

GLOBAL POVERTY AND INEQUALITY: HOW DEEPLY SHOULD WE BE CONCERNED?

The World Bank's Poverty Data for 2015 (the most recent date reported) estimates that over 700 million persons in the world live in extreme poverty, the majority of them women, who earn about half as much as men. Earlier data for 2010 showed that 100 million lacked access to safe water; 2,600 million lacked access to basic sanitation, 1000 million lacked access to adequate housing, 2000 million lacked access to essential drugs, 774 million couldn't read or write; 218 million children were forced to work for their subsistence, and 72 million elementary school age children attended no school. As of 2015, 35.2 percent of people inhabiting sub-Saharan Africa live in severe poverty, surviving on an income of less than $1.90 per day in purchasing power calibrated to what people inhabiting the United States can purchase.[1] Similar statistics

---

[1] According to how the World Bank (WB) calculates purchasing power parities (PPPs), the cutoff point for extreme poverty is $392/year indexed to 1993 purchasing power in the US and $785.76 for severe poverty. Adjusted to inflation, equivalent purchasing power cutoffs for 2007 would be $564 and $1,128 for a US citizen. By adopting these benchmarks for defining extreme and severe poverty the World Bank sets the bar low for gauging progress in eliminating poverty. In fact the International Poverty Line (IPL) chosen by the WB is the mean of the poverty line as determined by government bureaucrats in the world's fifteen poorest countries (nine of which have very small populations and thirteen of which are located in sub-Saharan Africa) who have political incentives to deflate the number of poor living in their country by adopting low domestic poverty lines. Moreover, the World Bank's current method for determining the cutoffs for extreme and severe poverty misrepresents the actual purchasing power of the poor in a number of respects. For instance, $1.90 – the recently adopted cutoff for extreme poverty that replaced the older threshold

for other regions are equally grim: 13.5 percent in South Asia; 4.1 percent in East Asia and the Pacific; 5.6 percent in Latin America and the Caribbean.[2] The good news is that those living in extreme poverty fell to 9.6 per cent of the global population, the lowest percentage ever recorded, down from the 2012 statistic of 12.8 per cent (902 million). Despite this progress, fueled in large part by rapid economic growth in India and steady growth in China (now diminishing) and by "investments in people's education, health, and social safety nets," World Bank President Jim Yong Kim noted that the goal of eliminating extreme poverty by 2030 will be difficult to achieve in a world racked by civil conflict and economic crises, including falling prices in natural resources (a chief export of developing countries). Most disturbing of all is the rapidly growing population of poor people in sub-Saharan Africa, which has traded places with Asia as the epicenter of a scourge of global poverty that in its less extreme but still severe manifestations still afflicts three billion of the world's inhabitants.[3]

Thomas Pogge (2008: 2) estimates that 18 million of the world's poorest die prematurely from poverty-related causes every year, one-third of all deaths, and from 2000 to 2014, more than the deaths caused by all the wars and genocides of the twentieth century combined. The daily toll from poverty-related deaths is 50,000, with 29,000 of them being children under the age of five. These data represent conservative estimates based only on family income. A richer understanding of poverty based on the United Nations Human Development Index inspired by Harvard economist Amartya Sen tracks the lower lifespan and quality of life – in terms of educational attainment, health, and living standards – of

---

of $1.25 – is supposed to cover nonnutritional as well as nutritional expenses, which may cost 50 percent more in developing countries. Also the purchasing power of the poor using their own country's currency is about ¼ of what it would be using dollars on global markets. Therefore, a more accurate accounting of the annual purchasing power (or consumption) of those living in extreme and severe poverty in 2007 with respect to global exchange markets would be $140 and $280, respectively. In fact, the average yearly consumption of those living in severe poverty in 2007 (2,533 million) would be $165, or about $.45/day. According to Thomas Pogge (2010: 67), a more adequate IPL for extreme poverty would by twice the WB's cutoff, which would suggest that many more people are living in extreme poverty than the WB indicates.

[2] Recent WB statics were unavailable for the Middle East and North Africa because of civil strife; 2010 statistics showed that 12 percent of the population in those regions lived in extreme poverty.

[3] In 1990 half of the global poor lived in Asia while only 15 percent lived in Africa; by 2015 those percentages were almost exactly reversed.

those at the bottom. But this index is insensitive to differences in gender, age, and social class.[4]

The World Bank calculations and the Human Development Reports show that the percentage of people living in poverty is declining. However, that statistic obscures the fact that improvements in China account for almost the entire decline.[5] A 2014 report, "The State of Food

---

[4] The Human Development Index (HDI) developed by Sen, Paul Streeten, Mahbub ul Haq, and others builds on the International Labour Organization's 1976 declaration that development should aim at satisfying the *basic needs* of everyone in the shortest time possible. As such it bypasses individual household and per capita income and consumption because these don't reflect the fact that different levels of income are required for people with different needs and different endowments to achieve basic or equal development of overall *capability* (see Chapter 2 n18 below). HDI takes the average of three indices (life expectancy, education, and gross domestic product (GDP)) scaled from 0–1 within countries. The Gender Development Index (GDI) uses the same components but penalizes for gender deviations by taking the harmonic mean of male and female scores. Thus, (supposing parity among male and female populations) if both men and women have an equal educational attainment of 0.6, the GDI is just 0.6. But if men have an educational achievement of 0.9 and women have an educational achievement of 0.4, the GDI is 4/9, or 0.45 (Pogge 2010: 86). By focusing on countrywide rankings, GDI and HDI take a step backward from the WB poverty headcount measure, which focuses on the impoverishment of individual human beings as these are aggregated. Furthermore, they obscure distributional inequalities within a country, so that great gains in HDI and GDI among the most affluent groups can easily make it seem that progress is being made, even though regression has occurred among the vast majority of poor, as is especially obvious in the case of income and life expectancy. Finally, GDI and HDI measure gross domestic product, or a country's output, the proceeds from which may be largely owned by affluent foreigners, rather than gross national product (GNP), which measures the domestic and foreign income of citizens (e.g., Angola recorded a huge increase in GPD between 2001 and 2007 even though most of its increase in domestic oil product went to foreigners and corrupt government elites). Improvements in GDI can be achieved by doubling 10,000 privileged women's incomes to $200,000 each rather than doubling to $2000 the incomes of 1 million female domestics (88). And because GDI, like HDI, summarizes all three indices, it obscures whether women's gains in one area offset losses in the other two. Pogge recommends that instead of just aggregating factors and dividing by population (as WB indices for income and consumption, HDI and GDI do) we need to begin with individuating factors of difference: age, gender, and social status. We need to know whether increases in literacy go to landlords or the landless, whether improved medical care benefits the young or the old, men or women, etc. We can then assess the relative deprivation of women, say, as the mean difference across population fractiles (divided by age, household income, situation, etc.).

[5] Poverty researchers at the World Bank (Chen and Ravallion 2008: 34ff) noted that the decline in extreme poverty (below $1.25/day) from 1981 to 2005 was greatest in China (627 million), East Asia outside of China (123 million), India (35 million), South Asia (12 million), and the Middle East (1 million). These declines were offset by increases elsewhere in sub-Saharan Africa (182 million) and a worldwide increase in people living in severe poverty (below $2.00/day) worldwide, despite a decline in this category in China (499 million).

Insecurity in the World," released by three UN agencies, the Food and Agriculture Organization, International Fund for Agricultural Development, and World Food Program, shows that the number of chronically undernourished people declined by 100 million over the past decade, but qualifies this statistic by observing that only 25 developing nations, including Brazil and Malawi, have succeeded in meeting the UN goal of halving the number of hungry people, and that some countries, such as Haiti, saw their hungry population increase (in Haiti's case, from 4.4 million in 1990–1992 to 5.3 million in 2012–2014). Altogether 1 in 9 persons inhabiting the planet (805 million) remain chronically undernourished.

The pledge by 186 nations who attended the 1996 World Food Summit in Rome, organized by the UN Food and Agricultural Organization, to reduce by *only* one half the number of hungry people by 2015, was furthered watered down in the UN's first Millennium Development Goal (MDG1), which promised not to halve the *number*, but only the *percentage*, of this demographic.[6] Given rapid population growth in the poorest nations, by 2015, the MDG1 will have been met if it succeeds in reducing the total number of hungry people by just 16.9 percent, from 1,089.6 million in 2000 to 905.2 in 2015. If the current 2015 WB estimate of 702 million for those living in extreme poverty is accurate, success has indeed been achieved. But success means that 158 million *more* people are starving than was aimed at in the original 1996 goal of 543.9 million.

Failure to significantly reduce global poverty appears especially glaring in light of China's rapid progress in reducing its poverty and the more than ample technical capacities that almost exclusively benefit the global

---

[6] The eight MDG goals were: 1. Eradicate poverty and hunger; 2. Achieve universal primary education; 3. Promote gender equality and empower women; 4. Reduce child mortality; 5. improve maternal health; 6. Combat HIV/AIDS, malaria, and other diseases; 7. Ensure environmental sustainability; and 8. Develop a global partnership for development. As Ian Goldin notes (Goldin 2016: 86–87) the MDG program was historically unprecedented in its alignment of donors' and recipients' aims and instruments, which included agreement on the definition and measurement of twenty-one targets and sixty intermediate indicators. The uneven success of the MDG program and its reflection of a top-down technocratic approach spearheaded by the UN and the OECD led to the 2015 adoption of the UN 2030 Agenda with its seventeen sustainable development goals (SDGs) under the auspices of a much broader set of civil society stakeholders. These goals build upon the MDGs by incorporating a broader spectrum of issues, including global climate change (goal 13); loss of biodiversity and environmental degradation (Goal 15), resource conservation (Goal14), sustainable growth (in agriculture [Goal 2], industry [Goal 9], urbanization [Goal 11], energy [Goal 7], and overall production and consumption [Goal 12]), and inequality within and among countries (Goal 10). The SDGs also expand the range of actors beyond markets and states to include businesses, cities, and private donors.

wealthy.[7] In 2005 the income ratio between the top and bottom decile was 273:1; the corresponding wealth ratio was 2730:1. The top 1 percent possessed 40 percent of global wealth; the top 10 percent possessed 85 percent. Today, average per capita consumption in high-income countries is thirty times greater than that in low-income countries (120 times greater when differentials in currency exchange rates are factored in), with the poorest 40 percent of the world's population accounting for just 1.7 percent of all household consumption in comparison to the top 15 percent, who account for 81 percent. As Pogge (2008, 10) notes, shifting just 1/70th of the consumption expenditure from the latter group to the former would provide the approximately $300 billion the former needs to escape severe poverty (calibrated at a $2 IPL). However, World Bank data show just the opposite trend: a growing disparity between high-income and low-income earners, with per capita real income in high-income OECD countries rising by 56 percent from 1984–2004 in comparison to the paltry 9.6 percent increase in income enjoyed by the bottom 10 percent during this period. Indeed, according to a frequently cited study by Branko Milanović (2002: 51–92), real income for the poorest 5 percent declined by 20 percent from 1988–1993, and then declined by another 23 percent from 1993–1998, while global wealth increased by 5.2 percent and 4.8 percent respectively. In sum, despite the impressive growth rates of many developing countries in comparison to the sluggish growth rates of most developed economies, today developmental inequality between and within developing nations is far greater than it is between and within developed nations, with the rate of relative inequality (or lack of social inclusion) – a key indicator of development – being higher in

---

[7] Using tax-based evidence from the United States, Britain, and France (extending back, respectively, to 1913, 1909, and the late eighteenth century), Thomas Piketty (2014) has convincingly tracked the growth in income inequality in a handful of representative affluent countries as well. He provocatively argues that the income differential between the top 1 percent and all other earners has returned to the level that existed during the Gilded Age (with the 1 percent receiving 20 percent of all income), before the era of progressive taxation had cut the top 1 percent's share in half (to around 10 percent by 1950). Driving this new age of "patrimonial capitalism" – in an era of slower economic growth and stagnating real wages (equivalent to 1970 levels) caused by declining technological innovation and population growth in the working-age population – are tax reductions on capital earnings, corporate taxes, and inheritance taxes. Paul Krugman (2014) notes additional factors not stressed in Piketty's analysis that contribute to this growing inequality: excessive CEO compensation and financial deregulation that rewards successful hedge fund managers, with only the latter laying legitimate claim to having "earned" their incomes through demonstrable market-based returns on investment.

middle-income countries (MICs) such as China, Indonesia, India, Nigeria, and Pakistan than in *lower*-income countries (LICs).[8]

Official Development Assistance

Probably most people would agree that living in a world where one-third of the world's population lives in severe or extreme poverty, in both absolute and relative terms, and lack the means to escape from poverty on their own, suffices to generate a duty to assist them on the part of high-income countries (HICs).[9] This duty is partly fulfilled in the form of global Official Development Assistance (ODA).[10] As defined by the Development Assistance Committee (DAC) of the Organization for Economic Cooperation and Development (OECD), ODA provides loans and grants from governments specifically targeting the welfare and development of the

[8] Simon Kuznets hypothesized that inequality tracks phases of development: the transition to industrialization increases inequality markedly, which gradually tapers off and then decreases as levels of education rise and birth rates decline. The hypothesis appears most applicable to the industrial phase of development, but is contradicted by growing inequality in postindustrial nations like the US and G-10 countries (see note 7). While absolute poverty has been reduced from 43 per cent of the world's population to between 10 and 15 percent, relative poverty within developing countries, defined as the percentage of those who fall below a level of income requisite for achieving a minimum threshold of social inclusion as measured by a rising mean of national per capita income, has not (Alonso 2016: 110–13).

[9] Peter Singer (1972) famously compared the duty to rescue a child drowning in close proximity to the duty to rescue a starving child living abroad. From Singer's strictly utilitarian perspective, the two are comparable: the death of one person is equivalent to the death of another, regardless of social connection or distance. Indeed, in response to a revision in Singer's drowning child example proposed by Paul Gomberg (2002: 45), in which the benefactor's rescue efforts require muddying boots that she plans to donate for famine relief to the benefit of saving many more lives, Singer agreed that the benefactor should forgo rescuing the drowning child. From a conventional moral perspective this is wrong. The duty of immediate emergency rescue of someone close at hand that does not place the benefactor at serious risk of harm reflects a powerful impulse – gorillas in captivity have protected small children that have fallen into their compounds – and moreover one that in human society has a rational basis in coordinating mutual aid efficiently without further calculation and, most importantly, without callous display of disrespect. Ultimately, as Richard Miller (2010: 25–26) notes, the expectation that others would rescue us in similar circumstances, instead of "looking straight through us," "makes us much less alone, much more at home in our social world." For Hegelians like Axel Honneth (see below), this kind of mutual recognition, or social affirmation, is the very essence of freedom.

[10] Of the approximately $300 billion in annual US charitable aid not included in ODA estimates, only about 10 billion goes to international aid, with a fraction targeting basic needs.

neediest countries. Approximately $149 billion was spent on ODA in 2013, a 69 percent increase since 2000 and a 350 percent increase since 1960, partly attributable to the expansion of DAC members from 8 to 28 (plus the EU).[11] In comparison to ODA delivered during the Cold War, which was largely used to prop up corrupt client regimes and therefore inefficiently managed, ODA today is more effective in targeting the neediest people (although much aid still flows to strategically vital countries, such as Afghanistan, Iraq, Columbia, and Egypt). ODA today is also better coordinated (although improvement is needed in this area as well).

To gauge whether this money satisfies the duty to assist we need to bear in mind that the OECD itself has determined that at least $320 billion a year will be required to help developing countries pay for mitigating and adapting to global climate change in addition to $130 billion in development aid. Altogether, it is estimated that implementing the SDGs will cost $2.5 trillion per year – more than twice the private and public investment in today's developing world (Goldin 2016: 111). The Global Recession of 2008–2012 has raised fears of another global financial crisis, so that ODA – which has now been surpassed by foreign direct investment ($650 billion), remittances ($350 billion) and other private funds ($320 billion) – will likely decline as donors reduce ODA in grappling with tight domestic budgets (Alonso 2016: 106–09).[12] And its future, relative to a plethora of new and innovative partnerships, such as the Global Partnership for Effective Development Cooperation (GPEDC), is highly uncertain, especially insofar as these partnerships are more effective in coordinating multiple efforts of regional and cross-regional sustainable development. As it stands, ODA comprises a very small percentage of Gross National Product (GNP). In 2005, the Millennium Project estimated that its goal for poverty reduction would require all high-income countries to donate .7 percent of their GNP, whereas the current level hovers around .2 percent. The biggest donor of ODA, and the wealthiest country in the world, the United States (at $31.5 billion), gave just .19

---

[11] One must not neglect the $23 billion in "south-to-south" donations provided by non-DAC members, chiefly Saudi Arabia ($5.6 billion). United Arab Emirates ($5.4 billion), Turkey ($3.3 billion), and China ($3 billion) (Alonso 2016: 124–25).

[12] Whereas developmental assistance targets economic redistribution, climate change development targets the creation and maintenance of international public goods (IPGs), such as reduced carbon emissions. Here again, MICs, which contribute 54 percent of CO_2 emissions, are especially important actors in promoting sustainable development in other developing countries since they constitute thirteen of the fifteen countries that the 2012 World Risk Report has determined are at the highest level of risk for suffering catastrophic effects of climate change (Alonso, 128).

percent of its GNP to ODA while Norway (at $5.6 billion) gave 1.07 percent. The United States currently ranks 20th in percentage of ODA it donates relative to GNP. To place these figures in perspective, the United States spends $496.5 billion for military defense, more than 16 times the amount it spends on ODA.

To be sure, capital flight has been a significant problem in China, India, Latin America, and Africa (the latter alone has lost upwards of $1 trillion in revenue since 1970 due to corrupt accounting practices in misstating the costs of imports and exports) (Goldin 2016: 98). It is estimated that reforming tax codes could more than compensate for shortfalls in needed ODA. Closing tax havens, which account for $32 trillion – one third of the world's wealth – could free up $189 billion alone (it is sobering to think what a "soak the rich" tax levied on the eight wealthiest persons on the planet might accomplish in this regard; their combined assets, totaling over $420 billion, exceed the $409 billion held by the world's poorest 3.6 billion).[13] Instead, governments are doing little to address this loss in revenue, with the recent trend favoring more regressive tax policies that benefit the rich and exacerbate domestic and global inequality. Alternatively, further gains in "aid" could be accomplished by forgiving the huge debts owed to lending institutions in the developed world that governments of developing countries are obligated to service or by reducing licensing fees that poor countries have to pay to transnational corporations in order to access value-added goods and services (during the peak of the debt crisis in the mid-1990s, for every $1 that was given in aid, $9 was taken back through debt repayments) (Goldin 2016: 96).[14]

---

[13] Oxfam Website, "An Economy for the 99 Percent" (January 16, 2017). The Panama Papers disclosure in April 2016 refocused public attention on the moral downside of tax havens. Tax havens – which are mainly wealthy nations like Switzerland, Hong Kong, the United States (especially Delaware and Nevada), and Britain (if one counts semi-independent former colonies like Bermuda, Cayman Islands, and Jersey) – shield the financial holdings of corrupt leaders from public scrutiny and deprive even wealthy countries of tax revenues and investment capital needed for creating jobs. Cutting corporate taxes at home to dissuade shell companies merely shifts more of the domestic tax burden to the workforce (Shaxson 2011).

[14] The debt crisis of the 1970s highlights the compensatory duties owed by developed countries to the developing world; the crisis was triggered by the United States drastically raising its interest rates to manage its own "stagnation" crisis, with the initially low-interest loans held by developing countries to help them "take off" on a course of rapid industrialization – aggressively promoted by foreign banks flush with excess petro-dollars from skyrocketing oil prices – subsequently being readjusted upward at higher unsustainable rates. It took almost twenty years of threatened and real loan defaults by developing countries before international institutions began to respond to this financial crisis. The

The amount of ODA that actually targets meeting "basic social services" is only a fraction – about 14 percent – of total ODA (in 2005, $7.63 billion out of $106.8 billion, with about one-fifth of the total amount going to Iraq).[15] Despite a recent shift toward targeting LICs instead of MICs,[16] little ODA trickles down to meeting basic needs. Part of the explanation for this is politics.

For example, until 2014 the US contribution to its Food For Peace Program (administered by USAID) – a relic of Cold War diplomacy whose funding has declined with the growing geopolitical insignificance of developing countries – had also served to rid American farmers of their agricultural surpluses. At the urging of Oxfam America, CARE, and the UN, the Obama administration determined that it could feed 4 million more people at a savings of $500 million if it could use $1.4 billion earmarked for the program to buy food vouchers for the needy to purchase food grown locally

world's thirty-eight heavily indebted poor countries (HIPCs) now have access to the HIPC initiative (in place since 1996 and continued under the G8's 2006 Multilateral Debt Reduction Initiative [MDRI]) whereby the IMF and WB provide concessional low interest loans for debt servicing (in 2005 the IMF also instituted a $3.3 billion debt relief measure for nineteen of the world's poorest countries, while the WB wrote off the larger debts owed to it by seventeen other HIPCs). When it was first introduced, the HIPC initiative was heavily criticized for requiring an excessive debt to exports (or debt to revenues) ratio of about 200–250 percent (280 percent based on debt/revenue calculations) for potential recipients of relief and for imposing structural adjustment conditions on qualifying governments. Over the next ten years the initiative was modified to allow for a lower debt to export ratio of 150 percent, and operate under a less austere Poverty Reduction and Growth Facility (PRGF) administration that replaced the enhanced structural adjustment facility (ESAF) regime. As noted above, thirty-nine countries have also received full or partial cancellation of debts owed to foreign governments and the IMF/WB. The two-thirds reduction in total debt owed by HIPCs still falls short of the Jubilee 2000 demands. Many of the eighteen countries (such as Zambia) that benefitted from cancelled loans were able to invest their savings in health, education, and other public services. Despite this progress, many poor countries did not qualify for debt relief or cancellation. As of 2012, the WB determined that developing countries owed $4 trillion in foreign debt (40 percent held by the BRICS group), with the poorest countries having to pay $34 million *per diem* to service loan repayments. As Goldin wryly observes (Goldin 2016: 99–100) "[i]n an irony of history, the advanced economies that preached macroeconomic orthodoxy failed to heed their own advice ... [and today have] levels of debt approximately similar to that of many of the developing countries during the 1970s and 1980s." To this he adds that the terrible lessons regarding failed structural adjustment policies learned in the 1970s–1990s have been forgotten with regard to Greece and other indebted countries.

[15] www.oecd.org/dataoecd/52/18/37790990.pdf

[16] From 2000 to 2011, MICs saw their share of ODA decline from 62.1 percent to 47.2 percent, LICs saw their share increase from 37.9 percent to 52.8 percent. ODA is still the largest source of international funding for LICs and represents 70 percent of foreign finance in least developed countries (LDCs) (Alonso 2016: 105–06).

in poor countries, thereby bypassing costs associated with transporting 1.44 million tons of basic foodstuffs and other bulk commodities across the Atlantic.[17] Most important, the new policy would stop driving local farmers out of business by "dumping" underpriced US agricultural goods in local markets. Opposition from the American Farm Bureau Federation, maritime associations, and other lobbying groups, who argued that vouchers invited corruption and would result in the loss of American jobs – this despite the fact that commodities shipped under the Food For Peace program account for less than two-thirds of 1 percent of US agricultural production and less than .5 percent of US agricultural exports – resulted in the passage of a diluted reform that sets aside only 20 percent of the money earmarked for food relief to be spent on vouchers serving 3.4 million fewer starving people than what had been projected under the original proposal (Abbot 2013).

Not only does 80 percent of the older form of "tied aid" continue to support policies that worsen poverty in poor countries, but also some of it – despite what critics of the Obama reform claim – is still used to prop up corrupt, authoritarian regimes who are more than capable of providing the basic necessities for their poorest citizens, but who prefer to squander their wealth on military expenditures and bloated government salaries. For example, South Sudan, the recipient of $600 million in US aid annually and the beneficiary of US state-building efforts since its independence from Sudan in 2005, is a country of stark contradictions, home to some of the world's worst poverty, health, and education problems as well as some of its richest oil deposits. Although its postindependence oil revenue has increased sharply, more than half of it has gone to paying for defense costs and bloated governmental salaries. Locked in an ethnic civil war with Nuer rebel leader and former Vice President Reik Machar that has left 10,000 dead and 800,000 displaced, the undemocratic government of Salva Kiir in Juba recently borrowed millions of dollars to pay its soldiers, after it shut down oil production over a dispute with Sudan over transit fees. As I write, over 100,000 people are suffering from human-made famine in north central South Sudan, with another 4.5 million facing acute food shortages. Although the US was instrumental in South Sudan's struggle for independence, US lawmakers now decry US developmental assistance as a crutch enabling the South Sudanese government to continue ignoring the needs of the poor while further entrenching its military rule (Dixon 2014).

---

[17] In 2013 Sudan, Ethiopia, Kenya, and Pakistan were among the major recipients targeted for emergency famine relief.

Development Finance Institutions (DFIs)

Public and private banks have been crucial players in development and poverty reduction since WWII. But development finance institutions (DFIs) are beholden to the political preferences of their shareholders, which in the case of the World Bank (WB) are the G-7 powers. During the Cold War, the WB provided concessionary loans to countries based mainly on their strategic value to the United States and its allies, with little attention to the goals of poverty reduction. Furthermore, the response of the WB and IMF to the debt crisis of the 1970s and 1980s produced catastrophic results, which we see being repeated today in Greece (Dixon 2014).[18] The resentment toward these institutions continues to this day and has generated backlash in the developing world. The emergence of the New Development Bank established by the BRICS consortium reflects this backlash, as does the establishment of the Chinese-initiated Asian Infrastructure Investment Bank. Today, the world's largest national development bank, the China Development Bank, has assets of over $1.2 trillion – twice as much as those held by the WB group. These latter banks have been crucial in developing high risk, long-term projects in "frontier markets," such as electrification and other forms of infrastructure. As MICs like China and India increase their budgetary capacity along with the development of capital markets, banks such as these will leverage their comparative advantage to fund costly public goods that markets and governments cannot fund (Goldin 2016: 89–96).

Trade

The example of South Sudan suggests that perhaps the US has a stronger duty to assist the poor living there given its responsibility for supporting that country's move to independence and its military security. If Pogge is right, high-income nations like the US collude in supporting corrupt authoritarian governments who steal their people's common patrimony of resources in exchange for economic and political favors. Not only have many of these high-income countries benefited from a violent history of colonialism, slavery, and genocide, but they also continue to benefit from lending and trading practices that harm poor countries in a multitude of ways. Even if the World Trade Organization (WTO) that was ushered in by the final Uruguay Round of GATT negotiations (1981–1994) has

---

[18] See note 14 and Chapter 4.

benefitted the poor in China and a few other places, it did not benefit many of the poor elsewhere. Despite the WTO's commitment to free trade, and its recent commitment in the Doha Round (2001) to furthering development, developed countries are still allowed to disproportionately "protect" their domestic industries through tariffs and subsidies at the expense of their poorer trading partners. At the end of the Uruguay Round, rich countries' average tariffs were 4 times higher than those of developing countries in sectors where developing countries were best positioned to compete (in agriculture, textiles, and clothing). The United Nations Conference on Trade and Development estimated that without such tariffs poor countries could export $1 trillion a year more, gaining up to $100 billion in additional exchange instead of suffering a net loss of $600 million, after bureaucratic costs and licensing expenses due to product patents are factored in.[19]

Apologists for the current trade regime sometimes argue that it will eventually benefit the world's worst off in the long run, but demanding that present generations of poor sacrifice for the uncertain benefits that will allegedly accrue to future generations bypasses difficult questions of intergenerational distributive justice. Furthermore, even if the current regime benefits the poor more than the regime it replaced, one might object that it does not benefit them more than a feasible alternative would. As Pogge puts it, a defense that rests solely on the fact that fewer people are dying than before is incredibly weak when no one has to die under a feasible alternative. The recent shift away from neoliberal orthodoxy toward neo-Keynesian policies promoting differential fair trade responsibilities – permitting governments of developing countries to phase out tariffs while leveraging a range of public services and economic interventions – has suggested such an alternative, as have the various

---

[19] Perhaps the costliest and deadliest provision of the WTO trade agreement is the 1995 Trade Related Aspects of Intellectual Property Rights Agreement (TRIPS) and related provisions that protect product patents for twenty years and beyond, thereby impeding and delaying the production of generic drugs that could save the lives of millions of people. Half of all poverty-related deaths are caused by disease, with tuberculosis and tropical diseases such as malaria accounting for 12 percent of the global burden of disease (GBD). A little more than 10 percent of global health research spending targets diseases that comprise 90 percent of GBD, with drug companies targeting the health needs of high-income customers. Only the latter can afford drugs whose prices, thanks to product patent monopolies, have been inflated to anywhere between ten to thirty times the normal market price and upwards of 100 times the cost of production. A country like India that, prior to 2005, had produced generic copies of drugs for its poor population using alternative production techniques, was forced by threat of trade sanctions to sign on to TRIPS. See also Chapter 4, notes 16 and 17.

schemes for mutually beneficial financial and trade arrangements that have been advanced along the southern corridor by Brazil, India, China, and South Africa (BICS). But these promising initiatives are also strained by power differentials and the inefficiencies associated with government corruption.

Global Warming

Other concerns about global distributive justice, however, suggest that unfair trade regimes might be the least injustice perpetrated against the global poor. Wealthy nations contribute a disproportionate share of the world's carbon emissions that drive global warming and exacerbate poverty. World Bank President Jim Yong Kim notes that, despite our best efforts to moderate global warming, "we could witness the rolling back of decades of development gains and force tens of millions more to live in poverty" (Kim 2013).[20] Absent more effective efforts, poverty will increase even more dramatically, unleashing new waves of migration. Rising temperatures are predicted to slash rice and corn yields, creating food insecurity for hundreds of millions of people.[21] Drought, rising sea levels, and extreme weather events also affect the poor disproportionately, with developing countries suffering 98 percent of deaths and 90 percent of financial losses.[22] Water and other resource scarcities, in turn, give rise to military conflicts, such as the

[20] Accounting giant PricewaterhouseCoopers reported that if current trends persist, the world will use up its "carbon budget"– the amount of carbon emissions compatible with limiting overall warming to 2 degrees Celsius above preindustrial levels – by 2034. To stay within this budget, by 2030 the G20 nations will need to reduce their carbon emissions by one-third, and continue doing so by one-half by 2050. The December 2015 Paris meeting of the Conference of the Parties (COP) to the United Nations Framework Convention on Climate Change resulted in an agreement signed by representatives of 196 countries, which recently became legally binding when 55 countries that contribute 55 percent of greenhouse gases ratified it in October 2016. Ratifying counties will be required to set a target for emission reduction, voluntarily chosen and administered, pursuant to the goal of reaching an increase over preindustrial temperatures of less than 2 degrees Celsius by the 21st century. However, signatories to the agreement committed themselves to "pursuing efforts" to limit the increase to below 1.5 degrees, which would require reaching zero emissions sometime between 2030 and 2050 (PricewaterhouseCoopers 2010).

[21] Half of the world's forests have been lost, and while deforestation has abated since the 1990s – it now destroys around 5 million hectares of forest every year – 12 million hectares are lost annually to land degradation and desertification, costing $42 billion in lost incomes (Goldin 2016: 120; Renton 2009).

[22] Rising sea levels, for instance, threaten to inundate coastal areas that are home to one billion people (25 percent of Bangladesh is less than a meter above sea level) (Goldin 2016: 122; *Global Humanitarian Forum* 2009).

current civil war in Syria.[23] Meanwhile carbon emissions exacerbate the acidification of the world's oceans, wreaking havoc on marine life and the food chain (Gillis 2012).

Persons in high-income countries bear a disproportionate responsibility for driving climate change. The World Bank estimates that OECD member countries generate an average of 10.2 metric tons of CO_2 per capita, while the least developed countries emit 0.3 metric tons of CO_2 per capita (World Bank Data).[24] In fact, the world's governments continue to encourage the production of fossil fuels through direct and indirect subsidies that amount to $1.9 trillion per year. Between 2005 and 2011, the 34 OECD member countries spent between $55 billion and $90 billion per year to support fossil fuel production and use (IMF 2013). Meanwhile, the largely voluntary and symbolic commitments ratified by 192 signatories to the Kyoto Protocol (1997) – which the United States did not sign – have been insufficient.[25] It remains to be seen whether the recently ratified Paris Agreement under the UN Framework Convention on Climate Change – from which the US, under the administration of President Donald Trump, recently withdrew – will result in effective carbon reduction legislation.

UNMET DUTIES

The brief summary of global poverty and global inequality recounted above suggests that inequities built into the global distribution of economic benefits and burdens – whatever their causes – impose greater duties beyond emergency assistance, duties that fall on everyone, more so on those living in high income countries and those who are comparably well off. Of course, causal factors cannot be ignored in determining

---

[23] Perhaps as many as 2 billion people suffer water scarcity, 660 million lacking safe drinking water (National Public Radio 2013).

[24] In 2004 the per capita carbon dioxide emission in the United States was 20.6 tons in comparison to China's 3.9 (6 as of 2014) and Bangladesh's 0.2 (the global average was 4.5). Growth in GDP is estimated to be eight times more important than population growth in explaining the rapid growth of China's carbon dioxide emissions, which now leads the world (China also leads in pioneering green technologies aimed at reducing emissions [Brown 2008: 246, 250]).

[25] Some parties to the agreement, most notably China and India, did not accept binding targets. However, in 2014 China and the United States signed a nonbinding agreement that commits China to capping its emissions and replacing 20 percent of its coal-generated energy with greener alternatives by 2030. This reduction is significant insofar as CO_2 emissions have risen in China and India, while recently falling in most developed countries. As of 2017, China leads the world in wind powered energy and ranks second in solar-powered energy.

responsibilities and their correlative duties. Do the poor themselves con-tribute to their own poverty through the suboptimizing choices they make? Perhaps, especially if these choices reflect adaptations to gender roles and customs that prevent women from being educated and entering the workforce and that discourage change and political activism leading to institutional reform. Do consumers who purchase goods made in sweat-shops contribute to poverty? Perhaps, especially if they don't use their purchasing power to leverage large retailers to increase wages and to improve conditions in the workshops they do business with. Do citizens contribute to poverty? Perhaps, especially if they don't ask their govern-ments to enact fairer rules governing international trade, lending, and developmental assistance (including doing more to encourage the creation of noncorrupt, accountable governments in the developing world).

I am sympathetic to the idea that fulfilling some of our duties will require compensating for past harms (taking into account a moral statute of limitations that extends no further, perhaps, than the past three gen-erations).[26] However, whether we have violated a human right, based on the fact that "the citizens and governments of the affluent countries... are imposing a global institutional order that foreseeably and avoidably

---

[26] In response to Pogge's demand for of a compensatory tax (Global Resources Dividend) – to be levied on affluent consumers of oil and other environmentally harmful resources – for unjustly imposing institutions on the poor that reduce them to poverty, for benefiting from crimes perpetrated against the descendants of the poor, and for benefitting from the unjust exclusion of the poor from natural resources, Richard Miller (2010: 59 and 271 note 4) observes that if people currently living in affluent countries benefited from past crimes of colonialism, genocide, and the like, their liability for restitution would have to be limited by a statute of limitations acknowledging their blamelessness. He also contests Pogge's insinuation that the poor should have an equal share in the world's resources, and that imposing trade embargos on tyrants who rob their country's resources would help the poor. Miller's desert-based, Lockean argument – that natural resources are rightly claimed by those who develop them – ignores the Lockean proviso, much insisted upon by Pogge, that private ownership of resources must be acquired in a manner that is just – the exception, not the rule, in the history of Western imperialism – and one, moreover, that allows the poor to access their fair share of the proceeds, preferably through remunerable employment. That said, I agree with Miller that trade embargos, withholding aid, and other sanctions targeting oppressive governments often end up harming the poor instead; indeed, the responsibility to protect against gross human rights violations has all too often assumed forms of intervention (typically military) that have harmed the victims more than their criminal assailants (as I argue in Chapter 6). Pogge's recommendation that newly minted democracies in poor countries be forgiven the debt accrued by former autocrats strikes me as more salutary, although instituting a global democracy panel of the sort he recommends for determining the democratic bona fides of postautocratic governments would have to be carefully devised so as not to favor powerful political interests.

reproduces severe and widespread poverty" via current trade practices and the like, as Pogge (2008: 207) suggests, is at least facially contestable. After all, many of these practices profit the poor as well, or at least do not make them worse off than they were. Sweatshops that exploit the poor are not imposed on them; indeed, they welcome the jobs that sweatshops offer.

Regardless of whether human rights are violated by our present global order – I believe that they are at the least not fully protected by that order and are very likely rendered insecure by it – one thing seems evident: If severe poverty remains a stubborn fact about a global economy that has made affluent people rich at the expense of the poor, then exploiting the poor in this manner is surely wrong. And, it is wrong because it violates a "relational duty," in the words of Richard Miller (2010: 59) and Iris Young (2007), to treat the poor fairly, showing equal concern for their interests. Fulfilling this duty will require making future changes in current practices and institutions, perhaps eventually leading to the abolition of capitalism as we know it.[27] Short of taking that radical step, we have duties to mitigate poverty and social inequalities in the global distribution of benefits and burdens.

But what is the proper way to frame these duties? Beyond a general duty to rescue those in emergency, or a general duty to reduce suffering when it entails not sacrificing something of comparable moral value, do we also have stronger duties with respect to the poor that emanate from a basic, higher-order duty to respect (and perhaps protect and promote) human rights? If so, how do these stronger duties affect our other duties of social justice?

HUMAN RIGHTS AND SOCIAL JUSTICE: TWO OVERLAPPING APPROACHES TO UNDERSTANDING OUR GLOBAL DUTIES

World Crisis and Underdevelopment aims to clarify the dynamics of capitalist underdevelopment and our duties with respect to mitigating poverty and inequality in a world of threatened resources and limited waste capacities. It also addresses changes in global governance and international law that would have to be implemented in order to effectively fulfill these duties. As I argue below, these are ambitious aims that require a multidisciplinary approach drawing from economics, political science, social science, and international relations, as well as from moral philosophy and psychology.

[27] See Chapter 4.

Utilitarianism

As a multidisciplinary approach, critical theory is well-positioned to address issues of justice and social underdevelopment. However, before discussing the peculiar advantages of the critical theory approach I adopt in this book, let me begin by briefly clarifying the strengths and weaknesses of standard approaches to justice, which for the sake of convenience I divide into approaches that focus on duties pertaining to human rights and approaches that focus on duties pertaining to social cooperation (or social justice).

Utilitarianism bases both sets of duties on an overarching imperative to maximize global well-being. But the efficient (cost-effective) mitigation of global suffering (say), cannot be the only method for determining our duties. Even a stalwart utilitarian like John Stuart Mill observed that "distinct and assignable obligations to any person or persons" can be based on other factors, such as social responsibilities, that might have only an indirect relationship to utility.[28] Some of these may be quite impersonal and far-ranging (such as the duty of emergency rescue); others may be based on personal ties, voluntarily or involuntarily assumed; and yet others may be based on rectifying harms (intended or not). Fulfilling these duties may not always harmonize with *directly* maximizing some generally agreed upon values or goods, even ones we regard as very important, such as reducing overall suffering.

Human Rights and Duties of Justice: The Global Poor versus the Local Poor

This book mainly explores several types of assignable duties: those stemming from human rights and those stemming from social justice. Human rights and social justice approaches undoubtedly overlap in supporting some of the same rights and duties. Individuals demand equal legal protection both as a matter of human right and as a matter of equal citizenship.[29]

---

[28] J. S. Mill, *On Liberty*, Chapter IV and notes 39 and 40 below.
[29] It may be argued (Waldron 1993: 25) that human rights duties are normally interpreted and fulfilled as social justice duties. The human right to national citizenship, for instance, presumes that human rights will be incorporated into the social justice duties governments owe their subjects, as I argue in Chapter 5. Should governments become incapable of fulfilling these social justice duties, then it falls on some outside source that might not be socially connected to that government's legal subjects to fulfill them as simple human rights duties. In general, the exercise of a right may require different agents to fulfill different kinds of duties, negative, positive, humanitarian, social justice, etc.; some of these may be linked in "successive waves of duty."

But human rights are rights enjoyed by persons simply in virtue of their humanity, regardless of whether or not they have entered into social relationships with us. For example, if we assume that persons have a human right to basic subsistence that others can satisfy without incurring significant hardship, then famine-stricken persons inhabiting an isolated island could demand that total strangers provide them with food relief as a matter of human right. By contrast, duties of social justice are owed to persons in virtue of their standing in some social relationship to the duty holder. A citizen of an affluent democracy may rightly demand that that society provide a standard of living well above that enjoyed by most people in the world, simply in order to receive his or her fair share of that society's social income and to participate with dignity and self-respect in that society's political life; but he or she could not reasonably demand that higher standard of living as a matter of human right.

There may be other differences between human rights and social justice duties that bear on the question of subsistence and economic equality. Social justice duties typically involve positive duties to act in such a way as to provide some good to others with whom one is socially connected and to whom one owes a duty. Parents owe their children a nurturing environment; contractors owe one another the goods and services they have promised to each other; persons who have harmed others through negligence owe them compensation; and, I will argue, all who are socially connected – and not just persons bound by common citizenship – owe each other fair treatment, including not taking advantage of each other; e.g., by exploiting a weakness or vulnerability from the vantage point of superior bargaining strength in order to gain unnecessary and excessive benefits at the other person's expense.

This latter example illustrates an important advantage that a social justice approach might have in comparison to a human rights approach in clarifying our duties with regard to poverty and inequality. It may well be the case that foreign sweatshops, which are contracted by wealthy retailers in developed countries, pay their workers above subsistence and above what might be owed to them as a matter of human right. Although these sweatshops might promote human rights by improving lives that might be made worse off if forced to survive on incomes generated by a local economy, they might reasonably be judged to be unjustly exploitative if (a) the incomes they provide do not provide opportunities for escaping deep poverty and (b) raising these incomes would not significantly reduce the profits of wealthy retailers in developed countries who could pass the marginal increase in labor costs onto their affluent clientele.

Human Rights

Indeed, even if, as I argue in Chapter 5, human rights stipulate thresholds of material provision and security that go beyond what sweatshop wages and conditions normally provide and designate moral aspirations targeting higher levels of development and flourishing that envisage a life without sweatshops, they do not expressly address injustices associated with extreme inequality. Although people who drive hard bargains typically set out to exploit their partner's weaknesses – and do so moreover, by threatening to withdraw their cooperation if their demands are not met – the extreme inequality in bargaining leverage between wealthy retailers and the local sweatshops with whom they subcontract creates a unique relationship of domination and coercion that amounts to vicious exploitation. In this case, social inequality as such rises to the level of a grave social injustice that may be every bit as harmful as a human rights violation. Indeed, social injustices of this type clearly impact the fulfillment of human rights. Local sweatshop owners and their workers lack the economic resources to bargain with multinational retailors for higher wages and better working conditions. The same applies to political power-leveraging; so long as the very wealthy leverage their demands with threats to transfer their assets abroad and/or withhold campaign contributions to aspiring office holders, persons of average means and, above all, the poor, will have little influence in shaping policies that protect their human rights.

There is another reason why some might find the social justice approach to be more attractive than the human rights approach. It is philosophically contentious whether human rights even require a socially guaranteed provision of subsistence. The Universal Declaration of Human Rights (1948) asserts that they do (Article 25), as do Catholic Social Teaching and classical natural law theory, but the current practice of humanitarian law and the modern, reason-based grounding of human rights, which narrowly equates human rights with basic rights of liberty against the state – the so-called "rights of man" – suggest that they might not. In practice, human rights violations are commonly understood to mean crimes against humanity and other grievous violations of international humanitarian law, not the absence of a good (such as water) needed to live whose deprivation (or insecurity) has been caused by an act of privatization that has been abetted and condoned by a legally sanctioned trade regime (as occurred in Cochabamba, Bolivia). The prevailing "interactional" account of human rights (as Pogge puts it) assumes that human

rights are claims against discrete individuals (mainly leaders of governments and militias) – not claims against institutions that have the impri-
matur of international treaty (Pogge 2008: 69–73). That explains why
poverty-related mortality and morbidity, when not intentionally caused
by criminal militias and governments, are treated as blameless evils, whose
victims can only plead for help as a matter of basic decency on the part of
well-off foreign donors (assuming that their own governments are too
weak to act on their behalf). In the modern theory of natural rights that
traces its lineage back to the eighteenth-century European Enlightenment,
"inalienable" rights are mainly (with few exceptions) identified with
liberty rights, or permissions to act without interference from state or
society. According to this modern liberal interpretation, such so-called
"negative" rights are guaranteed by "omissions" rather than by positive
acts; so long as society and state do not actively intervene in constraining
the conduct permitted by these rights (or intervene only to secure these
rights against malefactors), the individual's human rights are fully
respected.

John Rawls (1999a: 109–11) and Amartya Sen (2005), among many
prominent philosophers, have argued that respecting and promoting these
liberty rights alone might be the most important way to combat global
poverty and global inequality. In their opinion, corrupt and authoritarian
regimes that restrict liberty and patriarchal regimes that discourage
women from owning property and entering civil society impose the greatest impediment to economic development. In making this argument,
Rawls and Sen recognize that liberty must be accompanied by security
and development.[30] This concession of human rights to security and to
development, however, already implies a one-sidedness in the modern
liberal theory of human rights that has come under extensive scrutiny by
political philosophers. Henry Shue (1980) and Sen (2005) have persuasively argued that liberty rights are not only insecure when exercised apart
from security rights, but are also insecure when exercised apart from
subsistence and developmental rights (the rights to opportunities and
resources that build up basic capabilities essential to the rational exercise

---

[30] The Preamble to the Declaration on the Right to Development (1986) states that "development is a comprehensive economic, social, cultural and political process, which aims at
the constant improvement of the well-being of the entire population and of all individuals
on the basis of their active, free and meaningful participation in development and in the
fair distribution of benefits resulting therefrom." Note that the right to development is
framed as a group right, not an individual right. For further discussion of whether group
rights can be properly included in the category of human rights, see Chapter 7.

of informed choice) (Shue 1996; Sen 2005). One could extend Shue's thinking further and argue that no one can effectively exercise freedom of choice and action without having the right to participate in the political process that legally defines the scope of one's liberty. Anyone who accepts this train of reasoning should resoundingly endorse the conclusion drawn by the delegates to the 1993 World Conference on Human Rights in Vienna:

All human rights are universal, indivisible and interdependent and interrelated. The international community must treat human rights globally in a fair and equal manner, on the same footing, and with the same emphasis.

Understanding human rights in this robust sense justifies expanding the list of human rights beyond first-generation civil and political rights to include second-generation social rights, such as the right to welfare and security, and it may well justify expanding it to include third-generation ("group") rights to collective self-determination that are especially pertinent to women, religious and ethnic minorities, indigenous peoples and subnationalities (Ingram 2000, 2004, 2012). In this respect the human rights approach gains an advantage over the social justice approach, for it imposes duties on society at large to guarantee that each individual has free access to basic goods requisite for leading a minimally worthwhile life, no matter how socially *un*connected he or she may be to the persons on whom those duties might ultimately fall.

   Another advantage that the human rights approach has over its social justice counterpart is the greater weight that has traditionally been ascribed to human rights duties in comparison to other kinds of duties. This weight has been ascribed to human rights under the assumption that human rights are essentially liberty rights. Most conventional ethical approaches have held that it is worse to harm a person than to deny that person aid. Killing someone, for example, is generally thought to be worse than letting them die by denying them aid, even if the end result is the same. In short, harms inflicted on the agency of persons, who are distinguished from animals in virtue of their actual or potential possession of a free rational will, are violations of what is thought to be their essential humanity.

   At first glance, this way of defending the superior weight of human rights duties in comparison to social justice duties seems not very promising, because it adopts the narrow liberal interpretation of human rights mentioned above (the equation of human rights with liberty rights), thereby undercutting the view, defended by Shue and others, that denying persons aid can also constitute a human rights violation. Pogge (2008), however, argues that this is not necessarily the case. Instead of thinking of aid as something that is owed by a comparably weak duty of emergency rescue or by an even weaker duty of charity, he suggests that we think of aid as something owed by way of compensating for past and present harm. More precisely, he argues that the governments of the developed world share some portion of the responsibility for the mortality and morbidity caused by global poverty. According to Pogge, the developed nations of the world have benefited from (and abetted in) the violent colonial expropriation of the developing world's people and resources, thereby making most of the people inhabiting that world worse off than they would have been otherwise. They have also, along with corrupt ruling elites in the developing world, monopolized an unfair share of the world's common resources (and, by consuming them, contributed a greater share of the carbon emissions that particularly harm the most vulnerable and poor); and they have "imposed" (through their government's representatives) a trade regime that protects product patents that render lifesaving drugs beyond the reach of the poor even as it extends borrowing and resource vending privileges to corrupt rulers in developing countries. This trade regime encourages the underdevelopment if not destruction of local economies in those countries by allowing governments of developed nations to impose tariffs that make it difficult for poor countries to sell their goods in these wealthier countries and by forcing poorer countries to open their markets to underpriced and subsidized exports from these same developed countries.[31]

---

[31] The use by Japan, the EU, and the US of agricultural tariffs and quotas on exports, coupled with price supports, subsidies, and other policies aimed at mainly protecting a very small percentage of their wealthiest farmers, has also contributed to wide fluctuations in global food prices that severely harm the poor. Seventy percent of the world's poor live in rural regions, where subsistence farming, especially among women, provides the major source of employment. Unable to export their staple food crops and compete on the global market, farmers in the developing world specialize in unprotected agricultural products destined for consumption in the developed world, such as cocoa, rubber, and coffee. This shift toward a global monoculture geared toward standardized exports paradoxically contributes to food shortages at home. Forced to export these products in their primary (raw) form, farmers in the developed world lose the added value that comes with processing, and they remain vulnerable to shifting demand in developed countries for their products. Furthermore, because they cannot export their food staples, farmers who specialize in producing these commodities depend entirely on domestic consumer markets; but governments in developing countries often impose price controls on staples to protect poor urban workers (who, living in capitals, wield greater political clout), which in turn depress the income of poor farmers. Finally, rich countries that overproduce subsidized agricultural products "dump" this excess onto global markets, causing food prices to collapse globally. Attempts to seek redress for the harms and

In order to pay off their debt, poor countries may still be subject to conditions in taking out loans from the World Bank or International Monetary Fund, conditions that once typically required (and might still require in many instances) the devaluation of local currencies, the privatization and/or downsizing of government social services, and the deregulation of labor contracting, resource extraction, and environmental habitation. In short, Pogge argues that the rich owe compensation to the poor and have a duty to rectify the current trade regime, both as a matter of social justice and *as a matter of human (liberty) right,* insofar as the rich have *denied* the poor *free access* to the subsistence and security resources that are due them as human beings.[32]

Although Pogge presents his theory of human rights as primarily "institutional" rather than "interactional," his emphasis on seeking compensation for past and present harm obscures an important difference between the two models of human rights. Institutional accounts of human rights not only hold governments, global economic multilaterals (GEMs), and transnational corporations (TNCs) liable for damages caused by failing to protect secure access to goods that are guaranteed by human rights, but they also hold all of us who participate in maintaining said institutions responsible for changing them. Indeed, we have a duty to change institutions that threaten persons' secure enjoyment of rights especially when – as in the case of global capitalism – no agent can be held *individually liable* for bringing the institution into existence while virtually everyone is collectively responsible for maintaining it.[33]

To round out my summary of the relative advantages and disadvantages of the two approaches we have considered: Some philosophers have

---

injustices associated with escalating tariffs imposed by developed countries and other trade policies under the Doha Round of WTO negotiations – policies which predictably lead to chronic food shortages, collapsing food prices, and environmentally unsustainable forms of intensive, environmentally degrading, large-scale agribusiness – are discussed in Chapter 4. See Goldin (2016: 63–66; 134–37).

[32] See note 26.

[33] Collective responsibility for actively causing or passively allowing grievous human rights violations – Pogge's model for framing our *compensatory* duties – is distinct from collective responsibility for contributing (usually unwittingly) to the maintenance of unjust structures. The kind and degree of responsibility one has with respect to *changing* the sweatshop system, for example, depends on one's power, privilege, interest, and organizational capacity. Thus, while government officials and CEOs exercise direct power over the sweatshop system "from above," privileged consumers influence this power "from below" through their purchasing preferences. Sweatshop workers have the greatest interest in changing the system, while students have the time and education to raise public awareness of sweatshop injustice (Young 2007: 183–86).

challenged the view that human rights always impose stronger moral duties than social justice duties (Griffin 2008: 142–45). For example, it may be that the racial segregation imposed by the South African regime of apartheid – especially under the seemingly benign policy, adopted in the 1980s, of declaring parts of tribal South Africa extra-territorial "homelands" – caused worse harm to black South Africans than the denial of their human right to freedom of religion would have. The tribal homelands were created in an effort to legitimate the unequal and inferior treatment of black South Africans, who were prohibited from living in and traveling though certain places, by simply designating them as extra-territorial migrants (a status similar to guest workers). Reclassified in this way, South African blacks were subjected to the same ruthless exploitation and discrimination they suffered before the homelands system was instituted, but without the possibility of claiming that their equal rights *as South African citizens* had been violated. Indeed, assuming that the right to equal protection under the law afforded to *conationals* is a human right as well (pursuant to Articles 7, 13.1, and 15.2 of the UDHR), South African blacks could no longer claim that this *human* right and its corollaries (the human right not to be denied one's nationality; the human right to move freely within one's nation's borders, etc.) had been denied them. Regardless of whether the homelands system aimed to exploit a legal loophole by redefining the status of South African blacks as noncitizens who could no longer claim that the South African government was violating their human right to equal citizenship, South African blacks could still claim that they were suffering a social injustice every bit as evil as the injustice and harm they suffered under the earlier regime, when the violation of their rights (as citizens of South Africa and as human beings) had been transparent.

As the above example shows, the presumption that shifting "legal" borders can provide morally relevant grounds for delimiting the enjoyment of human rights raises deeper questions about the legitimacy of appealing to borders and national sovereignty as a moral and legal loophole for avoiding social justice duties to those who are defined as aliens. The right to have rights, as Hannah Arendt put it, cannot be reduced to the right to equal citizenship within a bounded nation so long as socially interdependent nations exist as vastly unequal spaces for the enjoyment of citizenship rights.

Regardless of whether or not we accept Arendt's problematic understanding of human rights as rights to social justice within a bounded state – a stipulation that leaves in limbo millions of trans-border communities and irregular migrants – it is clear that both human rights and social justice approaches play complementary roles in enabling a complete assessment of the peculiar wrongs associated with poverty and social inequality. The understanding of human rights as moral aspirations toward achieving a fulfilling and flourishing life for everyone envisages a life of dignity wherein domination caused by social inequality is eliminated. Even a more limited understanding of human rights as legal baselines determining thresholds of tolerable treatment implies social equality in the *equal* legal protection of said rights. The emphasis on ensuring just and fair participation in mutually beneficial social arrangements – equality in bargaining strength among social contractors – is one way of ensuring that the weakest members have their human agency and well-being respected and legally protected.

CONTROVERSIAL CLAIMS

As the preceding section shows, human rights and social justice duties are vague and ambiguous. Thus part of my task will be to clarify their meaning. This metaethical enterprise is perhaps easier to accomplish in the case of social justice. By "social justice" I mean, quite literally, duties that encompass fair dealing with others who are connected to us socially – including those who are impacted by our actions. Reliance on customary usage in parsing the meaning of social justice (in terms, for instance, of contractual duties, compensatory duties, duties of citizenship, etc.) will prove useful in explicating the meaning of human rights as well, although in this case more philosophical analysis may be required, as I argue below. Human rights have a complex moral and legal genealogy and their scope and meaning have clearly evolved. Although I maintain that human rights are best thought of as claims that individuals have with respect to governments and powerful, nongovernment agencies (including TNCs), to respect and, in some cases, protect, their access to a threshold of primary goods requisite for leading a life worthy of human dignity, one mustn't lose sight of their nonjuridical meaning as moral aspirations.

Among the controversial claims I will be defending are the following: determining the causes of poverty and economic inequality is not necessary for determining whether poverty is unjust and whether we have duties to remedy it; the coercive nature of extreme poverty in its disparate positioning of persons with respect to opportunities for leading a worthwhile life suffices to condemn it. Minimally, we have at least an imperfect duty to protect persons living beyond our national borders, if doing so imposes no significant burden on us; but the duty becomes more perfect, or unconditional, to the extent that we ourselves have contributed to rendering that life less secure.

Another controversial claim I will defend is that extreme socioeconomic inequality – whatever its causes – may also threaten secure access to primary goods requisite for the exercise of human rights. This is because one of the valued capabilities protected by human rights – rational agency – is distinguished by its normative and social structuration. Agents frame their pursuit of ends in terms of their own autobiographical self-understanding, which in turn refers to socially recognized norms and values. The deprivation or extreme diminishment of social recognition suffered by those who are judged to be of low socioeconomic or legally irregular status also diminishes their sense of self-respect and their self-understanding of what they can strive for. In some cases the lack of social status entails exclusion from the community and denial of opportunities to fulfill its norms and values. Extreme inequality also conduces to exploitative relationships that threaten agency. Such relationships enable the more powerful to extract concessions from the less powerful through superior threat-advantage, which amounts to coercion. Even if exploitative domination does not diminish minimum levels of agency in the short run, it may still diminish future opportunities for developing higher, perhaps more autonomous, forms of agency.

Another controversial claim I will defend revolves around paradoxes associated with the enforcement of human rights. On one hand human rights appear to be the most efficient means for respecting, protecting, and promoting agency. Current agency-depriving practices are universally recognized as criminal human rights violations that both national and international agencies legally sanction and seek to punish. For instance, illegal trafficking in human migrant labor can be prosecuted under humanitarian law that criminalizes the coercive – specifically nonconsensual – contracting of labor as a form of slavery, kidnapping, etc. On the other hand, forms of trafficking in which the "victims" rationally and voluntarily consent to their exploitation out of desperation, because they want to feed their families, are not easily prosecuted under human rights law. In fact, doing so subjects these "complicit" workers to risks of being charged with criminal offenses and deported back to their homelands, where they may face shame, abuse, or at the very least a repetition of the coercive social conditions that led them to their desperate criminal choice(s) in the first place. Complying with legal authorities to avoid deportation, however, brings risks of its own, as the "victim" or her family may be threatened with reprisals. Given this paradox in the current enforcement of humanitarian law, it might be better to supplement our human rights duties with social justice duties of a less overtly juridical nature. I argue that one way to do this is to decriminalize workers' consent to trafficking and to acknowledge the unjustly coercive background conditions from which they seek to flee. Duties of social justice may require the implementation of social legislation providing sanctuary for victims of trafficking. Furthermore, it may require us to rethink the paradox of humanitarian law by conceiving the coercive context from which victims of trafficking flee as itself a human rights violation (or deprivation). In that case, we may have to reconceive the dominant institutional understanding of a human right as a liberty to act without criminally coercive interference from an identifiable agent.

After we clarify what sorts of duties we have in making sure that human rights are respected and enforced, we face the difficult task of clarifying the myriad of other duties that are demanded of us as a matter of social justice. For example, what duties, if any, constrain trade relationships between rich and poor countries, or between multinational enterprises and the local sweatshops they employ? How should these duties be balanced with respect to duties that are owed to conationals or to stockholders? What incentives are there for the well-off to voluntarily comply with duties to reduce poverty and inequality?

If human-rights and social justice duties also aim to empower the poor, remedies will have to be tailored that avoid coercive forms of paternalism. For example, loan-agreements that impose stringent structural adjustment conditions, or forms of family planning assistance that exclude contraception and early term abortions, may force resistant recipients to reject aid. Conversely, microlending strategies that empower women's social and welfare agency might inadvertently reinforce adaptive preferences for traditional gender norms (including *purdah*) that diminish autonomous agency and gender equality.

A controversial solution to this problem that I shall propose encourages consensual dialogue between aid and loan providers. Common wisdom holds that aid workers and loan providers know better than their clients how to advance their clients' agency. Clients in the developing world are often characterized as suffering from backward ideas. This "wisdom" overlooks what indigenous peoples can teach the developed world about sustainable living. It also overlooks power imbalances between providers and recipients that undermine genuine collaboration. Finally, it overlooks the dilemmas that recipients face in choosing development. For instance, women may feel that they must choose between accepting their community's patriarchal norms or face agency-denying ostracism and violence. Conventional wisdom thus dismisses practices that might appear to be inefficient by Western standards but which are in fact efficient in sustaining community.

I argue that aid should be dispensed in such a way that discourages dependency and encourages local entrepreneurship and community self-determination. Collaborative projects should be responsive to local knowledge, experience, and culture. However, just as developmental expertise needs to be critically informed (and transformed) by local experience, so too local experience needs to be critically informed (and transformed) by expertise. Cross-cultural and expert-lay dialogue can spur reflection and promote a fuller range of agency, incorporating both social and autonomous forms, even if it goes no further than spurring reflection on how traditional customs, such as gender norms, can be reimagined in a more egalitarian way so as to advance the long-term empowerment of everyone.

Promoting the reduction of global poverty and social inequality through popular democratic movements – be they religious or secular – is one way to discourage the terrorism and civil unrest that exacerbates poverty and that also threatens the commercial interests of the United States and other hegemonic powers. To that extent, reduction of global poverty and social inequality, far from being a burdensome duty on those who inhabit relatively affluent nations, is rather a policy that serves their (and everyone's) long term interests. So looking at poverty reduction through the narrow lens of democratic reform and enlightened policies of economic development, I argue, goes a long way toward seeing how duty and self-interest harmonize.

But looking at the same problem through a wider lens suggests otherwise. Aside from reconsidering Islamic political movements, developmental policies, trade agreements, and perhaps even the fundamental tenets of a capitalist economy in the narrow sense, I argue that we will need to reconsider, more broadly, the very structure of global governance and international law in overcoming another kind of narrow, sovereign self-interest. The only realistic hope for avoiding the catastrophic levels of poverty and inequality that will likely accompany global warming is to designate global warming as a human rights and social justice threat of the highest magnitude.[34] The unequal

---

[34] A human rights framework was not incorporated into the United Framework Convention on Climate Change (1992) or the Kyoto Protocol (1997). However, in 2005 the Chair of the Inuit Circumpolar Conference submitted a petition to the Inter-American Commission on Human Rights on behalf of the Inuit of the Arctic regions of the United States and Canada arguing that the impact of global climate change caused by the "acts and omissions" of the United States violated the fundamental human rights of the Inuit peoples. Subsequent petitions by the Maldives and Small Island Developing States sought

distribution of costs and benefits that global warming portends does not encourage much optimism that high-intensity carbon producing nations will be politically motivated to strike multilateral agreements to drastically reduce their current rates of consumption and production. Indeed for a developing country like China the mere thought of reducing consumption and production must seem – at least in the short term – quite unbearable (and unfair); and given the pivotal role China plays in sustaining a vast network of global production chains, quite unbearable for the rest of us as well.[35]

The Paris Agreement confirms the view defended in this book that governments will need a more centralized governmental agency at the global level – such as the United Nations – to facilitate and monitor significant climate change policy. I therefore defend expanding the UN's role in global governance on logical and practical grounds. Constitutional reform of the United Nations General Assembly and National Security Council pursuant to cosmopolitan norms of democracy and rule of law must underwrite this change. Defending this claim will require addressing skeptical arguments from the Realist school of international relations. Above all, it will require showing how solidarity with a particular nation, religion, or political group can be extended in a cosmopolitan direction (Rawls 1999: 112–13).

A CRITICAL THEORY OF INJUSTICE AND UNDERDEVELOPMENT

The approach to moral theorizing I propose to adopt in this study is informed by the interdisciplinary methodology of the Frankfurt School tradition of critical theory. Following Marx's definition of critical theory as "the self-clarification of the struggles and wishes of the age,"[36] this approach grounds social criticism in historical reality. In contrast to ideal moral theories that adduce timeless norms of justice from human nature

to incorporate a human rights framework in the negotiating process of UNFCCC. A report entitled "Climate Change and Human Rights" (2008) that was developed by the International Council on Human Rights notes the advantage of shifting from aggregate cost-benefit analysis (emissions rights) to analysis of climate impact on individual human lives (human rights) in setting minimally acceptable outcomes and procedures for legal implementation (Tuana 2012: 410–18).

[35] To amplify upon the injustice of asking a developing economy to make the same sacrifice as a developed economy, much of China's carbon-emitting manufacturing industry is directly or indirectly owned by US-based companies; and much of its output is sold in the US.

[36] K. Marx, "Letter to Arnold Ruge" [September 1843].

or reason taken in abstraction from historical context, critical social theories seek guidance from the conventional norms that inform actually existing social practices and institutions.[37]

Natural law theory and classical social contract theory exemplify ideal theory; they postulate universal principles of duty and right that acquire real force and content only in their subsequent application to particular historical circumstances – the province of nonideal theory.[38] Utilitarianism, too, postulates an ahistorical principle of morality: the aggregate promotion of well-being. Although application of this principle engages circumstantial calculations of costs and benefits, this method of moral reasoning, unlike the natural (or rational) determination of rights and duties, is more likely to clash with conventional morality and conventional moral psychology. Utilitarians generally reject the conventional privileging of negative duties commanding forbearance from malfeasance over positive duties commanding beneficence. They also reject the conventional privileging of some persons' well-being based on accidents of birth and association. These unconventional features of utilitarianism find ample expression in the extreme measures proposed by utilitarians in

[37] The distinction between ideal and nonideal theory can be drawn in many ways and most theorists combine elements of both theories. Only a theory of justice, such as Plato's *Republic* (as interpreted by Leo Strauss, say) that methodically disregarded facts in constructing its political ideals and did not care about the possibility for realizing them, would count as purely ideal. This description would not apply to John Rawls' theory of justice, which appeals to general facts about history, psychology, economics, etc. in constructing an ideal theory of justice, whose utopian vision remains "realistic" enough to be capable of being striven for, even if it is unlikely to be attained. Rawls' ideal theory grounds his nonideal theory, which addresses situations involving *partial compliance* (e.g., injustice) or *unfavorable circumstances* (e.g., socioeconomic underdevelopment) (Rawls 2001: 13, 47, 101; 1999a: 90). Critical theorists also rely on ideal theories of justice (and development) in specifying the ultimate direction of change and comparing the relative merits of different historical possibilities for reform. However, unlike Rawls' theory, which can be accused of misdirecting attention away from present injustices and pathologies (see note 38), critical theories insist on more closely linking (ideal) theory and (nonideal) theory/practice, by appealing to genetic normative arguments and incorporating social scientific analysis of structural institutional contradictions (Stemplowska and Swift 2012).

[38] Sharply separating ideal from nonideal theory runs the risk of ideologically legitimating present injustice. According to Rawls's ideal theory of justice, access to scarce jobs and positions should not be qualified by morally arbitrary classifications, such as those based on race. The temptation to apply this ideal of justice to a nonideal world without adequate qualification risks "whitewashing" colorblind policies of employment, promotion, and admission to higher education that, given the after effects of past racial injustice (institutional racism), unwittingly perpetuate racial disadvantage. To identify injustice, critical judgment must occupy an ideal space of reasoning that stands in closer proximity to the real world (Azmanova 2012a).

addressing global poverty: Some utilitarians propose a "lifeboat" ethics calculated to stem unsustainable population growth by not intervening in overpopulated famine-stricken areas; others propose the opposite poverty reduction strategy of redistributing wealth from rich to poor until equality is achieved.[39]

The present study rejects the utilitarian dismissal of conventional moral priorities and respects the relative privileging of individual rights as well as special duties of justice based on social connectedness.[40] In doing so it shares common ground with natural law and social contract theories. However, unlike these ideal theories, it bases its understanding of human rights and social justice duties on evolving institutional practices, and has recourse to idealizing reconstructions only from within that

[39] Until recently, almost all moral discussions of global poverty and inequality were framed by utilitarian concerns. Using "lifeboat" ethics, some utilitarians (most notably Garrett Hardin [1974]) resurrected Thomas Malthus's argument that population growth outstrips food production and environmental carrying capacity, and so concluded that efforts at remedying starvation would backfire by producing more starvation. Conversely, other utilitarians (notably Peter Singer [1972]) deployed marginalist economic reasoning in defending an egalitarian redistribution of global wealth, coupled with developmentalist arguments that rising income security depresses population growth. Today, widespread acceptance of the four-phase *demographic transition* hypothesis confirms Singer's position. The hypothesis postulates an initial phase of high- birth/high mortality (typical of Europe during the eighteenth century and pre-WWII Asia and Africa), followed by a second phase of high-birth/low mortality population growth (typical of Europe during the Industrial Revolution and post-WWII Africa and Asia), concluding with a third phase of low-birth/low mortality population stability of about 2.5 children per family (typical of over half the developing world today) and a fourth phase of low-birth/low mortality population decline (typical of present-day Europe, Japan, and possibly China). According to demographic forecasts, world population will level out at about 12 billion sometime over the next fifty years (Goldin 2016: 57–58).

[40] Singer's preferred defense of a personal moral duty to contribute income and assets to poverty relief until one has sacrificed something of *comparable* and not merely of *significant* moral worth (pursuant to the principle of marginal utility) is rationally and logically unassailable, so long as one ideally abstracts from relational duties of social connection. In effect, Singer restricts the scope of our duties to moral obligations owed to persons as rationally indistinguishable bearers of equal human value and consideration. This latter (idealizing) abstraction is indeed essential to understanding our moral respect for human beings qua human beings. However, when coupled with Singer's utilitarian imperative of value maximization, it justifies not only human rights duties mandating that all persons be guaranteed minimally decent *thresholds* of basic resources. It mandates radically egalitarian distributive duties that require the redistribution of resources and capabilities without regard for concretely assignable social justice duties owed to family members, fellow citizens and national residents, producers and consumers, and others with whom we are institutionally connected. I discuss the derivative and secondary nature of rational (viz., abstract legal and moral) duties and rights vis-à-vis concrete duties of social recognition in Chapter 1.

practice.[41] These practices evolve in response to their own normative surplus. The rights and duties they prescribe realize the dignity, freedom, and equality of individual persons only partially; for as long as interpersonal, economic, and political institutions harbor social domination, equal opportunities for self-determination and self-realization will remain unfulfilled.

Obviously the method of *immanent critique* I adopt in this study presupposes a historically informed theory of social development. As I understand it, the theory of social development builds upon a tradition of political economy extending from early British empiricism to present-day neo-Marxian systems theory and beyond. However, in accordance with one strand of thought, I frame development in terms of a broader theory of social, cultural, and political *modernization*.[42] From this perspective, moral reasoning in terms of individual rights is a historical achievement

---

[41] Superficially critical normative theory resembles virtue ethics (of the contextual sort proposed, for example, by some feminist care ethicists) and communitarian political theory. However, critical theorists also invoke ideal normative reconstruction within the ambit of institutional social analysis. The interplay between ideal theorizing and conventional practice, which I discuss in Chapter 1, is not entirely unique to them. In this book, some of the social philosophers I draw upon who do not belong to the critical theory tradition, notably John Rawls, Richard Miller, Thomas Pogge, Allen Buchanan, and James Griffin, situate their ideal theorizing within specific institutional frameworks, although they seldom discuss the problematic interplay between their normative reconstructions and the global capitalist and Westphalian state subsystems.

[42] Development theory in its economistic form can be traced back to early modern moral philosophy. John Locke (Chapter V, *Second Treatise of Government* [1690]) famously extolled the greater industrial and agricultural productivity as well as individual progress in material well-being that a monetized exchange economy grounded in private property and a division of labor afforded, in comparison to the impoverished lifestyle yielded by North American Indian economies based on simple hunting and gathering. Enlightenment philosophies of history developed by Condorcet, Kant, and Hegel over a century later were more inclined to measure progress along moral and political dimensions, specifically in terms of the universal realization of individual freedom. During the heyday of European imperialism from 1840–1945, apologists for colonial rule, such as John Stuart Mill and Karl Marx, would appeal to both (economic and moral) strands of European thinking about progress and development (I discuss the racial subtext underlying this thinking in Chapter 2). However, talk of development during this period was overshadowed by the failure of capitalism to solve endemic crises of overproduction and proletarian impoverishment. In the wake of the new Cold War and anticolonial, national liberation movements in the developing world, post-WWII development theory, guided by the newly founded United Nations, evolved from a narrow focus on postwar *economic reconstruction* (promoting state-centered, Keynesian welfare policy for the sake of domestic and international peace) to a more ambitious theory of *modernization*. The architects of the latter theory of development, inspired by Walt Rostow's theory of economic stages and Talcott Parsons' theory of pattern variables, posited the First World (the industrial capitalist liberal democracies of Western Europe and the United States) – in opposition to the Second World (the authoritarian Communist regimes of China and the Soviet Bloc) – as the rational end-state for the undeveloped Third World.

of the modern world that shaped, and was shaped by, symbolic developments in other areas of culture and knowledge and by material developments in science and technology, economic production and consumption (including family life), legal and political order, and much else.

Modernization theory, which in Parsons' sociology derives from the neo-Hegelian writings of Weber and Durkheim, displayed a Eurocentric ethnocentrism in its understanding of modern values (it denigrated "traditional" social roles oriented toward maintaining collective identity and the intrinsically gratifying performance and display of ascribed character traits while extolling modern, technically specialized vocational roles whose performance could be evaluated by rational measures of achievement and rewarded in a manner conformable to individual self-interest and acquisitiveness). The theory also discounted obstacles to development presented by a history of imperialism. Marxists and "dependency-theorists," such as Immanuel Wallerstein, appealed to this fact in arguing that historical capitalism necessitates imperialism and underdevelopment. According to Wallerstein, global capitalism necessarily creates both a developed *center*, occupied by the United States, Western Europe, and Japan, *and* an underdeveloped *periphery*, comprising most of the Third World. Within this world system, the periphery sells low-value primary goods to the center in exchange for the center's value-added processed goods. While Marxists conceded the possibility of development under a global form of socialism, dependency theorists believed that global core-periphery dependency was systemically entrenched in a way that would likely perpetuate uneven development under any economic system. However, both Marxists and dependency theorists accepted a state-centric, Keynesian economic understanding of expanded or limited development. This understanding, which was largely embraced across ideological divides, was contradicted by the unanticipated "stagflation" that afflicted the US during the oil crisis of the seventies. The *neoliberal* paradigm of development that came to dominate development theory from the late seventies through the late nineties not only rejected state-centered economic development (and so diminished the role of the UN in development); it also rejected a values approach to development of the sort that had been favored by modernization theorists. For neoliberals, development, now limited to the single aim of poverty reduction through economic growth, would be driven by free trade and private investment. The failure of neoliberal orthodoxy to deliver on its promises in many parts of the developing world (see Chapter 4) provoked a renewed values-oriented approach to development led, once again, by the UN. The mixed success of the UN's MDG program included the rise of emerging economies (chiefly in China and India) and the restoration, especially in Latin America, of state-centered, neo-Keynesian economic policy. In tandem with the global economic fragility of the twentieth-first century and the potentially catastrophic specter of climate change impact on food production, water access, disease control, and much else, recent development theories and their corresponding practices have become more diverse in their aims, methods, instruments, and agents, involving: (a) reconsideration of the ills of "overdevelopment," such as climate change, environmental degradation, poor nutrition leading to obesity, diabetes, and coronary disease; (b) private-public partnerships; and (c) new collaborations among developing countries themselves. What remains core to the theory of development throughout these changes – a notion of universally protected human capabilities – reminds us of the singular achievements of modern culture: respect for the equal dignity of the individual as a bearer of universal human rights. Development theory must be sensitive to one-sided – ahistorical and culturally ethnocentric—interpretations of this universal legacy that reflect the ideological distortions wrought by socially dominant agents (as I argue in Chapters 2 and 5). For a brief reprise of development and postdevelopment theory, see Desai (2012) and Sahle (2012).

In saying that individual human rights are an achievement of the modern world I do not mean that they are necessarily *the* ideal logical endpoint of human moral reasoning. However, in contrast to purely conventional, ethnocentric "justifications" of (our) human rights, I do mean that human rights and the modern world(s) of which they are a part constitute, at the very least, path-dependent historical advances. On my understanding, modern rights and duties that first evolved in Europe over 300 years ago were more rational than, and therefore preferable to, conceptions of right and duty that historically preceded them. Following a vaguely Hegelian strategy of justification, we can say that rights and duties, along with the complex social, cultural, economic, political, and legal institutions in which they are embedded, were more successful than their premodern antecedents at solving social problems (or resolving social crises) that the latter themselves generated. For example, the ethical legacy of religion requires interpretation, which may lead to doctrinal schism and conflict that increasingly burden individuals with responsibility for having to reflectively choose their ethics according to their own personal conscience. Such ethical individualism may in turn spur demand for greater individual freedom and greater public accountability on the part of government elites. In conjunction with this ethical individualism, growth in population and material needs may further push economies regulated by rigid codes of artisanal production, commodity pricing, land usage, and the like to adopt less rigid rules of economic organization, exchange, and property ownership that are more efficient in meeting the growing needs of increasing numbers of individuals. In the words of Max Weber, we can discern an "elective affinity" between ethical individualism and economic individualism (self-interest, acquisitiveness, etc.), with both sets of practices – ideal (cultural) and material (socioeconomic, political, and legal) – conditioning the development of the other.

Explanations along these lines are typically offered by social scientists in explaining how modern market economies and liberal-democratic cultures arose in Europe and spread globally during the transformative period spanning 1350–1850. Islamic societies in Europe, North Africa, and Asia doubtless played a key role in preserving and advancing the moral and scientific core informing this legacy; but the legacy matured and spread throughout the world during the heyday of European colonialism (1800–1960). Thus, what I have designated as "modern institutions" have long ceased to be a strictly Western phenomenon with the consequence that their corresponding rights and duties have become universally accepted.

Critical theorists adopt the hypothesis that social development pro-
gresses along multiple paths of rational problem solving: through technical
development of efficient methods of economic production, on one side, and
moral development of schemes of cooperation and conflict resolution, on
the other.[43] Essential to this hypothesis, in their opinion, is the intersection
of these paths, producing collision (each maintaining its own, more or less
independent trajectory), convergence (each harmoniously reflecting a single
trajectory), or both. Orthodox Marxists (including Marx) were inclined to
believe in the inevitability of a technologically-driven trajectory of universal
progress (technological determinism), which for them would eventually
usher in the revolutionary establishment of a fully emancipated, contra-
diction-free communist society. Twentieth-century critical theorists reject
this simple convergence view, with some inclining toward a collision model
(Habermas) and others inclining toward a conversion-collision (or dialectical) view. Despite their disagreement on this score, all accept Marx's views
about the imbrication of modern technology and liberal individualism and,
like him, caution against labeling this normative fact unambiguously "progressive" (emancipatory and egalitarian).[44] Nonetheless, they adhere to the

---

[43] In contrast to the scientifically untestable predictions offered by orthodox Marxists,
today's critical theorists hang the plausibility of their logical reconstructions of social
evolution (species-specific learning) on empirically plausible explanations, often drawing
analogies with developmental psychology. See Habermas (1979) and Honneth (1996).

[44] The overly reductionist assumption that changes in ideological superstructures reflect
changes in the economic base, which in turn, are propelled by technological advances in
the forces of production compelling revolutions in property relations, contains a kernel of
truth. For example, in late eighteenth-century England the replacement of a domestic
cottage industry (the putting out system) based on human-powered implements by steam-
powered factories ushered in the demise of the extended family and the birth of the
nuclear family that would eventually have wide-ranging implications for configuring
Victorian sexual mores. In this context, Michel Foucault's controversial theses regarding
the capillary intersection of "microtechnologies" of disciplinary power – involving the
novel ordering of space and the temporal sequencing of corporeal motion in hospitals,
prisons, schools, factories, and military training – is intriguing (Foucault 1979a, 1979b).
The creation of humans who self-identify as individual subjects, that is to say humans
who have been subjected to apparatuses of self-governance qua "sexualized bodies" in
conformity with surveillance apparatuses of state and society geared toward engendering
productive bodies (what Foucault calls biopower), illustrates the power of technology in
"developing" individual capability and "freedom." Such techno-systems preserve individual capability and freedom in effective technical designs: For example, the factory
system's minute division of labor represents the *material sedimentation* of a certain
kind of individual agency whose "alienated" or "truncated" development, instantiated
in corporeal habitus, has achieved almost irreversible momentum to the point where it
has become highly resistant to "ideology critique." Foucault supplements this bleak
reductive account of development with an analysis of the human sciences. Besides
inventing individualizing techniques of observation, examination, and classification

idea that, once realized in material institutions (or techno-systems, to use Andrew Feenberg's term), this ideal normative legacy cannot be discarded (momentum implies irreversibility).[45]

Critical theorists have long observed that, at least within the ambit of capitalist and bureaucratic socialist society, technical progress and increased efficiency gained through scientific administration need not coincide with moral progress in realizing enduring values associated with freedom of choice, expanded intellectual and reflective capability, and democratic self-determination.[46]Authoritarian regimes, like China, may be remarkably efficient in reducing poverty and social inequality while discouraging dissent and democratic self-determination at higher levels of government.[47] Critical theorists also observe that the power conferred upon technical and managerial elites disempowers workers,

(the archive), these sciences elaborate discourses that serve to interpret and legitimate – and thus constitute – extant technological and governmental apparatuses. So construed, changes in moral reasoning regarding "scientific" standards of normalcy emerge alongside of technological changes rather than being determined by them. For an illustration of the imbrication of poverty expertise, methodological individualism, and techniques of disciplinary control in the name of empowerment, see Chapter 2. I compare Foucault's genealogical approach to social critique to the neo-Hegelian-Marxist approach favored by the Frankfurt School in Ingram (2005).

[45] Since Kant and Hegel, critical theory has endorsed the view that history will not witness any more normative revolutions beyond that which led to the universal recognition of the equal dignity of the individual as a free agent. This view is compatible with the possibility of future legal revolutions in our understanding and institutionalization of that singular idea. I thank Axel Honneth for suggesting this idea to me in a personal conversation.

[46] For a classical statement of the internal contradictions implicit in instrumental and moral-practical forms of societal rationalization, see Adorno and Horkheimer (1972); Marcuse (1964); J. Habermas (1987); and Ingram (1990).

[47] It should be noted that at the local level Chinese workers – perhaps more often than workers in the capitalist centers of the world—have successfully protested and struck for higher wages and improved conditions. Authoritarian governments in other developing countries have often not been as tolerant of and responsive to dissent. William Easterly, former World Bank economist and current codirector of the Development Research Institute at NYU, pointedly remarks (Easterly 2014) that partnerships between developmental technocrats (such as those funded by the Bill and Melinda Gates Foundation) and corrupt Third World autocrats (such as Ethiopia's former prime minister, Meles Zenawi) too often privilege poverty reduction and economic growth over human rights and democracy. Human Rights Watch's 2014 country report noted that Ethiopia's development projects, which were partly funded through foreign assistance, displaced indigenous communities without consulting or compensating them. Ethiopia, which imprisons non-violent opposition leaders and journalists and denies the right to assembly, receives $4 billion a year in developmental assistance. Easterly further notes that the World Bank, whose slogan is "Working for a world free of poverty," is forbidden by its charter to use the word "democracy."

consumers, and citizens. Because modern forms of institutional organization frustrate the realization of agency, it is no longer obvious that Western norms of rights, justice, and development that find effective material form in today's institutional techno-systems *are* progressive relative to the norms and techno-systems they replaced.

This ambivalent functioning of modern institutions has been appropriately highlighted by postmodernists and poststructuralists as well as by Frankfurt School critical theorists.[48] They call into question the emancipatory claims made on behalf of reason, and note that all institutions and their correlative norms of discourse and comportment are shaped by power-relations. Critical theorists must therefore confront the unpleasant fact that the conventional understanding of freedom, justice, and development on which they themselves rely for normative guidance is controversial. Thus some people find freedom supremely manifested in labor-saving technologies or in technically mediated monetary transactions and legal relationships. While technologies free us from work, monetary and legal transactions free us from being morally accountable to others, so that we can pursue our personal interests without needing to justify or coordinate them by engaging in risky, time-consuming conversations. Conversely, others find freedom supremely embodied in moral interactions that facilitate critical self-reflection and social detachment. Still others see freedom exemplified in social institutions that embed monetary and legal modes of strategic self-assertion in prior economic, political, and interpersonal relationships. Here individual freedom ceases to be defined by legally sanctioned egoism or morally sanctioned social detachment and assumes an expressly social valence, where the achievement of one person's aim is mutually recognized to require the achievement of other persons' aims in a scheme of social cooperation.[49]

---

[48] Among the more prominent "postmodernist" and "poststructuralist" critics of modern social institutions are Jacques Derrida, Michel Foucault, and Jean-François Lyotard (Ingram 1990; 1995). Postdevelopment and postcolonial theorists such as Arturo Escobar and Edward Said apply postmodernist insights to underscore how power relations impact the linguistic construction of social knowledge and social reality, resulting in what Said characterized as "Orientalism," or the social construction of "non-Western" societies as essentially different from their Western counterparts in their capability for development.

[49] Legal, moral, and social forms of freedom express progressive conditions for adequately conceiving and realizing freedom. The legal freedom to act on one's choices is impossible apart from moral freedom to deliberate on the goodness and rightness of those choices. Legal and moral forms of freedom, however, are exercised by persons in detachment from social relationships. By contrast, successful pursuit of morally considered choices

These competing visions of freedom motivate conflicting solutions to contemporary social ills. Technocrats, libertarians, and social democrats, for instance, frame the emancipatory yield of their respective solutions to global poverty in diametrically opposed ways: freeing economic markets from: (a) moral constraints that hamper efficient regulation; (b) regulatory constraints that hamper individual choice; and (c) social constraints (domination) that hamper fair, voluntary cooperation based on mutual recognition and open communication.[50] As befits their Hegelian-Marxist pedigree, critical theorists privilege social rather than technocratic or libertarian solutions to global poverty. From their perspective, the historical trajectory from *laissez faire* to welfare state capitalism progressively expanded and enriched the institutional meaning of emancipatory development, albeit not without generating new social pathologies of coercive misdevelopment caused by government over-regulation.[51]

Two critical theorists that have influenced my own thinking in this study – Jürgen Habermas and Axel Honneth – propose theoretical reconstructions of conventional practices that provide normative foundations for criticizing both social injustice and social pathology.[52] Habermas argues that a procedural conception of justice and democratic legitimation is grounded in conditions of communication oriented toward voluntary cooperation. What distinguishes this form of communication, which

---

ultimately depends on social cooperation in which that pursuit is made harmonious. For a fuller statement of this argument, see Honneth (2014).

[50] These different narratives of progressive economic emancipation occasionally overlap. The reigning neoliberal orthodoxy that celebrates the efficiency gains of free trade and unregulated markets combines libertarian and technocratic emancipatory narratives. Neoliberalism endorses libertarian individualism as a more technically efficient economic principle than welfare-based government regulation. This understanding of emancipatory progress is regarded as regressive from a critical theory perspective that highlights the normative and empirical connection between social welfare and nondomination.

[51] I follow Honneth (2014: 86–91, 113–18) in defining social pathology as a social – not psychological – development that "significantly impairs the ability to take part rationally in important forms of social cooperation" (86). Typically, the impairment in question involves failing to grasp the significance and purpose of such cooperation. For example, in child custody cases parents can forget the importance of the family as a loving and nurturing relationship. Likewise persons who rigidly act on scruples risk forgetting how to appropriately care for persons with whom they interact.

[52] Habermas and Honneth regard their moral theories as critical "reconstructions" of expectations persons inhabiting *modern* societies typically have. Such reconstructions differ from average persons' understanding of these expectations in drawing from evidence-based theories of economics, sociology, political science, and psychology, on one side, and conceptual analysis, intellectual history, and historical speculation, on the other. The decision to interpret history as if it were a progressive learning process is motivated, as Kant observed, by a rational, practical need to find meaning and hope in history.

Habermas claims is also crucial to noncoercive and undistorted socialization and identity-formation, is that any speaker can challenge or justify the relevant factual and normative beliefs underwriting interaction. Rational accountability at the level of everyday interaction constitutes a formal expectation for free and equal discussion (discourse) that, as Habermas understands it, unavoidably shapes our expectations regarding fully open, inclusive, and egalitarian ethical deliberation. Having penetrated all social practices and normative institutions in the course of modernization, such expectations normatively guide a critical theory of human rights, social justice, democratic legitimation, and individual development.

In this book I qualify Habermas's theory of communicative action in two ways. First, I am skeptical whether the principle of discourse that Habermas claims tacitly informs our procedural expectations regarding rational disputation is sufficiently determinate to motivate challenges to specific injustices. The "rights" and "duties" attached to free and equal speech are not equivalent to the rights and duties that attach to persons who relate to each other as moral equals, as even Habermas himself observes. Masters and slaves can hold each other rationally accountable for the superficial beliefs underlying their joint cooperation without either of them questioning the deeper background consensus underwriting their unequal status.[53] In order for a slave to challenge the morality of her status, she must first experience indignation from the disrespect she suffers from her bondage. Her *cognitive* demand that her master justify their unequal relationship follows from a *felt* violation of her deep-seated need to be recognized as an integral personality aspiring to freely develop her agency.

Second, I qualify my use of Habermas's theory of communicative action by rejecting its overly sharp distinction between areas of social life coordinated by communicative interaction and areas of systemic functioning coordinated by strategic, success-oriented interaction. Habermas relies upon this bilevel theory of society to explain an important kind of underdevelopment (or distorted development), which he characterizes as the "colonization" of the lifeworld by the system: Economic markets and administrative legal bureaucracies that have become detached from the value- and norm-laden context of everyday life in the course of modernization increasingly insinuate their single-minded success-oriented logic back into everyday life under compulsion from the ambivalent growth dynamics

---

[53] For instance, a slave owner might solicit advice from his skilled slave, who in turn might be expected to offer an independent judgment.

of late, state-administered capitalism. This technicization of everyday life causes pathological (or one-sided) forms of agential development that find iconic expression in hyper-competitive consumer- and work-obsessed individuals who identify themselves in terms of marketable assets, or commodities. Such persons withdraw into their private lives, care little about social justice and the common good, passively accede to hierarchies of knowledge and power, and live their lives without higher meaning or purpose.

Leaving aside the accuracy of these symptoms and Habermas's classification of them as pathological,[54] the diagnostic tool Habermas uses to explain them problematically presumes that economic and administrative mechanisms of coordination are *completely* unregulated by moral expectations of justice and integral well-being. This presumption renders struggles for fair trade, nonexploitative contracts, business ethical practices, green capitalism, and worker-managed market socialist schemes inexplicable. Likewise rendered inexplicable is the *political structure* of a global economy whose neo-liberal understanding of freedom, justice, and development (the so-called Washington Consensus) constitutes a coercive norm imposed on the developing world by the United States and its imperial allies.

Commensurate with this understanding of the global economy as a value-laden ethos of selective underdevelopment, I argue that trade, loan, and contractual agreements between powerful governments, global economic multilaterals, and multinational corporations and their weaker partners, should become less strategic and adversarial and more dialogical, consensual, and preferential toward the weakest and most vulnerable. In addition to reforming international relations and trans-border policies affecting refugees and migrants, Habermasian "discourse ethics" can also underwrite more collaborative forms of social knowledge between poverty experts and their "clients," thereby encouraging deeper understanding of the coercive nature of both poverty and technocratic poverty amelioration. Finally, Habermas's discourse theory of law (1996) can provide a model of democratic legitimation that remains sensitive to different levels and types of deliberation, from domestic to global governance.[55]

Honneth pursues a different justificatory strategy that better serves my purpose in reconstructing a richer account of agential development.

---

[54] Since the 1990s Habermas has recast his critique of juridification in terms of democracy-stunting pathologies associated with a one-sided legalism favoring liberal or welfare paradigms of conflict resolution.

[55] For a statement of the connection between Habermas's discourse ethics and his views on human rights, law, and democracy, see Ingram (2010) and Chapter 5 in this book.

Rejecting Habermas's bi-level model of society as lifeworld and system, Honneth grounds his pluralistic understanding of social justice and development in a functionalist account of distinct spheres of social action that mutually complement each other. Key to this account, which is inspired by the social theory of Talcott Parsons, is a form of social understanding that both developmentally precedes and encompasses rational communication: mutual recognition. In contrast to Habermas's Kant-inspired deontological ethics of justice and rights, Honneth draws upon Hegel's teleological account of self-actualization propelled by struggles for recognition.[56] On this account, the concept of a fully developed and free personality entails living in harmony with society, knowing that one's individual identity and sense of self are affirmed by one's peers in: personal relations of love, friendship, and care; moral and legal relationships founded on equal-respect; political relationships based on solidarity and the common good; and economic and cultural relationships fostering self-esteem. I draw upon this robust theory of agency to show that human social development encompasses both *objective* factors, such as capability, and *subjective* factors, such as experience of well-being, fulfillment, and happiness.[57] Using this dual perspective theory, I then show how social injustice intersects social pathology.

As with Habermas, I apply Honneth's theory with qualification. First, the attempt to explain all injustices and social pathologies in terms of failed or distorted recognition is too ambitious. Distinguishing good (freedom promoting) from bad (conformist-promoting) forms of social recognition will require appealing to non-psychological determinants of action that lie outside the scope of recognition theory. Second and related, no social action theory – including Honneth's – can afford to neglect the non-intentional determinants of norm-guided action: power relations, embodied habits, structural constraints, and technological systems. Herein lies the partial truth of Habermas's bi-level theory of society: Some injustices (e.g., cutbacks in government anti-poverty programs due to economic recession) and some social pathologies (e.g., hyperconsumerism and social apathy) appear to have their source in the relatively impersonal functioning of the economic and administrative systems characteristic of late

[56] See Honneth (1996, 2104).

[57] *The World Happiness Report, World Values Surveys*, the World Gallup Poll and the Commission on the Measurement of Economic Performance and Social Progress (2010) headed by Joseph Stiglitz and Amartya Sen, all recognize the need to include measurements of subjective satisfaction alongside measurements of objective capability and achievement.

capitalism. Global capitalism has increasingly reduced all social relationships to strategic relationships between buyers and sellers who, to a large
extent, no longer feel that they need to recognize each other as free and
equal compatriots bound in solidarity.

Third, by focusing on solidaristic relations of recognition based on
common values and norms, Honneth's theory has little to say about social
relations that transcend the nation state. In contrast to Habermas's discursive proceduralism, which is capable of providing a universal (i.e,
rational) deontological justification for basic human rights that transcend
different cultural visions of human goodness and agential development,
Honneth's teleological ethic expressly finds support in the cultural expectations of human fulfillment embedded in Western traditions of liberal
democracy. The question thus arises whether this particular cultural
understanding can be extended globally, across cultures.

Even if it is true that beneath our culturally fragmented, economically
integrated world there exists a shared normative background underwriting
global struggles for recognition, Honneth's theory seems incapable of
explaining this fact. When Honneth presents his theory in the guise of a
formal philosophical anthropology, its success in grounding culturally
independent needs for recognition comes at the expense of prescriptive
determinacy; in other words, it suffers from the same incapacity to explain
why persons in a specific situation experience disrespect as Habermas's
proceduralist theory. When he presents it in the guise of sociology of
modern Western values, its success in explaining these culturally embedded
experiences comes at the expense of its universal applicability.

My own approach to the above dilemma is to split the difference
between Habermas's procedural account of critical rationality and
Honneth's substantive reconstruction of cultural expectations. Recent
history has shown that Western values of individual dignity, freedom,
equality, and democracy emerged as responses to social changes that have
now become global, so that this cultural legacy, too, has become global. In
that case, we can rightly speak of a universal pathway of development that
has ramified into multiple sociocultural branches. A procedural understanding of rationality, along with a deontological understanding of basic
human rights, is one component of this theory; another is the more
substantive ethical expectations of mutual recognition that underwrite
modern interpersonal relations, market economies, and democratic polities. Taken together, these formal and substantive components ground a
thin conception of the human good. Recognition theory can appeal to an
evolutionary account of development pegging individuation and social

inclusion as twin pillars of fulfilled agency, but it cannot dispense with rational discourse in determining which culturally specific manifestations of these ethical goals are genuinely emancipatory.

In sum, the conceptual difficulties inherent in the two critical theories on which the present study relies are on balance no more challenging than those besetting ideal theories.[58] Moreover, these theories give us an account of agency, coercion, and social contradiction that is phenomenologically richer and sociologically more accurate than accounts put forth in ideal theory. Although their account is superior to technocratic or libertarian variants for purposes of capturing what we mean by human rights, social justice, and individual development, I do not defend it as necessarily superior in all respects. In particular, these critical theories are still too ideal in their neglect of the material (viz., corporeal, environmental, and technological) embodiment of normative agency and human values.[59]

---

[58] See notes 37 and 38.

[59] German Idealists (especially Schiller and Hegel) as well as political economists (beginning with Adam Smith) antedated Marx in their ambivalent assessment of the emancipatory potential of technology, which could just as easily cripple and deskill human capability as express and realize it. Rejecting the Weberian view of technology as value-free neutral instrument, Martin Heidegger and Jacques Ellul condemned modern technology for what they perceived to be its inherent objectification of human existence, stratification of society into technocratic dictators and manipulated masses, and misdevelopment of human capabilities. Herbert Marcuse, the critical theorist who most devoted himself to this critique, believed (as did Marx) that modern technology was neither essentially innocent nor essentially alienating, but reflected in its design the dominant political values of the time. Marcuse's student, Andrew Feenberg (1999, 2017), has elaborated this thought in his distinction between primary and secondary forms of instrumentalization, the former abstracting technical elements from their contexts and reducing them to quantifiable process suitable for control; the latter reversing this process by concretely synthesizing technical elements into a value-laden design. Like the legal system, technology functions as a mechanism for steering human behavior, while also expressing and embodying – and potentially realizing – human freedom. Feenberg criticizes capitalist production technology for incorporating designs that selectively reinforce hierarchy and deskilling in order to efficiently manage a minute division of labor oriented exclusively toward the single value of profitability. He presents information-communication technology (ICT) as having the potential to enhance higher capabilities associated with democratic debate and action. Today, critical theorists debate the ambivalent impact of ICT on development, which in its present social configuration under global capitalism can either institute a digital divide that exacerbates hierarchies of knowledge and power, or create a decentralized, egalitarian global public space suitable for disseminating information and arguments. As I argue in Chapter 2, the technological development of human agency depends on the appropriate design and use of ICTs and other instruments vis-à-vis the specific needs of local communities. For further discussion of these points and the relationship between technology and development generally, see Ingram (2010: 278–81); Ingram and Bar-Tura (2014); and Alampay (2012).

PART I

AGENCY AND DEVELOPMENT

Recognition, Rational Accountability, and Agency

The concept of social development refers to at least two distinct processes, one of which concerns the central topic of this chapter. Societies are said to develop, or evolve, by becoming structurally more complex. This kind of social development is connected to another kind: the social development of individuals. As social structures become more complex, individuals interacting within them are forced to assume new roles and develop new capabilities. In short, the more structurally complex their interaction becomes, the more deliberate (and less habitual and routine) their way of relating to themselves and to others becomes.

This chapter explores the basic rudiments of how persons' agency – their way of relating to their social world and to themselves – develops in response to structural change. I begin by discussing a normative concept of agency that depends on social recognition as well as material welfare. A brief survey of the inadequacies of psychological and political conceptions of recognition leads me to take up Hegel's more trenchant contribution to developing this concept within a broader explanation of freedom and personal identity. I conclude that Hegel's concept imposes a reciprocal responsibility on one who is recognized to give account of her action.

Using Habermas's notion of discourse to illustrate the weak egalitarianism implicit in holding others rationally accountable, I turn to the dynamics of agential development. I argue that agential development (self-actualization) transpires in the course of critically disrupting and re-establishing identity-based agency. I proceed to clarify this crisis-driven dialectic by appeal to Axel Honneth's account of three ethical kinds of recognition that supplement Habermas's discourse conception. After adopting Nancy Fraser's principle of participatory parity, which I believe combines the strengths of Habermas's and Honneth's respective theories of discourse and recognition, I conclude by discussing gendered micro-credit programs as vehicles for recognition and empowerment.

AUTONOMY AND IDENTITY-BASED NORMATIVE AGENCY

Poverty and social inequality impact human rights and social justice in a very specific sense: they adversely affect persons' well-being and agency. Well-being and agency are distinct (albeit intertwined) goods: one can be empowered to act as an agent but still be deprived of a sense of well-being; conversely, one can feel good about one's life and yet be deprived of agency. The question therefore arises: Are human rights' deprivations and social injustices bad because they harm people's sense of well-being or because they harm their agency?

Assuming that the answer is "both," several considerations favor agency as the central moral concern. Well-kept slaves can be socialized into feeling content with their lives of ignorance, unfreedom, and subordination. Condemnation of their slavery as an injustice would therefore have to be grounded in something besides their psychological deprivation of well-being, namely in the harm done to their agency, understood as an *objective*, or nonpsychological, state of potential human functioning or flourishing.

This latter understanding of human flourishing, which Martha Nussbaum (2000) and Amartya Sen (1999) have famously reinterpreted under the heading of basic human capabilities (Sen 1999; Nussbaum 2000), is fraught with the following dilemma (to cite Ann Cudd 2014: 198): "The way that capabilities are framed sets a standard that some poor would not wish to meet, or else it allows too much to be mere aspirational capability and does not require an adequate level of functioning because the poor's standards are set by their circumscribed experiences" (Cudd 2014: 198). This objection foreshadows a tension in the very concept of agency I intend to explore further in this chapter: Freedom is both a state of mind and an objective capability. I am free to the degree that I subjectively experience myself as being fulfilled, in harmony with my society and (socially constructed) environment; but that experience must be informed by an understanding of the objective possibilities for humans like myself, however differently situated, for becoming capable of doing things in general. Lacking this reflective (indeed, philosophical) understanding of how my psychological experience of being environmentally supported and socially recognized relates to the objective world as it has socially evolved renders that experience limited and potentially delusional.[1]

Let us leave aside the experiential dimension of agency for the time being and focus exclusively on its objective (conceptually and empirically determinable) meaning. If we insist that agency entail a strong conception of individual autonomy in choosing values and norms *solely* on the basis of one's own self-reliant critical introspection (as Kant would have argued), we impose a standard that *no one* can meet, since no one can act in total disregard for at least some social norms that authoritatively guide reflection. On the other hand, if we opt for a weaker account of autonomy that sets the standard of agency too low, we open the door to slavish patterns of action that automatically adapt choices to the dictates of others without regard to personal reflection of any kind.

We will explore this dialectic of socially mediated self-reflection in greater detail below. For the time being, let us clarify a less problematic, more common understanding of agency. Minimally, agents must be capable of acting intentionally, pursuing aims by doing things that are designed to achieve those ends. Some animals and very young children possess this capacity, but they are not agents in the full sense of the term. Agency also requires the capacity to choose between alternative aims and courses of action, a capacity for entertaining future possibilities. Furthermore, these possibilities must be ones that an agent ascribes to his or her self. Agents understand themselves to be in possession of a personal identity, or of living a single life that has been shaped by their choices in the past and that will continue to be shaped by their choices in the future (albeit in a way that need not be described as planned out, or even cohering consistently).

So construed, agency designates a spectrum of agential capacitation: Persons suffering from advanced memory loss such as Alzheimer's or multiple personality disorder exercise diminished agency. Following Derek Parfit (1984), I can even question whether the person I am now is really the same person I was (or will be). More importantly, each of us identifies his or her self with multiple social roles, autobiographical narratives, and ideal personas that increase or diminish in relation to each other depending on the social context in which we find ourselves. Our

---

[1] Nussbaum (2000) seems to prematurely dismiss the importance of the subjective, or psychological dimension, of free agency by insisting on the purely objective determination of capability.

strong inclination to mitigate any psychological dissonance between them – a source of volitional uncertainty and confusion, and therefore of potential diminished agency – by suppressing or rejecting one or more of them is itself fraught with risk of agential psychopathology.

So, care must be taken to avoid the dilemma I noted above in which we uncritically posit either (a) an ideal notion of agency as unified around a single, rationally coherent self that exists throughout a lifetime and sovereignly (autonomously) manages its various aspects as mere effects of its controlling power or (b) a phenomenalist notion of agency as fragmented and dispersed into warring centers of desire and choice, however secondary and reflected each might be from a particular standpoint. In any case, choosing ends and means toward realizing a plan of life cannot be equated with Rawls' liberal moral power to reflectively form, revise, and pursue a conception of the good unqualifiedly, because this power is exercised from the standpoint of an isolated individual who values personal liberty above social recognition that comes from caring for family and participating in community.

Conversely, agency cannot be equated with acting in terms of one's own values, "whether or not we assess them in terms of some external criteria," as Sen suggests (1999: 18). This last idea may suffice as a minimal description of agency that applies to even the extremely poor (who, after all, are agents). But, following Cudd's argument, it cannot suffice as a norm for criticizing the agency-stunting effects of severe poverty (as Sen himself would be quick to acknowledge). At some point, failure to exercise an internal agency capacity due to severe malnutrition, social brainwashing, and ignorance of options counts as a diminution of agency *simpliciter*, even if the person suffering incapacitation merits respect as a rights-bearing agent (Griffin 2008: 67). Furthermore, citing Deepa Narayan (2000), Cudd notes that poverty stunts agency by excluding the poor from full membership in a community that sustains that agency. The poor suffer humiliation, dependency, social stigma, and – at the extreme – feel coerced into violating social norms, even to the point of engaging in criminal behavior (Cudd 2014: 204).

What Cudd means by *normative* agency thus incorporates a basic social dimension: "Our ability to guide our actions by social norms and to contribute to their maintenance through holding ourselves and others to account for them" (Cudd 2014: 205). Cudd maintains that this account of agency is neutral between liberal "autonomy agency" and collectivist "identity agency," yet she acknowledges a dialectical interplay between social accountability and individual accountability that appears to underscore their complementarity. In fact, although Cudd does not say it, this interplay is the hallmark of a distinctive, social conception of freedom that philosophers since Hegel have discussed under the rubric of *recognition.*

HEGEL ON RECOGNITION AND SELF-CERTAINTY: FREEDOM AND IDENTITY AS CONDITIONS OF AGENCY

Since the publication of Charles Taylor's *Multiculturalism and the Politics of Recognition* (1994), the concept of recognition has re-emerged as a central, if not dominant, category of moral and political philosophy. Taylor's use of Hegel's seminal category to defend group rights aimed at securing legal and public recognition of the distinctive identities of groups resonated with critical theorists such as Jürgen Habermas (1998a: 203–36), Seyla Benhabib (1992, 2002), Nancy Fraser (Fraser and Honneth 2003), and above all Axel Honneth (1996), who elevated the category of recognition to the most foundational of moral and social categories. Honneth, for example, drew on the research of developmental psychologists, such as Jessica Benjamin (1988) and Donald Winnicott (1965), as well as pragmatists, such as G. H. Mead, all of whom had used the category of recognition (or something analogous to it that involves taking into account the perspective of the other) to explain how a sense of self emerges from the empathetic identification with primary caretakers. The accent here on social recognition as a precognitive basis for individuation has been variously understood to also imply a condition for psychological wholeness and well-being or, more radically, a transcendental condition for the bare possibility of reflectively relating to one's self as a self. In the meantime, critics – many of them influenced by poststructuralist currents of thought – have argued that the category of recognition, with its alleged identification and reconciliation with the other, designates an impossible and perhaps even undesirable abnegation of individual autonomy and authenticity (McNay 2008; Markell 2003).

The critics are right, *if* recognition exclusively means a condition for *identity* agency rather than *autonomy* agency. In Hegel's iconic account of recognition, achievement of a stable and integral identity – or certainty of self – represents only half the story.[2] Indeed, Hegel reminds us

[2] Robert Pippin (2008: 259), for one, argues that Hegel's mature concept of recognition is properly understood as an *ontological* category referring exclusively to what it means to be a free, rational individual, or *agent.*

that self-certainty is itself a dialectical process: Unthinking confidence in my self-understanding that comes with feeling secure in the performance of my concrete social roles remains uncertain until I have reflectively ascertained the truth of that understanding, which by its very nature opens up a divide between the part of myself that is reflecting and the part of myself that is being reflected upon. This *internal* division (non-identity) reflects (mirrors) an *external* (social) division: I reflectively recognize who I am through others recognizing me.

Although Hegel insists that such social recognition normally affirms (conforms to, reflects back) the person I recognize in myself, this happens at best partially, only when social relationships approximate a state of harmony. This approximately happens whenever social relationships and social identities are relatively fixed and stabilized in specific (clearly identifiable and distinguishable) *concrete* social roles, in such a way that actors hold one another accountable and recognize each other according to the common, uncritically accepted institutional norms of their particular society. However, social relationships seldom attain that level of stable harmony.

As society develops greater complexity and persons accordingly expand their repertory of concrete social roles in ways that complicate their lives, role conflicts emerge that can rise to the level of social and personal crisis. Crisis impels actors to transcend their concrete roles and adopt more abstract, autonomous points of view in keeping with more inward-looking individual-centered forms of reflection. Such "alienation" from self and society need not undermine recognition as a basis for identity agency, but it does necessitate translating recognition from a collectivist mode of mutual validation into a higher, more reflective register of rational accountability, mutual questioning, and social critique. Commensurate with this change, personal identity itself becomes more fluid, more abstract (or less singularly attached to concrete social roles), and more freely owned.

Thus, to say that recognition is a category of *both* freedom and identity refutes the critics' concern that it privileges identity at the expense of individual freedom and self-transformation. Insofar as Hegel regards freedom, rationality, and individuality as historical achievements of the human spirit, recognition, too, acquires for him the status of a historical achievement and the outcome of protracted struggle. Therefore, Hegelian recognition does not designate a *transcendental* condition for the bare possibility of subjectivity, selfhood, relation to self, or self-consciousness, insofar as these capabilities can be attributed to children as well as adult human beings prior to acquiring access to skill sets and institutional opportunities associated with responsible agency.

Nor does it exclusively designate a condition of psychic wellness and self-esteem of the sort that figures in the political struggles for recognition discussed by Taylor and Honneth (such affirmative aspects of social freedom and identity are but partial aspects of healthy recognition). Rather, to the extent that Hegel develops what Robert Pippin calls a "recognitive politics" as an alternative to other liberal political rationales of a consequentialist or rights-based nature, such a politics will be first and foremost grounded in a prior capability: rational accountability, albeit a form of accountability that originally – and perhaps in modern, complex society, normally – finds its limit in institutionally defined social roles, or shared identities grounded in concrete norms (Pippin 2008: 242, 250, 258, 265).[3]

In sum, no matter how important recognition might be for personal psychological health, basic self-awareness, and political justice between groups, it is not the sort of recognition that Hegel philosophically defends as the *telos* of fully actualized *agency*. Although Hegel might be wrong to dismiss these other forms of recognition as central to a full account of social freedom and agency (as I argue below), he is correct to point out that they are of a different caliber – less socially primary – than recognition understood as mutual accountability.[4] Taylor may be right that a group's

[3] See Hegel's remark (1991: 276) that "rationality consists in general in the unity and interpenetration of universality and individuality" and his claim that "every individual has his station in life, and he is fully aware of what constitutes a right and honorable course of action" (1975: 80). Hegel's point, of course, is not that consequences and rights never count as legitimate political reasons but that they do so only as qualified from the standpoint of some socially recognized role and its proper standpoint.

[4] In his reply to me (Ingram 2010b: 470–89), Pippin (2010: 515–17) notes that there may not be any disagreement between us, insofar as he acknowledges Hegel's affirmation of the material and psychological background conditions requisite for exercising rational agency. However, he *does* believe that Hegel's distinction between civil society and state would render a politics of social recognition in Taylor's and Honneth's sense problematic from a Hegelian point of view. As Pippin understands it, that point of view would rule out legal enforcement of social recognition (as he notes, one cannot "compel" solidarity). From this remark, it is unclear whether the distinction between state (or law, as a rational expression of universal interests) and civil society (as a sphere of particular needs) would rule out civil rights movements on behalf of affirmative action, special exemptions for religious minorities, and guaranteed political representation for women and subnationalities. Equally unclear is whether it would rule out class struggles aimed at overcoming oppression and domination. If Pippin intends his reading of Hegel to imply the kind of dualism between the political and the social emblematic of Hannah Arendt's political philosophy, then Hegel (and perhaps also Pippin) and I *do* disagree. For as I argue in Chapter 2, the exercise of practical discursive reason is always a process that is constrained by racial, gender, class, and cultural power relations.

achieving mutual recognition from other groups regarding the worth of its own members' distinctive racial, gender, or cultural identity may be a necessary condition for intergroup dialogue so essential to achieving political justice, understood as equality in the legal and political distribution of social esteem, say, but it is not a necessary condition for enabling the group's members to act in a rational and responsible manner as agents. Likewise, Honneth may be right that achieving emotional bonding and identification with caretakers may be a necessary developmental stage in the process of becoming a fully balanced human being, and it may well be that absent such bonding, infants could never become persons who experience themselves as subjects living in a meaningful world of objects.[5] But having been recognized in this precognitive, emotive, or empathetic manner of identification is not part of what it means to be a rational agent.

As we shall see, both Honneth and Taylor extend their respective psychological and political accounts of recognition to incorporate Hegel's linkage of recognition and rational agency. This linkage expressly contradicts our conventional understanding. Conventional wisdom conceives of freedom as a causal power innate within the individual. In the empiricist tradition of Hobbes, Locke, and Hume, the will can be said to be free if its decision to pursue this or that desire is unhindered by external impediment. The transcendentalist tradition inaugurated by Kant goes further than this by reasonably insisting that the mere faculty of choice (*Willkür*) provides a poor foundation for freedom so long as the rational, calculating will remains in thrall to pre-rational inclination. But Kant's idea of a spontaneous "uncaused" volitional agency that inhabits some otherworldly *noumenal* realm while somehow acting in the real world – interrupting bodily desire through exercise of moral choice – is scarcely philosophically satisfying. How can mere respect for an abstract, empty conception of formal practical reason that commands never making an exception for oneself, never treating others simply as means, and never acting on a maxim that could not be logically willed as a maxim all others should follow (the categorical imperative) provide sufficient reason to act this way rather than that, apart from worldly desire?

Hegel's solution to this dilemma involves radically reconceiving the way in which Kant's idea of autonomy as submission to one's own moral reasoning (self-legislation) is understood. Instead of thinking of autonomy

---

[5] For a discussion concerning the importance of emotional bonding to the achievement of perspective sharing and objective experience, see Tomosello (1999), Hobson (2002), and Honneth (2008).

simply as a function of *individually* exercised practical reasoning in accordance with a formal procedure, Hegel thinks of it as a *dialogical* accomplishment in which agents invest their desires in the rational form of validity claims whose reasonableness they then justify to other agents in concrete terms that these other agents recognize and accept. The rational need to acquire self-certainty of my own agency – to know who I am and what I am doing – intersects with the need for justificatory self-assertion. I actively justify – literally take ownership of – both aspects of my agency, my freedom and my identity, only through others that recognize me.

Hegel's defense of this recognitive account of freedom proceeds at many levels. Early on in the *Phenomenology* (1807) he focuses his attention on the dialectical confrontation between the claims and counterclaims of human beings who seek recognition of their distinctive, nonanimal status as free, self-aware agents. As is well known, the section of the *Phenomenology* in which Hegel discusses the dialectic of self-consciousness (culminating in the relationship between master and servant) disabuses us of any conceit in our own autochthony in its compelling account of why *natural* consciousness (e.g., a being who acts solely on survival instinct) cannot be free on its own without risking life itself in struggle with another who risks the same, with each mirroring back to the other (and subsequently internalizing) the self- and freedom-constituting meaning of their struggle.[6]

The logic behind risking oneself in order to gain oneself back in the form of freer, more self-aware agency is repeated in a later section of the *Phenomenology*. Whereas the *asocial* recognition culminating the earlier existential struggle can only be one-sided and partial – the victorious master only recognizes himself through the eyes of an unfree and self-less servant[7] – the *social* recognition between persons who voluntarily limit their freedom and selfhood in the course of cooperating with each

---

[6] This account rearticulates an earlier argument that Johann Gottlieb Fichte had developed in his *Grundlage des Naturrechts* (1796): to wit, that autonomy first arises when human beings distinguish themselves from animals by transforming their immediate, natural desires into *claims*, or demands, addressed to others and requiring their recognition.

[7] The problem with the master-servant relationship that supposedly resolves the existential struggle to the death between persons who demand unreciprocated recognition of their freedom is its incapacity to rise above the fundamental contradiction that recognition cannot be compelled and, indeed, cannot affirm the superior sovereignty of one when given unfreely from another who is deemed to be little more than an object. Although the servant achieves a certain awareness of his own freedom in fearing death, postponing satisfaction of natural need, and dominating nature through labor, neither he nor the lord can achieve subjective certainty of their autonomy and, indeed, cannot be free, because they lack the moral, legal, and ethical preconditions in which they might transform their immediate demands into rationally justifiable validity claims requiring mutual recognition.

other succeeds in mutually constituting the meaning of their action along with their respective individual and social identities. Unlike the free action of an actor abstractly considered, social action expresses each actor's concretely limited and secured agency as an individual embodiment of socially recognized roles, values, and norms.[8]

Later on in the *Phenomenology*[9] we encounter the dialectic of social recognition played out on the higher register of communicative action. Once they have achieved moral self-awareness, social actors cease to passively conform to socially recognized roles, values, and identities. They now judge the moral significance and rightness of each other's conduct. Hegel shows that the subjective convictions of moral agents remain essentially incomplete and indeterminate in meaning – lacking in conviction and objective reality – until they are *justified* before other persons whom the actor recognizes as having the right to judge (paras. 645, 653). Each no doubt asserts his own convictions as normatively binding for everyone else (paras. 655–56).[10] But the actions which express a person's convictions are motivated by a host of interests, some of them base (fame, ambition, etc.). Others accordingly interpret them in a different light and judge them to be hypocritical (para. 665).

Coaxing a confession from the actor regarding his true motives, the hard-hearted judge can scarcely claim with certainty that she and not the actor is right. Indeed she too can be accused of hypocrisy in proclaiming the moral purity of her judgment, which, unlike that of a "beautiful soul" who refuses to act at all, is also tainted by ulterior motives (paras 658,

---

[8] In the section concluding the chapter on reason, entitled "Individuality which Takes Itself to be Real in and for Itself," we learn "that a person cannot know what he [really] is until he has made himself a reality through action" (para. 401). The "purpose" and "matter at hand" in his acting, however, comes to light only as it is expressed and taken up by others, thereby showing that the pure integrity of one's willing is a chimera. Agents may "pretend that their actions and efforts are something for themselves alone in which they have only themselves and their essential nature in mind," but "in doing something, and thus in bringing themselves out into the light of day, they directly contradict by their deed their pretense of wanting to exclude the glare of publicity and participation by all and sundry" (para. 417).

[9] Chapter 6, subsection (c), entitled "Spirit that is Certain of Itself: Morality."

[10] Jay Bernstein equates the "beautiful soul" with a "deliberative community" that produces agreement on norms in abstraction from ethical action, while he interprets the conscientious actor as one who acts out of individual conviction without considering how the consequences of his actions impact the community (1996: 36–38). Bernstein then compares this dialectic to that contained in Hegel's treatment of Antigone and Creon, and concludes that the *Phenomenology* effectively ends when both the conscientious actor and the beautiful soul recognize the truth of the "absolute other," namely, the prior context of shared ethical norms that frames their one-sided forms of understanding.

663–65). Forgiveness comes when both actor and judge mutually confess their hypocrisy and recognize their mutual accountability to one another. Each must now exit the sanctum of inner moral conscience and submit their claims to mutual criticism. And each must accordingly risk his or her identity as a moral agent if the reasons he or she gives in identifying and justifying what he or she has done fail to convince the other (paras. 667–71).

To paraphrase the moral of this story in a way that Hegel might have accepted had he lived in our post-Wittgensteinian world, we could say that intentional action and free, self-aware agency do not fully exist unless they enter into a language game of mutual question and answer. Any gap between the agent's and the public's assessment of what the agent did marks a gap in recognition and, therewith, a gap in the agent's own certainty that what he or she thought she did *is* what he or she did in fact; and *that* experience of *self-alienation* is tantamount to an experience of unfreedom.

Leaving aside the importantly relevant question whether the formal legal institutions of a modern liberal state are needed to secure the universal moral agency of citizens who are free to question publicly recognized standards of right and wrong,[11] a further point bears mentioning with regard to Hegel's substantive conception of practical reason: Justification will be constrained by or reconciled to the particular social roles, values, and norms that are publicly recognized in one's society and will not be free to methodically detach itself from these roles as if aspiring to become a formal test for determining how any rational speaker, hearer, actor, or judge would justify the action in question.

---

[11] Hegel's mature writings in the *Philosophy of Right* and in the *Encyclopedia* flesh out the legal and political implications of this conception of recognitive freedom. The important points developed in these writings are as follows: If freedom, or taking ownership of one's inclinations, volitions, and intentions, requires transforming these subjective events into rationally justifiable *validity claims* addressed to and recognized by others (as Habermas would say), then it also requires an intersubjectively recognized framework in which asserting and redeeming individual claims makes sense. That framework is the modern state, understood not merely as government but as shared political understanding firmly anchored in what we today would loosely identify as a liberal and democratic ethos. In other words, it is only within a modern state that objectively recognizes individual freedom and responsibility through legal institutions such as private property, accountable legislative representation, and so on and further grounds these formal institutions in substantive traditions expressing common values, aims, and meanings as well as concrete narrative identities based on intersubjectively recognized roles, that something like genuine individual self-ownership can happen.

The philosopher's temptation to think that there must be a general, abstract reason supporting the social justifications proffered by everyday agents is apparently mistaken, for such a reason could not provide a motive for acting that would be more concretely meaningful and prescriptive than the substantive reason institutionally provided. Habermas's formal pragmatic account of rationality accountability, which I discuss below, succumbs to this folly when considering most ordinary cases. Playing institutionally *unbound* social roles of speaker (truth claimer) and listener (claim critic) apart from institutionally *bound* social roles of, say, doctor and patient, adds nothing to the sorts of specific claims and justifications that a doctor and patient might raise or make with respect to a course of proper treatment.[12] In justifying the rightness of a prescribed regimen of care to the patient the doctor should not have to appeal to a general moral theory. In contrast to respecting the concrete guidelines offered by the Hippocratic Oath, respecting the inherent dignity of the human being, as Kant's deontological moral theory admonishes us to do, normally fails to condemn a physician's decision to countermand the wishes of a quadriplegic patient who requests to be removed from life support. Radically questioning the appropriateness of this oath and any other professional code of ethics is merely the idle fancy of philosophers, who are free to adopt wholly abstract and transcendent notions of rational justification, truth, and rightness in their ivory towers.

RATIONAL DISCOURSE AND AUTONOMY AGENCY

Is Hegel right about recognition remaining within the limits of collectivist identity agency as I have described it above? Hegel himself noted that revolutionary shifts in developing autonomy agency, leading up to our present-day understanding of freedom and human rights, were propelled by moments of social crisis in which persons were compelled to stand back from their concrete social roles and defer to more universal norms. Indeed,

---

[12] Habermas's distinction between institutionally unbound speech acts that raise universal validity claims to truth, rightness, and sincerity and institutionally bound speech acts that raise nongeneralizable claims based on particular social roles was first developed at length in the 1973 essay, "What is Universal Pragmatics" (in Habermas 1998b). Although Habermas adopts Stephen Toulmin's model of informal argumentation as an alternative to deductive forms of reasoning, he places no restrictions on the reasons that can justify criticism, noting that any medium of social communication and understanding can be challenged as ideologically distorted and constrained from the counterfactual standpoint of rational dialogue. See J. Habermas, "Wahrheitstheorien" (in Habermas 1984).

even without the fragmenting impact of societally induced identity crisis, persons inhabiting complex modern societies can scarcely exclude counterfactual moral reasoning from the recognized play of mutual accountability. A comparison between Hegel's account of rational accountability and two contemporary analogs that were inspired by it – Habermas's discourse ethics and Robert Brandom's inferentialist semantics – suggests why.

Brandom's inferentialist account of action posits mutual recognition as a prior condition of rational agency. Persons hold one another accountable for the commitments that can be inferred from the assertions they make about themselves, others, and the world around them. But Brandom understands the role that communication plays in this process as mainly passive; we listen to what others say, observe what they do, and keep score of who is committed to what, being ever vigilant to ferret out commitments that conflict with one another or with the collectively recognized commitments of our society. We do not, however, seek to find a *new* basis for mutual recognition by demanding justification of the truth and rightness of our commitments by appeal to reasons that *lack* social recognition.

As Habermas observes (2003b: 163), Brandom understands a commitment to truth and rightness as a commitment to whatever society happens to recognize as such.[13] But this can't be right. In claiming that our assertion is true or right we imply that *all* persons could be rationally persuaded to accept it. Of course, we cannot assume that any finite exchange of arguments would ever justify a controversial claim once and for all. Habermas therefore concludes that justification is essentially *counterfactual;* in other words, our inconclusive finite conversations anticipate a temporally unlimited, spatially inclusive *ideal speech situation* (Habermas 2003:248).

The implication of this ideal of dialogical accountability for a recognitive theory of agency is unsettling. Recognizing oneself as a free and responsible agent must remain a desideratum; in retrospect, conversation is always constrained by time limits, institutional norms, and entrenched forms of power. Full self-certainty (self-ownership) regarding who one is

---

[13] It is not always clear whether, for Brandom, objectivity is (as he says) a *structural presupposition* of language use that forces speakers to adopt an autonomous, critical standpoint vis-à-vis collectively recognized facts and norms (Brandom 2000: 360). His assertion (Brandom 1994: 625) that "fact-stating talk is explained in normative terms and normative facts emerge as one kind of fact among others" commits him to conventionalism (Lafont 2002: 185–209; Ingram 2010a: Appendix C).

and what one is doing ideally depends on what an indefinite number of our fellow interlocutors *would* decide one is doing according to an ever-changing matrix of shared reasons. Complete agreement with and recognition from others being impossible, free agency remains forever deferred (as Jacques Derrida would say), a project under development.

This conclusion would appear to contradict Hegel's own optimistic claims about the fully realized fact of freedom for those inhabiting modern liberal societies.[14] The cunning of reason (*List der Vernunft*), as Hegel understands the developmental logic culminating in European modernity, must have already actualized its *telos* – freedom – in order for it to have been retrospectively reconstructed by philosophy. But the proper way to interpret Hegel's account of historical development is to stress the role that imperfectly rational agents play in constituting their own agency across time.

Take the example of the dissident who refuses to reason about society in the way that conventional roles would dictate. Hegel is not claiming that one must always account for one's action by appeal to conventional roles, least of all when those roles collide. This situation arises in moments of social breakdown, when our ethical identity (*sittliches Wesen*) is shattered. Hegel's famous gloss in the *Phenomenology* on Sophocles' portrayal of the conflict between Creon and Antigone illustrates the breakdown of an imperfectly rational ethos, in which roles of citizen and family member cannot be harmonized because neither citizen nor family member can give a satisfactory rationale to the other that could justify what he or she is doing.

Contrast this breakdown with our modern form of social crisis. In a modern society that has incorporated robust rational accountability all the way down to its core, individuals identify with their multiple social

---

[14] Such triumphalism has led Honneth (1996:59–63) and Habermas to conclude that Hegel jettisoned the forward-looking, dialogical account of rational justification so strikingly evident in his *System of Ethical Life* and *First Philosophy of Spirit* dating back to 1802–1804 for the backward-looking, monological justification present in the Jena *Phenomenology of Spirit* of 1807. Beginning with this latter work, Hegel putatively defends the absolute incarnation of reason, namely, a final true understanding of ourselves as completely free, by direct appeal to humanity's inevitable, divine-like march to the modern state, behind the backs of agents and quite independently of any dialogical reflection they might have undertaken in enlightening themselves about the imperfect rationality of their social relations. For early statements of Habermas's position, see "Labor and Interaction: Remarks on Hegel's Jena Philosophy of Mind" (in Habermas 1973b: 167; and Habermas 1971: chapters 1 and 2). For later versions of the same see Habermas (1987a: 39–42; 2003b: 202–11).

roles less rigidly and dogmatically. Our cultural conflicts don't lead to a wholesale abandonment of rational accountability toward others, even if they produce skepticism and alienation. Such skepticism now appears to be reasonable to the extent that questioning authority finds institutional support. One draws from science in questioning religion; or one draws from religion in questioning science. It doesn't matter that the sources of socially recognized reasons aren't strictly universal, so long as there remains at least one overarching institutional support that is: morality.

Persons who are asked to render an account of their behavior in terms of universal morality are asked to do so in ways that any rational human being might accept. The universal validity they claim for their reasoning will require that they abstract from the particular ethos they inhabit, or at the very least, hypothetically imagine the possibility of such abstraction. That is to say, they must be able to hypothetically free themselves from the limits of their own ethos and even (perhaps) radically question this ethos, e.g., by reconfiguring it in more secular and universally appealing narrative about human rights.[15]

PATHOLOGIES OF ABSTRACT INDIVIDUALISM

Hegel's account of recognition does not extinguish the individual moral agent's legitimate right to demand rational justification of what contingently exists. The danger in such a demand – what makes it unreasonable and pathological – is its absolute withdrawal from the public realm of social accountability into the private realm of fanatical self-certainty. Pathological is the self-imposed alienation and self-reification that comes from forgetting the discursive preconditions underlying one's own claim to be rationally justified. As noted above, this kind of pathology is not inherent within counterfactual forms of philosophical reasoning.[16] But it is inherent in societies marked by extreme social fragmentation and personally felt identity crisis. "Conscience," "Beautiful Soul," "Absolute Freedom and Terror," and similar Hegelian epithets directed against abstract moral individualism suggest that the highway of despair traversed in the *Phenomenology* goes well beyond philosophical skepticism to encompass

[15] I discuss secularization in Chapter 7. Hegel's point is that critical moral detachment from our social ethos cannot – nor should not – be absolute. We can selectively criticize some institutional roles but we cannot deny all of society's duties at once.

[16] See, for example, my discussion of Rawls in Chapter 2.

social pathology.[17] The delusions of a few Nietzsche-inspired postmodernists notwithstanding, the totalitarian moral experiments in fascist and Islamist social engineering of our era are less a testimony to philosophical imagination gone amuck than they are a reaction to social disintegration.

Hegel's indictment of abstract *moral* individualism and its totalitarian counterpart highlights a singular modern pathology that also manifests itself in the form of abstract *legal* individualism. Forgetfulness of social ties (e.g., to children and significant others) in pursuit of one's narrow rights leads persons (e.g., married couples) into destructive legal battles when proper consideration of these ties counsels more consensual, other-regarding forms of conflict resolution. Widespread pressure to convert social relationships involving mutual accountability into juridical relationships involving obligation-free spheres of private dominion can also degenerate into social pathology. Such examples of *systematically misunderstanding* the "rational meaning of a [social] form of institutionalized practice," as Honneth puts it, conspire with modern *misdevelopments*. Regressing behind the level of universal need satisfaction, contractual fairness, and ecological well-being achieved by mid-twentieth-century modern social democracy, neoliberalism's detachment of market economy from ethical regulation finds its pathological complement in today's economic individualism, which celebrates the new entrepreneurial worker who can embrace increased responsibility and flexibility along with increased risk of unemployment.

Other modern developmental pathologies and misdevelopments are less easily explained in terms of Hegel's social recognition model. Ideological misrecognition, or mistakenly believing in the fulfillment vouchsafed by social recognition itself (in conforming to society's recognized functional roles), represents a case in point. The same can be said about self-reification (e.g., viewing oneself as a commodity or thing to be marketed and manipulated). Along with narcissistic hedonism and consumerism, self-reification deforms development of an integral identity properly anchored by moral values and social purposes. Other examples of social pathology – connected to the colonization of domains of communicative interaction by monetary and legal media, the one-sided

---

[17] Following Honneth's gloss on Hegel (Honneth 2014: 114–20), we can distinguish two main types of moral pathology: the uncompromising moralist who listens only to her own self-legislating conscience and forgets or rejects her concrete social duties to family, friends, and loved ones, and the fanatical terrorist who sacrifices all ethical social life as a means to achieving transcendent moral ends.

cultivation of instrumental rationality at the expense of critical reasoning, and the loss of meaning, purpose, and unregimented freedom in alienated labor – have legal as well as economic causes. In order to explain why they are pathological, recourse to a theory of ethical recognition somewhat richer than the one Hegel provides will be required. In my opinion, that theory has been developed by Axel Honneth.

HONNETH ON RECOGNITION AS AN ETHICAL CATEGORY

If recognition designates more than an ontological status attached to socially accountable agents but also marks a historical achievement whose meaning is captured by the dignity of the individual as a self-actualizing agent, then it will also designate a normative standard against which social injustices and social pathologies can be measured. The transition from a premodern society, in which only persons of noble rank are accorded recognition based on their dignified status and honorable distinction to a modern society in which even the humblest individual is respected for the dignity of her humanity and esteemed for her social contribution, marks out the historical trajectory of this struggle in the West (and worldwide).

Merely recognizing someone as an agent like oneself who merits equal respect, what many have thought to be definitive of the moral point of view, however, leaves out other dimensions of recognition that are just as vital to the exercise of agency. Also important is moral recognition of what makes us different and unique: our individuality (or as Taylor, following Rousseau, puts it, our authenticity). Because our individuality is interpolated though the particular social statuses we occupy, the particular social roles we play, and the particular social values we embody, basic trust in who we are, or confidence in ourselves as persons with a stable character and identity, requires recognition of these social markers by others, beginning with the loving emotional support provided by our parents.[18] These markers become sources of positive social esteem based on acquired attributes and accomplishments rather than on inherited statuses. Being recognized as a good citizen, good mother, good Muslim, and good person enables one to act with confidence and assurance from peers. Stigma associated with unemployment, poverty, social deviance, and social marginalization inhibits social interaction and can undermine

---

[18] "In becoming sure of the mother's love, [children] come to trust themselves, which makes it possible for them to be alone without anxiety." A. Honneth (1996: 104).

opportunities for living a free and worthwhile life with others. Struggles for racial, gender, religious, and economic recognition overlap the struggle for moral recognition, insofar as they counteract forms of discrimination that deny equal human rights to members of subaltern groups. However, such struggles go beyond the struggle for human rights insofar as they seek recognition of the particular social value (merit) of persons within society, struggles including, but not exclusive to, so-called multicultural identity politics.

Finally, as noted above, recognition from parents, friends, and loved ones enables adults as well as children to acquire the self-confidence necessary to master the multiple moral and social roles that they will be expected to play while retaining a strong and relatively stable sense of who they are. Because our personal identities are embodied, showing disrespect to another's body by raping, torturing, or otherwise abusing them violates their psychological as well as physical integrity. Absence of emotional support produces pathologies of self-abnegation and delinquency that can undermine social agency, not only by diminishing self-confidence, but by stunting the cognitive and empathetic capacity to recognize others as human beings and to imagine what it is like to be in their particular situation.[19]

---

[19] Honneth distinguishes emotional recognition necessary for forming healthy personal identity from antecedent recognition, or "spontaneous non-rational recognition of others as fellow human beings" (2008: 152). Whereas antecedent recognition identifies persons as selves with unique needs (as opposed to things), emotional or loving recognition nourishes others' cultivation of their own needs. That said, Honneth observes that autism and other psychopathologies associated with failed antecedent recognition also stem from failures or incapacities to emotionally bond with others. Such failures (or incapacities) to identify with (recognize) others as selves have cognitive as well as affective consequences. Although the capacity to assume the perspective of others is essential for grasping an objective world, forgetfulness and/or suppression of our primal emotional bonding with persons, Honneth submits, can lead to reifying ourselves, other human beings, and our natural environment. Of course, the capacity to emotionally bond with others can itself assume healthy or unhealthy, morally acceptable or morally unacceptable, forms; scam artists and torturers are highly capable of "empathizing" with their victims, albeit for purposes of psychological manipulation and coercion. So what Honneth calls "primary" (or precognitive) recognition is normatively neutral; upon this elemental product of infant/mother bonding develops a complicated psycho-sexual network of object-relations involving primary caretakers. Such relations can embody norms of love that engender a learning trajectory culminating in higher levels of care, empathy, and solidarity for others along an expanding arc of concern, but they need not. See *Reification* (ibid.) and especially the critical comments by Judith Butler, Raymond Geuss, and Jonathan Lear, who question the adequacy of Honneth's attempt to conceptualize reification as a forgetfulness or suppression of primary recognition.

The preceding account adopts the simplified taxonomy of levels of recognition suggested by Axel Honneth, whose most recent explanation follows Hegel's tripartite scheme, developed in the *Philosophy of Right*, of three formative levels of social agency (ethical life): intimate personal relationships between friends, lovers, and family members; moral-legal relationships between rights claimants bound together by economic dependency; and solidaristic relationships between citizens and persons who hold one another in mutual esteem based on their associational contributions.[20]

HONNETH'S THEORY OF RECOGNITION

Paraphrasing Honneth, prior to acquiring role competencies necessary for engaging in rationally accountable forms of speech action, children must first bond emotionally and identify with the perspective of their primary caretakers. [21] Development toward adulthood takes the form of an emotional struggle for recognition between parent and child in which child and parent come to accept each other as individuals with independent needs that merit satisfaction. Entering civil society, the young adult further assumes responsibility as an impersonal bearer of rights who is at once legally independent from others while remaining morally accountable to them for her choices. The resulting struggle for recognition between self-asserting rights-holders who possess different traits, abilities, and claims to social contribution[22] must be resolved on a different social stage in which, for example, each acknowledges that the satisfaction of her own needs and, therewith, the realization of her own economic freedom depends on the reciprocal satisfaction of others' needs and the

---

[20] This scheme excludes Honneth's discussion of "antecedent" recognition (see note 19). Early on Honneth (1996) drew almost exclusively from Hegel's Jena period writings from 1801–1806 (see note 14). However, recently Honneth has based his theory of recognition on the *Philosophy of Right* (1820), where Hegel argues that *abstract rights* that ground negative (external) freedom from interference and *moral duties* that ground reflective (inner) freedom presuppose more concrete *ethical relations* of family, civil society (economic life), and state (political life) for their full *social* realization. My book incorporates the ideas of both early and late Honneth without examining their interconnection. For a brief comment on their mutual coherence, see note 25.

[21] The table below modifies similar diagrams found in Honneth (1996: 129) and Zurn (2015: 46) by combining taxonomies of recognition developed in both early and late Honneth.

[22] Honneth singles out traits and abilities as markers of esteem in his earlier work on recognition, while emphasizing social (civic, economic, etc.) achievements as markers of esteem in his later work on social freedom (see note 20).

TABLE 1 *Types of Recognition (Honneth)*

	Antecedent Recognition	Love Recognition	Respect Recognition	Esteem Recognition
Practical relation to self	Antecedent self-affirmation	Self-confidence	Self-respect	Self-esteem
Type of relationship	Social interaction	Love and friendship	Moral/legal relations and rights	Solidarity
Mode of regard	Primordial engagement	Emotional	Cognitive	Esteem
Object of recognition	Human personhood	Needs and emotions	Moral autonomy and authentic existence Legal autonomy	Traits, abilities, contributions, and achievements
Aspect of personhood acknowledged	Human existence	Particular physical being	Universal humanity; personal and group identity Abstract legal personality	Individual life of accomplishment, merit, and social value
Community of recognition	Interaction partners	Intimates	Fellow moral subjects Fellow legal subjects	Members of communities of value and cooperation
Paradigms of disrespect	Reification [pathology, not injustice]	Abuse and rape	Denial of moral rights, equal consideration of interests Denial of legal rights, legal exclusion and discrimination	Cultural denigration, refusal to acknowledge partnership, share of social contribution
Primary social action spheres	All	Romantic attachments, friendships, and families	Moral deliberation and dialogue Legal transactions and proceedings	Economic transactions, political public spheres, socio-cultural associations
Type of freedom	X	Social	Positive Negative	Social

realization of their economic freedom. Indeed, from this perspective, each should recognize others as esteem-worthy contributors to both the economic and legal-political reproduction of society.[23] Citizens, for instance, not only assert their rights but also recognize their fellow citizens as loyal compatriots joined together in a cooperative enterprise in which questions of fairness and social justice come to the fore.

Honneth here reminds us that the moral autonomy (reflexive freedom) and legal independence (negative freedom) that individuals assert against society emerge out of society. Both *negative* freedom from external interference and *positive* (reflexive) freedom to inner self-determination remain but abstract potentials for developing real freedom. As we have seen, negative freedom without reflexive freedom remains in thrall to external sources of desire and motivation; conversely, reflexive freedom without negative freedom remains objectively impotent. Each of these one-sided conceptions of individual freedom achieves satisfactory realization only in higher forms of institutionalized *social* freedom. Legal institutions that protect negative freedom reliably function only when democratically legitimated in ways that reflect the moral and ethical consensus achieved in public discourse. Moral discourses that engender reflexive freedom reliably function only when institutionalized throughout civil society in various legally protected private and public spheres.[24]

What makes these institutional spheres of personal, economic, and political life essential for developing individual freedom is that individuals bound together by love, economic cooperation, and democratic self-determination self-consciously recognize the freedom of the other as a precondition for, rather than as a limit to, their own freedom. Although the ethical sphere of personal relationships represents the clearest (and perhaps least problematic) example of living freely without inhibition in the presence of another who emancipates one's personality and allows one to fully be oneself, the ethical sphere of democratic deliberation represents the most reflexive level of collectively determining the very institutional (legal, economic, political,

---

[23] Here I follow Honneth in distinguishing strategic conflicts of material (self-) interest from moral conflicts of self-recognition, wherein one party feels disrespected by the other. For further clarification of this point, see Zurn (2015: 55–59).

[24] Honneth (2014: 38–41), however, regards reflexive freedom – exemplified in three moral modalities of rational self-legislation (of universalizable norms), personal self-realization (of authentic desires), and collective self-actualization (of sociopolitical identity) – as a higher form of freedom than negative freedom, insofar as it can only be effectively exercised through a social procedure of rational discourse. As he notes, in the writings of Habermas and Apel, this ideal of discourse anticipates an ideal, unlimited community, although in practice it presupposes a real, finite community (42–43).

and social) parameters that define one's freedom in general.[25] Here personal self-realization and collective self-actualization converge around the shared aim of maximizing equal freedom for all. In addition to social justice something similar to the solidarity found among intimates re-emerges here. For, duties of civic friendship in a liberal democracy extend beyond duties of reciprocity; like a family whose members are willing to make unreciprocated sacrifices for the most vulnerable among them, the state is properly perceived by its members as a collective project of self-determination in which the protection and enhancement of each citizen's agency ethically requires that those who are privileged contribute more of their income to improving the lives of the worst off in the name of solidarity.

The liberal democratic notion of civic solidarity illustrates a tension at the core of any recognitive account of agency. Solidarity, like loyalty to family and friends, implies a willingness to assume risks, shoulder burdens, and make sacrifices for those with whom one shares a unique bond of trust and concern. The recognition of accountability is here bounded, unlike that associated with universal morality. Nonetheless, we can detect a tendency toward more encompassing forms of group loyalty, from small hunting bands (which at one extreme resemble extended families) to large states. As social units expand and become more differentiated, face-to-face familiarity diminishes and the basis for ethical recognition becomes more abstract. Something like nationality, usually coupled with a civic religion (early modern European confessional states come to mind) eventually subsumes more parochial loyalties. In the case of modern constitutional democracies, especially multicultural states reliant upon immigration, national solidarity is further abstracted from ethnic, linguistic, and religious ties. Loyalty to the state in this case means: self-conscious participation in an ongoing project of large-scale self-determination encompassing, in addition to reciprocal cooperation for mutual benefit, civic friendship.

I will suggest at the conclusion of this book that this abstract form of civic solidarity, which no longer calls forth patriotic sacrifices in the name of imperial aggression but instead demands concern for the welfare of all residents who constitute what is fast becoming a global community of shared fate, can be extended beyond the state to encompass transnational

[25] Honneth argues that moral, legal, economic, and socio-political relationships not only build upon the ethical care that originate in parent-child relationships but also incorporate such care into their underlying norms (2012: 205). Honneth's thinking here arguably conflicts with the stronger Hegelian structural differentiations in his Parsonian account of social action spheres that inform his late theory of social freedom. I thank Todd Hedrick for this observation.

and supranational (cosmopolitan) forms of solidarity. However, until we have a clearer notion about how the dynamics of recognition enable persons to recognize each other as bound together in solidarity, such an abstract possibility can only appear enigmatic. Is global solidarity – indeed, any solidarity – an outgrowth of persons perceiving what they already have in common, or is it something that is constituted by means of their extended struggle and interaction?[26]

RECOGNITION: ASCRIPTION OR PERCEPTION?

I have argued that the category of recognition is a normative category that captures both an *ontological* feature of adult rational agency in modern society (what, following Habermas, I dub discursive accountability) and an *ethical* dynamic of self-realization that precedes and encompasses rational agency. So far, I have discussed the ontological but not the ethical aspect of recognition.[27] Several questions immediately come to mind in thinking about this latter aspect: Does recognition *perceive* another's qualities and accomplishments or does it *constitute* them? Does recognition always entail positive affirmation? Does everyone deserve recognition?

In addressing the first question, Honneth argues that recognition cannot be understood as the driving force behind self-realization if it does not incorporate both perception and attribution. Take the perceptual model of recognition. If recognition means that the recognizer merely defers to how the recognized perceives himself, the person so recognized is already certain of his status and can dispense with recognition. As Hegel persuasively argues, this can't be right. A serf in twelfth-century France could not have perceived himself to be a person possessing worldly dignity and stature equal to that of a nobleman even if the thought had occurred to him, because no socially recognized value system would have been available to him by which he could have perceived himself that way. Slaves in the antebellum American South, by contrast, could (and did) draw upon their own African heritage as well as the egalitarian humanism of the Anglo-American Enlightenment to convince themselves of their dignity. Assuming (with Hegel) that egalitarian humanism culminates a developmental logic, we can *retrospectively* attribute equal moral dignity to serfs as well, and accordingly judge them to have been misrecognized by the society of their time.

---

[26] I take up this question in Chapter 7.

[27] I discuss the dynamics of discursive accountability in greater detail in Chapters 2 through 7.

A second problem attends the perception model: Merely discovering something about another person which that person already knows to be true of himself does not help realize that person's self-agency. Letting a person be who he is, for example, by granting him opportunities upon discovering that he is, say, an officially documented free person rather than a slave, can help that person legally exercise the free agency that he knows he already has, but it does not contribute to enhancing his own understanding as a free person.

By contrast, attributing something to a person which that person does not know he already possesses in some degree – e.g., treating an *abject* slave with dignity – can indeed enable him to see himself as something more than chattel. However, there are two problems with saying that recognition bestows (constitutes) the slave's newly awakened dignity. First, it undercuts the normative distinction between proper recognition and misrecognition. Until the slave is recognized as a free agent possessing dignity, he is nothing more than the chattel he is initially recognized to be. Second, making a slave's agency dependent on the constitutive affirmation of a free person appears to reinstate abject dependency; for then the freedom acquired is not the result of a *self-actualizing* struggle on the part of a free agent demanding the full realization of what is already properly *his* by moral right.

Honneth thus concludes that the correct explanation of recognition "represents a middle position between pure constructivism ... and mere representationalism."[28] Recognizing a living being as worthy of moral recognition involves perceiving the dignity that being already possesses and asserts, which in turn imposes a duty on the recognizer to treat the recognized as a moral equal. Fulfilling this duty bestows added dignity upon the one recognized. To take our earlier example, recognizing the dignity of a slave who has already resisted his bondage can awaken within him a deeper self-awareness of his own dignity. Being confirmed in his dignity by another in turn enables him to relate to others as a moral equal

---

[28] As can be seen from the following quote (Honneth 2002: 510), Honneth endorses a socially qualified value realism with respect to agential capabilities that resembles Nussbaum's: "I can really affirm only those capabilities that are reinforced as valuable through the recognitional behavior of those with whom I interact .... [and] although we make manifest, in our acts of recognition, only those evaluative qualities that are already present in the relevant individual, it is only as a result of our reactions that he comes to be in a position to be truly autonomous, because he is able to identify with his capabilities." For a more detailed discussion of Honneth's and Nussbaum's effort to steer clear of constructivism and representationalism, see Zurn (2015: 51–54) and chapters two and five.

and, as well, to struggle for more expansive recognition of his dignity. In the course of this struggle, he may discover for the first time that freedom of choice, learning to read and write, being able to express his opinion, and being an equal member of a racially integrated society are more developed aspects of living a life of dignity. So, demanding recognition of the dignity one already possesses – even if it is more than just a shred of dignity – can unleash a chain of events that progressively actualizes one's living a life of fuller dignity.

Recognizing persons as worthy of love or social esteem displays a similar structure: One cannot genuinely possess self-esteem without having already contributed socially, but one's self-esteem and desire to contribute socially can be encouraged by having one's social accomplishments recognized. As for love, one cannot possess self-confidence without having already successfully learned to be oneself and do some things on one's own, but one's confidence in being oneself can be lovingly nurtured by others.[29] Love opens up an intimate social space for physical and mental freedom of expression.

If internalizing positive recognition from others is essential to further developing the agency one already "self-consciously" possesses, then – as per the concern raised by my second question – recognition would appear to stymie rather than promote the self-realization of *authentic* individuals with distinctive personalities. Stated somewhat differently, if social conformism is the price of recognition, then persons bent on being true to themselves should heed Rousseau's and Emerson's advice to abjure the temptation of ethical recognition altogether.

Honneth responds to this objection by reminding us that recognition grows out of social conflict and struggle in which recognized social statuses – especially those characteristic of modern, developed societies – enjoin autonomous self-determination against social pressure to conform. We know from the ahistorical, anthropological object-relations theories of Benjamin and Winnecott, which Honneth cites in discussing the psychodynamics of parent-child bonding, that parental love typically incites infantile aggression (Honneth 2012: 217–31). Such resistance to affective bonding is essential to healthy individuation. Adult stages of recognition draw upon this reservoir of individuation to foster healthy anticonformist individualism. In fully developed modern societies, moral recognition

---

[29] But note the disanalogy: Recognizing an infant or very young child as worthy of love is typically unconditional, involving no perception whatsoever of what that child has already successfully accomplished.

encourages autonomous self-assertion while social recognition encourages appreciating unique differences (individuality) in group memberships and social contributions.

In short, struggles for recognition originate out of conflict, which remains a permanent motor driving historical progress along all three dimensions of recognition.[30] Progressive inclusion *and* individuation mark struggles for recognition within all three spheres, albeit in different ways.[31] Just because recognitive relationships have become progressively inclusive, individuated, and anticonformist, however, does not mean that we must explain this fact by exclusive appeal to struggles for recognition. As we shall see below, the conflict between autonomy agency and collectivist agency recounted above remains a problem for recognition theory within traditional and transitional (modernizing) societies. In these societies, development of women's agency often requires sacrificing moral recognition and empowerment for the sake of social recognition and self-esteem. This trade-off appears to be all the more unavoidable so long as systemic constraints (e.g., economic pressure to adopt cottage industry sweatshop production), power relations (e.g., patriarchal modes of valuation), and embodied habits (e.g., feeling comfortable with submissive patterns of movement, speech, domestic confinement, etc.) condition *ideological* norms of social recognition and esteem externally. Resolving this tension may therefore require going outside of recognition theory to consider a more basic principle: that of equal political participation in discursively negotiating social agency and identity from more objective, critical points of view.[32]

---

[30] "On one hand, we see here a process of individualization, i.e., the increase in opportunities to legitimately articulate parts of one's personality; on the other hand, we see a process of social inclusion, i.e., the expanding inclusion of subjects into the circle of full members of society" (Honneth and Fraser 2003: 184–85).

[31] In more recent writings Honneth has maintained that intimate relationships historically progress in fostering more inclusive and individuating forms of recognition, along with moral-legal and meritocratic relationships. For example, we now include criminals among those whose bodily integrity must be respected and we recognize the need for persons to explore their sexual identities. Legal rights, too, have progressively been extended to more people even as they have progressively expanded to protect all dimensions of individual agency, from civil rights to democratic participatory rights and, finally, welfare rights. Meanwhile, social esteem has been detached from the exclusive honor attached to noble birth and become universally available to persons according to their individual merit.

[32] Lois McNay's concern (2008: 196) that "the idea of recognition is constraining for an analysis of gender because it remains committed to a face-to-face model of power that obscures the systemic ways in which sexual and other inequalities are reproduced" is

This objection, however, does not impugn recognition theory as an essential component of a more comprehensive critical theory. So, let me now turn to our last question: Does everyone deserve recognition? Answering this question compels us to reconsider the preceding social dilemma as a political dilemma. Although all persons deserve love, moral respect, and social esteem when the question is posed abstractly, when the question is posed concretely the answer would appear to be "no": We have no duty to recognize groups that negatively misrecognize other groups.

Nancy Fraser argues that a theory of recognition such as Honneth's does not have the normative resources to identify legitimate demands for recognition.[33] Honneth disputes this claim: Although all persons should have an equal opportunity to acquire self-esteem in reciprocal relations of recognition based on socially valued contributions, anyone who denies this right to others should not be esteemed in any capacity that relates to *this* part of their identity. Thus, we can exclude white supremacists from those meriting recognition. Indeed, any group whose identity is premised on denying reciprocity and equal opportunity to other groups *must* be so excluded.[34]

apropos of the need to discuss not only systemic (structural) determinants of action but also power relations and embodied habits that condition recognitive relationships from without. Critical theorists such as Habermas and Honneth both acknowledge the need to adopt the standpoint of a sociological observer; moreover neither dismisses the impact of power shaping their own sociological descriptions and rational normative reconstructions, which, as I remark in the Introduction and Chapter 2, bear the indelible effects of modern techno-systems and the always questionable normative/factual generalizations of the human sciences. My qualified defense of Honneth and Habermas contrasts sharply with the Foucault-inspired critique of these thinkers developed by Amy Allen (Allen 2016:106), who argues that they do not adopt a sufficiently critical standpoint with respect to such modern moral categories as individual autonomy, reflexivity, and rational normative universalization. Whether Allen's assessment of these thinkers is more accurate than mine is a matter of judgment. She and I both agree that confronting ethical relativism requires defending at least some norms of individual and societal development, while conceding their contingent emergence out of disciplinary practices and discourses as well as their disempowering side.

[33] Unfortunately, Fraser mistakenly equates Honneth's theory of recognition with a theory of multicultural identity politics, thereby ignoring Honneth's discussion of emotional and moral recognition. Elsewhere she wrongly asserts that "In Axel Honneth's theory ... everyone is morally entitled to social esteem," regardless of their political values (Fraser 2001: 28).

[34] As Zurn notes (Zurn 2015: 71), one must distinguish social struggles for the universal esteem of one form of ethical life (say, democratic socialism) from esteem-based social struggles aimed at overcoming discrimination against groups. Furthermore, one must distinguish Honneth's defense of a "formal conception of ethical life," which consists of "the entirety of intersubjective conditions that can be shown to serve as necessary preconditions for individual self-realization" (Honneth 1996: 173) from other teleological theories of a more substantive nature, such as virtue ethics and communitarianism,

This position converges with Fraser's own view about the politics of recognition.Noting that refusal to extend recognition to some identity groups (white supremacists, for instance) is not unjust, Fraser adds that legitimate complaints about not having been properly recognized almost always accompany economic and political injustices or harms caused by the *maldistribution* of material welfare and decision-making powers essential to the exercise of agency. So, in contrast to white supremacism, Black empowerment promotes equal opportunity to achieve esteem, specifically in response to a status order marked by white privilege.

RECOGNITION, REDISTRIBUTION, AND PARTICIPATORY PARITY: THE HONNETH-FRASER DEBATE

Fraser's effort at distinguishing legitimate from illegitimate complaints about cultural misrecognition raises an important question. Legitimate complaints typically refer beyond the injustice of cultural misrecognition to include economic and political injustices (Fraser 2010: 17). This observation raises a more basic question about the relationship between (mis) recognition and injustice. Occasional lack of recognition from this or that person might not be harmful to one's self-confidence, self-respect, or self-esteem,[35] but general lack of societal recognition is often harmful and, for that reason, appears to be *prima facie* unjust unless, as in the above case involving groups that negatively misrecognize other groups, there is a good reason for it.

Lack of recognition does not imply injustice, but perhaps injustice implies lack of recognition. To begin with, it seems that anyone who suffers injustice also experiences disrespect or lack of proper recognition. If injustice and lack of positive, proper recognition always accompany each other, it is important for purposes of remedial action to know which (if either) of these dyadic terms is explanatorily primary.

One reason for thinking that misrecognition is explanatorily primary – the view held by Honneth – is that some injustices involve nothing more than misrecognition. For example, members of the LGBTQ community in the United States are not, as a group, economically oppressed. Nor are

---

which recommend one hierarchy of values and one concrete form of life as supremely good (Zurn 2015: 67).

[35] This claim cannot stand without qualification. Isolated incidences of socially shunned hate speech, when not directed toward a specific person or when directed toward a specific person to whom it causes no personal harm, can still cause harm to the targeted group of which that person is a member.

their political rights diminished (in fact, gay, lesbian, and transgender persons have sometimes been very effective in leveraging their political power to obtain equal rights). However, many communities and organizations exclude them from membership or ostracize them on the basis of cultural norms.

By contrast, misrecognition seems to be present wherever there is economic and political injustice. For example, English miners who lost their jobs during Thatcher's administration also lost a part of their identity and dignity. Again, institutional racism – the aggregate effects of past intentional discrimination coupled with present-day residential segregation – partially explains why so many inner-city African Americans do not enjoy equal educational and economic opportunity and find themselves politically marginalized, even in areas where they constitute a majority or plurality of the population.

Honneth explains these facts by arguing that economic and political injustice is *caused* by a prior lack of social recognition. It is because the social contribution of British miners was not esteemed by the Thatcher regime that that regime sought to suppress the miners' union and deprive them of economic well-being. It is because the equal dignity of African-Americans was not recognized by law until very recently that they continue to suffer effects of institutional racism even in the absence of overt discrimination.

In her debate with Honneth, Nancy Fraser acknowledges the close overlap between recognition-based injustices and economic and political injustices but objects to explaining all injustices in terms of misrecognition. To illustrate her point, imagine for a moment that the loss of a small subsistence farm caused by market competition from high-tech foreign agribusiness is unjust because rules of trade are mainly set up by the rich and powerful to profit themselves. This injustice, at once economic and political, intends no disrespect to the anonymous farmers who suffer the consequences. Or take the example (mentioned by Fraser) of someone who loses her job due to corporate merger, "outsourcing," or technological redundancy. Competitiveness and profitability explain these outcomes, just as "supply and demand for different types of labor; the balance of power between labor and capital; the stringency of social regulations, including the minimum wage; the availability and cost of productivity enhancing technologies; the ease with which firms can shift their operations to locations where wage rates are lower; the cost of credit; the terms of trade; and international currency rates" largely explain different rates of remuneration (Fraser and Honneth 2003: 215).

That said, many economic injustices might well be explained in terms of misrecognition. Take , for example, the corporate contracting of sweat-shop labor. The desire of very wealthy businesses to extract the most work for the least pay, even if guided by the laws of market competition, mis-recognizes the contractual relationship between employer and employee as a purely strategic relationship. On the contrary, contracts create moral expectations and voluntarily assumed obligations that, although legally enforceable, depend on all parties mutually recognizing that their terms of cooperation ostensibly benefit all parties fairly. Exploitation violates this ethical consensus; it disrespects the moral agency of workers and denies them proper esteem for their productive contribution. Especially pertinent here (and to my own analysis of gender-based misrecognition in develop-ing societies) is Honneth's extended discussion about how women's unre-munerated reproductive and childrearing activity as well as their consignment to lower paying jobs (e.g., in sweatshops) and their receipt of unequal payment for equal work can *only* be explained in terms of patriarchal estimates of achievement and social contribution.

The above examples show that Honneth's *weaker* claim that a "recog-nition order" *preconditions* any economic system is descriptively more accurate than his *stronger* claim that it determines that system's distribu-tive outcomes. Laws governing property ownership, market competition and monopoly formation, creation and conduct of corporations, con-scionable and enforceable contracts, collective bargaining rights, labor-safety and environmental standards, nondiscrimination in employment and provision of services, and fraud all reflect cultural valuations about fairness and the public good. In addition to these legal values, capitalism depends on psychological incentives, work ethic codes, and other socially recognized expectations regarding esteem-worthy social contribution.

Violation of any of these expectations can provoke outcries of injustice: job discrimination, unfair taxation, contractual coercion, occupational endangerment to health and safety, inadequate compensation, denial of equal opportunity in accessing basic services, and so on. At its most extreme, violated expectations that social wealth generated by social labor ought to be democratically controlled can galvanize a struggle for democratic socialism. This struggle for justice converges with a struggle for integral self-realization on behalf of those who resist pathologies associated with hyper-consumerism, alienated labor, and environmental/ ecological degradation.

The weak claim that a recognition order *invariably* conditions eco-nomic relationships but only *variably* influences distributive outcomes might well seem unsatisfying from the standpoint of remedial action, for it leaves unsettled the causal diagnosis of many social injustices and pathologies. To take my earlier example: Is high unemployment among young African American men living in poor urban communities caused by cold economic calculation on the part of private investors, coupled with public development programs whose fortunes rise and fall relative to the heavily indebted government agencies that fund them? Or is it caused by intentional or institutional racial discrimination entrenched in both private and public sectors? If the former is the case, then raising and redistributing public revenue and offering private investment incentives, leading to the provision of better infrastructure, schools, police security, and social services might grow decent-paying jobs in poor African American communities. If the latter is the case, then aggressive consciousness-raising campaigns targeting racial discrimination in private and public institutions, leading to legal promotion of integration and affirmative action policies, becomes imperative for improving the economic opportunities of young African American men.

In the final analysis, only finer-grained socioeconomic investigations than those currently available can conclusively clarify the complex causal nexus underlying chronic underemployment among young African American men. Absent such an unequivocal diagnosis, the unmistakable presence of racial misrecognition as one contributing factor to economic injustice will dictate a multipronged remedy. That said, criticism of injustice and pathology need not await a fully developed diagnosis. When submitted to the legitimating tribunal of public scrutiny, feelings of disrespect, coercion, and unhappiness can guide critical theory.

Both Fraser and Honneth endorse variants of this proposal. I will briefly comment on Fraser's insofar as it combines the advantages of Habermas's discourse ethics with Honneth's recognition theory. According to Fraser, a single principle of *participatory parity* suffices to ground criticism of *all* injustices, be they economic, political or sociocultural.[36] Pursuant to Habermas's discourse ethics, Fraser maintains that the basic framing

---

[36] The meta-ethical disagreement between Fraser and Honneth regarding choice of theory (deontological versus teleological) overshadows their desire to find a third alternative between these extremes: Honneth's "teleological liberalism" and Fraser's "thick deontological liberalism" (Fraser and Honneth 2003: 230). According to Honneth, "the point of recognition is the same as that of participatory parity: the development and realization of individual autonomy" (259). Honneth continues: "Fraser defines the 'why' and 'what for' of equality with reference to the good of participation, whereas I understand this 'what for' as the good of personal identity formation, whose realization I see as dependent on relations of mutual recognition" (176).

questions – concerning who should have a right to deliberate and decide, what injustices are at stake, and how they should be fairly mitigated – must be dialogically resolved. As with Habermas, Fraser understands this to entail questioning the territorial sovereignty of states, not to eliminate it, but to show how it contributes to global injustices, such as statelessness and poverty, while at the same time obstructing their mitigation. But agreeing with Honneth, she insists that the motives guiding social criticism and political struggle must appeal to socially recognized norms, values, narratives, and identities that possess greater normative substance than formal conditions of rational discourse.[37] To cite Christopher Zurn, a key advantage of recognition theory over Kant-inspired discourse theory is that "the connections between moral feelings of violation, the conditions of personal integrity, and social misrecognition serve to anchor the theory's normative aspirations in actual social processes" (Zurn 2015:68). In other words, recognition theory takes up everyday feelings of moral outrage, encourages theoretical elaboration of new concepts by which to name and identify the harms that occasion that outrage, and thereby provides theoretical guidance to the formation of social movements aimed at overcoming a vast array of distinctive types of social injustices beyond those concerning the violation of universal human rights.

CONFLICTED AGENCY AND THE SELF-SUBORDINATION SOCIAL RECOGNITION PARADOX: EMANCIPATING WOMEN IN DEVELOPING COUNTRIES THROUGH MICRO-FINANCE

Having briefly examined the complex relationship between economic, cultural, and political injustices, let me now return to a problem I mentioned earlier regarding the tension between social conformism and anti-conformism within recognition theory. Women in the developing world must sometimes choose between recognition, welfare, and empowerment. Prohibited from working outside the home to feed their children and having an equal voice in decision-making, women who seek to be economically and politically empowered suffer stigma and ostracism from

---

[37] Fraser (Fraser and Honneth 2003: 238) prefers narratives – specifically, "folk paradigms of social justice" that motivate social movements – over psychological feelings and expectations because the former have already been reflectively formulated in intersubjective discourse. As I read Honneth, feelings and expectations, too, must be filtered through intersubjective discourse in order to assess whether they aspire to greater inclusion and individuation.

family and community, and as a consequence suffer from diminished agency in their simple pursuit of the welfare requisite for agency.

The above dilemma – the modern-day equivalent of Antigone's – sheds light on paradoxes of women's development associated with one controversial form of empowerment: microcredit.[38] Often, women in the developing world have access to welfare and status recognition only through their husbands. According to Naila Kabeer, women who become self-employed through microcredit can become empowered independently of their husbands without sacrificing recognition and welfare. Although some women who receive microcredit sometimes do so in order to work at home in compliance with *purdah* (domestic seclusion) they can at least acquire bargaining leverage to exact some concessions from their husbands. Furthermore, their sense of self-esteem is likely to increase to the extent that they are valued by their husbands and community for contributing to their family's upkeep. So, even though microcredit interventions do not immediately emancipate women from the weight of material oppression and patriarchal domination, they set in motion a chain of events that appear predestined to do so (Kabeer 1998: 63–84).

Can we conclude that microcredit unequivocally develops women's agency in a way that meets the three requirements of justice and well-being noted above? No doubt, women's capacity to bargain and the expanded opportunities for choice afforded to them by accessing microcredit have enhanced their welfare and social status (they can now stay at home *and* feed their families). But enhanced self-esteem comes at a price. Serene Khader (2014) observes that the price in question involves "opportunity costs" in the form of diminished *autonomy* agency (to use Cudd's term) and, more specifically, diminished *feminist* agency, or freedom from restrictive and self-subordinating gender roles that deny women an equal

---

[38] Only about a third of households studied prefer micro-finance institutions (MFIs) to other, more flexible, sources of loans, such as local moneylenders and family. The vast majority of the more than 137 million who participate globally – an 18-fold increase since 1997 – are women (they compose 97 percent of Mohammed Yunis's Grameen Bank's clientele). MFIs were heralded as an innovative anti-poverty program and driver of development, providing liquid assets to meet a variety of needs and encouraging savings. However, recent studies on the short- and long-term effects of MFIs suggest that MFIs may have little impact on development, as measured by increases in welfare, health, education, consumption and women's empowerment. These results partly reflect the small size of loans in question, which on average are repaid at an APR of 37 percent, running as high as 70 percent, mainly due to transaction costs. Very few MFI loans enable the hiring of employees for larger enterprises. MFIs, however, encourage positive changes in consumption (from nonessential goods to durable, business-related goods) (Banerjee 2015).

voice at home and in their community. Even their heightened self-esteem as microcredit beneficiaries comes at the cost of further entrenching patriarchal domination. Indeed, instead of being respected as a moral equal, some of these women appeared to have increased their value to family and community by being reduced to property, or mere collateral – in fact, reduced to a status not so different from that of a slave or source of dowry (Khader 2014: 223–48).

This dilemma – and the temptation to renounce genuine agential development for the immediate fulfillment promised by an ideology of patriarchal recognition – leads Khader to question two assumptions about the agency-empowering effect of microcredit that have been made by Kabeer and others. The "cumulative assumption" holds that agency is all of a piece: Expanding options through increased welfare implies expanded options with respect to self-determination as a woman and as an autonomous individual (autonomy agency). The "substantive assumption" links enhanced agency to the acquisition of substantive moral beliefs about one's right to self-determination (Khader 2014: 229). In line with this thinking, Susy Cheston and Lisa Kuhn (2002: 71) argue that self-efficacy implies greater self-esteem, which in turn implies belief in the right to self-determination as resistance to patriarchy. Kabeer adds that bringing income into a household implies a belief that one is entitled by moral right to a fair or equal portion of what one brings in (Khader 2014: 230; Kabeer 2001: 71).

Khader questions both assumptions by observing that the dilemma faced by poor women in traditional developing societies – to resist patriarchal subordination or increase their welfare agency by acceding to subordination – is at root a dilemma about which social roles to identify with, whose social recognition matters, and what kind of rationally accountable agency is most desirable. Khader dubs this classical Hegelian dilemma the "Self-Subordination Social Recognition Paradox": Access to certain opportunities and goods (income, self-esteem, etc.) that may be essential to the exercise of autonomy agency depends upon conformity to socially recognized patriarchal gender roles, which effectively require limiting autonomy agency to meet the demands of collective identity agency. Antipoverty interventions may incentivize not only compliance with sexist norms but even their internalization. The latter happens when rewards for compliance (increased familial love, social esteem, material benefits) align with one another in a way that encourages strong personal identification with sexist norms. Although autonomous women who have acquired a belief in their feminist agency can outwardly comply with sexist norms out of mere expediency, the psychological costs of acting against their conviction can be great.[39] Rationalizing a repeated violation of a deeply held conviction in an effort to mitigate one's sense of having committed a practical contradiction reduces one kind of agency-threatening cognitive dissonance by increasing another: self-deception.

The cognitive dissonance between achieving welfare agency through socially recognized identity agency and achieving feminist agency through non-socially recognized autonomy agency can be reformulated as an identity crisis, or lack of self-certainty, about which kind of recognition is most valuable to one's exercise of agency (Khader 2014: 231). Rawls, Honneth, and Taylor link self-esteem to a personal belief that one's life plans are of value; but being certain that they are valuable depends on others recognizing them as such. Although one might think that a reflective moral commitment to unpopular values may be strong enough to withstand widespread social disapproval, the ambiguities played out in being a "good woman" as judged against conflicting standards of social responsibility and agency are a recipe for feelings of moral failing, guilt, self-denial, and diminished (divided) agency (Khader 2014: 233; Meyers 2014: 212).

Of course, the self-subordination social recognition paradox discussed above depends on the viability of patriarchal norms in the face of powerful economic forces. Bucking patriarchy and risking social ostracism – which studies show to be among the worst evils cited by poor women, since it results in denying them the social pathways for acquiring all other goods (Narayan 2000; Kabeer 2001) – might be worth it if globalization itself should render male control over income more precarious (Khader 2014: 234). As Honneth points out, social crisis can be fertile ground for struggles for recognition that can nurture more abstract (autonomous) and more inclusive (cosmopolitan and humanitarian) communities of social recognition and agency. If so, then (paraphrasing Fraser) one should be reluctant to extend equal recognition to cultural

---

[39] Martha Nussbaum (2000: 236–39) mentions the intriguing case of Hamida Khala, an educated Indian woman who autonomously chooses as her life plan – against her husband's initial enlightened protestations to the contrary – a life of moderate *purdah* permitting some outside activities in modest full-body covering. In this instance, there is no contradiction between asserting one's right to autonomy and reflectively accepting restrictive gender-roles. The reflective submission to gender roles (sometimes undertaken as an expression of female empowerment) must be distinguished from uncritical submission to gender roles in deference to patriarchal norms that one has internalized as a function of one's identity agency.

identity groups that make subordination a condition for women receiving an adequate distribution of welfare.

Indeed, thanks to consciousness-raising efforts by the UN and global NGOs, local and national governments in the developing world have promoted a new communal awareness of women's rights. The World Bank's *World Development Report: Gender Equality and Development (2012)* notes that, in addition to establishing legal and constitutional reforms guaranteeing these rights, developing countries have narrowed gender gaps in primary and secondary education, improved the nutrition, health, and life expectancy of women in particular, and have encouraged women's participation in the labor force.[40]

The question Fraser and others raise is whether these local changes in the social recognition of women's equality are enough to offset global obstacles to their realization. The *WDR 2012* encourages strengthening women's ownership and control over productive assets (in developing countries most small landholders are women), ending gender discrimination in labor markets, and supporting women's cooperatives and support networks, all of which speak to the importance of combining microcredit interventions with autonomy-empowering social support networks of recognition.[41]

These recommendations for local reform and consciousness-raising must be accompanied by economic changes at the global level. However, as Alison Jaggar (2014: 170–94) and Shahra Razavi (2012: 1–14) have argued, the Report's assertion that "globalization can help" by opening

---

[40] The Report still counts as serious problems violence against women, high levels of maternal mortality, especially in sub-Saharan Africa and South Asia (1), gender selection abortion and infanticide in China and India contributing to abnormally low female to male ratios (13–16), under-representation of women in government, exceptionally low levels (10–20 percent) of female property ownership; substantial gendered gaps in earnings, with unpaid domestic and low-paying care work being done primarily by women (17).

[41] The *WDR 2012* advocates governmental and nongovernmental interventions aimed at increasing women's ownership, inheritance, and control over resources such as land as well as the provision of credit, extended agricultural services, and access to broader and more profitable markets (WDR 2011: 27–28). The latter is especially important, for as Cudd notes, microcredit aimed at local, small-scale needs is unlikely by itself to provide the resources for quick, large-scale improvements without partnerships involving commercial (especially multinational) enterprises (Cudd 2014: 217). The Report also recommends desegregating labor markets, introducing occupational training and placement for women, ending discriminatory labor regulations, and supporting women's networks and cooperatives. The Report encourages release time from domestic caregiving for part- or full-time employment outside the household, facilitated by publicly subsidized child care (2011: 28–30, 223).

up trade and transcultural communication neglects the way in which macroeconomic institutions and policies advocated by the World Bank, the IMF, and the WTO have worked against the Report's own recommendations (WDR 2012: xxi). With the backing of wealthy developed countries, above all, the United States, these institutions and policies have permitted the destruction of small holder subsistence agriculture, the downsizing of government social services (which mainly benefit women), and the use of tariffs, subsidies, and patents on the part of wealthy countries to unfairly protect their own domestic economies to the detriment of developing nations' economies (Jaggar 2014: 183, 187). If we accept the view, defended in this chapter, that protection of agency is what human rights are mainly about, then it is hard not to conclude, in paraphrase of Thomas Pogge, that the leaders and representatives of the richest nations on earth are complicit in perpetrating a massive human rights crime against the world's poor (Jaggar 2014: 185–86; Pogge 2008).

In sum, globalization can expand economic opportunity for women and increase their agency across multiple dimensions (welfare, feminist, etc.) only if the scope for social recognition at the level of global institutions is also expanded in a truly cosmopolitan direction. Paraphrasing Fraser, this extension of the dialogical norm of participatory parity will require submitting the current Westphalian frame of state-centered political decision making to transformative critique in light of the fact that the boundaries of hegemonic governance and techno-economic globalization extend beyond national borders (Fraser 2010). Besides counteracting "transnational cycles of gendered vulnerability" (Jaggar 2014: 191),[42] wealthy nations must become rationally accountable to poor nations (and above all, the poor people in those nations) by exposing their global policy commitments to reciprocal critique. At the local level, developmental aid must shed its conditionality "by engaging in dialogue with the poor about their needs" so that "the poor receive recognition for their community knowledge and social norms" (Cudd 2014: 217). In the words of

---

[42] Building on the work of Susan Moller Okin and Iris Marion Young, Jaggar (2014: 178–82) notes that the cycle of exploitation and dependency that female domestic caregivers experience in marriage is not only reinforced by local patriarchal norms that make it difficult for women to live outside of marriage but by global norms that define care work as exclusively women's work. In tandem with global economic inequalities between South and North, these norms conspire to create a vigorous global trade in "maids" in which desperately poor women migrate to wealthy countries abroad, where they work in hotels or in wealthy households (whose female members may have escaped domestic drudgery for more lucrative occupations). I discuss the impact of female migration on families and agential self-realization in Chapter 3.

Cudd, empowering aid "builds their identity agency [and] by engaging the poor in reflection and dialogue about what they want and how best to achieve it, their capacity for autonomous agency (ibid)." Furthermore, following Jaggar's recommendation (Jaggar 2014: 191), the global community of peoples must be premised on a rejection of sovereign privilege, coupled with a strengthening of global democratic friendship and governance. Indeed, if we have learned anything from Hegel's account of agency, it is that it can only be realized collectively, in dialogic solidarity with, and in mutual recognition of, all who have a rightful stake in the shared fate of the planet.

2

Agency and Coercion: Empowering the Poor through Poverty Expertise and Development Policy

In the previous chapter, I argued that agency depends on recognition in at least two ways. To begin with, who we are and what we do (and how freely we do it) depends on others recognizing our actions as rationally justifiable. It may be true that self-interested forms of strategic interaction bypass this kind of cooperative accountability. Nevertheless, many familiar types of strategic action depend on institutions whose underlying norms imply such accountability. For example, persons engage in self-interested economic or legal transactions with the mutual understanding that these competitive interactions serve a higher, constraining purpose: they facilitate cooperation for mutual benefit. When economic and legal systems fail to benefit everyone fairly, or treat consumers, producers, citizens, and clients, simply as depersonalized individuals in a cold calculus of costs and benefits, those in charge of their regulation can be held democratically accountable. By contrast, strategic action that is not institutionally embedded openly manifests a power struggle in which contestants seek only to impose their will, no matter the cost to others. Second, in addition to constituting the conditions for rational cooperation, recognition secures the *telos* of agential development. Whereas accountable cooperation harmonizes potentially antagonistic wills in mutually enhancing everyone's freedom, identity-building recognition develops agential capabilities through nurturing and self-affirming personal relationships. Especially important in this regard is recognition of social contribution, which builds esteem.

Accountable cooperation and identity-building recognition do not always function to enhance agential development. They frustrate agential development to the degree that they subordinate individual autonomy to the constraints of oppressive social norms. Criticism of such norms requires adopting more universal and abstract social perspectives. As we saw in the case of women who seek welfare and empowerment through participation in micro-lending programs, the choice between social esteem (conforming to traditional patriarchal gender roles) and autonomy (conforming to modern individuating roles) creates a new dilemma of recognition that can only be resolved by overcoming patriarchal domination. Overcoming patriarchy requires institutionalizing participatory parity, in which, for example, men and women learn to reflectively govern their association as equals. Recognizing the principle of participatory parity, in turn, presupposes the provocation of social crisis: in this instance, the experience of patriarchy as dysfunctional in a modern, globalized world.

In this chapter, I examine different pathologies of development and developmental assistance that revolve around what sociologists, when speaking about underdevelopment in advanced developed societies, call "the culture of poverty." Although some of these pathologies articulate a tension between traditional forms of social agency and modern forms of autonomy agency, many of them do not. Rather, they articulate distinctly modern forms of social alienation, atomistic individualism, and reification. Not all of these pathologies comprise a "culture of poverty." Some comprise a syndrome that might be characterized aptly as a "culture of poverty *expertise*." Welfare dependency and family breakdown, which contribute to feelings of disempowerment, low esteem, educational underperformance, and predisposition to antisocial behavior and political apathy, symbiotically coexist alongside government antipoverty programs that legally classify their "clients" as administrative cases whose behavior can be molded through strategic incentives and disincentives. Both of these disempowering cultures exemplify forms of distorted or inadequate recognition in which the agential pathologies of the poor are treated as exclusively self-originating or structurally determined. Left unrecognized is the experience of the poor themselves and more basically, their personal narratives about how an impoverished social environment has coerced them into making suboptimal choices.

Taking antipoverty policy as an illustration of development assistance gone awry, I argue that an alternative kind of expertise informed by discourse ethics could better recognize the experience of the poor in developing a deeper understanding about how the institutions and social norms that shape their agency can be changed. I begin my argument by addressing the culture of poverty thesis. The Culture of Poverty: The American Debate discusses this diagnosis within the context of the United States, followed by a brief reprise of similar diagnoses that have been made with respect to underdeveloped societies (The Culture of Poverty: The Global Debate). I then expose the classism, racism, and ethnocentrism of the science that purportedly diagnoses this pathology (Poverty Expertise as Ideology: The American Experience and Development and Theory as Ideology: The Global Experience). The Social Contractarian Foundations of Development Theory and the Limits of Rational Choice continues this analysis by examining the ethical underpinnings of development expertise. In both American and international contexts the dominant ethical aim, I argue, has been social contractarian: development should promote economic, social, and political integration by empowering the poor as equal partners in fair and mutually beneficial cooperation. I submit that two paradigms of social contract theory, which appeal to different economic assumptions (Keynesian and neoliberal), have grounded development science from the postwar period to the present day. I contend that in both instances reliance on rational choice reasoning prevented purveyors of these social contract theories from appreciating the coercive impact of poverty on the poor. From this perspective, welfare-oriented and liberty-oriented strands of contractarian ethics recommend development policies that have regressive implications; neglecting the recognitive grounds of freedom, these policies engender their own varieties of agency-stunting coercion. Coercive Environments as the Hidden Foundation of Injustice and Social Pathology develops this charge in greater detail by examining the possibility that poverty constitutes everyday life as a coercive environment that constrains the poor to make suboptimal choices. I argue (Discourse Ethics and the Disclosure of Coercive Environments: Toward a Reform of Poverty Expertise) that development expertise that critically accounts for this fact will have to be guided by social epistemological norms of a discourse ethical nature. I conclude (Applying Discourse Ethics and Recognition Theory to Global Development Policy) by discussing several attempts to incorporate discourse ethical insights into development policy designs.

THE CULTURE OF POVERTY: THE AMERICAN DEBATE

In today's America, the persistence of crushing poverty in the midst of staggering affluence no longer incites the righteous jeremiads it once did. Resigned acceptance of this paradox is fueled by a sense that poverty lies beyond the moral and technical scope of government remediation. The failure of experts to reach agreement on the causes of poverty merely exacerbates our despair. Are the causes internal to the poor – reflecting their more or less voluntary choices? Or do they emanate from structures beyond their control (but perhaps amenable to government remediation)? If both of these explanations are true (as I believe they are), poverty experts will need to shift their focus away from politicized narratives of causation to a hitherto undertheorized concept: coercion.

Socioeconomic environments are agency-restricting. As I described earlier in my discussion of social recognition, poverty forces the poor to choose between options that expand choice in one area (welfare agency) at the expense of narrowing choice in another area (autonomy agency). Choosing to maximize welfare by either obeying or violating socially recognized norms can do violence to an important aspect of one's normative agency. Social stigma attached to dependency and deviance prevents the poor from fully owning their actions. In this respect, their lack of freedom reflects a psychopathology that, in Hegelian terms, might be described as a kind of self-alienation.

The psychopathology of the poor has long been a *leitmotif* in American discussions of poverty, but not in the sense I have just described it. Rather, the poor are simply viewed as defective agents, where agency is measured against an abstract, individual-centered model of rational choice. The poor are regarded as incapable of making rational choices as a result of some personal defect in their character, or they are seen as helpless victims of social forces beyond their control. Little or no mention is made of the social-pathology of an economic system that treats everything as a commodity, reduces all values to quantifiable calculi of costs and benefits, and undermines the egalitarian conditions of social recognition requisite for a healthy sense of agency. Yet the kind of objectifying social science that comports with the pathological logic of late capitalist society, as I have just described it, continues to parlay its common-sense stereotype of the poor as morally and rationally defective.

In her pathbreaking work, *Poverty Knowledge: Social Science, Social Policy, and the Poor in Twentieth Century US History* (2002), Alice O'Connor traces the failure of public policy aimed at eradicating poverty to ideologies about the poor that still find wide acceptance among academic elites. As she notes, these ideologies have a venerable pedigree, dating back to the Progressive Era's preoccupation with working-class vices such as alcoholism and sexual promiscuity, then re-emerging with a vengeance sixty years later when Daniel Moynihan published his controversial report, "The Negro Family" (1965), in which he asserted that the single-parent, female-headed household structure of the urban African-American family had become "the principal source of most of the aberrant, inadequate, or anti-social behavior that did not establish, but now serves to perpetuate the cycle of poverty and deprivation" (Moynihan 1965: 31; Steinberg 2010: 2). Attacked for his insensitivity to the institutional racism and economic underdevelopment that underlay this family structure as well as for his neglect of its functional adaptability within an extended kinship community of pooled resources and child rearing, Moynihan's diagnosis was largely dismissed by poverty experts, only to be resurrected twenty years later by conservative social scientist Charles Murray in his highly influential anti-Great Society diatribe, *Losing Ground* (1984), in which he claimed that preferences for unemployment, illegitimacy, and welfare dependency were economically rational in light of the incentives provided by excessive entitlements.[1] Reappropriating Gunnar Myrdal's 1940s depiction of the poor as an "underclass," even progressive social scientists such as William Julius Wilson, who was keenly aware of the impact of institutional racism and structural underdevelopment on perpetuating disadvantage, sought to shift partial blame onto the urban poor by once again invoking Oscar Lewis's post-War reference to a "culture of poverty" (Lewis 1987; Myrdal 1944; Wilson 1987). As of this writing, examining poverty through the lens of culture continues to find great appeal among social scientists, as evidenced by the 2010 publication of a widely heralded critical study, *Reconsidering Culture and Poverty* (Small 2010). Most surprising of all, despite the termination of government-funded welfare in 1996 and its replacement by workfare – and despite the statistical reduction of those receiving food stamps and other government assistance prior to the economic recession of 2008 and its subsequent reversal owing to causes that were generally regarded as structural – government leaders across the political spectrum still trade on old stereotypes about the poor and their behavioral pathologies to justify their neglect of them.

Nothing that I have said above should incline us to dismiss the kernel of truth in the culture of poverty thesis; but it does compel us to situate that thesis within a broader context of pathological tendencies at work in government and society at large. To the extent that higher rates of teen pregnancy, low educational achievement, mental illness, drug addiction, domestic violence, and criminal behavior are especially concentrated among the poor (Noble 2015; CDC 2016; Chaloupka, et al. 1999; Bobo 2009; Aizer 2011),

[1] Having argued that the economic divide between whites and blacks was a result of inherited intelligence (Murray and Herrnstein 1994), Murray today attributes this gap to a differential assimilation of cultural values revolving around hard work, educational achievement, and stable marriage (Murray: 2011).

and especially among the poor who inhabit urban and rural locations marked by residential and occupational segregation, one might justifiably infer that the poor who inhabit such communities not only expect these outcomes but that some of them accept these outcomes as cultural norms, conformity to which yields social recognition and self-esteem. In the absence of education and economic opportunities, having children of one's own or joining a gang confers status recognition and prospects for meaningful relationship. Defiance of these norms can be isolating. In the context of a harsh and competitive environment, violence rather than dialogue becomes the preferred, habitually ingrained and socially recognized, form of conflict resolution. Social alienation and anomic disrespect for mainstream social norms encourages gaming the system, successful pursuit of which becomes another source of social esteem. The sociopathic mentality of the poor who succumb to a life of crime mirrors society-wide cynicism about the law as a necessary restraint on others whose loopholes ought to be strategically exploited for one's own benefit. The pathological colonization of everyday life by strategic forms of interaction goes beyond the infusion of economic calculation to include coercive, legal forms of pacification and conflict resolution. The concentration of police violence and racial profiling in racially segregated communities complements a criminal justice system that incarcerates a larger percentage of its population – mainly composed of poor minorities and immigrants – than any other country. Deprived of potential breadwinners and parents, families who lose members to the criminal justice system face greater risk of breakdown and criminal predation. Meanwhile, once released from prison, convicted felons suffer from social stigma and, in some states, political disenfranchisement. Pathological juridification also manifests itself in the form of so-called government assistance programs that subject the poor – many of whom are single mothers – to various forms of bureaucratic-therapeutic intervention. Denied federal welfare payments, poor women and men are generally forced to work outside the home in order to qualify for benefits, which in the case of single mothers interferes with childrearing (government subsidized day care, when available, still removes mothers from their youngest children) and misrecognizes (undervalues) reproductive labor.

THE CULTURE OF POVERTY: THE GLOBAL DEBATE

Similar stereotypes inform the social science that has guided international development programs since the sixties. Developmental theory emerged alongside a white supremacist ideology aimed at "civilizing the world" in a decidedly Eurocentric mold – the so-called "white man's burden." By the eighteenth century the advantages in geography and biodiversity that gave European civilization a head start in developing the "guns, germs, and steel" requisite for conquering the world were conveniently mistaken for racial advantages (Diamond 1997). As Thomas McCarthy notes, the most influential universal histories of the late eighteenth and early nineteenth centuries elaborated by Kant and Hegel expressly presumed that progress in human freedom was a providential gift bestowed on white men only. Because nonwhite races were biologically excluded from this legacy, their "development" could only consist in learning subservience and dependence.

Today's culture of poverty thesis trades on more subtle stereotypes about the developing world. To a large extent this thesis recapitulates the social recognition–subordination paradox that I discussed in Chapter 1, which pits conformity to traditional social roles against modern recognition of moral autonomy and individual self-assertion. Put simply, developing societies in which traditional roles highlighting communal obligations and patriarchal subservience prevail are judged to be "culturally backward" to the extent that they resist more individualistic – ostensibly rational and economically productive – familial, economic, and political forms of organization.

The relatively less racist and less ethnocentric articulation of this thesis can be traced back to the classical social theories of Marx, Durkheim, and Weber. Durkheim and Weber especially focused (as did Hegel and Kant before them) on the importance of religion and secularization in obstructing or advancing this process. Weber, for instance, believed that an active orientation to social change uniquely resided in the ethical heritage of Abrahamic faiths and that only Christianity – specifically Protestantism – provided the "spiritual" conditions for realizing modernity as a distinctly rational form of capitalist society based on individual responsibility (Weber 1958), thereby relegating non-Western religious worldviews (including Islam) to the status of economically and politically backward cultures.[2]

---

[2] Weber did not live to finish his study of Islam to complement his other volumes on sociology of world religion (1920–1921): *Ancient Judaism*, *The Religion of China*, and *The Religion of India*. His scattered remarks on Islam (Weber 1965: 263–64) argue that "Islam was never a religion of salvation" that could inspire worldly asceticism conducive to capitalism in the way that Christianity could. Islam, he contended, was disseminated by warriors who sought salvation through holy war (*jihad*) and territorial expansion. The feudal property system they established tolerated slavery, serfdom, and external, ritual deference to *shari'a* but no internal ethical commitment to personal responsibility. Complementing Islam's legalism, which vested the *qadi* with *ad hoc* law creating powers

Variants of this controversial "orientalist" thesis[3] continue to circulate today among those who posit a fundamental "clash" between the egalitarian individualism of Western civilization and the rest of the world (Huntington 1997).

Weber was mistaken in his assumption that rationality undermines religion, but religion and indeed any worldview that has not made peace with secular reason must be judged backward and, to that extent, pathological. Patriarchal worldviews that insist on domiciling women child bearers contribute to unsustainable rates of childbirth even as they deny them opportunities to become educated and more productive. Indeed, the culture of poverty based on the patriarchal family has other far-reaching economic and political ramifications, insofar as it stifles individual initiative and comports with authoritarian attitudes. Thus, it is not surprising that Rawls and Sen justifiably target gender discrimination as central to corrupt and authoritarian political cultures that stifle economic development.

The culture of poverty in the developing world represents an opportunity that has not been wasted by the developed world. As in the American context, the global context has called forth regressive responses: on one side, developmental aid that encourages dependency and corruption, while undermining local economic enterprise; and on the other side forced privatization of collective farms and public services, coupled with neoliberal, free-market approaches that expose already vulnerable domestic markets and strained government support systems to foreign competition and destructive downsizing and deregulation. The unleashing of consumer frenzy in the developing world among the educated and wealthy reflects a distinctly Western pathology wherein social esteem is measured by individual success rather than social contribution. Among the poor, this rapacious form of unequal development is met with a combination of

---

in interpreting the vague and unsystematic corpus of *shari'a*, was an inward-looking, but mystical and otherworldly, Sufism.

[3] Bryan Turner (1974: 230–43) argues that much of Weber's explanation for Islam's failure to provide fertile ground for capitalism – its alleged lack of inwardness and asceticism, formal systematic legal structure, and acceptance of commerce – is faulty. The *Qur'an* discusses commerce in a noncondemning tone and exhorts the believer to ethical conduct conducive to ascetic salvation; meanwhile Anglo-American common law with its judge-made case law approach parallels *qadi* law in its lack of systemic unity. But Turner observes that one part of Weber's explanation *does* ring true, although it is extrinsic to his discussion regarding the spirit of Islam: patrimonial war lords destroyed a once-thriving money economy by seizing property and land through arbitrary taxation and confiscation.

cynicism, resignation, and sociopathic behavior culminating in criminality and/or ideological fanaticism.

Progressives dismiss mainstream stereotypes about cultural backwardness, if not the pathological culture of poverty outlined above, as symptomatic of a wider neglect of poverty producing causes that have nothing to do with the culture of the poor. Granting that patriarchal gender norms, traditional stigmas associated with race and caste, religious condemnation of contraception and abortion, and indifference and/or hostility to education and cosmopolitan outlooks have at times negatively influenced the way the poor think about their options in life, there can be little doubt that the cumulative effects of past discrimination and institutional racism working in tandem with neoliberal economic policies and top-down technological interventions have contributed to the persistence of poverty in the United States and elsewhere around the globe. So, the question arises: How did poverty expertise come to focus exclusively on reforming the poor rather than society?

POVERTY EXPERTISE AS IDEOLOGY: THE AMERICAN EXPERIENCE

Taking the United States as her example, O'Connor shows how the professionalization of government-funded poverty research that came to rely increasingly on quantitative measurements contributed to blaming the poor rather than society for poverty. In keeping with the dominant scientism that insinuated itself in sociology as early as the 1930s, such measurements were touted as the *sine qua non* of objective knowledge. In truth, the reduction of poverty to measurable factors such as household income presupposed a kind of methodological individualism that was anything but value-free. By refusing to study poverty in terms of more holistic categories of class, race, and gender – the categories Progressive Era sociologists living within urban communities used in developing descriptions based on members' first-person accounts of their living conditions – the independence from partisan politics the professional school of poverty expertise hoped to gain turned out to be a deceptive illusion. Quantitative rigor was achieved by abstracting from the broader field of political economy pertaining to unemployment, low wages, labor exploitation, political disenfranchisement, and social isolation. As the focus of poverty research increasingly centered on the nuclear family, the causes of poverty came to rest on individual

behavior.[4] In the words of Foucault, two complementary learning processes that had been underway for four hundred years – the *discursive*
construction of "responsible individuals" initiated by the governmental/
human scientific/industrial complex, in tandem with the *technical* construction of productive, individuating (privatizing, isolating, and seg-
menting) spatial configurations in homes, factories, hospitals, and
schools – conspired to construct the social category of the "delinquent,"
the "unproductive social parasite," and other types of pathological
abnormality whose behavior would require disciplinary modification.[5]

In sum, although poverty research had always been championed by
progressive liberals, its statistical formulations, informed as they were by
methodological individualism, were far from politically neutral. At best,
such formulations were susceptible to multiple interpretations. The cultural explanations of poverty and pathological behavior that progressive
researchers provided from the early decades of the twentieth century up
through the Great Society reform were generally linked to deeper structural explanations centered on economy and society. As I noted in
Chapter 1, the social-recognition submission paradox that explains why
poor women in developing countries choose patriarchal dependence over
empowerment is also conditioned by economic factors. Absent pensions
and social welfare systems, giving birth to many children will likely
increase the number of potential male progeny who can provide shelter
and support in later life (through their wives); but absent decent employment opportunities for males – caused by globalization, for instance –
women are often compelled to work outside the home.

The above example illustrates how cultural explanations of individual
behavior that neglect the broader political economy paint only a partial
picture of poverty. Yet even in their most superficial form, when centered
solely on individual measurements of educational underachievement (to
take an enduring example drawn from the US), cultural explanations for
poverty adduced by pioneering progressives were offered as justifications
for government reforms that were aimed at improving school funding,
nutrition, health, and welfare rather than the behavior of the poor. In the
hands of conservatives, such statistics provided the fodder for an all-out
attack on these very same reforms. By the 1980s, the welfare reform that
replaced the war on poverty eventually became the catchword for weaning

---

[4] As I remarked earlier (Introduction, notes 44 and 59), the nuclear family and its contribution to modern individuation is itself a techno-subsystem of capitalism (Feenberg 2017).
[5] See note 44 of the Introduction.

the undeserving poor from their pathological dependence on a bloated bureaucracy that was feeding upon the earnings of the middle class.

Ironically, it was another kind of dependence – of poverty researchers on government funding – that contributed to the redirection of poverty studies away from poverty reduction to behavior modification. These academics tied their knowledge to the shifting fortunes of the welfare state. As the welfare state became increasingly destitute as a result of adopting neoliberal fiscal and monetary policy, its minions sought to reduce welfare rolls rather than eliminate poverty. Poverty expertise was now called upon to explain and legitimate this new strategy. Statistics were used to underscore the failure of chronically underfunded antipoverty programs so as to eliminate them entirely; the punitive correction of individual behavior through incarceration or mandatory workfare combined with entitlement caps wholeheartedly endorsed the conservative ideology of individual responsibility.

Even if the academy's statistical findings paint a more accurate picture of the complexity and variability of poverty – the value of which should not be underestimated – its methodological individualism and, above all, its animus toward structural holism create a narrative vacuum in which families and individuals end up playing the decisive roles. Hence the all-consuming obsession with individual behavior, followed by pathological culture and government codependency, as the leading cause of poverty.

DEVELOPMENT THEORY AS IDEOLOGY: THE GLOBAL EXPERIENCE

In 1986 the United Nations General Assembly declared the right to development, which affirms that "every human person and all peoples are entitled to participate in, contribute to, and enjoy economic, social, cultural and political development, in which all human rights and fundamental freedoms can be realized" (Art 1.1). This new right reflected the utopian vision of Senegalese jurist and former president of the UN Commission on Human Rights, Keba M'Baye, who in 1972 urged the establishment of a New Economic Order that would redress global inequalities between North and South and firmly link first-generation civil and political rights to the fulfillment of second-generation economic, social, and cultural rights (1986 Annex, A. 1 and 9).

No sooner had the UN adopted the right to development than critics on both the left and the right began to point out its practical and theoretical shortcomings. Practically speaking, corrupt government officials in Africa and Asia used the right to development to leverage wealthier countries for foreign aid, much of it spent on nonessentials (such as military hardware) and showcase ("white elephant") projects designed to placate the oppressed masses, and almost all of it conditional on the receiving government playing a subservient role as dependent client to imperial power. So, despite the $2.3 trillion spent on aid in the last fifty years, almost a billion people are still suffering from severe poverty. The poverty reduction policies imposed on poor nations by the IMF and the WB have decimated the economies of poor nations and made them more dependent than ever on rich countries.[6] Citing Michel Foucault's analysis of modern biopower and its disciplinary regime, Amy Allen (2014) suggest that this spectacular failure is functional for maintaining current relations of power and domination.

It might be justly argued that the practical failure of development policy was caused by Cold War geopolitics, inflexible macroeconomic ideology, and inefficiencies that have gradually receded in importance since 1989, thanks to more effective targeting and monitoring of aid. The real successes of development policy over the last twenty years, which I discussed in the introduction, should not blind us to continued geopolitical manipulation of development projects that perpetuate domination, nor should it occlude the role of development theory in maintaining imperial power relations down to the present day.[7] Beginning in the sixties, development

[6] See Chapter 4 and the Introduction for further details on the debt crisis and IMF/WB structural adjustment policy. Timothy Mitchell (Mitchell 2002) documents how USAID's intervention in Egypt in the 1980s was premised on the social construction of that country as one immersed in a chronic food crisis stemming from overpopulation and inefficient farming. This construction justified purchasing three billion dollars of grain from the United States. Left out of this construction was an inconvenient truth: Egypt's grain shortages were caused by diverting its domestic grain production toward satisfying the growth of its livestock industry, which was needed to meet the consumer demands of its upper classes.

[7] These theoretical shortcomings are visibly manifest in the way that developing countries have been labelled by leaders of the developed world, as can be seen as early as Point 4 of President Harry Truman's foreign policy agenda announced in his 1949 Inaugural Address. Although Truman expressly rejects "the old imperialism" in favor of "improvement and growth of underdeveloped areas," his labeling of these areas as economically "primitive and stagnant," along with his proposal to relieve global suffering through "imponderable resources and technical knowledge" that are "growing and inexhaustible," tacitly attributes the cause of poverty in the developing world not to the imperial policies of the developed world but to the cultural backwardness of the developing world and its inability to emulate the industrial model of the West. A less distinctive trace of ethnocentric paternalism found expression in French demographer Alfred Sauvey's term

policy began applying Weber's modernization thesis in tandem with very different geopolitical aims. Guided by Talcott Parsons' "structural functional" analysis of modernization, with its binary (traditional versus modern) scheme of "cultural pattern variables," important policy centers such as the Harvard Department of Social Relations (headed by Parsons), the Social Science Research Council's Committee on Comparative Politics, and the MIT Center for International Relations advanced linear models of economic and political development that adopted Western (largely American) models of technology transfer, capital investment, and top-down democratic elitism.[8] Once the danger of allowing "backward" countries to elect their own popular leaders became apparent, foreign policy experts who had initially pinned their hopes on the depoliticization of the masses through increased consumption (the American way of diffusing class warfare), quickly switched to supporting tutelary dictatorships. The failure of those developmental experiments culminated in the neoconservative and neoliberal strategies of the 1990s: forced imposition of "democracy" through military intervention and forced liberalization of markets through threat of trade and lending sanctions. Despite paradigm shifts in global poverty expertise (most notably from Keynesian to neoliberal economic models),[9] the basic methodology has

"*tiers monde*" (Third World) to capture the ideologically nonaligned status of the postcolonial world during the height of the Cold War in 1952. This reference to the Third Estate within the old feudal order was meant to emphasize not only the economically lower status of Third World countries but also their historical diversity and independent pursuit of distinctive paths of economic development (non-aligned with either capitalism or socialism). In the 1970s, the pejorative connotations associated with "underdeveloped" and "third world" led to the introduction of "newly industrialized countries" (NICS) to describe countries with emerging manufacturing-based economies. More recently, the relatively neutral expression "global South" has gained currency as a less pejorative moniker for developing countries in Asia, Africa, and South America (Schafer 2012).

[8] Parsons (Parsons and Shils 1951) held that traditional and modern societies select different action patterns – revolving around binary-coded solutions to typical social dilemmas – that enable them to fulfill AGIL functions (economic Adaptation; Goal attainment; social Integration; and Latency, or cultural motivation). Traditional societies select roles whose performances value immediate affective gratification, ascription of status, diffusion (or combination) of multiple social functions, particularism regarding behavioral expectations, and collective orientation. Modern rationalized social systems select action patterns that value delayed gratification, achievement, functional specialization, universalism regarding behavioral expectations, and individualism. Using this framework, Parsons stressed the poverty-mitigating function of the modern nuclear family as a specialized subsystem headed by stay-at-home mothers whose sole function was the socialization of children into responsible, hard working adults with stable, gendered identities (Parsons 1955).

[9] See Introduction, note 42.

remained the same: extrapolate a single model of development from Western (largely American) experience and impose it on "culturally backward" nations in the name of liberation (McCarthy 2009: 200–20).

The tragic history of forced development from above raises profound questions about critical theory's own reliance on "grand enlightenment narratives" in elaborating an emancipatory theory of development. Critical theorists like Allen and McCarthy who incorporate Foucault's genealogical methodology in criticizing Eurocentric ideals of individualism and freedom and their neoliberal analogues are reluctant to discard the Enlightenment legacy. However, any defense of individual autonomy and other so-called universal (or permanent) norms of development would appear to succumb to the same criticism that critical theorists (including Marx himself) leveled against all metaphysical appeals to human nature. Once we concede the genealogical claim that historically contingent technologies of knowledge and power historically shape theoretical conceptions of reason, agency, and development (and therewith conceptions of freedom, equality, and justice) critical theorists are left with the difficult task of showing how these conceptions can be universally justified. Separating the emancipatory idea from the institutional constraints in which that idea is effectively (albeit inefficiently) realized poses a necessary, if indeed interminable, ethical responsibility to reflect critically and dialogically.

What moral should we draw from this story? The critical theorists I cite in this study inherit a Marxist legacy that understands all too well the ideological potential of any norm to legitimate hierarchies of domination. That Marxism itself succumbs to developmentalist ideology – identifying progress with industrialization, for instance – reminds us that a *positive* idea of development, as distinct from *negative* experiences of powerlessness and deprivation, must be invoked with extreme caution, and with more than a hint of irony given the imbrication of colonialism and "underdevelopment."[10] Critical theory must therefore be receptive to empirical

---

[10] Many theories have been advanced to explain the uneven development of countries but none seems so basic as that of colonialism. Besides cultural explanations, developmental theorists like Charles Beitz have argued that the possession (or lack thereof) of resources is a significant factor impacting development. However, as Rawls and Sen point out, this can't be the whole story, because sound economic policy can counteract scarce resources (as in Japan). However, there appears to be a more sinister connection between resources and underdevelopment. Daron Acemoglu, Simon Johnson, and James Robinson argue that in regions with abundant natural resources and high population density, such as the Belgian Congo, colonizers established "extractive regimes" that recognized few if any limits on government power, in contrast to settler colonies that, at least in theory if not in

evidence demonstrating the contextual nature of societal and individual potentials for "development." Furthermore, such empirically underdetermined theorizing that acknowledges its political preferences cannot but remain receptive to multiple developmental pathways chosen by people who are concerned about taking control over their own development democratically. To what extent the emergence of a monocultural global economy impacts receptivity to alternative political frameworks for theorizing development by replacing local folkways with uniform standards of technical capacitation cannot be underestimated.[11] Theorizing social

practice, recognized the sovereignty of indigenous peoples, respected property and treaty rights, and established limited government (for settler communities). The legacy of the first kind of colonialism – justified by a right of conquest in the name of a civilizing mission, not by a right of discovery in claiming "uncultivated and uninhabited land" – deprived many developing countries of good governmental institutions and paved the way for murderous civil wars and pillaging of resources (as many as 5 million people have died in the Congo since 1994 from starvation and disease caused by endless warfare to gain control of the country's vast resources; under the brutal rule of Belgian King Leopold II, as many as 10 million may have died). Geography, too, has been cited as a cause of underdevelopment. Tropical zones pose developmental challenges in the form of higher rates of insect-born disease (causing a lower rate of productivity) and substantially lower grain yields due to pests, extreme weather, and poor soil. As Jared Diamond argues (1997), geography may have explained why Europe got a developmental head start that enabled it to dominate the world (Goldin 2016: 46–53).

[11] The conceptual problems surrounding the definition of development parallel those confronting the definition of disability. In both instances, a nonmetaphysical (nonbiological and nonessentialist) norm of agential functioning (capability) must specify historically based contextual determinants of successful social adaptation without uncritically reducing itself to those determinants. Female foot binding may have been supremely adaptive for women of genteel birth relative to nineteenth-century Chinese cultural norms, but no enlightened theory of development would hesitate to label those norms oppressive and their corresponding performance disabling. In today's high-tech global economy, low levels of literacy and formal education qualify as disabling in a way they might not have two hundred years ago. Indeed, in today's high-tech global economy it might be argued that the deskilling of labor that was once performed as craft work and is now reconfigured to adapt to automated assembly lines – what Marx famously critiqued under the heading of alienated labor – is disabling as well. Even if the division between mental and physical labor is not an intrinsically disabling structural feature of the organization of production under capitalism, a one-sided cultivation of technically demanding work skills to the detriment of other social and reflective capabilities might well be. This disabling of sociopolitical aptitudes could more likely be mitigated under a different, market socialist scheme based on worker managed businesses, as I argue in Chapter 4. For a more detailed discussion of this problem, including a critique of the UN's distinction (contained in the World Programme of Action Concerning Disabled Persons [1983]) between cross-cultural standards of *impairment* (loss or restriction of normal physical and psychological functioning), standards of *disability* (restriction of normal *activity* resulting from impairment) and culture-specific standards of *handicap* (disadvantage in adapting to social roles and norms) see Ingram (2004: 91–116).

development and individual capability thus remains a necessary, if fraught, enterprise.[12]

The practical lessons that can be inferred – especially regarding the eliminable causes of underdevelopment – are more contentious. For conservatives who do not subscribe to neoracist variants of cultural determinism *á la* Murray and company, there remains but the simple fact of individuals making bad choices. Progressives who wish to counter this explanation can no longer appeal to social structure as causally determinative without denying the possibility of community empowerment and self-determination. Once it is conceded that the causes of poverty are multiple and embedded in opposed but equally compelling background narratives about "healthy" social functioning and agential development, poverty experts must still confront the apparent contradiction that the persons they seek to empower rationally and autonomously choose courses of action that may be suboptimizing precisely because they are coerced into doing so by circumstances beyond their control.

To summarize: If poverty researchers are to address this kind of coercion, they will have to do a better job of communicating with and understanding the poor. O'Connor, for example, points out that academic policy wonks, like political elites generally, tend to come from the upper echelons of society and identify strongly with the policy imperatives that governments impose on them. Not only do they share common biases about class and race, but they typically have had little contact with the poor. The vast social distance separating them from the poor contributes to a lack of empathic understanding. The poor are both misunderstood and pathologized.

The lesson we should draw from this, O'Connor reminds us, is not that poverty expertise must be set on the proper path of a purely quantitative science liberated from partisan ideological attachments. On the contrary, given that any social science is partial in its framing of reality, the most we can hope for is a research practicum that qualifies its individualizing and

---

[12] Arturo Escobar's post-development thesis correctly questions whether "industrialization and urbanization [are] inevitable and necessary progressive routes to modernization" (Escobar 1995: 39). I agree with Escobar that hunters and gatherers can achieve "development" following their own cultural, social, and political lights without pursuing the *over*development and *mis*development characteristic of modern industrialization (literacy, it might be argued, is only developmentally *essential* in areas where the encounter between urban and rural cultures leaves the latter vulnerable to legal and pedagogical domination). But I believe that Escobar is misguided in romanticizing indigenous societies in the false belief that they fall on the other side of a premodern/modern binary (Sahle 2012).

disaggregating methods relative to more holistic contexts that can only emerge in the course of conducting community-based field work of the sort pioneered by Jane Addams and the Chicago Settlement movement. This requires returning social science to its progressive origins. Today, the most exemplary *global* collaboration between poverty/development experts and popular social movements occurs in the World Social Forum (WSF), whose founding in Porto Alegre, Brazil, in 2001 has encouraged countless researchers to insert themselves into the struggles of the global poor and advocate for their empowerment.

THE SOCIAL CONTRACTARIAN FOUNDATIONS OF DEVELOPMENT THEORY AND THE LIMITS OF RATIONAL CHOICE

Why should poverty experts think that empowering the poor is so important? One answer is that they subscribe to the social contractarian idea of society as a cooperative venture among free agents who regard themselves as equals. Although Hobbesian variants of this idea allow that the decision to cooperate may be constrained by strategic threats (and hence be coerced) other variants (descended from Locke and Kant) deny this. They insist that consent be conceived as the outcome of a fully (ideally) rational and voluntary decision that respects the equal moral dignity of all parties to the social contract. On this reading, social institutions and structures that impose unequal benefits and burdens on persons are to be considered prima facie unjust unless those who are negatively impacted (e.g., the poor) could rationally consent to them as advancing their interests better than any other feasible alternative.

In keeping with this reading of the social contract, it becomes apparent that welfare-liberal and libertarian varieties of social contract theory, exemplified in the moral philosophies of John Rawls and Robert Nozick, respectively, provided background justifications for the two opposing paradigms of poverty expertise that gained wide acceptance in America during the 1960s war on poverty and the 1980s war on welfare dependency. They also provided background justifications for the two opposing paradigms of development that have dominated discussion at the global level – Keynesian and neoliberal – since the Bretton Woods regime was inaugurated in 1944. Both varieties of social contract theory endorse models of agential freedom and fairness that find purchase in modern liberal democratic society: freedom as moral self-determination (evident in Rawls's Kantian constructivism) and freedom as legal independence (evident in Nozick's Lockean entitlement theory). Each therefore departs from what Hegelians, such as Honneth and I, regard as abstract and one-sided aspects of a more comprehensive social conception of freedom grounded in economic and political institutions. Most problematic, because both theories conceptualize rational consent from the standpoint of procedures that incorporate methodological individualism into their design, neither appreciates the importance of democratic discourse in disclosing injustices and pathologies related to social coercion and domination.[13] In short, while the libertarian view of consent remains blind to the poverty-inducing constraints generated by "free" market exchanges, the welfare-liberal view remains insensitive to coercive interventions aimed at reducing these constraints.

Let me begin by briefly sketching what I take to be some conceptual parallels between the welfare-liberal and libertarian varieties of contractarian thinking, on one side, and poverty expertise, on the other. Despite its consideration of structural economic inequality, the economistic poverty expertise that emerged during the heroic age of Lyndon Johnson's Great Society program advocated for egalitarian income redistribution in a manner that was largely insensitive to sociohistorical contexts of race, gender, and class in the same way that its Rawlsian counterpart was. While reacting to forms of racial and class oppression, it did so without the consent or participation of its targeted beneficiaries. Yet, for all of its bluster about disempowering the working poor through welfare dependency, the libertarian paradigm of poverty knowledge that all but replaced its welfare-liberal counterpart by the mid-nineties had nothing to say

---

[13] This criticism applies to the social contract theory that Rawls developed in *A Theory of Justice* (1971). The social contract theory he elaborated in *Political Liberalism* (1999b), however, deploys three kinds of arguments, one of which appeals to democratic discourse. In *Political Liberalism* Rawls continues to appeal to arguments that hypothetical contractors reasoning behind a veil of ignorance might give in support of principles of justice. To this monological exercise in rational choice reasoning he adds reasons that persons living in a liberal democracy guided by an ideal conception of moral personality might give in support of them. However, in addition to these theoretical modes of reasoning, he appeals to reasons that you and I, deliberating here and now, might give one another. These justifications are of three types: a. *pro tanto* – justifying a freestanding conception of justice relative to reasonable standards of coherence, completeness, and conformity to intuitive judgments of justice pursuant to achieving narrow reflective equilibrium; b. *full justification in civil society* – justifying a conception of justice as the substance of an overlapping consensus among nonpolitical values and comprehensive doctrines pursuant to achieving wide reflective equilibrium; and c. *public justification in political society* – justifying a conception of justice based on public reasons not essentially dependent on comprehensive doctrines, which I discuss in Chapter 7 (Rawls 1999b: 385–89; Hedrick 2010: chapter 2).

about disempowering the poor through structurally induced poverty. Blaming poverty on the perverse incentives of the welfare state and on the pathological culture of the poor, this paradigm recommended harsh "workfare" requirements, benefit cutoffs, and regimes of supervision that were arguably more coercive in their punitive orientation than earlier forms of "welfare paternalism."

Although Rawls and Nozick developed their social contractarian philosophies within the context of a distinctly American debate about income distribution and inequality, their arguments appealed to ostensibly universal principles of morally constrained rational choice that found wide application in the economic theories of their time. Post-war development policy, both at the domestic and international levels, was guided by Keynesian economic principles that counseled extensive government economic regulation and egalitarian income distribution as the *via regia* toward a consumer-driven pathway of economic growth and development. Development policy since the eighties, by contrast, has taken its bearings from neoliberal economics, which eschews regulation, egalitarian redistribution, and protectionism in favor of pro-investment strategies involving tax reductions on income and capital assets, cut-backs in government services, and elimination of barriers to free trade and investment.

The failure of Rawls and Nozick to fully appreciate the threat to the social contract posed by welfare- and market-dependency partly stems from their use of the very same rational choice models for conceptualizing voluntary consent that informed poverty expertise. In both instances, the subjects for whom choices were modeled were considered in abstraction from their social contexts, and more importantly, from their experience and understanding of these contexts. The methodological individualism endorsed by these models, in turn, led Nozick and Rawls to underestimate, respectively, the coercive nature of poverty and welfare paternalism. Ultimately, it led poverty knowledge experts inspired by these models of government- and market-based empowerment to propose policies that exacerbated rather than mitigated poverty.

Rawls's *A Theory of Justice* (1971) achieved popularity among social theorists and policy makers in the wake of the war on poverty in part because it incorporated rational choice methods that were just then coming into vogue. Ignorant of their social position and averse to taking major risks under conditions of uncertainty, Rawls's hypothetical contractors are rationally compelled to choose a scheme of justice that institutionalizes equal civil and political rights and permits social inequalities only when they benefit the worst off. Declining to trade basic equal liberties for greater shares of income, these rational choosers nonetheless reject a libertarian scheme that maximizes property rights and economic freedoms at the expense of equal social opportunity and equal democratic citizenship.

Rawls's theory of justice reflected the optimistic view of many progressives that economic growth would solve the paradox of poverty so long as sufficient increases in overall wealth trickled down to the poor and educational opportunity generated widespread vocational skills that would find a growing market. His later writings on political liberalism (Rawls 1999b), penned during and after the Reagan administration's assault on the welfare state, reflect the views of a somewhat less optimistic generation of poverty experts who were beginning to question the feasibility and correctness of aggressive programs of income redistribution and urban redevelopment. Rawls accordingly re-elaborated his contractarian model in ways that underscored its incompatibility with social welfare dependency while at the same time reaffirming its emphasis on dispersing wealth and eliminating poverty. In contrast to the egalitarian requirements of the difference principle that informs his preferred account of justice as fairness – an account that favors a property-owning democracy in which wealth is widely dispersed (Rawls 2001: 135–40) – Rawls endorses a social safety net as necessary and sufficient for minimally just democracy.

Rawls's retreat from the strong egalitarianism of his "comprehensive" theory of justice may reflect more than a shift toward a more philosophically neutral liberalism when we recall the critique leveled against it by Robert Nozick (Nozick 1974). Appealing to libertarian sentiments, Nozick held that implementing Rawls's proposed income transfers would violate the reasonable expectations of many, if not most, of his targeted readership. Specifically, these transfers would ostensibly entail a fixed pattern of distributive outcomes that would be experienced by those whose incomes were taxed as an unjustified act of government coercion, a violation of commonly shared notions of just desert. Taking his cue from Locke, Nozick accordingly recommended an entitlement account of justice.

Although this account would eventually inspire a new generation of conservative poverty experts, its full political impact was far more ambivalent. The theory may have legitimated economic outcomes that were neither egalitarian nor necessarily beneficial to the worst off, but it did so pursuant to the Lockean proviso, which upheld subsistence rights (a principle unknown to Rawls until his later work) and required that the history of property acquisition and transfer leading up to present-day accumulations accord with norms of procedural justice. Leaving aside its neglect of the structural coercion underlying facially just market systems, the chief virtue of Nozick's desert-based model of natural property rights – at least from the standpoint of progressive poverty experts – is its condemnation of current distributions of wealth originating in slavery, colonialism, legal discrimination, and other unjust procedures of appropriation and exchange.

Despite acknowledging the injustice of coercive acquisition, Nozick dismisses much that is wrongfully coercive about poverty by departing from a theoretically impoverished understanding of freedom that exaggerates the capacity of individuals to rationally control their destinies on their own, without support from government safety nets, pensions, education, and health services. He fails to appreciate how free, rational choices are subject to forms of domination and coercion, and he fails to appreciate how they can diminish or restrict the very freedom of those who make them. Multiplied across a population, the aggregate effect of such choices can be globally irrational, creating unintended and in some cases unforeseen economic and environmental obstacles to the free pursuit of otherwise rational aims. Hence, we see the communitarian rationale for legally compelling people to care for their environment, health, and future economic security. If we assume that people would choose such collective remedies for individual short-sightedness given sufficient knowledge and rational consideration of how their own freedom and happiness are at stake, then "forcing them to be free" through more far-sighted government policies may be less "coercive" and paternalistic than libertarians like Nozick think.

In contrast to Nozick, Rawls has a more robust appreciation of how government acts to protect against collective risks to freedom. But he underestimates how these acts disempower the very people they are supposed to empower by subjecting them to bureaucratic regulation. For single mothers who comprise a substantial portion of welfare recipients, regulation means living under constant surveillance to ensure that conditions for receiving assistance are not violated (Fraser and Gordon 1994). Coercion, in the form of legal threats to terminate benefits, becomes more palpable in the physical eviction of tenants from public housing in the name of urban renewal, or the closing of under-enrolled and under-performing schools in the name of efficiency. The top-down manner in which these policies are implemented (often without consulting those adversely affected by them and almost never with their consent) makes a mockery of the empowerment aims that inform Rawls's ideal of equal citizenship.

COERCIVE ENVIRONMENTS AS THE HIDDEN FOUNDATION OF
INJUSTICE AND SOCIAL PATHOLOGY

Despite their different presumptions about agential freedom, welfare-liberal and libertarian contractarians agree that, along with reducing neediness, social stigma, and loss of self-esteem, empowerment is the most important value to be furthered by antipoverty policy. Libertarians worry that poverty disempowers the poor by limiting their negative freedom to pursue desired goals and by exposing them to threatening situations (poor schools, unsafe neighborhoods, and insecure access to vital services). Consigning the poor to political irrelevance and inferior legal capacity, it also renders them vulnerable to domination by others. Welfare liberals worry that poverty disempowers the poor by limiting their positive (moral) freedom to reflect on a broad range of choices concerning who they want to be and how they want to live. Denied equal educational opportunity, the poor are also denied opportunity to develop their reflective and judgmental capabilities; and thus, find themselves alienated from political life and vulnerable to manipulation.

Leaving aside disempowerment caused by lack of resources and opportunities, most of us would agree that disempowerment caused by threatening legal action certainly involves an element of coercion. I submit that severe environmental threats, analogous to the threats posed by a hostile workplace environment, do so as well.

We typically speak of coercion when one person is constrained to choose a less desirable course of action by the threat of another person who has power to inflict a significant harm on her. Poverty is coercive in the sense that it makes the poor susceptible to this kind of constraint. Indeed, it may well be that whenever domination (or any social relationship marked by a large disparity in power) obtains, there also obtains the threat of coercion. Marx maintained, for instance, that the relatively weak bargaining position of an employee in comparison to that of her employer is necessarily coercive, because the employer's threat to fire the employee constitutes a greater threat than the employee's refusal to work. Given that some unemployment is mandated by the requirements of a stable market economy and that unemployment is generally much less desirable than employment, the employer's threat is coercive. However, in another sense we would say that the employer is not coercing the employee insofar as the employee is legally free to refuse the offer and the offer is otherwise legal (entails no violation of rights).

Marx himself denied that employers coerce their employees in this legal sense, however much they exploit them. Yet he always maintained that capitalists as a class had historically dispossessed the working class, *legally forcing* the latter into their state of relative powerlessness. However, if we adopt a more charitable (perhaps naïve) view of capitalists, holding that they do not act intentionally (as a class) to dispossess their workers, we might still blame the economic environment in which they act for constraining them to exploit them.

Before discussing the possibility of designating an environment rather than a discrete act as coercive, I will simply note that the poor are vulnerable to domination (and therewith coercion) by persons besides their employers, including government agents, utility providers, and landlords who have the legal right to deny them needed services unless they conform their behavior to legally sanctioned threats. While none of us is free from having to pay our bills and conform to government regulations, only the poor generally experience such demands as threats to their very dignity and livelihood.

Let me now turn to a different kind of coercion that does not involve a relationship of domination. I noted above that an environment such as a market economy may be described as coercing a class of persons into positions of relative powerlessness whereby they then become vulnerable to domination (coercive threats) by others. Persons participating in any system of contractual exchange have threats at their disposal aimed at constraining other parties and perhaps they must tacitly rely on such threats simply in order to compete in the system. The threats in question can be coercive, and the system that compels the making of such threats can also be coercive. But coercion in both of these senses is legally innocent. It may be morally innocent as well, if (to use a parallel argument made by defenders of paternalistic coercion) the coercion in question serves to advance the long-term rational interests of the coerced.

If the preceding arguments hold true, imagining poverty as embedded in a coercive (hostile and threatening) environment that is *morally* non-innocent will pose no great challenge. I would now like to extend this argument further by suggesting that an impoverished environment (a state of poverty) might also be *legally* noninnocent. The legal context for discussing coercion might strike some as infertile ground for elaborating the wrongfulness of poverty. As legally defined, wrongful coercion involves cases where person A illegally threatens another person B with harm (typically entailing the violation of B's rights) unless B does something she doesn't want to do. Do these threats exhaust the meaning of wrongful coercion?

Diana Meyers points out that civil law classifies hostile workplace environments as illegally coercive insofar as they leave women and minorities with no choice but to suffer unbearable hostility or resign (Meyers 2014b) The cumulative impact of words and actions that, taken singly, do not rise to the level of hostility, or that might not even have been maliciously intended, nonetheless may create a hostile workplace environment. Here the assignment of liability shifts from the agents who *cause* the hostile environment to the employer who knowingly *permits* the environment to persist.

Meyers argues that this analogy can be extended to discussions about poverty. The disparate impact of poverty on poor women may leave them with no viable option but to starve or deliver themselves over to the tender mercies of labor and sex traffickers. The coercive impact of poverty is largely ignored in the 2000 UN Protocol's definition of illegal trafficking as involving "threat or use of force or other forms of coercion." This definition overlooks the fact that some of these women "freely" and "rationally" choose this escape from poverty. Repatriating them or returning them to their original situation as currently permitted by law does not address the coercive nature of the environment within which their choice was exercised. By contrast, recent cases of amnesty law involving trafficked women draw explicit analogies between political and economic refugees, thereby suggesting parallels between political (agent-centered) and economic (environment-centered) threats (Haynes 2006).

Again, it might be objected that, even if poverty does coerce women to consent to their own illegal bondage, such consent does not rise to the level of a legal violation, since there are many cases of coerced consent that are (and perhaps ought to be) legal. Alan Wertheimer notes that consent decrees offered by government prosecutors to companies that have violated antidiscrimination or antiregulatory statutes are both coerced (since the companies have no real option but to consent) and valid (Wertheimer 2014). By parity of reason he concludes that the right of poor women living in developing countries to consent to undergo risky drug trials that offer only cash payments but no other medical benefits is likewise legally innocent. This consent may be coerced by the absence of viable options, but it is nonetheless valid insofar as it does not lead to the direct violation of rights.

Does the validity of coerced consent in these cases refute Meyer's argument? Nothing about what persons can validly consent to out of desperation speaks for or against the illegality of the circumstances that "force" them to consent. From Meyer's perspective, women who are forced into trafficking by poverty may well have a right to choose this option, just as women fleeing from political oppression may have a right to choose this option. That does not render the political (or economic) oppression any less illegally coercive. In short, extreme poverty rises to the status of a human rights violation to the extent that it forces desperate people to choose illegal pathways for exiting it.

DISCOURSE ETHICS AND THE DISCLOSURE OF COERCIVE ENVIRONMENTS: TOWARD A REFORM OF POVERTY EXPERTISE

Throughout his career Habermas has formulated his social theory as a dialogical method for exposing the coercive nature of social environments. If we assume that condemnation of coercive association is what makes social contract theory the most compelling moral foundation underwriting the empowerment aims of poverty expertise, we find in Habermas's discourse theory of law and democracy a contractarianism that specifically exposes the limitations of welfare-liberal and libertarian alternatives (Habermas 1996: 393–414).

Especially relevant to our purposes is Habermas's penetrating analysis of the legitimation crisis besetting the welfare state, which examines the contradiction between the administrative regulation of a crisis-prone market economy and the democratic imperative to hold government accountable to universally recognized norms of distributive justice (Habermas 1975). Habermas contends that the empowerment of technical social engineers devoted to the singular cause of stable economic growth coupled with the depoliticization of apathetic masses absorbed in their everyday private lives comes at the expense of a robust public debate over the justice of government income redistribution. He also observes that social policies that compensate for severe inequalities – specifically antipoverty programs that aim to empower the poor – necessarily rely on coercive legal classifications and eligibility requirements that effectively *dis*empower the poor. Poor urban communities are thus literally "colonized" (taken over) by government-appointed social workers, housing authorities, planning agencies, school boards, and other "poverty police" (Habermas 1987b: 356–73).

To a large degree, this diagnosis converges with Honneth's diagnosis of modern social pathology. The encroachment of technocracy and bureaucracy into spheres of public and private life replaces or systematically distorts face-to-face communicative relationships by means of which agents hold one anther rationally accountable, resolve their conflicts consensually, develop reflective capacities for autonomously shaping their

identities, critically reappropriate traditions, and reimagine the techno-
systems within which all these processes occur. The technical outsourcing
of knowledge, deliberation, and decision-making to specialized experts,
along with the deferential (ideological) worshipping of scientific and
technological elites as unquestioned authorities in all areas of life, promotes widespread fragmentation and impoverishment of critical aptitudes
throughout the population. This pathological misdevelopment, which
gives free rein to the repetitive compulsions of unthinking routine, finds
its natural complement in another pathological assault on voluntary social
cooperation: the subordination of discursive modes of coordinating
action to strategic modes of interaction. The single-minded pursuit of
personal success detached from any recognitive ethos entitles actors to
treat others as mere hindrances or means to the achievement of their ends.
When naked bargaining accompanied by threats and manipulation
becomes the contractarian social norm, coercion itself is rendered invisible. Once the social environment descends to this level of coerciveness, it is
but a short step to a politics of friend versus foe, in which the stakes reduce
to hegemonic legal domination of one group by another and everyone
games the system regardless of social costs.

These Hobbesian contractarian dispositions appear pathological only
insofar as the recognitive relationships that establish the ethical preconditions for market economy and democratic polity evince a deeper moral
contractarianism. Although it is closer in spirit to the Kantian contractarianism advocated by Rawls than to the Lockean contractarianism advocated
by Nozick, Habermas's contractarianism goes beyond both of them by
advocating for a radical democratization of all areas of public life, precisely
as a hedge against forms of coercion and domination emanating from
government and marketplace. It acts on the principle that legitimate government must be fully transparent and fully accountable to the people, which
means that it must consult the people directly, by submitting its poverty
programs to fully inclusive and unrestricted public scrutiny. Public consent
to principles of distributive justice and their applications cannot be presumed on the basis of hypothetical models of rational choice.[14] It can only be

---

[14] Habermas insists that persons consent to norms for the right reasons, and that the
rightness (justice and impartiality) of reasons be tested in real dialogue in which persons
check their biases through mutual questioning rather than through the less reliable
method of individual-centered, context-bracketing, rational choice (Habermas 1998a:
57–90). Despite Habermas's critique of Rawls' use of rational choice reasoning, something analogous to his own discourse theoretical approach to justification finds purchase
in Rawls's linkage of legitimacy and public reason (see note 13).

determined by democratic procedures[15] that adequately approximate the ideal of rational dialogue wherein all affected parties have equal opportunities to voice their concerns, question social arrangements, and withhold their consent, free from the "constraints of action," especially constraints of legal and economic power, of neediness and fear, that emanate from administrative and economic systems.[16]

Because of its appeal to theoretically reconstructed normative ideals of a very abstract nature, Habermas's discourse theory of law might be vulnerable to some of the criticisms it lodges against rational choice contractarianism.[17] Fortunately for us, Habermas's interest in reaching mutual understanding through dialogue predated his interest in rational argumentation (discourse in the technical sense of the term). I therefore propose that we return to the origins of discourse theory in his early writings on social epistemology and critical social science. There Habermas defended a descriptive, interpretative social science oriented by a knowledge-constitutive interest in mutual enlightenment and emancipatory empowerment, a collaborative sociology with practical intent, in which (to paraphrase Marx) the experts would be educated by those whom they would seek to educate and empower (Habermas 1971; 1998b).

Discourse theory's main contribution to redirecting poverty research towards a qualitative study of social coercion thus resides in the domain of pedagogy, where it models a procedure for achieving mutual understanding and self-transformation. From the very beginning, Habermas saw discourse as a political analog to the clinical conversation between analyst and analysand, but without the latter's asymmetrical, theoretically mediated interaction. In both instances, dialogue was regarded as combining enlightenment and emancipation. Resistance from questioning others would sensitize us to the cognitive distortions wrought by attachments, identifications, and social standings that had been conditioned by a coercive environment whose underlying relations of power and domination had been "repressed." Such knowledge would be a necessary condition for

[15] Habermas insists that only his "proceduralist" or "democratic" contractarianism explains how welfare and liberal contractarian (legal) paradigms can be harmoniously developed. For a more detailed discussion of his approach, see Chapter 5.
[16] For a discussion of the links between mass media and social power and their impact on (mis-)shaping rational public opinion, see Ingram and Bar-Tura (2014) and Habermas (2009).
[17] As I note in Chapter 5, this convergence is most apparent in Habermas's deduction of unsaturated basic rights from his principle of discourse (D).

freeing us from the coercive entanglements of unconscious bias and ideology. But just as psychoanalytic self-reflection required an emotional transference between the analyst and the analysand, so too discourse required an empathetic bond with the other. Reconciling Kohlberg and Gilligan, Habermas observed that affirming my equal right to speak and participate in a just community of communicative cooperation would be misunderstood by me if I did not fully appreciate the solidarity binding my freedom and happiness to that of my fellow consociates.

So construed, the empathy that flows from my recognition of our communicative solidarity constitutes a cognitive act of "reciprocal perspective taking" that is "methodologically" compelled by the very structure of discourse. It is therefore not an emotional identification that "affectively" induces "concessions" toward those with whom one empathizes. As a moral agent, one is committed to resolving differences by listening and responding to other's reasons, including their personal narratives. In the words of Hannah Arendt (here echoing Kant on political judgment), one must "enlarge one's mind" to acknowledge and, whenever reasonable, incorporate the way others understand social reality as appropriately modified by critical insight (Habermas 2011: 289).

Habermas explicates this duty in terms of a controversial philosophical understanding of social cooperation, self-constitution, and autonomy. According to him, social cooperation cannot be conceived *primarily* as a strategic coordination among self-interested persons who *exclusively* steer their behavior through negative or positive incentives. Rather, the primary coordinating mechanism is "communicative action," or spoken interaction in which persons commit themselves to obligations based on making certain kinds of unavoidable claims whose validity is presumed to be rationally justifiable to others. The competence required to claim (implicitly or explicitly) that one's invitation to cooperate is guided by reliable knowledge of reality (true beliefs) and appropriate norms (right evaluations) builds upon a long process of socialization. In order to communicate, persons must acquire mastery of first-, second-, and third-person speaker roles and, along with that, an ability to identify with different social perspectives, including, as George Herbert Mead noted, the moral point of view of the "generalized other" or "we standpoint." Each of us is forced to "decenter" ourselves from our initial egocentrism as we learn to play multiple roles, identify with multiple perspectives, and expand our horizon of self-understanding to include the universal standpoint of humanity as well as the particular standpoints of concrete others.

The subject's capacity for achieving selfhood and autonomy also emerges during this process. Individuation – experiencing myself as a distinctive "I" – presupposes socialization involving the internalization and creative mastery of socially recognized roles and values. To recall my earlier discussion of Honneth's social recognition theory of psychological development, even before the acquisition of language, emotional bonding between parent and child sets the stage for the first acts of empathetically identifying with others, of experiencing affirmation from others as well as resistance and rejection from them. These affective attachments and struggles, so well documented in object-relations theory, generate feelings of guilt and anxiety that extend beyond our immediate kith and kin. Those "out-groups" who resist or threaten our particular idealizations of security and happiness are perceived as threats to our very identity as well, and so call forth additional feelings of guilt, resentment, and anxiety. We objectify them as if they were "outside" the bounds of empathetic identification and we demonize them by blaming them for our problems, projecting onto them our own insecurities and feelings of inferiority. This is part of the hidden psychology underlying our resentment toward the poor, especially those who are also marked as culturally and racially different.

Genuine disclosure of how the poor are impacted by their coercive environment therefore requires mutual understanding and dialogical critique involving both the poor and their academic and government interlocutors. In order for this exchange to satisfy demanding discursive norms of inclusion, poverty expertise will have to become accountable to the broader lay public as well. The benefits of representative citizen advisory boards and other experiments in deliberative polling (Fishkin 2005; Neblo 2007) in guiding policymakers are too numerous to mention; but the greatest benefit would consist in a fruitful exchange of perspectives and expertise in which all participants – experts as well as ordinary citizens – are forced to question their own biases (Druckman 2004).

The pedagogical benefit of citizen advisory boards recalls, once again, the importance of redirecting poverty research and policymaking away from narrow governmental agendas and isolating academic ivory towers that incline toward overly abstract, methodologically individualizing constructions of agency and moral responsibility. These technologies of poverty knowledge conspire with governmental policies aimed at disciplining the poor, and encourage their practitioners to identify with people who look and behave like themselves while distrusting those who don't. Discourse ethics, I contend, provides a necessary theoretical and practical framework for conceptualizing this pedagogy of the oppressed, thereby mitigating the blind stereotyping and scapegoating of the poor that currently informs public policy.

Confirmation of the advantages of discourse ethics and recognition theory in guiding poverty expertise toward its presumptive goal of emancipating and empowering the poor can be found in global development policy. In the past thirty years development policy has become more sensitive to Western technocratic biases. The difficulty of specifying universal norms of development sufficiently substantive for purposes of evaluation and reform remains a work in progress. However, the universal quality of life factors listed in the UN's Human Development Index (HDI), which measures development in terms of living a long and healthy life, having access to knowledge, and having a decent standard of living, and the Gender Inequality Index (GII), which measures reproductive health, empowerment, and access to labor markets, can be used to critically assess institutional discrimination and disempowerment.[18] The focus on developing

---

[18] See Introduction, note 4, where I discuss the advantages and disadvantages of measuring poverty using HDI and GDI metrics. The UN Human Right to Development (1986) addresses the development of states, and HDI and GDI function principally to compare and rank state averages across specific developmental indices instead of head counts of individuals who fall below minimal thresholds of household income and consumption (the approach used by the WB in measuring poverty and development). The focus on agential development instead of household income and consumption owes much to the capability approach developed by Sen and Nussbaum as an alternative to Rawls's use of income as an all-purpose means for acquiring other primary goods. The debate between these competing methods is laid out in detail by Sen (1982: 353–69) and Nussbaum (2000, 88–89). The argument for the capability approach can be summarized accordingly: Unlike capabilities, such as health, intelligence, and the like, primary goods, such as wealth and income, are not goals in their own right. As Marx famously argued in the *Economic and Philosophic Manuscripts* (1844), the goal of development is *emancipation* – being able to *do* and *be* something, rather than to *have* something. And given persons' different natural capacities for converting income (resources and goods) into capabilities (opportunities for doing and being something), development science as a mechanism of redistribution should focus on capabilities, not resources, as the primary currency to be distributed. Rawls resists this conclusion, however, arguing that capabilities are difficult to measure and, as a function of natural endowments, fall outside the purview of social justice. He therefore does not consider health, vigor, intelligence, and imagination as primary social goods, regarding them instead as natural goods that are influenced, but not directly controlled, by the basic structure of society (Rawls 1971: 62). Nussbaum disagrees, and rightly points out that the same could be said of social respect, which Rawls does include as

capabilities within institutions supporting social freedom and autonomous agency is in keeping with the general spirit of recognition theory, while allowance for contextual variation and inclusive democratic appropriation respects values emphasized by discourse ethics.

As for the problem of technological dependency and technocratic elitism, critical theory from Marx to Foucault has long emphasized the linkage between capacitation, individuation, governmentality, and technology, with the latter simultaneously conditioning both the development and efficient implementation of moral values, albeit in ways that are ambiguously empowering and disempowering, emancipating and constraining.[19] Mainstream theorists of development (those who believe that development can be politically and theoretically redeemed) thus warn of the power imbalances, epistemic distortions, and self-defeating consequences of "technological cooperation" between modern, industrial societies and their pre-modern, pre-industrial counterparts:

[O]ver-reliance on "technical cooperation" is a never-ending scandal, sustaining an enduring rationale for power. Technical cooperation, i.e., the provision of experts from donor countries and scholarships for study there, is a gigantic

---

a primary good. She concludes that because society is responsible for providing the social bases underlying natural goods, it makes sense to compare different societies in their provision of equal opportunities for ensuring that each person can realize his or her natural endowments in the form of basic capabilities. Although actual measurable achievements in health, as with other capabilities, do not perfectly measure the degree to which a society has guaranteed their social bases, when combined with other data regarding natural contingencies, such measurements can provide a rough estimate regarding the degree of socially guaranteed capability. More important, the capabilities approach can provide a philosophically convincing explanation for moral (and, with qualification) legal human rights (see Chapter 5) as well as guide the selection of primary goods. Furthermore, inequalities in measurable capabilities across gender, region, social class, etc. can signal inequities in the distribution of resources. Despite the usefulness of a capability approach in these areas, the idea put forward by Sen and Nussbaum that capabilities could replace primary goods as the principal *lingua franca* of an egalitarian, prioritarian, or threshold-satisfying theory of distributive justice is quite problematic. As Pogge notes (Pogge 2002: 167–228), in order to compensate those with fewer natural endowments for capability, there would have to be universal agreement on a list of valuable capabilities, a method for measuring their achievements, a calculus for weighing achievements of different capabilities, and a method for measuring the relative value of a person's diverse overall endowments with respect to overall capability achievement. More philosophically worrisome is the presumption that persons can be *vertically* ranked according to natural capability endowments, rather than assessed along a *horizontal* axis of different capability endowments, which is more in keeping with the democratic, egalitarian tenor of modern liberal political thought.

[19] I discuss the imbrication of normative and technological development in notes 44 and 59 of the Introduction.

presence, 29% of net bilateral official developmental assistance in 2006. Despite the dedication and skill of individual foreign experts, statistical findings, anecdotal evidence and common sense all suggest that this much reliance on foreign expertise neglects local knowledge and local ties. The correlation of economic growth with reliance on technical cooperation is negative (Miller 2010: 227–28).

While some technological coordination can promote the aim of development, over-reliance on the kinds of unsustainable, hierarchical forms of technological development pioneered by the West merely replicates the ideological fetishizing of technological elites characterized by Habermas as toxic to the spirit of noncoercive cooperation in advanced liberal democracies. Educating local technological elites in advanced donor countries encourages dismissal of their local knowledge and skill base, makes them dependent on expensive schooling, licensing, and technology transfers, entices them to resettle abroad where their technical knowledge is more easily applied and more highly remunerated, and thereby contributes to yet another siphoning of local resources and capital to wealthier and more technologically advanced countries.

Successful development that relies on technological cooperation must insist on standards of appropriateness (requiring fewer resources, costs, and environmental footprints) and democratic appropriation. As I noted in the introduction, the causal pathways linking technological development and social development are complex: technological designs geared toward narrow definitions of efficiency distort not only economic development but political, social, and cultural forms of development as well. Given their Marxist critique of technologically alienated work and leisure (the culture industry), critical theorists must continue to evaluate the positive and negative potentials of information and communication technologies (ICTs) in our (rapidly becoming) postindustrial, global information society even as they welcome experimental microtechnological innovations, which unlike large-scale developmental engineering, are susceptible to impact evaluation using randomized control trials (RCTs).[20] All other things being equal, open technologies that allow for multiple

---

[20] Late comers to development, such as Africa, originate less than .6 percent of patents and accordingly pay huge fees in purchasing and licensing drugs (average annual per capita health expenditure in sub-Saharan Africa is $100 compared to the equivalent expenditure of $9,150 in the US) and agricultural technologies (70 percent of biotechnology patents are owned by the five largest companies; 90 percent of genetically modified seed patents by just one: Monsanto). On the positive side, ICTs enable leap-frogging of expensive fixed-line infrastructure so that rural as well as urban communities can cut costs of financial transfers (such as Kenya's M-PESA program), access digital markets for cheaper goods, and access medical information and health services (Goldin 2016: 138–42).

adaptations (interpretations) and perform multiple functions simultaneously – such as information and communication technologies – are
generally preferable to closed technologies that do not. This is partly
because open technologies by their very nature more easily lend themselves to applications that are both appropriate *and* democratic.[21]

Technological cooperation typically comes with other conditions –
some political and others economic – that reinforce dependency and
promote underdevelopment. The political conditions – e.g., transfer of
military equipment and other forms of technology and training in
exchange for loyalty – need little commentary. The economic conditions
are more complex. Some of them require that receiving countries adopt
neoliberal policies imposing free trade, structural readjustment in local
finance, and government downsizing of services.

One way to avoid these pathological forms of developmental dependency is to offer developmental assistance in the form of unconditional
monetary gifts. However, former World Bank Economist David Ellerman
notes that gifts create different pathologies of dependence; they undermine
internal motivations to become self-reliant and, when received in the form
of in-kind assistance, such as food or clothing, replace domestic sources of
production. It is significant that Ellerman's alternative – *indirect* aid, which
comes in the form of untied, no-strings-attached monetary gifts that supplement developmental projects that are initiated, controlled, and mainly
funded by receiving governments and communities (Ellerman 2006: 11),
deliberately promotes self-reliance by tapping into local knowledge and
local networks.

By diagnosing the agential pathologies that attach to unconditional and
conditional forms of direct assistance, Ellerman's alternative moves us in
the direction of a discourse-ethical development policy. However, not
only does it fall short of this goal, it does not even escape the dilemma it
seeks to avoid. As Ann Cudd remarks, client governments and communities may intentionally pretend to be needier than they are in asking for
supplemental gifts. Combined with wasted aid from mismanagement and
corruption, this consideration invariably inclines thoughtful donors to

---

[21] For further discussion of critical theory and technology, specifically related to technology
transfer through patents and licensing, ICTs, social power, capitalism, and the digital
divide, see Chapter 4 (notes 16 and 17) and Introduction (notes 44 and 59). Meanwhile
the extension of intellectual property protection to forms of traditional knowledge that
abound in the developing world, such as folk-medicines and health treatments as well as
indigenous designs and art, is wanting due to lack of access to affordable legal
representation.

attach conditions to their aid. Furthermore, as we saw in the case of microfinance, donors are reluctant to offer aid if they think it will reinforce discrimination (Cudd 2014: 209).

Cudd believes that the only way to avoid Ellerman's dilemma is to bypass developmental aid altogether. She accordingly recommends that development policy focus on macro- and microeconomic reforms that build upon instrumental motivations to earn income through nonexploitative work and fair trade. Arguing that just and inclusive economies benefit everyone in the long run, she observes that men are harmed by the socioeconomic exclusion of women just as affluent consumers are harmed by the exploitation of cheap foreign labor. Until exploitation and discrimination are eliminated, the considerable economic contributions that could otherwise be expected of potentially talented producers and consumers will remain untapped. Seen from this perspective, fair trade policies that protect vulnerable markets in developing countries while lowering trade barriers in developed countries advance the interests of both the poorest workers and the wealthiest consumers (Cudd 2014: 211–13).

Cudd's appeal to strategic self-interest as a sufficient motive for reforming the global economy presumes that enlightened long-term self-interest trumps blind short-term self-interest. This position not only belies past experience but also ignores the unavoidable ethical motivations for reform that reside within the global economic system as a whole. It is true, as I observed earlier, that all market transactions project strategic features. Bargaining involves leveraging threats and exploiting weaknesses. However, underneath the war of wills common ethical assumptions necessarily limit the extent of morally permissible coercion and exploitation. As Richard Miller forcefully argues, there is a difference between merely exploiting persons' desires and taking advantage of them. In the latter case, the difference in neediness and threat potential is so vast, that the one being taken advantage of really has no viable option but to accept whatever offer is made to them. Cooperation under circumstances in which one of the beneficiaries is still left very badly off in comparison to the other beneficiary is coercive and violates duties of mutual moral respect and reciprocity (Miller 2010: 60–66). Unlike a local caterer that must pay its workers less, a globally subcontracted sweatshop can afford to pay its workers more, simply by passing along increased costs to affluent consumers.[22]

---

[22] Added costs in contracting sweatshop labor abroad would justify lower wages and benefits to foreign workers were it not for the fact that these costs are dwarfed by the

Miller extends this critique of sweatshop exploitation beyond the usual call for uniform collective bargaining rights by insisting that labor negotiations should be structured according to the same discourse ethical rules he proposes for transnational trade and finance negotiations.

> In general, willing acceptance of a joint binding commitment is the outcome of reasonable deliberations among countries' representatives if and only if everyone involved fulfills all responsibilities in these negotiations. These responsibilities are of three, interacting kinds. First, representatives must fulfill their responsibilities of good faith toward one another. This responsibility involves two duties of reciprocity. On the one hand, each must seek an arrangement that all representatives can responsibly and willingly accept, provided that all the others have the corresponding commitment. On the other hand, the representatives must observe reciprocity in their reasoning, backing their own proposals with morally relevant reasons and giving weight, in proportion to seriousness, to relevantly similar reasons offered by others, *so that the importance of a consideration is assessed by its strength rather than by the identity of those affected by it.* Second, the representatives must fulfill their responsibilities to those they represent, so that they only accept outcomes that that they can justify to the people of their country in terms that these people can accept while regarding their interests and autonomy as no less important than others'. Third, the people of each country must live up to their responsibilities. For example, they have a duty to live up to their demanding political responsibilities to compatriots. This is a duty to foreigners, as well, since it is violated when the citizens of one country insist on arrangements that shift what are properly their own burdens of responsibility onto foreign shoulders (Miller 2010: 72, my stress).

The three responsibilities for transnational trade and finance negotiation mentioned by Miller appeal to universal contractarian duties of reciprocity that are presumed to hold between partners engaged in mutually beneficial cooperation. However, it is the first responsibility that expressly enjoins "reciprocity in reasoning." More precisely, negotiation must not descend to the level of strategic bargaining, but should weigh the reasons and interests of others impartially, without taint of nationalistic bias.

huge profits that foreign workers generate. These profits explain the eleven-fold increase in foreign direct investment from 1990–2005 in low- and middle-income countries in comparison to the fourfold increase of investment in high income countries. For instance, in 2000 hourly labor costs in manufacturing in Malaysia were a tenth of what they were in the US; in Thailand and China the relevant ratio was one-thirtieth and one sixtieth, respectively (Miller 2010: 64). To be sure, no corporation compensating its foreign workers at levels approximating levels in developed countries will retain its competitive pricing structure unless competing corporations adopt the same policy – hence, the importance of adopting uniform fair labor standards globally as proposed by the International Labor Organization (ILO) and the Ethical Trading Initiative (ETI), (Miller 2010: 67–69). See *World Development Indicators 2007*, table 6.

Without this ethical presumption, motivation for voluntarily submitting to competitive markets lacks (in Honneth's words) "legitimacy in the name of .... economic security and social recognition" (Honneth 2014: 187).[23]

In this respect, it is significant that Cudd's discussion of *micro*economic developmental policy departs from her *macro*economic instrumentalism in endorsing discourse ethical norms of transacting loans and other forms of mutually beneficial cooperation. For example, her critique of Muhammad Yunus's Grameen Bank's supreme preference for microcredit lending not only targets its economic viability – microfinancing businesses in oversaturated informal sectors offers no sustainable basis for job creation and public taxation (Bateman 2011) – but it raises concerns about the social recognition-submission paradox experienced by women who take advantage of this option. Cudd's preference for cooperative worker-management experiments uniting local businesses and transnational corporations partly reflects her estimation of the greater growth potential of economies of scale, but it also reflects her belief that these cooperative enterprises enable the poor to "receive recognition for their community knowledge and social norms" by engaging them in dialogical reflection in a way that increases their autonomous agency (Cudd 2014: 216–17).[24]

CONCLUDING REMARKS ON THE STRUCTURAL OBSTACLES TO IMPLEMENTING DEVELOPMENT POLICY

No development plan relying exclusively on fair cooperation between development experts and their clients, transnational corporations and their subcontracted employees, banks and borrowers, can escape distortions wrought by power imbalances between involved parties. Nor can they become fully effective so long as systematic injustices in background conditions persist. Weak, corrupt, and undemocratic institutions of governance represent one such obstacle, alongside structural adjustment

---

[23] Citing Émile Durkheim, Honneth adds "equality of opportunity as an essential condition [of an economic] relation of mutual recognition": "Only if all market participants have the chance to discover and develop their true capacities; only if they find fulfilling work and can enter into employment contracts without any internal or external compulsion can they view themselves as equals among equals in the division of social labor" (Honneth 2014: 194).

[24] Cudd cites approvingly the example of CEMEX in Mexico, which consulted a poor community about a plan to install cement floors in their houses while at the same time providing them with the skills and favorable terms of financing requisite for them to do so affordably.

policies that prevent poor recipients of international loans from fulfilling their social contractarian obligations to their own citizens (Brock 2014: 124–25; Green 2008: 12). Of special concern is the inability of poor governments to monitor an informal economy dominated by noncontract labor, thereby making the collection of tax revenue extremely difficult. Trade agreements that eliminate tariffs – often the only accountable source of tax revenue available to poor countries – and international laws permitting needy states to set up "tax havens" to attract businesses also divert revenue from governments, costing developing countries $385 billion annually in lost revenue (Cobham 2005). One example of this kind of legal gamesmanship, transfer pricing, enables a company in a high tax zone to misreport the true market price for a good it produces by selling it below cost to a subsidiary (often disguised as an independent buyer) located in a tax haven. Doing so enables the company to report the sales as a loss, thereby evading taxation, while the subsidiary resells the good to consumers at full market price, without having to pay sales tax.[25]

Another obstacle to development should not go unmentioned: the migration of skilled workers and professionals in developing countries to developed countries (Brock 2014: 131–33). The phenomenon of "brain drain" leaves many poor countries without educators, health providers, technicians, and other skilled professionals needed to build stable institutions and develop human capacities. One ought not to condemn those who have good reasons to migrate, but practices of predatory recruitment of skilled foreigners run afoul of the code adopted by the World Federation of Public Health Associations, which recommends following "[r]eciprocal strategies [that] include sending developed country health workers in an exchange program, remunerating the source government for its investment in a workers' education program, or offering continuing education that a foreign health worker could apply in the home county" (cited by Brock 2014: 132).

I have withheld discussion of the unjust background conditions that fuel migration until the Chapter 3. While the choice to migrate to a rich

[25] Solutions to this form of tax evasion range from the "world-wide formula apportionment" model proposed by the US Treasury, which assigns corporate tax bases across jurisdictions in a way that more accurately reflects a corporation's true profits, to harmonizing tax rates across countries and disbursing tax revenue according to a corporation's activity within the various jurisdictions in which it and its subsidiaries operate. The Extractive Industries Transparency Initiative (EITI) also sets up independent methods for public monitoring of taxes and royalties paid to developing countries by corporations that extract resources within those countries (Brock 2014: 127, 129–31).

country might be economically rational given lack of opportunities for career advancement, inadequate working conditions, and lower rates of compensation, it is seldom morally reasonable. This is especially so for the women I discussed earlier who collude in their own trafficking. In Chapter 3, I show how discourse ethics can be leveraged to criticize the international framework that criminalizes these and other migrants while disclosing the circumstances that compel their desperate action.

PART II

GLOBAL CRISIS

3

Forced Migration: Toward a Discourse Theoretic Policy Governing Political and Economic Refugees

Agency requires economic welfare, social recognition, and political empowerment for its realization and robust exercise. Poverty threatens misdevelopment of all three conditions. Antipoverty development policy also induces pathologies of developmental dependency and disempowerment unless it incorporates discourse ethical principles of mutual accountability. But no policy works well within the context of failed government institutions. Under these circumstances, migration often becomes the best option for escaping poverty.[1]

But migration, threatening misdevelopment, is a poor substitute for development. Besides contributing to societal underdevelopment through the exportation of skilled labor, migration negatively impacts the development of the migrants themselves. Enhancement of welfare agency[2] often comes at the expense of social recognition and democratic

---

[1] Today about 3 percent of the world's population (around 250 million persons) are migrants, a percentage that has remained constant despite population growth, principally because of the increase in the number of countries and restrictive borders. 91 million migrants move between developing countries, 86 million move from developing to advanced countries, and another 73 million move between advanced countries or from advanced countries to developing countries. Most migrants move for economic reasons (Goldin 2016:147).

[2] Remittances undoubtedly enhance the welfare of migrants' families who reside in their communities of origin, thereby diminishing the poverty that causes migration in the first place. Officially declared remittances alone (not counting informal transfers) amounted to $436 billion in 2015, a fourteen-fold increase over the level recorded for 1990, with India (over $70 billion) and China. ($64 billion) being the major beneficiaries. Remittances account for between 20 and 50 percent of GDP in developing countries such as Tajikistan (49 percent), Nepal (25 percent), Haiti (21 percent), Tonga (24 percent), and Gambia (20 percent) (Goldin 2016: 148).

empowerment. When parents migrate abroad for gainful employment and leave their families behind, their children are deprived of loving relationships they need for development. Migrants also suffer loss of citizenship rights in their country of destination as well as loss of social respect and esteem. A worse fate befalls undocumented migrants and victims of trafficking.[3]

This chapter focuses on the failure of developed countries and international institutions to frame policies that protect the human rights of this latter category of migrant. Treatment of undocumented migrants as outcasts and criminals ignores the coercive circumstances that compel them to break the law in the first place. I not only refer to the unreasonable quotas, legal conditions, costs, and lengthy processing that make regular migration impossible for many desperate persons; I also have in mind a global state system that subjects people to arbitrary abuse (or neglect) by their own governments and by the inequities of international trade agreements and unregulated markets – circumstances that have in large measure been condoned, if not created, by the very countries in which they now seek their welfare.[4] Recognizing these circumstances for what they

---

[3] Many of these victims are slaves, whose number today – 35 million – is greater than the equivalent number during the Atlantic Slave Trade two centuries ago. India (14.5 million), sub-Saharan Africa (5.6 million), and China (3.2 million) account for most of them (Goldin 2016: 146).

[4] To cite just two blatant examples, beginning in 2005, the United States began charging undocumented migrants with the crimes of illegal entry and illegal re-entry (Operation Streamline). As of 2013, nearly a quarter of all prisoners in federal institutions (more than 60,000) were convicted of these crimes, second only to drug-related crimes. Those convicted serve between a month and twenty years of prison (the median term is fifteen months). The number of persons charged each year under this criminal statute now numbers around 100,000 – more than those charged with any other federal offense. Many of these prisoners are housed in privately run "Criminal Alien Requirement" prisons that have been sued for mistreating their inmates (more than 100 migrant prisoners have died while serving sentences). A more sinister example of criminalization involves Syrian refugees fleeing civil war and oppressive refugee camps in Jordan, Turkey, and Lebanon, where food vouchers have been reduced to as little as $13.50 per *month*. Under a law passed in September 2015 designed to stem the crush of refugees crossing into Hungary in transit to Germany and more affluent European nations, refugees crossing the Hungarian-Serbian border, where (unlike the Croation border) any official entry is denied, are arrested and immediately tried in criminal courts that often ignore their claims to asylum. Charged with illegal breach of a border fence, they face up to three years in prison. Lesser penalties involving deportation and denial of re-entry technically entail being banned from the twenty-six European nations (including such welcoming nations as Germany) that make up the Schengen passport-free travel zone of which Hungary is a member. In April 2017, Hungary began admitting only fifty persons per week for asylum processing, housing them in detention camps (Dickson 2014, 2015).

are – as unlawful, rights-violating circumstances analogous to circumstances that compel asylum seekers to enter sanctuary states illegally – should force developed countries to protect the human rights of these economic refugees by providing them with opportunities for economic, social, and political inclusion.

The understanding that many irregular (undocumented) migrants are themselves victims of circumstances beyond their control and that "policies that criminalize cross-border movements" and subject migrants to detention should therefore be "reviewed" (l.33) has been officially endorsed by the 193 nations who signed the 2016 New York Declaration for Refugees and Migrants, which culminated the September 19, 2016 United Nations Summit on Addressing Large Movements of Refugees and Migrants – the first of its kind in the seventy-one-year history of the UN. The Declaration declares "solidarity with, and support for, the millions of people in different parts of the world who, *for reasons beyond their control, are forced to uproot themselves and their families from their home*" (l.8 – my stress). The Declaration continues by acknowledging "a *shared responsibility* to manage large movements of refugees and migrants" for *humanitarian reasons* and to "address [their] root causes" (l.11–12).

The Declaration also condemns antiimmigrant xenophobia (l.14), recommends special humanitarian consideration for unaccompanied minors (l.23, 32), and urges increased financial expenditure and international cooperation in providing for the needs of migrants and the resettlement of refugees (l.38, 40). It does not, however, recommend any changes in the status quo beyond urging states to review prevailing policies regarding their duties toward refugees and migrants. Official humanitarian law holds that governments in general have at most an unspecified duty to rescue selected persons fleeing *political* oppression by offering them temporary sanctuary, and says nothing about persons fleeing civil wars, economic insecurity, and environments devastated by pollution, coastal flooding, and catastrophic weather-related events. Fulfillment of such an unspecified duty of political rescue is left to the discretion of governments acting on the wishes of their citizens. This *communitarian* right to self-determination collides with the *cosmopolitan* duty to protect the human rights of all persons to migrate freely.

Communitarian and cosmopolitan views regarding duties to migrants find equal purchase in both recognition theory and discourse ethics. In this chapter, I argue that a qualified application of these theories would favor an ethics of migration that would be neither strictly communitarian nor cosmopolitan. Such an ethics commands respect for the human rights of both political and economic refugees to resettle abroad while at the same time endorsing the rights of democratic peoples to set priorities for normal immigration subject to qualification. In addition to respecting duties of kinship, social contribution, and compensation in setting immigration priorities, discourse ethics implies that democratic nations should acknowledge a metapolitical duty to open their borders in a way that permits graduated or disaggregated rights of citizenship. By conceiving of the responsibility to protect the human rights of refugees as a cosmopolitan responsibility addressed to both single states and the community of nations taken collectively, it enjoins the creation of global democratic institutions by means of which nations can democratically resolve on a just policy for distributing the burdens and benefits of admitting and resettling refugees, similar to the way in which the European Commission has proposed to do regarding the resettlement of refugees within the EU. Finally, by transforming adversarial immigration hearings into dialogical fora permitting full disclosure of the (unlawfully) coercive economic and political threats arrayed against undocumented migrants, discourse ethics partially shifts the burden of proof that undocumented migrants shoulder onto the state.

Because my argument supporting the right of undocumented economic migrants to safe haven hinges on an analogy between their situation and the situation of political refugees, I begin by discussing the current refugee crisis and legal conundrums surrounding the enforcement of humanitarian refugee law (Political Refugees: A Humanitarian Crisis). The failure of developed countries to secure the rights of refugees hinges on several factors: an outdated legal definition of who counts as a refugee accompanied by wide latitude in discharging an unspecified duty to rescue. I argue that recent changes in the legal definition of refugee imply that persons fleeing life-threatening poverty have a claim to foreign protection regardless of how they enter their chosen sanctuary (The Evolving Definition of Refugee Status and the Discretionary Application of Humanitarian Law). Although considerations of national security and limited economic capacity strengthen the discretion of receiving governments in choosing to rescue or not, other considerations weaken it (Refugees' Rights versus States' Rights and Compromising Refugees' Rights on the Altar of State Sovereignty: The Evolving Role of the UNHCR). Economic Refugees Reconsidered shows how far the UN High Commissioner for Refugees (UNHCR) has gone in its efforts to placate countries that host its refugee camps. Many of these camps, I argue, combine protection and prevention in ways that violate refugees' human rights; meanwhile the UNHCR's laudable aim of repatriating refugees is tarnished by the coercive (but politically expedient) way in which it is pursued.

The Analogy between Hostile Work Environments and Poverty continues the argument begun in part two, defending the claim that most economic refugees are political refugees. This argument hinges on the premise that government oppression can consist in criminally neglecting the welfare of legal subjects. The Special Duty to Decriminalize and Protect Victims of Human Trafficking extends this argument by recalling my earlier analogy between hostile work environments and illegal coercion. The example of migrants who enter through illicit forms of trafficking illustrates how official neglect of structural coercion leads to misclassifying economic refugees as "illegal aliens" and criminals.

The remaining sections survey the dominant approaches to the ethics of migration that frame the rights of migrants and the duties of states: libertarian cosmopolitanism, utilitarian cosmopolitanism, welfare-liberal cosmopolitanism, communitarianism, and discourse ethics. Cosmopolitan theorists tend to frame their ethics to apply to an ideally just world wherein the current realities of political community that normally justify restrictive borders are regarded as temporary or less normatively compelling (Cosmopolitanism and the Case for Open Borders). Libertarian cosmopolitans who prioritize an individual's innate right to mobility insist that transnational migration should not be legally restricted for the sake of political community but only for the sake of preserving individual liberty. Utilitarian cosmopolitans defend open borders for a different reason, namely that free movement of labor as well as of goods and capital maximizes global economic well-being. Welfare-liberal contractarians, by contrast, defend the human right to migrate as essential to justice. I argue that all three variants of cosmopolitan migration ethics depart from impoverished conceptions of agency that abstract from the vital importance of social recognition and political empowerment and discount the costs of migration on development: brain drain, familial separation, and community abandonment. Stressing the importance of territorially bounded political communities in instituting these agential conditions, communitarians rightly broaden the sorts of practical reasons that polities might give for restricting (or at least regulating) immigration (Communitarianism and the Case for Restrictive Borders). I argue, however, that the communitarian privileging of solidarity undervalues the human rights of migrants and exaggerates the degree to which communal relationships may require restrictive borders.

My discussion of the dilemmas faced by parents who are compelled by economic necessity to migrate for the sake of their children (Parents Who Migrate: The Hidden Cost of Divided Agency) illustrates the need for an alternative to cosmopolitan and communitarian approaches. I begin by discussing the most radical contribution discourse ethics makes to theorizing about immigration: a metapolitical challenge to the borders within which immigration policies are assumed to hold (Discourse Ethics and Border Policy). Discourse ethics admonishes us to reconsider how borders wrongly exclude persons from participating in policy deliberations that deeply affect their human rights. Taking as my illustration the Israeli-Palestinian conflict, I argue that the historical violence and contingency that underlie contested borders, in conjunction with the emergence of new political solidarities, justifies re-examining their democratic legitimacy. Here, discourse ethics inclines toward ideal (or counterfactual) theorizing in a way that pushes toward cosmopolitanism. The EU's model of disaggregated citizenship, in my opinion, suggests that this is already happening under nonideal conditions.

Discourse ethics has a more practical application in domestic and international debates questioning the justice of immigration policy, where it makes realistic concessions to communitarian political concerns without, however, embracing the de facto priority of these concerns over cosmopolitan concerns. I propose (Discourse Ethics and Immigration Policy) a discourse ethical norm that shifts the burden of justification from needy refugees onto affluent governments (taken singly and collectively) and condemns as unjust immigration policies that do not balance the cosmopolitan human rights claims of economic refugees against the communitarian democratic rights of sovereign peoples. Unlike cosmopolitan approaches, however, it qualifies arguments prioritizing the human rights of immigrants vis-à-vis arguments on behalf of the human rights of citizens and other rationally justifiable duties to the community, not limited to the protection of national security but also including protection of group rights. Balancing the rights of refugees and peoples ultimately requires that discourse ethics be institutionalized at the supranational level, where the benefits and burdens of admitting and resettling refugees can be democratically resolved pursuant to an inclusive discussion setting forth the different capabilities and interests of each nation.

I conclude my nonideal theorizing of the political realities facing irregular migrants by examining how discourse ethics could guide reform of deportation hearings (Discourse Ethics and Immigration Courts). Instead of the mass plea-bargaining spectacles found in many US courts in which migrants are charged with criminal entry,[5] deportation hearings guided by discourse ethical principles would cease being adversarial and would require courts to incorporate into their deliberations migrants' narratives chronicling their experiences of violence and economic coercion.

POLITICAL REFUGEES: A HUMANITARIAN CRISIS

In an ideal world composed of well-ordered nations Rawls's optimistic view that "the problem of immigration ... is eliminated as a serious problem" may well be correct (Rawls 1999a: 9). But until we achieve a "realistic utopia" in which all people can exercise their human rights fully, live without fear of discrimination and political oppression under governments that are accountable to them, and enjoy the fruits of a satisfactory and sustainable standard of living, immigration will remain a serious problem.

I will argue that the migration of economic and political refugees is especially problematic for reasons that Rawls (following Walzer) only partly appreciated: The uprooting of communities of recognition, on one side, portends the disempowerment and marginalization of migrants, on the other. Most affected are undocumented migrants fleeing extreme poverty who suffer the greatest marginalization: criminalization. (A similar stigma attaches to the 13 million "stateless" persons who are currently denied legal status within their country of birth.)[6] In order to see why their law-breaking should be excused and their legal status normalized, I recommend that we turn to the fate of political refugees, especially asylum seekers, whose entry into sanctuary states often skirts normal legal avenues for processing petitions.

Before developing the analogy between economic and political refugees, I would like to remind the reader of the enormity of today's political refugee crisis. This crisis is not simply about numbers, but reflects the failure of states and international relief agencies to resolve a legal tension

---

[5] Criminal trial sessions typically involve five or more suspects pleading guilty to a judge simultaneously (as per the advice of their court-appointed attorneys, who often represent many clients at once, speaking with each of them for as little as a few minutes or longer, depending on whether they are multiple offenders whose convictions merit longer sentences) (Dickson 2014).

[6] Bangladeshis, Rohingya Muslims, and Haitians, whose legal status has been denied by the Myanmar and Dominican governments, respectfully, stand out as especially egregious examples of statelessness.

between rights of sovereignty and human rights of refugees. This tension pervades all discussions regarding the ethics of immigration.

The UN High Commissioner for Refugees (UNHCR) recently reported that 2014 witnessed the largest surge of forcibly displaced persons ever recorded – 65 million, surpassing the 50 million refugees at the end of World War II (UNHCR 2014).[7] The addition of 20 million forcibly displaced persons since 2000 has been spurred by drug wars in Mexico and Central America and by civil conflicts in Europe, Southeast Asia, sub-Saharan Africa (origin of one-third of all refugees) and the Middle East (chiefly in war-torn Syria, origin of one-fifth of all refugees). Approximately 90 percent of refugees migrate to safe havens in poor developing countries that can least afford to support them (Turkey now hosts more refugees than any other country, with 2.7 million, followed by Pakistan, with Lebanon recording the highest concentration of refugees, roughly 25 percent of its population). By contrast, the world's wealthiest nations, including the United States, Australia, and member states of the EU, under pressure from citizens who are hostile to immigrants, are devising ways to keep out and contain the unparalleled wave of refugees.[8]

This disparity is not surprising. The Geneva Convention on Refugees designates the first foreign safe haven a refugee enters upon exiting his or her country of origin as having primary legal custodianship over that refugee. Such havens are typically adjacent to refugees' countries of origin and, like them, are often poor and institutionally weak. Furthermore, the nonrefoulement provision of the Convention prohibits states from repatriating foreign arrivals, regardless of whether they meet the stringent definition of a refugee or asylum seeker, if doing so would place their lives and liberties in jeopardy. To circumvent this responsibility, wealthy countries, which are typically not adjacent to the countries emitting refugees, do everything in their power to prevent refugees from entering their territory, from building walls and intercepting smuggling vessels to setting up border checks in foreign as well as domestic ports. The incentive to block entrance is further strengthened by the moral presumption prevalent among wealthy democracies that refugees must not be detained in

---

[7] Syria is the origin of 3.9 million refugees, followed by Afghanistan at 2.6 million and Somalia at 1.1 million. Palestinians constitute the largest group of refugees at 5.1 million.

[8] 1.7 million persons applied for asylum or refugee status in 2014. Leading countries receiving applications were Russia (275,000), Germany (173,000), and the United States (121,000). Only 105,000 were admitted for resettlement in twenty-six countries. The United States was the recipient of 73,000 of them (UNHCR 2014).

camps beyond a reasonable time and should be resettled as normal residents.

Current law thus conspires to ensure that the burdens for receiving and resettling refugees will not be equitable, despite the fact that all nations share responsibility for a state system, which legally sanctions disparate treatment of the world's peoples.[9] Thus, having witnessed a 51 percent increase in the number of refugees seeking asylum since 2013, Europe has put in abeyance plans to admit legitimate asylum seekers in a manner equitable to member states (in effect, modifying the "first safe haven" provision of the Geneva Convention) due to strong resistance from its Eastern flank, with the latter responding by setting up more border checkpoints, fences, and detention centers.[10] In stark contradiction to the discourse ethical spirit underlying the European Commission's voluntary resettlement program, the recent agreement between Turkey and the EU permits the EU to send new migrants (chiefly from Syria and the Middle East) arriving in Greece back to Turkey, their "first safe haven."[11] This regression in policy is doubly ironic, given that Turkey's

---

[9] 2017 witnessed the mass exodus of 500,000 Rohingya fleeing ethnic cleansing by the Burmese army; a poor country – Bangladesh – not Australia, has provided them refuge. As Joseph Carens remarks (2013: 215–17), the political obstacles to sacrificing domestic resources for the sake of agreeing on a fair method for distributing burdens of resettlement are formidable; likewise, uncoupling duties to provide temporary asylum from duties to resettle that might seem to be a promising way to encourage rich nations to accept a greater number of temporary asylum seekers, encourages them to export their refugee population to other nations for permanent resettlement that have far fewer resources for guaranteeing their human rights.

[10] In 2008 the EU Parliament approved new guidelines for detaining and expelling illegal immigrants – an area of law that had previously come under the exclusive jurisdiction of individual member states. The new guidelines permit the detention of illegal immigrants for up to eighteen months before being expelled and a re-entry ban of up to five years (for those who are noncompliant or who are deemed a threat). Illegal immigrants would be given a chance to leave voluntarily within thirty days of apprehension (similar to a recent provision proposed by Immigration and Customs Enforcement [ICE] in the US); otherwise they may be detained for six months, with longer periods of detainment for those who are deemed potential security risks (however, as of 2015 the processing time for asylum and refugee applications has well exceeded that period, with living conditions in detention centers in Bulgaria and other ports of entry so bad that a European court ruled against returning refugees to detention centers there). The EU is also constructing a wall on its eastern flank to seal its borders from undocumented immigrants coming from non-EU member states of the former Soviet Union. In the US, the "invasion" is also being treated as a military problem, requiring the extension of a wall along the US-Mexico border (Faiola 2015: 1:15).

[11] Based on the Commission's proposal, EU member states agreed for the first time to relocate 160,000 asylum seekers from Greece and Italy to other member states by September 2017 and to relocate another 22,500 asylum seekers outside the EU to member states (European Commission Report: Refugee Crisis in Europe [July 2016]).

own human rights record is so bad that one out of five Turkish citizens who apply for asylum in the EU are granted it by European countries.[12]

Humanitarian concerns have taken a backseat to politics.[13] The increase in the number of refugees drowning in transit from North Africa and the Middle East to Italy during the first four months of 2015 increased fifteen-fold (to about 1600) over the same period a year earlier after Italy cancelled its costly search and rescue program (Mare Nostrum) because of fear that it would encourage more illicit smuggling (the program is credited with having saved more than 150,000 lives in 2014). Meanwhile, EU plans to blow up empty smuggling vessels have been resisted by the UN, and the disastrous capsizing of a smuggling boat with a loss of 900 lives has subsequently forced the EU to renew its search and rescue programs amid protests by human rights advocates.

Europe hopes to build political resolve for rescuing refugees by getting the United States, Canada, and Australia to agree on hosting some of them. But the kind of multination cooperation that led to the resettlement of over 2.5 million Vietnamese refugees after the Vietnam War will be hard to replicate in the current anti-immigrant climate. The Australian government is hostile to the idea that it should provide safe haven to the more than 25,000 refugees – most of them poor Bangladeshis and Rohingya Muslims, whose citizenship status has been revoked by the Myanmar government. While many of the Malaysian and Indonesian smuggling vessels on which they flee are denied entry and left to drift with the expected tragic consequences, those refugees that make it to land

---

[12] The legal technicality invoked by the EU to avoid processing these asylum seekers hinges on the "first safe haven" clause of the Geneva Convention: If migrants have entered Turkey as their first safe haven then they should have applied for asylum there instead of trying to reach the richer and safer sanctuaries of the EU. The precise terms of the EU-Turkey agreement ensure that Turkey's current population of 2.7 million refugees will remain stable: for every Syrian refugee returned to Turkey from Greece the EU will accept in return one refugee from Turkey. The deal also stipulates that Turkey will receive fast-track processing of billions of dollars in EU aid to defray the cost of maintaining its refugee population, concessions amounting to visa-free travel of Turks to the EU, and talks aimed at expediting Turkey's application for membership in the EU. Meanwhile, the UNHCR has already condemned substandard conditions in Turkey's refugee camps, with Amnesty International's director for Europe and Central Asia, John Dalhuisen, characterizing this so-called humanitarian deal as "doublespeak" intended to "hide the European Union's dogged determination to turn its back on a global refugee crisis and willfully ignore its international obligations" (Cook and Hadjicostis 2016: I.6).

[13] Anti-immigrant nationalism is now global, as evidenced by the Brexit vote in Britain, the election of Donald Trump to the American presidency, and the rise of populist right-wing political movements, spearheaded by Alternative für Deutschland (in Germany), Geert Wilders (in Holland) and Marine La Pen (in France).

are either immediately repatriated (the fate of most Bangladeshis) or are kept in sparse camps awaiting UN processing of asylum requests that can take months.[14]

The same resistance to refugee resettlement pervades public opinion in the United States, as was recently documented by the popular backlash against a 2015 Obama administration proposal to resettle 10,000 (reduced from an original goal of 100,000) Syrian refugees by September 2016. Resistance was partly fueled by widespread fear that Muslim refugees pose significantly greater security risks than other groups.[15]

More pertinent to my argument is American resistance to resettling Central American migrants fleeing regional violence. This crisis illustrates the legal challenges that attend an evolving definition of asylum seeker while highlighting moral duties to compensate migrants who are fleeing from hardship caused in part by the government to which they are now appealing for sanctuary.

In 2014, 70,000 children (most of them unaccompanied by an adult caretaker), streamed across the southern border of the United States fleeing violence and economic chaos in Honduras, El Salvador, and Guatemala (Nicaragua, the second-poorest country in the Western hemisphere but relatively violence-free, has not experienced an exodus of refugees). In this instance, the violence – mainly from government security forces exercising a free hand (*mano dura*) and the drug gangs they are attacking – was abetted by US foreign policy. Among the major gangs reaping terror are MS-13 and Calle 18, which were formed in Los Angeles, the home of many Salvadoran refugees fleeing the Central American wars of the 1980s. Denied legal refugee status (in sharp contrast to Nicaraguan refugees, whose Sandanista government the Reagan Administration was

---

[14] 2017 witnessed the mass exodus of 500,000 Rohingya fleeing ethnic cleansing by the Burmese army; a poor country, Bangladesh (not Australia), has provided them refuge. The Australian government defends its harsh policies as a humanitarian response aimed at stopping smuggling, but refugees detained – sometimes for more than two years – in processing centers in Nauru and Papua New Guinea that are funded by the government but run locally have been raped and threatened with violence (a Somali woman raped at the Nauru center was returned to the center after having received an abortion in Australia). Instead of following the lead of Europe in providing asylum to refugees, Australia is negotiating the permanent resettlement of refugees in the Philippines (Kaiman and Bengali 2015: 1:16).

[15] The reasoning behind the 2017 federal court decision to strike the Trump administration's temporary suspension of visas for persons entering from selected Muslim countries shows that hostility to Muslims, rather than simple fear of terrorism, was arguably the chief intention underlying the Trump ban. Numerous studies show that opposition to immigration among Americans is mainly directed at Muslims, Mexicans, and migrants with dark skin.

trying to overthrow), Salvadoran refugees and the children they brought with them formed their own underground drug businesses, which they exported to other American cities, and a decade later were deported in large numbers back to their homeland. Meanwhile, the US government, under the pretext of supporting the war on drugs, had resumed its funding for the training and assistance of the Honduran military, which had joined police forces in repressing the political allies of former left-wing president Manuel Zelaya, who was overthrown by the right-wing military in 2009 (Honduras claims the dubious distinction of having the highest homicide rate in the world, with an impunity rate of over 90 percent). Importantly, the political policies that have promoted violence have worked in tandem with US economic policies in the region, where the neoliberal provisions of the Dominican Republic-Central America-United States Free Trade Agreement (CAFTA-DR) in force since 2006 have stifled economic growth in the Northern Triangle region (at a rate of less than 1 percent) and increased poverty (Main 2014).

The Obama and Trump administrations' response to the migration of unaccompanied children has been mixed. Many of the children and their families have been housed in detention centers under sparse conditions where they await bond hearings to determine whether they can be released to family members in the United States. Initially bond was refused to many of those detained in order to deter other migrants from crossing but, after a federal court in February 2015 excluded deterrence as a ground for denial, the Office of Homeland Security began releasing detainees who had been in centers for over six months. The Victims of Trafficking and Violence Protection Act (2000), reauthorized and amended in 2008 under the Bush administration, guarantees unaccompanied children a right to an asylum hearing. However, it does not guarantee them a right to legal counsel and understaffed immigration courts that were unprepared to deal with the surge of cases made hasty decisions that had tragic consequences for some of the children who were quickly deported.[16] Indeed, the Obama

---

[16] Unaccompanied child migrants who are not classified as refugees are "misrecognized" in a variety of way; they are either treated as adults – specifically, as delinquents – or as dependents who are victimized by broken households. Denied adult agency, they have no right to initiate legal relief on their own; denied the innocence normally accorded to children, they are subject to legal detention. Although much has been written about the social stigma of undocumented children who are deported after residing in the US for most of their childhood, those who are deported after having recently arrived also suffer social condemnation and exclusion (Heidbrink 2013). Indeed, from 2014–2015 researchers documented over eighty killings of deportees (some of them minors) following their repatriation (Brodzinsky 2015).

administration's public relations campaign announcing that illegal migrants would be immediately deported,[17] combined with its increased funding of militarized border patrols in the Northern Triangle, effectively endorsed the Republican criticism that these migrants have no legitimate claim to asylum and are simply migrating for economic reasons, encouraged by the prospect of eventually receiving amnesty.[18]

THE EVOLVING DEFINITION OF REFUGEE STATUS AND THE DISCRETIONARY APPLICATION OF HUMANITARIAN LAW

In order to properly assess the legality of US policy regarding the recent wave of Central American migrants one must turn to humanitarian law and practice, which has witnessed a redefinition of the status of asylum seeker favorable to the argument I am developing in this chapter.

The discretion regarding to whom sanctuary must be given has been narrowed over the years. In years past states could refuse sanctuary if they determined that a migrant's claim to political persecution did not rise to a level calling for emergency rescue. In recent years, however, *endangerment*, and not just political persecution, has been added to the list of factors obligating states to open their doors to refugees.[19]

Indeed, an argument can be made that endangerment should replace persecution – which sometimes can be relatively mild – as the most salient

---

[17] In September 2014, the Obama administration approved a plan to allow several thousand children to join family members residing in the US legally.

[18] However, in April 2015 the Obama administration began implementing a program, the Central American Minors (CAM) Refugee/Parole Program, that allows children under the age of twenty-one from Guatemala, Honduras, and El Salvador, and in some cases their mothers or fathers, who would normally not be admitted as refugees, to be admitted if they are deemed to be "at risk of harm" and have a sponsoring parent lawfully residing in the US. Children who qualify can obtain Green Cards and eventual citizenship; spouses who qualify can be paroled into the US and receive some benefits.

[19] As of 2016 the UNHCR has adopted the expanded definition of refugee contained in the Organization of African Unity's Convention Governing the Specific Aspects of Refugees in Africa (1974) which includes "every person who, owing to external aggression, occupation, foreign domination or events seriously disturbing public order in either part or the whole of his country of origin or nationality is compelled to leave his place of habitual residence in order to seek refuge in a place outside his country of origin or nationality." The Cartagena Declaration on Refugees (1984), adopted as a nonbinding resolution by Mexico and other Latin American countries, builds upon this definition to include "persons who have fled their country because their lives, safety or freedom have been threatened by generalized violence, foreign aggression, internal conflicts, massive violation of human rights or other disturbances which have seriously disturbed public order."

consideration in defining refugee status. Many countries already allow entry to persons fleeing natural disasters, civil wars, and threats of violence from which they cannot be protected by their own government.[20] The United States, for example, allows persons fleeing from domestic violence and other forms of endangerment to apply for "temporary protected status" if their own government will not act to remedy the danger.[21] Under this provision, at least some Central American migrants fleeing gang warfare have been granted relief.

This looser practice of migrant protection also accords with the UNHCR's "extended definition" of a refugee as anyone outside their country of residence who faces "serious and indiscriminate threats to life, physical integrity or freedom resulting from generalized violence or events seriously disturbing public order" and other "man-made disasters."[22] Threats to life, physical integrity, or freedom resulting from events seriously disturbing public order can include severe, life-threatening poverty. Hence, under this broader definition of refugee, persons fleeing poverty should qualify as refugees.

This change in the institutional practice of who counts as a refugee lends support for my argument that economic refugees should be given the same protections as political refugees. It might be objected that this consideration would be relevant only for economic refugees who migrate legally. But the (il)legality of migration has no bearing on the moral merits of whether or not a refugee should be granted sanctuary. Immanent endangerment provides a particularly compelling reason why persons fleeing political persecution must sometimes forgo the formality of applying for asylum (or a transit visa) and enter a foreign port illegally. Lack of trust and desperation may further compel such persons to lie to border officials and asylum judges regarding the exact reasons for their entry. As Joseph Carens notes, such "illegal" (and depending on local statutory law, criminal) behavior is no more reprehensible than what some Jews did

[20] This policy conforms to the original "responsibility to protect" (R2P). framework that was drafted by the International Commission on Intervention and State Sovereignty (ICISS) in 2001. I discuss this framework in Chapters 5 and 6.

[21] US Citizenship and Immigration Services (USCIS) permits nationals of selected foreign countries who currently reside in the US on a continuing basis to apply for Temporary Protected Status (TPS), a status distinct from asylum status, if they are fleeing "on-going armed conflict," "environmental disaster," or "other extraordinary and temporary conditions."

[22] UNHCR Resettlement Handbook, chapter 3.2.2; Procedures and Criteria for Determining Refugee Status.

when they sought to exit Nazi Germany using false identification (Carens 2013: 210–11).

In principle, undocumented economic migrants have as much moral (and arguably, legal) claim to sanctuary as political refugees. However, international humanitarian law exhibits an unresolved tension between its recognition of the rights of refugees to safe haven and its recognition of the rights of sovereign states to determine their duties in this regard. Understood simply as a duty of humanitarian beneficence, the duty to rescue refugees depends on the discretion of the benefactor regarding whom to give aid and by what means.

It need hardly be said that governments find technical loopholes to skirt their legal obligations under international law. Article 14 of the Universal Declaration of Human Rights (1948) asserts a right to asylum for anyone fleeing persecution "for reasons of race, religion, nationality, membership of a particular group or political opinion." Aside from the narrowness of this definition, which reflects the traumas of World War II and the Cold War, the UDHR nowhere imposes obligations on states or other entities to guarantee this right. The Geneva Convention Relating to the Status of Refugees (1951) and the Protocol added in 1967 require that signatory states not forcibly return refugees and asylum seekers to their countries of origin if doing so endangers their freedom or existence.[23] However, it

---

[23] But application of this provision is also subject to judicial discretion. In the wake of 9/11 US Atty. Gen. John Ashcroft expedited the current process of reviewing immigration and asylum appeals by reducing the three-court appeals panel from three judges to one. Under this mandate the sole presiding judge was required to issue only a one-sentence opinion. As a result of this "streamlining" many persons were wrongly deported. A particularly chilling example of this process is the case of Nourain Niam, a member of a persecuted Sudanese opposition party, who was repatriated in 2003 on an order issued by Judge James Fujimoto in 2001 on the grounds that there was no record of Niam having applied for asylum and that he did not "face a probability of torture" ... "despite Sudan's apparently poor human rights record" and the fact that he was a member of a "disrespected group." After being denied a "withholding of removal" (or stay of deportation), Niam fled to Chad, where the US embassy denied him a visa. He was beaten by Sudanese secret service agents and has since returned to the US, thanks to the Seventh Circuit US Court of Appeal headed by Judge Richard Posner, who has been instrumental in overturning 40 percent of the deportation decisions that have been appealed. More recently, the Inspector General's Report highlights serious abuse of immigrant and asylum-seeking detainees in US prisons, including lack of adequate food, medical treatment, and access to lawyers. Beatings and sexual harassment were also reported. Despite this record of abuse, the Report continued to recommend that Immigration and Customs Enforcement Agency

allows these states to satisfy this principle of *nonrefoulement* by transporting refugees to safe havens in other consenting countries, erecting safe havens in their country of origin, or by simply denying them entry in the first place.[24]

It goes without saying that the second option noted above – involving the erection of safe havens in the country of origin – best serves migrants' interests in having their welfare, social esteem, and empowerment restored, but only if the causes that compelled them to migrate are securely removed, thereby eliminating the need for displacing and detaining them in camps within their own national borders.[25]

Because wealthy democracies have found it politically inexpedient or morally risky to shelter refugees themselves, they either detain them in safe havens in their country of origin or farm them out to less wealthy and less democratic countries. As I noted earlier, the Geneva Convention abets in this avoidance maneuver by designating the first sanctuary a refugee enters as having initial responsibility for his protection.

Leaving aside international law, there appear to be sound reasons for holding that safe states that border crisis states have a greater duty to provide temporary asylum, all other considerations being equal. Refugees have urgent needs that normally require their immediate settlement upon exiting a crisis state; those who have left behind loved ones and a life which envelopes their very identity have urgent needs to return home as soon as it is safe to do so. For this reason, Turkey (assuming that it is a safe and humanitarian haven) appears to have a greater *prima facie* duty than the United States or Europe to temporarily shelter, if not permanently resettle, Syrian refugees. However, given the ease of air travel and the overburdening of poor border states, the prima facie argument for imposing a duty based on geographical proximity is not very compelling.[26]

(an agency within the US Department of Homeland Security) police itself. See Dow (2004). For a critique of similar abuses in the EU, see note 10 above and Harding (2000).

[24] Examples of the second alternative include the Mexican government's detention of 425,000 Central American migrants between 2014–2016 at the request of the US and the protected sites that the UK erected in Sri Lanka to encourage Sri Lankans to "displace themselves" internally rather than seek asylum abroad. The penetration of UK legal authority into the sovereign territory of another country mirrors the penetration of extra-territorials into the UK; both of these border "violations" place in doubt the legitimacy of borders as such. See Harding (2012: 56).

[25] Overthrowing brutal dictatorships (as President Clinton did in restoring Jean-Bertrand Aristide to power in Haiti) or developing depressed economies (as the EU did for Spain and Portugal in the 1980s) can reduce migration if done in a way that respects national sovereignty.

[26] I thank Drew Thompson for this observation.

Considerations besides proximity also factor into the moral calculus determining how much discretion governments have in deciding who they admit. Governments whose citizens are of the same ethnicity or religion as refugees fleeing ethnic or religious persecution have a greater duty to rescue members of their own tribe, if for no reason other than that doing so will uproot them less from a familiar community of recognition. The same kind of reasoning explains why nationality or *i*deological kinship imposes greater responsibilities of rescue on some countries rather than on others.[27]

Considerations of national security and economic capacity also temper a government's decision to shelter refugees (Walzer 1983: 51). How much these factors should weigh in comparison to the human rights of refugees remains a hotly debated question. In the 1970s, the number of refugees was relatively small in comparison to today's mass exodus, and when a wealthy country like the United States was confronted with a large mass of asylum seekers from Vietnam and Cambodia, it could accommodate them without incurring a substantial burden. However, as I noted above, asylum seekers and refugees displaced by today's regional conflicts have almost entirely been resettled in poor developing countries that lack sufficient resources to maintain them.[28]

COMPROMISING REFUGEES' RIGHTS ON THE ALTAR OF STATE SOVEREIGNTY: THE EVOLVING ROLE OF THE UNHCR

In his history of the United Nations High Commissioner for Refugees, Michael Barnett, former officer of the US Mission to the UN during the Rwanda crisis (1993–94), recounts how bolder humanitarian interventions on behalf of refugees since the end of the Cold War in response to growing regional conflict has forced the UNHCR to adopt a pragmatic approach in accommodating opposing realities that, in turn, has compromised its original legal goal of protecting the human rights of refugees.

[27] The former factor is illustrated by Greece's absorption of Greek minorities forcibly expelled by Turkey in the early 1920s, the latter factor is reflected in the automatic asylum the US government once extended to Cuban dissidents fleeing Cuba's communist regime). Last but not least, causal responsibility for contributing to a refugee crisis explains why the US government has a duty to temporarily shelter and permanently resettle Iraqis who collaborated with coalition forces following the overthrow of Saddam Hussein.

[28] The sole exception to this generalization is Germany, which in 2015 alone received over one million refugees, twice the number of refugees received by the remaining fifty European countries (Goldin 2016: 152).

Reflecting the conflict between states' sovereign right to advance the interests of their people and its own humanitarian concerns, the UNHCR during the Cold War presented its mission as apolitical and noninterventionist, and accordingly limited itself to mainly facilitating the legal status of a very narrow range of "persecuted" persons who had successfully fled from Communist bloc nations in Europe to Western nations (Barnett 2010: 87). By the end of the Cold War – and in response to the explosion of regional conflicts and civil wars in the developing world and Yugoslavia – the UNHCR had dramatically shifted its mission from providing permanent integration of asylum seekers in host countries to preventing a wider class of refugees from migrating by facilitating their "protection" within their home country or by repatriating those who had already migrated and were living in temporary refugee camps as soon as UNHCR officials determined that it was reasonably safe to do so.

The reasons for this change were largely principled and laudable. Once the category of "persecuted person" had been expanded to include anyone fleeing from endangering "disturbances of public order" – and the category of "displaced persons" expanded to include internal subnationalities, such as Bosnians in the former Yugoslavia and Kurds in Iraq, Turkey, and Syria – the focus shifted to attacking the political sources of migration, with the expectation that, once these sources were removed, refugees would want to return to their homeland (which many were doing anyway, assisted or not by the UNHCR).

There were somewhat less laudable but nonetheless legitimate reasons for this change as well. Refugee camps are expensive to maintain and the "safe haven" they offer often provides little in the way of protection, seeming more like sparse prisons to those housed within them. As noted above, hosting refugees often imposes a huge burden on host countries, and further strains their political relationship with the country generating the refugees.[29] Finally, the UNHCR believed that it would lose credibility and efficacy if it stood by while exhausted or unsympathetic host countries forcibly expelled their refugee populations (Barnett 2010: 90–92).

---

[29] The largest refugee center in the world (population 329,000), located in Dabaab, Kenya, houses Somalian refugees fleeing famine. Although living conditions in the center are poor and lacking government police protection, many residents are economically self-employed. By 2016 more than 100,000 refugees had voluntarily submitted to repatriation. But on May 6 of that year the Kenyan government announced its intention to close the center and the Kakuma refugee camp on the grounds that the center and camp had been infiltrated by al Shabaab, the militant group ostensibly responsible for an attack on a shopping mall in Nairobi.

By placing its own financial and organizational interests on the side of states' interests, the UNHCR may have abdicated its initial duty to protect the rights of refugees. Because the UNHCR's original policy of not repatriating refugees without their written consent created enormous bureaucratic obstacles, the UNHCR redefined the "voluntariness" of repatriation in terms of an "objective" determination by UNHCR officials that conditions in the home country are safer or marginally more humane than conditions in the host country. Thus, without consulting refugees – who, having no knowledge of conditions "on the ground," were judged to be unreliable agents of their own best interests – these officials sometimes repatriated them against their will. Justified in the name of benevolent paternalism, this coercion acted as a prior restraint on, or deterrence to, would-be refugees contemplating migration.

Coercion of adults in the name of paternalism is only justified if its aim is to prevent the person being coerced from abdicating, destroying, or permanently disabling his or her agency and is based on sound knowledge. Granting that UNHCR paternalism intends to protect refugees from threats to their agency – ranging from the relatively benign effects of protective detention to the hostile violence of host populations – it is doubtful that it is based on sound knowledge. As I observed in the case of poverty and developmental expertise (Chapter 2), the knowledge guiding UNHCR officials is often distorted by failure of officers in the field to adequately consult with all affected groups. This was made manifest in 1994, when UNHCR began forcibly repatriating some 250,000 persecuted Burmese Rohingyans who had fled to Bangladesh. The judgment that conditions in Burma had improved enough to warrant this act hinged on testimony from just a few field officers in Burma, who could not have visited all the remote villages and who, in any case, were almost always accompanied by representatives of the Burmese government – the very persons most highly motivated to cover up human rights abuses. More accurate assessments of the oppression awaiting repatriated Rohingyans offered by the UN Human Rights Commission were not heeded. Instead, UNHCR officials attributed the continuing exodus of Rohingyans – many of whom had been recently repatriated – to the most commonly cited "push-pull" factor: comparative economic advantage (Barnett 2010: 96–98).

Today the same reasons are given for repatriating Bangladeshis, Africans, and Central American children. In fact, economic distress, political oppression, and civil unrest mutually condition each other. This fact – and the expansion of protected persons to include not just refugees but internally displaced populations (IDPs) – has led the

UNHCR to increasingly shift its focus away from the relatively apolitical task of protecting the rights of refugees to exit oppressive circumstances to the very political task of assisting states in managing and
containing their unwelcome minorities without grossly violating their
rights. The end result may be the most feasible economically and
politically speaking (and sometimes the most humanitarian as well)
but it often comes at the expense of not fully protecting the human
rights and agency of at-risk populations. Barnett succinctly summarizes this dilemma by noting that

> UNHCR's developing involvement in the internal affairs of states, the desire to
> eliminate the root causes of refugee flows, the desire to give refugees an
> alternative to fleeing their homes, and the interest in getting them home as
> quickly as possible can all be seen as progressive shifts in the humanitarian
> agenda. But these developments also join up with a sovereignty-driven
> humanitarianism that can curtail the rights and numbers of refugees. The
> result is that humanitarianism can become implicated in a system of
> deterrence and containment (Barnett 2010: 100).

To summarize: The UNHCR's financial and organizational interests converged with interests of sovereign states in fabricating a policy of deterring
and containing would-be refugees – all in the name humanitarianism.
Discouraging dislocations and encouraging repatriation under appropriate circumstances restores refugees to communities of recognition. Too
often, however, knowledge of circumstances on the ground has been
distorted by failure of field officers to be held accountable. Worse, the
UNHCR's complicity in sorting political refugees from a mass of economic refugees obscures the real question at hand – migrant endangerment – and reinforces the suspicion that migrants are presumed to be
illegal unless proven otherwise.

ECONOMIC REFUGEES RECONSIDERED

The distinction between political and economic refugees that I reject is
premised on the correct idea that certain kinds of harms are generally
worse than others. It is generally thought to be worse to inflict harm on
persons than to let harm happen to them, and it is even worse to do so
intentionally, with malice, rather than unintentionally, by accident. This
explains why so-called negative duties to refrain from torturing, enslav-
ing, kidnapping, and murdering someone are said to be more "perfect" or
"unconditional" in what they command and with regard to whom they

apply than so-called positive duties to aid others in distress (since refusing aid does not make the other person worse off than he or she already is).

It also explains why many believe that "first-generation" human rights that protect civil and political liberties are thought to have priority over "second-generation" economic rights that protect welfare. According to this reasoning, forcibly deporting an asylum seeker back to a state where he or she will likely suffer persecution, imprisonment, torture, or murder makes the deporting agent complicit in a crime (the violation of a civil right) should the worse come to pass.[30] By parity of reasoning, refusing entry to political refugees fleeing from criminal predators, while not quite as bad as delivering them back to their enemies, still makes the border guard an accomplice to a crime. In this sense, it is not quite accurate to say that our duty with respect to political refugees and asylum seekers is exclusively an imperfect duty of beneficence; for failure to help in protecting against criminal harm to others when it poses no risk to oneself is worse than being uncharitable.

However plausible this rationale might seem, it is utterly irrelevant to the realities confronting modern refugees. If the recent genocidal wars in the Horn of Africa have taught us anything, it is that governments can kill unwanted minorities under their jurisdiction by simply not rescuing them from starvation caused by natural disasters.[31] A government's failure to protect the rights of its own inhabitants to access food when it can do so alone or with the help of outside agencies amounts to criminal neglect; and neglecting to fulfill assignable positive duties of care toward others is

---

[30] See Kant's essay On Perpetual Peace (1795), especially the Third Definitive Article for Perpetual Peace, subtitled: "The Law of World Citizenship Shall Be Limited to Conditions of Universal Hospitality." As the sole cosmopolitan right governing conduct between individual persons and foreign states, the right to hospitality (*Wirtbarkeit*) "means the right of a stranger not to be treated as an enemy when he arrives in the land of another." Kant adds that "one may refuse to receive him when this can be done without causing his destruction (*Untergang*); but so long as he peacefully occupies his place, one may not treat him with inhospitality." He then (somewhat inconsistently) qualifies this otherwise unconditional right to "asylum" by noting that "it is only a visitation right (*Besuchsrecht*)" and not a right to be a permanent guest (*Gastrecht*).

[31] In January 2010, the Centre for Research on Epidemiology of Disasters published an article in *The Lancet* estimating that between 178,000 and 461,500 excess deaths had occurred in the Darfur region, mainly as a result of starvation and disease caused by the civil war between the Omar al-Bashir-led Sudanese government and non-Arab Muslim rebels, which began in 2003 and continued until 2010. The UN estimates that that close to three million persons have been displaced (many by means of coerced migrations) in what the International Criminal Court describes as mass genocide and other crimes against humanity perpetrated under the auspices of the Bashir government.

equivalent to nonfulfillment of a negative duty to avoid harming them, and so constitutes a violation of a basic human right.

To be sure, neediness and failure to protect against it are scalar concepts. Does the Mexican government's failure to protect its citizens against drug wars and police- and military-sponsored violence constitute criminal negligence? Does its failure to cushion the economic dislocations caused by the privatization of communal farming lands (*ejidos*) and the North American Free Trade Agreement (NAFTA)? When does failure to protect reach the point of criminality (equivalent to violating a human right) as distinct from some less culpable and less actionable form of negligence?

Following Thomas Pogge's lead (Pogge 2008: 46–50), if we were to rank human rights shortfalls along a scale, then intentionally mandated harms, numerically extensive harms, nonrandomized harms that affect select populations, harms possessing a greater likelihood of occurring, and harms posing a greater risk to life are worse *ceteris paribus* than harms that are legally permitted (or legally forbidden but not prevented), infrequent, random, or nonlife-threatening. Key to this metric is the notion that states and other responsible entities can be held liable for omitting to protect against unreasonable risks that jeopardize the secure enjoyment of basic rights; deliberate violations of human rights and humanitarian crimes – the human rights deficits currently selected for possible foreign intervention by the responsibility to protect (R2P) framework unanimously approved at the 2005 UN World Summit—designate only the most extreme form of legal and moral culpability (Pogge 2008: 46–50).

A further consideration to bear in mind is that in our post-Westphalian world liability for human rights deficits extends across political jurisdictions. It is hard to deny that the government of the United States shares some liability with the Mexican government for putting vulnerable Mexicans at risk for human rights deprivations. US domestic and foreign drug policy has arguably contributed to maintaining a black market in illicit drugs that feeds the cartels and gangs that profit from it; building a wall along the southern frontier has only exacerbated turf wars between gangs seeking ways around it. Lax regulation of gun purchasing and registration in the US facilitates a ready supply of illegal arms across the border. US-trained and -armed security forces in Central America sometimes work clandestinely with the very drug cartels they are supposed to be fighting against and routinely violate the civil rights of civilians during the course of "doing their job." Finally, US government sponsorship of and support for NAFTA, CAFTA-DR, and other free trade agreements that have been in force in the region has contributed to economic stagnation and increased levels of poverty, both of which feed corruption and the underground drug economy.[32]

Migrants fleeing natural catastrophes unrelated to civil strife also count as political and economic refugees whenever failure to provide them relief stems from avoidable government "negligence" that in a world of enormous concentrations of wealth can only be described as transnational in scope.[33] Indeed, virtually all migrants fleeing destitution can be so counted, once we assume that most governments, multinational corporations, and global economic multilaterals share liability for international trade agreements, resource extraction privileges, and lending and borrowing conventions that cause their destitution (Pogge 2008).[34]

THE ANALOGY BETWEEN HOSTILE WORK ENVIRONMENTS AND POVERTY

This last point introduces another reason for considering poor economic migrants as refugees: Wealthy nations are liable for causing (or at the very

[32] In 2012 the percentage of Mexicans living in poverty (52.3) was virtually unchanged (52.4) from when NAFTA was enacted 20 years earlier, resulting in a net increase of 14.3 million poor Mexicans when adjusted for population growth (Weisbrot, et al. 2014).

[33] Amartya Sen's empirical analysis of four famines (Bengal, 1943; Ethiopia, 1972–1974; Sahel, 1972–1973; and Bangladesh, 1974) concludes that government irresponsibility, not food shortage, was the main cause of mass starvation. Citing Sen's study (1981), Rawls remarks that "a government's allowing people to starve when it is preventable reflects a lack of concern for human rights" (Rawls 1999a: 109).

[34] Governments of developing countries also encourage the exportation of labor to the developed world in order to take advantage of remittances from abroad that mitigate domestic discontent caused by poverty (see note 2), joblessness, and lack of social services (the latter stemming from government diversion of tax revenue toward debt payment). Working with corporations in the developed world, they have sought to expand the WTO's Mode 4 program, which regulates the global flow of skilled workers, executives, independent contractors (medical professionals, engineers, etc.), to include construction workers, domestic workers, and less skilled laborers. The WTO strongly opposes regulating conditions of employment and insists that these be determined in accordance with voluntary standards set forth by the International Labor Organization (ILO). Organizations such as Migrant Rights International and National Network for Immigrant and Refugee Rights justifiably oppose Mode 4 as an extension of guest worker programs that cause brain drain from the developing world and exploit "temporary" workers whose rights to movement and unionization are curtailed and who are vulnerable to deportation upon the termination of their jobs. Mode 4 also runs afoul of the UN International Convention on the Protection of the Rights of All Migrant Workers and Members of Their Families (1990), which extends basic human rights to all migrant workers (documented or undocumented), supports family reunification, mandates rights to employment and education equal to those possessed by citizens of the host country, and prohibits collective deportation (Bacon 2008).

least, failing to prevent) an economic environment that forces the poor to make legally unconscionable choices that put themselves and their families at risk. The argument I elaborated in Chapter 2, which hinges on an analogy between hostile workplace environments and a coercive economic system, suffices to show that governments that legally support a global economic order that forces a poor person to make an unconscionable choice – culminating in a decision to embark on a course of illegal transit – are analogous to business owners who permit a workplace environment that forces an employee to leave her job, with its attendant risks and insecurities, or stay and face demeaning misrecognition.

THE SPECIAL DUTY TO DECRIMINALIZE AND PROTECT VICTIMS OF HUMAN TRAFFICKING

The choices facing economic migrants fall along a spectrum: while all are voluntary, some are coerced by circumstances. Most unconscionable among them are decisions to migrate illegally. Those who contract smugglers suffer the additional indignity of paying exorbitant smuggling fees, suffering indentured servitude, and enduring risks of abandonment, kidnapping, criminal detention, and much worse.[35]

Should smuggling and trafficking be dealt with as criminal violations? Should they be dealt with as human rights violations? If we simply view smuggling and trafficking as problems of global injustice – for example, as actions in which victims freely (albeit illegally) contract services to exit poverty in a nonideal world – there is a danger that the criminal aspects of recruitment, coercion and exploitation will become less visible or even excusable. Victims of migrant trafficking and smuggling arguably have a greater claim to asylum than ordinary economic refugees fleeing global injustice, since they have suffered above and beyond the coercive circumstances compelling their migration (Francis and Francis 2014: 145–48). Conversely, criminalizing trafficking makes victims accomplices to crime, subject to punishment unless they cooperate in criminal prosecution of recruiters and exploiters.

The source of the above dilemma, to recall my earlier discussion of trafficking,[36] resides in theorizing the legal significance of coerced consent.

---

[35] Contracting the services of a trafficking agent for purposes of legal immigration also poses risks of being victimized by fraud, labor exploitation, sex trafficking, illicit organ harvesting, or slavery upon arrival at the port of destination.

[36] See Chapter 2.

Is consent to trafficking coerced by the criminal threats and bribes of traffickers or is it coerced by the circumstances (perhaps equally unlawful) of an impoverished environment? The UN Convention on Transnational Organized Crime (UNCTOC) appears to endorse the former description in its definition of trafficking as the "recruitment, transportation, transfer, harboring or receipt of persons, by means of threat or use of force or other forms of coercion, of abduction, of fraud, of deception, of the abuse of power or of a position of vulnerability or of the giving or receiving of payments of benefits to achieve consent of a person having control over another person, for the purpose of exploitation" (UN Office on Drugs and Crime 2004). By defining victims of trafficking as unwilling accomplices, the UNCTOC effectively treats trafficking as a simple case of criminal coercion, thereby ignoring the extent to which victims of trafficking voluntarily choose this recourse as the only viable solution to living in poverty.

The fact that victims of smuggling are often willing accomplices to their own criminal trafficking invites a third hypothesis, to wit, that their consent is not coerced. This hypothesis has not been vigorously pursued by local jurisdictions, to which the UNCTOC delegates primary responsibility for interdicting trafficking, except when trafficking violates humanitarian law, as when minors are recruited into the ranks of soldiers committing war crimes and crimes against humanity. Because of the ambiguities surrounding consent[37] and the sympathy shown to victims and in some cases beneficiaries of trafficking (including people seeking organ donations, illegal adoptions, and the like) governments often choose not to enforce their own antitrafficking laws.[38]

Such *official noncompliance* does a grave injustice to victims of trafficking who might be harmed by two kinds of unlawful coercion: agential and circumstantial. However, governments who seek to prosecute illegal traffickers who have acted upon the offers of their victims face a dilemma: The victim ceases to be a victim once she is classified as an accomplice. Governments can then threaten such a person with deportation or worse unless that person cooperates with police authorities in convicting their trafficker. Trafficked persons might resist cooperating for the sake of protecting a "friendly" trafficker; more likely they will do so to protect their families from retaliation by an "unfriendly" trafficker.

---

[37] Mail-order brides, for example, act as their own traffickers (Francis and Francis 2014: 150–57).

[38] Some governments (notably Thailand and Cambodia) defer interdiction in favor of reaping the benefits from sex trafficking tourism.

The current US policy of offering T-visas to trafficking victims suffers from this defect (Francis and Francis 2014: 164). In effect, this carrot-and-stick approach adds another layer of coercion to the circumstantial and agential coercion trafficking victims have already endured. By contrast, the Council of Europe Convention on Action against Trafficking in Human Beings (2005) acknowledges the circumstantial coercion of victim-accomplices by providing them assistance, safety and protection, living standards sufficient for subsistence, emergency medical aid, legal assistance, and access to education for children (Francis and Francis: 149). Providing trafficked migrants with sanctuary has the advantage of eliminating a fear of deportation that traffickers use to keep their clients in line (Francis and Francis: 163).

To conclude, while one must not lose sight of the criminal harms inflicted on migrants by traffickers, it is shortsighted to focus only on this fact and ignore the coercive circumstances of poverty that compel migrants and other victims of trafficking to consent to their own exploitation in the first place. John Christman observes that consent to exploitation has a social (or group-based) dimension that the individual-centered, criminal liability model of coercion overlooks. Victims of trafficking often consent to their exploitation from peer pressure (family and community members), typically against the background of patriarchal models of social recognition and identity agency which I discussed earlier (Christman 2014: 333).[39] Disclosure of this "culture of trafficking," Christman adds, could benefit from a theoretical perspective marked out by Habermasian discourse ethics (Christman 2014: 334), which provides "a template within which the voices of those [coerced into trafficking] can be expressed, so that policy instruments, legal structures, and procedures are organized around [their] inclusion" (341).

COSMOPOLITANISM AND THE CASE FOR OPEN BORDERS

I have argued that the migration of at least the most desperate economic refugees – those without jobs and alternative sources of income – is coerced by poverty, or more precisely, by a global capitalist economy that produces extreme inequality and uneven development. The inability of small-scale, labor-intensive economies in the developing world to compete with the large-scale, high-tech economies of the developed world leads to the destruction of these economies and a corresponding loss of

[39] See Chapter 1.

jobs. Within these economies, workers with jobs (especially within trades and professions) may be less constrained by circumstances to relocate abroad in search of better-paying jobs. But jobless workers may be left with no other alternative but to uproot themselves from their families in search of employment elsewhere – an alternative whose harm to themselves and their families can scarcely be compensated by the prospects of meager employment abroad.

Of course, not all approaches to the ethics of immigration assess these market pressures the same way I do. Some of them simply deny that migration is coerced by poverty. Others accept this fact but find it morally benign or morally defensible in light of the aggregate benefits of a market system involving unrestricted flows of goods, services, and labor.

Three cosmopolitan ethical approaches support the moral innocence of open border migration to the extent that this comports with border security and domestic law and order requirements:[40] libertarian, utilitarian, and welfare-liberal. Libertarian cosmopolitans who define free agency in terms of abstract negative (legal) freedom, as action unconstrained by other agents, judge immigration restrictions but not the choice to migrate as coercive. According to them, the natural right of an individual to migrate in pursuit of his or her well-being ought to be legally constrained only if it interferes with others' right to do the same.

Utilitarian cosmopolitans defend an ethics of unrestricted migration through a different route. Demoting individual freedom to the same status as other values that contribute to well-being, they concede that the choice to migrate may be harmful in some respects, but argue that it will be beneficial in the long run.[41] From an economic perspective, all decisions involve "opportunity costs" – sacrifices as well as gains. The emotional,

[40] Cosmopolitan and communitarian ethics fall along a spectrum of open/restrictive borders, with both ethics accepting the need to accommodate ideal human rights duties and political realities, depending on different weights they attach to these two values. While cosmopolitan ethics shifts the burden of justification onto border-restriction-minded polities; communitarian ethics shifts the burden onto open-border-minded migrants. Discourse ethics splits the differences between these approaches, albeit in a manner that privileges cosmopolitan priorities.

[41] Economists agree that migration benefits both originating and receiving countries. The standard charge that immigrants take jobs away from domestic workers is mistaken to the degree that migrant consumer demand drives job growth, often at higher skill levels and sectors of production that do not employ migrants. The World Bank estimated that a growth in labor migration to three percent of the global workforce between 2005 and 2015 would add $365 billion to the global economy, with developing countries receiving two-thirds of this gain (Goldin 2016: 150; Peri, et al. 2012:152–97). Today, $27 billion – more than its revenue from oil exports – flow into Mexico in the form of remittances.

physical, and monetary costs of dislocation are therefore justified if they are outweighed by the benefits.

As for coercion, any economic system can be said to affect our fortunes adversely and, in so doing, compel us to make painful decisions. Following this line of reasoning, poverty and habitat destruction caused by climate change may be said to act as an inducement by compelling those who are caught in its web to flee to more promising circumstances.[42] The migrant's curse at his miserable predicament thus appears to be unfounded when seen from the vantage point of the wise economist.

The migrant's curse finds a more sympathetic ear in the welfare liberal, who nonetheless agrees with her libertarian and utilitarian counterparts that uninhibited migration represents an opportunity – not for facilitating the unconstrained pursuit of personal ends or reaping the aggregate benefits of global wealth maximization but for respecting moral autonomy (freedom of conscience and self-determination) and realizing an ideal of impartial justice. A global order regulated in accordance with Rawls's liberty principle would ideally maximize individual freedom of movement compatible with an equal freedom for all, limited only by nonideal circumstances in which freedom of movement must be restricted for the sake of preserving the law and order requisite for its exercise. A global order regulated in accordance with Rawls's difference principle mandating that inequalities benefit the worst off could be structured to improve the circumstances of the worst off where they currently reside (Rawls's own preference) or by allowing them to freely migrate to better circumstances, a position advocated by Joseph Carens (Carens 1995: 338–39).[43] A quasi-cosmopolitanism of the sort advocated by Richard Miller, who condemns wealthy countries for violating their quasi-contractual duties to their poor trading partners, also comports with wealthy countries loosening

---

[42] Presumably "climate refugees" in MICs who possess sufficient liquid capital can migrate from stricken agricultural regions to cities that provide them with better income opportunities than they had as farmers, while contributing to a "developmental shift" toward industry and manufacturing that will benefit the country as a whole. Post-developmentalists such as Arturo Escobar (Chapter 2, note 12) rightly question whether this Western pattern of development through urbanization and industrialization is sustainable and appropriate for developing countries. Even the economists who propose this optimistic windfall from climate change concede that many subsistence farmers in very poor countries will lack the capital to migrate (Cattaneo and Peri 2015).

[43] Carens endorses Rawls's prioritization of liberty over welfare in arguing that under the nonideal circumstances of today's world, unrestricted cross-border migration should be permitted unless doing so endangers the liberties and rights of host communities (Carens 1995: 336–38).

restrictions on admitting poorer, unskilled migrants for the sake of compensatory justice while compensating the unskilled domestic workers these migrants displace.[44]

Significantly, even when welfare-liberal cosmopolitans like Carens concede that migration can leave communities depleted of human resources and expose migrants to discrimination in the countries that host them, they do not think it a danger to agency (Carens 1995: 338). Carens himself sees no morally relevant difference between domestic and global migration.

But there is indeed a difference between an unemployed automobile worker in Detroit who moves to Kentucky in search of work and a similarly situated Mexican *campesino* who migrates to the United States. The different degrees of economic desperation each encounters from being unemployed as well as the freedom, social recognition, and well-being each surrenders in relocating are not equivalent. The displaced American worker is typically less compelled by economic circumstances into moving (he or she can rely on unemployment benefits, welfare/workfare payments, or the surplus income provided by other extended family members). Even if he or she must endure the hardship of relocating, which might include separation from family, the hardship does not typically involve cultural uprooting and loss of citizenship rights.

To summarize, despite the fact that welfare liberals endorse a richer understanding of moral agency than their libertarian and utilitarian counterparts, they tend to dismiss the importance of communal attachments for fostering social recognition and intact identity, both of which, I have argued, are essential to *social* freedom.[45] The development and exercise of moral faculties within interpersonal-familial, economic, and political institutions depend on belonging to a prior community of mutual recognition in which others deeply care about us and in so doing nurture within us a sense of self-confidence, self-respect, and self-esteem (Honneth 1996).

---

[44] Miller (2010: 79, 220) cites studies showing that a modest 3 percent increase in developed countries' workforce by workers from undeveloped countries with no bias against the unskilled would result in additional remittances of up to $100 billion: "At present a 10 percent per capita increase in remittances to people in a developing country from relatives working abroad is on average independently associated with about a 3 percent decline in the proportion whose income is below $1 a day (79)" (Adams and Page 2005:2 f).

[45] See Chapter 1 for my defense of the priority of social freedom over negative (legal) and positive (moral) freedom.

COMMUNITARIANISM AND THE CASE FOR RESTRICTIVE BORDERS

Here we see how the liberal prioritization of individual freedom passes over into the communitarian prioritization of social freedom founded on the egalitarian solidarity of citizenship. But solidarity is a fraught concept. My earlier examination in Chapter 1 of the dilemmas of social recognition highlighted its regressive as well as progressive possibilities. Traditional forms of solidarity problematically presuppose the bounded nature of communities whose memberships do not spill over into other communities. The linkage of boundedness and homogeneity of identity – another questionable presupposition – feeds into ethnocentrism. Modern forms of solidarity emphasize civic attachments grounded in democratic self-determination over homogeneous identity. But both forms of solidarity build upon a distinction between in-groups and out-groups, such that those who determine the identity of the group from within have near-perfect freedom to decide whom from the outside they will admit.

But how perfect is this freedom? Regarding immigration, Walzer (following Rawls) suggests that governments have a minimal duty to aid those in distress if it can be done without burden – a principle of mutual aid the meaning and application of which, like any imperfect duty of beneficence, depends on the duty holder (Walzer 1983: 33). Accordingly, preservation of national identity – however racially informed it might be – is no less legitimate a reason for denying burdensome migrants entry than is preservation of economic affluence. Following their communitarian impulses, even multicultural democracies like the United States and Australia have notoriously embedded racial and ethnic restrictions into their immigration policies during the twentieth century. From Walzer's communitarian perspective, such repugnant policies are nonetheless legitimate to the extent that they reflect the will of the majority (and do not foreclose migration to uninhabited territory).[46]

Walzer does not say whether such racial exclusions contradict the more progressive, liberal features of American and Australian democracy. Assuming that racial nondiscrimination counts as one of these features, he could have concluded that American and Australian immigration policies (and the majority of white citizens in those countries who

[46] Walzer (1983: 46–47) observes that the "White Australia" policy could only have withstood moral challenge if white colonists hadn't staked their right to the continent by brutal force and had respected the principle of mutual aid by ceding some of its vast and sparsely populated territory to desperate Asian migrants.

supported them) missed the deeper communitarian impulses coursing through American and Australian democracy. Assuming further that these impulses run deeper than *Herrenvolk* (white settler) democracy and reach down to more abstract principles of democratic pluralism of the sort advocated by welfare-liberal cosmopolitanism and discourse ethics, then white supremacist identity politics stands less as a refutation of communitarianism than as an indictment of one instantiation of it.

Relying on this deeper democratic ethos, Walzer draws very different communitarian consequences for the treatment of immigrants who have already been legally admitted. Such immigrants should be recognized for their social contribution by having ample opportunity to reunite with their families under liberal rules of sponsorship. Policies that prohibit guest workers from permanently integrating with their host country violate another principle that recalls discourse ethics, to wit: the principle that what affects all should be decided by all (Walzer 1983: 60–63). The former (communitarian) principle speaks against denying guest workers the same civil rights accorded to permanent residents; the latter (noncommunitarian) principle speaks against denying permanent residents the opportunity to become citizens.

Walzer does not address moral dilemmas posed by so-called illegal migration. However, it would be relatively easy to see how the two principles annunciated above might apply to granting amnesty to undocumented migrants who have resided in their host country for a reasonably long period of time. Extrapolating from the politics of recognition, it seems wrong that persons who have laid down roots in a community should ever be subject to deportation.[47]

Needless to say, absence of self-esteem and/or *mis*recognition define(s) the condition of many migrant workers, regardless of whether or not they are legally documented. They may feel a sense of self-esteem for sending vital remittances to their families back home but still suffer from societal discrimination based on their appearance and "alien" origins. The degree of misrecognition is magnified even further for those who enter and stay

---

[47] Walzer, of course, might qualify the duty to grant amnesty based upon a prior communitarian duty to the welfare of legal residents. However, in the United States, from 1998–2012 4.5 million US citizens (660,000 of them children) lost undocumented parents to deportation (Human Impact Partners Family Unity, Family Health Report, June 2013). The agential harm to young children who have been separated from parents suggests a strong communitarian duty to grant amnesty for this latter class of undocumented migrants.

illegally; for they are additionally threatened with deportation (which for some means removal from family and community).

PARENTS WHO MIGRATE: THE HIDDEN COST OF DIVIDED AGENCY

Communitarians are the first to acknowledge the agency-threatening impact of migration on communities. However, by wrongly postulating the ontological priority of community over individual, welfare over autonomy, they often exaggerate the importance of stability, harmony, and homogeneity requisite for maintaining intact relationships based on solidarity.[48]

A case in point is the policy adopted by Romania to discourage parents from migrating. This policy reflects the sound *counter-cosmopolitan* intuition that unrestricted emigration can harm the development of children but ignores the equally sound *cosmopolitan* intuition that parents should be free to migrate for the sake of procuring their family's welfare.

Parents have a responsibility to both provide for their children materially and give them continuous love and guidance. However, in today's imperfect world of rich and poor nations they are faced with the constrained choice of choosing one over the other – leaving their families for sustainable employment abroad or remaining with their families in a condition of desperate shame. No matter how they choose, they violate their moral responsibilities and socially recognized role expectations.

Women remain responsible for children's care in most places, so it is hardly surprising, given the growing global demand for female caregivers and maids in the postfeminist developed world, that economic migration has become increasingly "feminized." Women (or men) who leave their children with a temporary caretaker rather than a spouse or intimate family member, however, might be harming their children psychologically,

---

[48] Citing Michael Walzer's assertion that a world without restrictive borders would be a cosmopolitan dystopia of deracinated men and women bound together only by the flimsiest of self-interested commercial ties (Rawls 1999a: 39; Walzer 1983: 39), Rawls advances the idea of a closed political community that "reproduces itself and its institutions and culture over generations" and whose "members enter only through birth and exit only through death" (Rawls 1999a: 12, 18, 26) as both an ideal to be approximated as well as a working hypothesis for a law of peoples – even to the extent of apparently endorsing John Stuart Mill's disturbing biological understanding of national identity as "common sympathies" rooted in "race and descent" (23).

socially, and developmentally, even if their remittances are improving their children's welfare (Gheaus 2014: 301).[49]

The 1989 UN Convention on the Rights of the Child (Articles 9.1, 9.3, and 20.3) asserts that a continuous loving relationship between parent and child is a child's right that can be waived by parent and state only under exceptional circumstances. This right is justified on both epistemic and moral grounds. Parents who interact with their children on a daily basis have unique knowledge about the peculiar needs of their children and thus have both the insight and motivation to function as the best advocates for their children. Morally speaking, love between parent and child is essential for building self-confidence and stable identity.

This explains why breaking a continuous parent/child relationship is often traumatic for the child (Gheaus 2014: 305). Studies of Romanian and Polish children whose parents have migrated show that their temporary foster homes were less stable and that children reported feeling traumatized by the absence of a loving parent. One can conclude that the children cited in this study were harmed despite improvements in their material welfare, insofar as they fell below a minimally acceptable threshold combining both adequate material provision *and* adequate parental care (Pipemo 2007: 63–68).

It goes without saying that parents should not be accused of child abandonment if, under economic duress, they can secure adequate material provision for their children only by migrating. True, those who migrate are typically not the worst off in their society; many possess education and marketable skills, have social connections and enough capital to apply for visas and the like. Still, they are constrained by the *t*hreat of poverty – they come from countries plagued by corruption and degraded welfare states (such as Romania). Hence, in keeping with my earlier argument, they and their families do not have secure access to goods guaranteed to them by human rights.[50]

---

[49] Between 1998 to 2013, 660,000 children in the United States lost a parent to deportation. From 2012 to 2015 almost 20,000 children were deported, many of them separated from parents and relocated to countries whose language they were not fluent in. Studies show that these children suffer from higher rates of mental and physical illness, low educational achievement, and poverty. Family Unity, Family Health Report for 2015, in collaboration with Health Impact Partners. www.humanimpact.org/projects/hia-case-stories/family-unity-family-health-an-inquiry-on-federal-immigration-policy/

[50] As specified by the UDHR, these goods include social security (A.22); voluntarily chosen just and favorable working conditions (A.23); healthcare and provision of welfare, with special care and assistance for motherhood and childhood (A.25); elementary education

But the more compelling point to be made here, to recall my earlier analogy between a poverty-producing economic system and a hostile workplace environment, is that, no matter how the poor choose, they are forced to give up some essential part of their agency. Migrating parents, in the words of Anca Gheaus, "lack full moral autonomy as well as truly voluntary choice" (Gheaus 2014: 310). They violate their moral responsibility toward their children and surrender their identity as parents regardless of whether they stay or leave. Nor can their voluntary choice to have children under uncertain circumstances be faulted, since having and raising children is itself a fundamental human interest worthy of human rights protection (Gheaus 2014: 311).

Given the double-bind recounted above, Gheaus argues against the Romanian policy that makes it illegal for parents to migrate without securing adequate legal guardianship for their children. This coercive policy acts as a prior restraint on parental options insofar as foreign employment abroad often becomes available without advance notice and must be filled immediately, leaving no time for lengthy legal paper-work to be processed. In the final analysis, such coercive policies fail to deter (as noted in the cases of mass migration cited earlier in this chapter, migrants will risk imprisonment and much worse for the sake of helping their families) and violate a fundamental right to migrate which desperate parents must be free to exercise (Gheaus 2014: 313).

Gheaus herself recommends that governments encourage potential migrants to seek good custodial care for their children and provide counseling to children who are left behind. Alternatively, she could have recommended that host governments make it easier for legal residents to petition for family reunification visas.[51] But because these measures are at best palliative and do not eliminate the economic conditions that generate the double-bind parents face – and because poor governments, which often find themselves caught in the double-bind of having to accept

---

aimed at full development of the human person (A.26); and "a social and international order in which [these] rights. ... are fully realized" (A.28).

[51] One justification for doing so builds on already recognized human rights of children and familial membership to adduce a human right to family reunification. Depending on the reasons for vesting the family with intrinsic and instrumental value commensurate with such a strong right, reunification could apply to extended family members and even caregivers. Problems affecting the human rights of legal residents due to the effects of chain migration would have to be resolved in a manner that fairly balanced the reasonable interests of both residents and families seeking reunification. For a defense of a discourse theoretic approach to this problem, see Drew Thompson, "A Human Right to Family Reunification: A Discourse Ethical Approach" (unpublished manuscript).

harsh measures imposed on them by global multilateral economic institutions or face trade retaliation, loan embargos, and other unsavory options, can't fund custodial care centers and counselors – she urges an international reform of the entire global economic order as the only solution to the problem (315).

Gheaus does not address the politics of such a reform. As we have seen throughout this chapter, the question regarding who has the right to decide "who owes what duty to whom" finds no adequate response in communitarian or cosmopolitan thinking. Indeed, to the extent that these alternatives presuppose a fixed framework for deliberating and deciding on these questions, they beg a further question that only discourse ethics is equipped to answer.

DISCOURSE ETHICS AND BORDER POLICY

Discourse ethics draws quasi-cosmopolitan implications from communitarian premises. It reflects a deep social fact about the ethos of mutual accountability informing modern and above all liberal democratic societies. Its reliance on face-to-face deliberation as a mutual check on unreasonable self-interest and cognitive bias provides a needed corrective and complement to monological forms of practical reasoning that rely more heavily on personal introspection. However, in addressing ethical conflicts of widely different scope, both real *and* hypothetical dialogue find equal purchase in this ethics. Practically speaking, normative disagreements that occur within a bounded community can only be legitimately resolved through face-to-face deliberation, even if this process must be dispersed over many "publics" and "condensed" and "filtered" by mass media. Ideally speaking, however, some matters requiring deliberation affect everyone, including future generations. Deliberating on these matters may be spatially and temporally bounded but the reference point for ultimate justification refers to an unlimited community, whose possible opinions about ideal justice only personal hypothetical speculation can entertain.

The importance of face-to-face dialog over personal speculation regarding immigration ethics, policy, and practical application varies considerably. Moral reasoning about metapolitical questions concerning appropriate boundaries of deliberation and decision-making and universal human rights principles will rely on personal speculations (ideal theory) that abstract from time and place and imagine possible worlds. Political reasoning about domestic immigration policy will rely on situational discussions taking place in parliament and public arena (nonideal theory). Judicial reasoning in deportation proceedings will rely on private conversations between judge, defendant, and legal counsel. In some instances, all three types of reasoning may be elicited. Judges, for example, typically recur to policy rationales in applying the law to individual cases; in adjudicating cases that are recalcitrant to mechanical resolution they are often thrown back on their own moral intuitions.

Let me begin by addressing one theoretical concern about immigration that discourse ethics is uniquely positioned to illuminate: the justice of borders. Most discussions about the ethics of immigration assume that legal inhabitants within a political territory have a stronger moral claim than others to occupy that territory. Had not the United States annexed half of Mexico's territory in an aggressive war of conquest, Americans living in the Southwest might have justly claimed this privilege against Mexican nationals.[52] But that war and subsequent US interventions in

---

[52] As David Miller (2016) reminds us, realism counsels us to bracket the morality of how political boundaries have been established, with the wisdom of this advice increasing as the event of establishment recedes ever more distantly. But that wisdom seems misplaced when a majority of Mexican nationals believe they have just claim to inhabit land that was once their rightful patrimony. Like Walzer, Miller subscribes to a communitarian defense of such boundaries as essential to fostering the communitarian solidarity requisite for establishing special duties of distributive justice, including collective political rights to self-determination (28). Although Miller concedes that respect for human rights, principles of non-discrimination, and duties of repair constrain immigration policy, he insists that the duty to aid refugees is a matter of humanitarianism, not of justice (163) and that "justice permits us to do less for would-be immigrants than we are required to do for citizens" (30). However, Miller's communitarianism is weakened by his endorsement of a weak cosmopolitanism that commands that "states must consider the impact of the policies they pursue on those who live outside of their borders" and are therefore forbidden to "give zero weight" to their interests in such matters. (24). Furthermore, his claim that "if there are no relevant differences between people, we should afford them equal consideration" (24) poses a significant challenge for his theory given his recognition of a human right to internal freedom of movement. His argument defending an asymmetry between intra-border migration (the human right to freedom of internal movement contained in Article 13.1 of the UDHR) and cross-border migration appeals to questionable empirical assumptions regarding the special burdens that a policy of open borders would impose on states' capacities to fulfill their human rights duties to their own subjects, and the unique role that the human right to freedom of internal movement plays in counteracting policies of apartheid and other forms of discriminatory segregation (52–55). In the final analysis, Miller's own awareness of global social connectedness, including his understanding of how economic and environmental policies of developed countries adversely impact the lives of vulnerable people in the developing world, seems understated in comparison to his emphatic insistence that citizens of a state have a superior right to occupy its territory regardless of historical contingencies. I thank Drew Thompson for making clear to me these shortcomings in Miller's position.

Mexico and Central America – economic and military – make claiming such a privilege highly dubious.

The justice of borders comes into special relief whenever a historically disputed border impinges on the self-determination of stateless minorities and refugees who are denied full citizenship rights in their own homeland.[53] Israel's current immigration and naturalization policies aim to restore a Jewish homeland to diaspora Jews but their ancillary purpose – to preserve a dominant religious identity in the face of non-Jewish (more specifically, Palestinian) migration and settlement – denies Palestinians full access to and citizenship rights within *their* homeland.

Discourse ethics not only questions the ethical coherence of a state whose political identity is claimed to be simultaneously Jewish and liberal democratic, or secular. It also questions the justice of Israel's expansion and reconfiguration of its borders through its policy of Jewish settlements in land formerly occupied by Palestinians and its system of walls, checkpoints, and passes that obstruct Palestinian freedom of movement.

Conflicting claims to national security and human rights that swirl around the debate over Israel's border politics clearly call for discursive resolution involving all affected parties. Palestinians living in the West Bank, Gaza Strip, Lebanon, and Jordan as well as Israeli nationals (Jews and non-Jews) have more at stake in the outcome of this debate than anyone else, but inhabitants scattered throughout the Middle East, not to mention Africa, Europe, and United States, have a stake as well. Appropriately weighing all the relevant arguments will invariably raise additional metapolitical questions about Israeli and Palestinian "identities": Should these identities be incorporated into a single nonreligiously identified state, separated into two states, or radically reconfigured into a complex confederation of multiple, semi-sovereign states?

I will leave it to others to decide how a speculative "metadiscourse" addressing this "metapolitical" question might be democratically institutionalized. That such a discourse is being so institutionalized throughout the world is a fact to be marveled at. Europe is one place where it has already happened. Europe's "disaggregated citizenship" policies build upon free labor and residential mobility by enabling foreign nationals from EU member states to access social benefits and vote in municipal

---

[53] Current Middle Eastern conflicts illustrate the disastrous legacy of Europe's dissection of the African-Asian region into colonial territories whose boundaries – far from being discursively resolved by all affected parties – often disrespect the integrity of established linguistic, religious, and tribal communities.

elections. In Belgium, Denmark, Sweden, Finland and the Netherlands, third-country nationals can participate in local elections as well.

Europe is not the only place where foreign residents enjoy extensive citizenship rights. Many British Commonwealth countries permit citizens of other Commonwealth countries to vote in elections (today, mainly restricted to local elections). Other countries (e.g., Chile, Philippines, and Malawi) and Hong Kong require only permanent residency to vote in *all* elections (Earnest 2009).[54]

To summarize: discourse ethics' signal contribution to theorizing about the normative parameters of immigration reminds us that the political frameworks for addressing questions about "who should decide what about whom" cannot be taken for granted in the way that cosmopolitan and communitarian responses traditionally have.[55] As we have seen, the EU has already embarked on a path toward rethinking these questions specifically as they apply to internal migrants and asylum seekers from outside the Union. Its proposal to distribute the burden of resettling refugees among all member states provides a template for revising the Geneva Convention's state-centric principle for assigning responsibilities to shelter and resettle refugees that anticipates a more centrally organized response to this crisis under the auspices of a democratically reconstituted UN[56] As we shall now see, discourse ethics' signal contribution to policy debates shifts the burden of justification from needy migrants to the affluent governments that deny them entry.

DISCOURSE ETHICS AND IMMIGRATION POLICY

The most striking contribution discourse ethics makes to our reasoning about immigration consists in expanding the community of deliberation

---

[54] Some municipalities in the US permit foreign residents to vote in local elections.
[55] The fact that "post-modern" immigration flows have diverse causes, including the willingness of skilled members of the middle class to uproot their identities so as to take advantage of global economic opportunities, has received considerable attention in recent years. Persistent back-and-forth cross-border migrations coupled with diverse forms of dual (multiple) citizenship, legal residency, and so on simultaneously call forth more flexible modes of negotiating immigration and immigrant rights and more secure (less flexible) human rights guarantees for immigrants generally, both of which increasingly extend beyond the capacity of the isolated nation state. Hence the need to secure the rights of all migrants in a cosmopolitan legal order – extending beyond bilateral and multilateral international treaties between nations – that has its democratic, legitimating basis in a global public sphere. For further discussion about why current patterns of global migration necessitate this response, see Pensky (2008) and Chapters 6 and 7 below.
[56] I discuss such a proposal in Chapter 6.

to include migrants. Most policy debates only take account of domestic opinion. Discourse ethics demands that policy debates take account of the interests of everyone who is impacted by that policy, so that the debate proceeds "not just from the one-sided perspective of an inhabitant of an affluent region but also from the perspective of immigrants who are seeking their well-being there; [viz.] a free and dignified existence and not just political asylum" (Habermas 1996: 511). A policy that spells the difference between life and death for some persons obviously impacts their human right to life, which explains why humanitarian arguments for asylum made by economic refugees – and not just political asylum seekers – should carry so much weight.

Indeed, the "growing interdependencies of a global society that has become so enmeshed through the capitalist world market," which impose on all of us an "overall political responsibility for safeguarding the planet," also impose special obligations on affluent nations to compensate peoples of the developing world for "the uprooting of regional cultures by the incursion of capitalist modernization" (Habermas 1998: 231). Here we see the second contribution that discourse ethics makes to our reasoning about immigration. Not only must the claims of immigrants be factored into policy debates but they must weigh equally. Indeed, they might weigh more than the claims of relatively affluent peoples who are trying to deny them entry into their country. This would especially be the case if the relative differences in standard of living separating these two groups stemmed from past and present injustices of colonialism and imperialism. Giving fair weight to migrants' claims shifts the burden of justification onto affluent nations. Thus, instead of expecting migrants to justify why they should be granted admission as privileged beneficiaries of charity, discourse ethics requires that affluent nations justify to migrants why their claims to compensation should not compel some form of restitution. In discussing immigration quotas,[57] Habermas insists that the needs of migrants count as much (or more) than the economic needs of

[57] Quotas and queues contribute to irregular migration. The 1965 US Immigration and Nationality Act (amended 1976) ended quotas based on national origin, race, and ancestry that reserved 70 percent of all slots to the UK, Germany, and Ireland and very few to Asia and Africa. At the same time, it extended per country quotas to the Western hemisphere for the first time (allotting a yearly total of 120,000 to that region, with a per country limit of 20,000). Unlimited family reunification visas with long queue lines extending over twenty years, combined with very low work visa quotas, fueled a wave of irregular migration from Mexico to the US from 1970 to 2008.

the host country "in accordance with criteria that are acceptable from the perspective of all parties involved" (232).[58]

Extrapolating from this example, I propose the following principle for assessing the justice of a country's immigration policy:[59]

An admission policy is just only if both current members and applicants could not reasonably reject it after fully and impartially discussing the moral rights and interests at stake for all affected parties.

The astute reader will notice that I did not stipulate that all who are affected by an immigration policy must be able to rationally assent to it. The rational assent of persons who are only tangentially affected should not weigh as heavily as the assent of those who are affected directly and deeply. Furthermore, stipulating universal consent as a criterion of justification as Habermas does is impractical when talking about real debates within public and parliamentary spheres. Given that some dissent is likely, what matters is that it is reasonable and carries weight. Because very needy migrants have comparably strong reasons for migrating, the burden of justification generally weighs heavier on affluent parties who would deny them entry. Taking all these considerations into account, needy migrants who could reasonably *not* assent to an immigration policy after concerted efforts have been made to persuade them can be understood as exercising a veto right over that policy.

---

[58] The argument as presented here would require some qualification. The concept of compensation presupposes problematic conceptual and empirical criteria for identifying victims and beneficiaries. Furthermore, the argument in favor of balancing interests can only sensibly apply to the interests of immigrants who are actually trying to immigrate (and not the interests of potential immigrants, which would include all outsiders). In "balancing interests" it matters whether we are talking about balancing the interests of, say, an individual applicant to admission against the interests (individual or collective) of some subset of residents or whether we are balancing the interests of a large mass of applicants with respect to the interests (individual or collective) of some subset of residents. I thank Drew Thompson for this observation.

[59] Seyla Benhabib proposes a somewhat different principle:

[I]f you and I enter into a moral dialogue with one another, and I am a member of a state of which you are seeking membership and you are not, then I must be able to show you with good grounds, with grounds that would be acceptable to each of us equally, why you can never join our association and become one of us. These must be grounds that you would accept if you were in my situation and I were in yours. Our reasons must be reciprocally acceptable; they must apply to each of us equally (Benhabib 2004: 138).

Unlike Benhabib's principle, which emphasizes a reciprocal burden of justification that is perfectly symmetrical, my proposal stresses the practical implication of such a burden, which is to shift the current burden asymmetrically borne by migrants onto affluent peoples. For further discussion of the concept of asymmetrical reciprocity see Young (1997).

Using my principle, it becomes immediately apparent that policies that restrict entry of economic and political refugees whose basic human rights are at stake are unjust. Also unjust, it seems, are policies that deny guest workers full civil rights and, if their immigration status is more permanent than temporary, a pathway to citizenship.[60] Importantly, immigration policies that exclude candidates because their cultural beliefs and practices are different from those of the host country are unjust as well.

Habermas himself argued this point in criticizing Germany's guest worker policy and its *jus sanguinis* policy regarding naturalization and citizenship:[61] "The ethical substance of a political integration that unites all the citizens of the nation must remain 'neutral' with respect to the differences between the ethical-cultural communities within the nation, each of which is integrated around its own conception of the good" (Habermas 1998a: 227). He further claimed, out of deference to a discourse ethical principle of multicultural recognition, that immigrants should not be expected to assimilate to "the way of life, the practices, and the customs of the local culture across their full range" if this means having to give up "the cultural form of life of their origins," unless that form of life is politically unreasonable (in Rawls's terms) or intolerant of other reasonable cultural forms of life (Habermas 1998a: 229). At most, states might expect immigrants to "enter into the political culture of their new homeland" which "safeguards the society from the danger of segmentation" and from a "separatist disintegration into unrelated subcultures" (Habermas 1996: 513). In other words, the only permissible

---

[60] Guestworkers could reasonably dissent to laws denying them civil rights or a pathway to citizenship insofar as these legal entitlements protect their political right to effectively advocate and lobby on behalf of their interests.

[61] Writing in the wake of revisions (1993) made in Germany's Basic Law concerning the right to asylum, Habermas was alarmed by the xenophobic reactions he saw among his compatriots and Europeans in general to the wave of immigrants from Africa and war-torn Yugoslavia. Reserving some of his harshest criticism for Germany's immigration law, he underscored the injustice of a policy that granted "ethnic Germans" (*Statusdeutschen*) a constitutional right to citizenship while denying this same right to Germany's unmarried male guest workers, who were recruited from southern and southeastern Europe to work as cheap labor from 1955–1973 and forced to wait fifteen years before applying for citizenship. He also argued against Germany's restrictive immigration policy, which (with the exception of ethnic Germans) virtually cut off immigration from all but the wealthiest and most highly skilled. Rejecting the idea that Germany's national political identity could remain ethnically centered given its multicultural composition, Habermas invoked the discourse principle of equal inclusion to defend a conception of civic solidarity ("constitutional patriotism") based on democracy and human rights. For a more detailed discussion of this conception, see Chapter 7.

cultural reason for refusing to admit an applicant would be demonstrative disloyalty to the principles underwriting a nation's liberal democratic constitution.[62]

Seyla Benhabib offers a somewhat different understanding of what discourse ethics demands in this regard. Qualifications for immigration that require immigrants to possess ascriptive properties that are generally not of their own choosing – such as "race, gender, religion, ethnicity, language community, or sexuality" – are unacceptable and run afoul of the nondiscrimination provision of Art. 2 of the UDHR. Acceptable qualifications are "skills and resources [such as] language competence, a certain proof of civic literacy, demonstration of material resources, or marketable skills" (139).

Benhabib concedes that these criteria might be abused in practice and that past historical injustices have played a significant role in distributing assets and talents among the different races and nationalities of the world. So, it is far from clear whether her criteria could comport with discourse ethical principles unqualifiedly.

More interestingly, Benhabib appears to deviate from Habermas's thinking in maintaining that ethnic and religious *preferences* might accord with these principles, if they were intended to protect members of vulnerable or persecuted groups (such as Israel's preference toward diaspora Jews). Indeed, discourse ethics differs from cosmopolitan ethics in conceding that migrants' human rights can be qualified by, and balanced against, the human rights of citizens and other rationally justifiable duties to the community, not limited to protection of national security but also including protection of groups.[63] In conflicts like this, the responsibility to protect a migrant's human rights falls on the entire community of states. Coordinating their efforts at the supranational level, they must resolve on the most equitable policy for admitting and resettling refugees.

---

[62] As Habermas notes (Habermas 1998a: chapter 8), immigration cannot but alter "the composition of the population in ethical-cultural respects as well." Habermas here criticizes Charles Taylor's defense of Quebec's controversial language laws (Taylor, et al. 1994), which required immigrants and Francophone Quebecois to send their children to French-speaking schools, noting that these laws appeared to stifle a basic freedom of communication and correlative right to interpret one's own identity (and presumably, the identity of one's children).

[63] Interestingly, neither Benhabib nor Habermas addresses the possibility that small polities possessing strong religious identities – Israel and some aboriginal communities come to mind – might reasonably restrict immigration to preserve those identities and offer sanctuary to their historically oppressed adherents.

DISCOURSE ETHICS AND IMMIGRATION COURTS

Discourse ethics shifts the burden of justification from needy migrants to affluent peoples by insisting that the weightier claims of migrants for just compensation and humanitarian treatment under the law be factored into policy discussions. For most refugees, however, the only venue where they can press their claims with any hope of receiving an impartial hearing is before an immigration judge.

Adjudication of an appeal may be routine but often it involves judicial discretion in choice, interpretation, and application of statutes. Judges rely on open-textured constitutional principles in undertaking this endeavor. The principle mandating equal due process that often crops up in immigration cases, for instance, is not a rule that narrowly dictates a single correct application but a regulative ideal that requires interpretation in light of the relevant case history (past, present, and future) and the entire body of relevant law. The hermeneutical circle wherein legal precedents, constitutional principles, statutes, and case law mutually interpolate each other can produce new holdings that reverberate throughout the legal system.

Discourse ethics prescribes a judicial procedure requiring that all relevant perspectives bearing on the most comprehensive description of a case be considered and that all relevant principles (and statutory rules) be weighed in determining which rules and principles are most applicable. Crucial to this process is a courtroom procedure, which should not be structured simply as an adversarial contest, whereby all sides have equal opportunities to state their cases freely, cross-examine witnesses, and introduce evidence (Habermas 1996: 172; Ingram 2010a: 210).

I would like to conclude this chapter by examining a real-life case to illustrate how discourse ethics might regulate a typical immigration hearing. Elvira Arellano was an undocumented Mexican worker in the United States who founded Familia Latina Unida, an organization that fights against deportations that separate spouses from one another and their children. She founded this organization after she herself was apprehended by immigration authorities in 2002 and taken from her then three-year-old son, who having been born in the US, was an American citizen. She and her son had been claiming sanctuary in a Methodist church on Chicago's Southside, waiting to see if Homeland Security would carry out the deportation threat it issued in August 2006. A year later while in route to a political rally in Washington D.C. Homeland Security officials apprehended her in Los Angeles and deported her to Mexico (her son later joined her there).

Thanks to an Illinois congressional delegation, she had been granted three stays of deportation since 2003 in order to care for her son, who was diagnosed with ADHD and other health problems. Unfortunately, her request for a private bill that would grant her an exemption from deportation was not supported by lawmakers, who argued that it would be unfair to other undocumented workers. After residing in Mexico for seven years, Arellano presented herself, her teenage son, and her 4-month-old baby to US Border Patrol officials in San Diego, requesting asylum from drug-related violence and because she had received threats for her work as a human rights activist on behalf of undocumented Central American immigrants in Mexico. She has since been released from detention, and has resumed her activism in Chicago while her case is pending.

In what follows I will examine whether it was right for the US to have deported Arellano in the first place. I will also assume that Arellano did not satisfy US requirements for asylum at that time. Finally, I will assume that a general statute permitting the deportation of persons who have knowingly entered a country illegally is just, even though I have argued that it could be so only with considerable qualification. Are there extenuating circumstances in Arellano's story to which a judge might appeal in granting her relief from deportation?

Arellano left Mexico as an economic refugee during the Mexican monetary crisis of the 1990s. Not only was she the mother of a juvenile American citizen with special needs but Arellano was a political spokesperson for immigrant families whose parents or children were facing deportation. She occupied a low-paying unskilled job that most Americans have no desire to do and she paid her taxes. Her family in Mexico – to which she was repatriated – lives in Michoacán, one of the poorest and most violent states in Mexico.

In bringing to bear these extenuating circumstances in deciding Arellano's case, a judge would also need to recur to additional principles (embodied in US executive orders, judicial decisions, and legislation):

P.1   No one who has resided sufficiently long in a country should be deported unless they have committed a serious crime.[64]

---

[64] This principle is reflected in Senate Immigration Bill 744, passed by the Senate in June, 2013, which provides for conditional amnesty and a pathway to citizenship for undocumented workers who have resided in the US since 2011. This principle is also reflected in the Obama Administration's three most important executive orders: Deferred Action for Childhood Arrivals [DACA], Deferred Action for Parents of Lawful Permanent Residents [DAPA], and the replacement of President George Bush's Secure Communities policy with a policy implementing amnesty for virtually all undocumented persons who have not

P.2 Persons should not be deported, if this risks separating them from their parents, children, or persons who depend on or care for them.[65]

P.3 Persons should not be deported, if doing so endangers their lives in violation of international humanitarian legal practice.

In my opinion, the combined weight of these principles, conjoined with a fair assessment of her extenuating circumstances, should have exempted Arellano from deportation, and they should now compel the courts to grant her asylum.

I mentioned above that deportation hearings should not be structured mainly as adversarial contests. They should be structured as dialogues whereby petitioner's request for understanding and mercy imposes a reciprocal discourse ethical duty on the part of the presiding judge to empathetically place himself in the shoes of the petitioner. Letting petitioner tell her story of the events leading up to her decision to enter illegally is the first step in a process leading toward exempting her from deportation.

In light of the importance of face-to-face testimony in eliciting empathetic understanding from the court, it seems fitting that I conclude this chapter with an uplifting story in what has otherwise been a tragic tale for thousands of Central American refugees fleeing violence. 32-year-old Alba Cruz and her 3-year-old daughter had been detained at the Dilley, Texas trailer compound awaiting an immigration hearing. An Immigration and Customs Enforcement Official had determined that she and her daughter had a "reasonable fear" of being physically abused by her ex-boyfriend in

---

recently entered the country. The Obama administration created DACA in 2012 to provide temporary but renewable legal status to children who entered the US illegally prior to their 16th birthday and have resided in the US for five years. In 2014 the Obama administration created DAPA, which provides temporary but renewable legal status to undocumented parents of citizens or legal residents. A more far-reaching executive order put into force in mid-2015 essentially narrows enforcement of deportation proceedings to just three categories of persons: convicted criminals, recent arrivals apprehended mainly at ports of entry, and suspected terrorists. Deportations for 2015 were projected to be around 227,000, almost half the 409,000 deported in 2012 (a record high). Homeland Security Secretary Jeh Johnson gave the following rationale for the change in policy: "We are making it clear that we should not expend our limited resources on deporting those who have been here for years, have committed no serious crimes and have, in effect, become integrated members of our society." On June 23, 2016, a divided Supreme Court let stand a ruling by the 5th US Circuit Court of Appeal in *United States v. Texas* that upheld an injunction against enforcing DAPA (Marron 2015: 1:18).

[65] P.2 and P.3 also find support in the official rationale for DAPA, CAM, and US prioritization of visas emitted for family reunification.

El Salvador. Because of the high demand placed on immigration courts, her hearing took place in a compound trailer, by teleconference with Judge Lourdes de Jongh in Miami. Her attorney, who worked for a pro bono immigrant defense project, was seeking temporary asylum for her and her daughter, deferred removal, and a work permit for herself.

Judge Jongh began the questioning: "You're going to be telling me your story." Through a translator and with her lawyer by her side, Cruz began her story. She had been victimized twice by domestic violence, once in 2004, after she entered the US the first time, and a second time, just before she re-entered the US in 2014 with her daughter. The first time her alcoholic boyfriend threated to stab her with a knife, followed her to work, and smashed the windows on her car (all of which was corroborated by a police report). After returning to El Salvador, she became pregnant by her second boyfriend, who demanded sex from her in return for a five dollar per diem living allowance to support herself and her baby. With prodding from her lawyer, Cruz recounted how her boyfriend screamed at their daughter, yanking her hair and slamming her down in a chair. He threatened to keep the child if Cruz tried to escape. When Cruz complained to her boyfriend's mother she told her that she would have to suffer the abuse in order to "have a home." Cruz did not go to the police because she feared they would do nothing to protect her and that it would only make her boyfriend angrier, repeating what had happened in the US the first time around.

Finally, the lawyer representing the government asked how she entered illegally. She answered that she had help from her relatives, who raised $5000 to pay a smuggler for the trip across the Rio Grande, from Ciudad Acuna, Mexico. After a sympathetic hearing from the judge, Cruz emerged from the trailer, scooped up her daughter and announced, "We Won!"[66]

---

[66] As narrated in "Lives on Hold in Holding Center," Chicago Tribune (July 1, 2015), sec 1: 18.

4

Imperial Power and Global Political Economy: Democracy and the Limits of Capitalism

This book is dedicated to defending the thesis that coercion ought to occupy center stage along with economic injustice in discussing global poverty. Chapter 3 pursued this claim by arguing that no economy which drives the poor to uproot themselves from their communities and risk life and fortune at the hands of smugglers, border guards, and criminal law enforcement agencies is morally or legally innocent. Although a cosmopolitan legal order permitting untrammeled freedom of movement would reduce this risk, it would not eliminate it. Even if such an order did a better job of respecting human rights, maximizing global welfare, and promoting social justice, it would not respect valid communitarian concerns about loss of democratic control and, most importantly, would not compensate for loss of agency experienced by those who migrate out of economic desperation. They leave their families and communities reluctantly, knowing full well that they also leave behind recognitive relationships that are vital to their sense of identity and freedom.

Neither cosmopolitanism nor communitarianism adequately addresses the coercive nature of a global order that criminalizes economic refugees in the name of national sovereignty or subordinates democracies to the imperatives of unrestricted mobility in labor, commodities, and capital. I have argued that discourse ethics provides a better approach to theorizing the moral injustices and harms experienced by economic refugees. In this chapter, I will make a similar claim regarding the injustices and harms associated with a global economy premised on the unrestricted flow of goods and capital.

My indictment of our present global order as unjust and inimical to the aims of development would be groundless if the structures that underpin the global economy were fixed or inherently rational. This might be the case, for instance, if they were naturally moral, conforming to God-given rules of private property ownership and freedom of contract. Alternatively, it might be the case if they were instrumentally rational, maximizing production and consumption more than any other conceivable alternative. The former line of reasoning, reflecting what I have dubbed libertarian cosmopolitanism, holds that only a free market economy fully embodies the highest moral end: negative (legal) freedom from government constraint. The latter line of reasoning, reflecting what I have dubbed utilitarian (or neoliberal) cosmopolitanism, denies that a market economy embodies any moral value, including that of individual freedom. Instead of extolling the intrinsic justice of contracts between "free and equal" individuals, neoliberalism endorses increasing global wealth as an all-purpose means for realizing any preferred goal. Its appeal to "value-free" economic science poses an especially grave challenge to an ethics of development premised on realizing the supreme value of agency.

Libertarianism and neoliberalism presuppose that free markets are, or ought to be, beyond political debate. Presumably, only juridical and scientific elites possess the expertise requisite for managing the economy properly, so that democracy and the discourse ethical principles that I have hitherto suggested inform it find a limit here. I will argue, on the contrary, that libertarianism and neoliberalism are blind to the fact that the global economy is a *political* economy. Neoliberalism is oblivious to the social contractarian values that necessarily underwrite both domestic and global market economies; libertarianism grasps this ethical truth, but interprets the values in question in terms of an undeveloped conception of agential freedom. Discourse ethics and recognition theory, by contrast, provide a compelling narrative of agential development that interprets these values in terms of a more robust moral and social conception of agential freedom.[1] From the perspective of these theories, moral right and economic efficiency designate politically contested norms, the legitimate meaning of which should be resolved democratically by all who come under their constraint.

Commensurate with the political understanding of the global economy outlined above, the following chapter begins by examining the imperial

---

[1] See Chapter 1 for a discussion of the difference between abstract and subjective notions of (negative) legal and (positive) moral freedom, on one side, and concrete, objective (institutional) conceptions of social freedom, on the other.

power exercised by the United States and other developed nations in imposing a global regime of trade and finance that perpetuates an imbalance of capital distribution favoring these economic blocs in their dealings with developing countries. I argue that imperial power not only violates the social contractarian ethos underlying international relations in the postwar period but that the current imperial regime fails to live up to ethical duties concomitant with the "paternalistic" exercise of that power (Imperial Power and International Relations: The Logic of Underdevelopment and Unsustainable Economies and Contractarian Duties and the Moral Burden of Empire). I then turn my attention to the social contractarian ethos underlying our global market economy and examine the claim that free trade is the most efficient and just path toward reducing poverty, inequality, environmental degradation, and global warming (Free versus Fair Trade). My objection to this claim chiefly centers on the theory of comparative advantage that policy makers working within global institutions invoke in touting the benefits of free trade in reducing poverty and advancing development. In place of unqualified free trade I recommend macroeconomic models of poverty reduction (such as import substitution) that rely less on trade. Eliminating trade barriers hindering the free flow of goods from developing to developed countries, while phasing out trade protections in the developing world, is a short term fix that does not solve the problem of wage competition, which hurts workers worldwide (Markets and Negative Externalities: Dependency, Environmental Degradation and Global Warming). The remainder of my argument emphasizes the gains in environmental protection, global climate control, and community development offered by economic democracy (Toward an Efficient and Just Reduction of Negative Externalities: Market Strategies versus Government Regulation). Sustainable development, I argue, might not be well served by the growth dynamics driving capitalism, which in today's financialized economy severely limit any form of democratic control (The Limits of Capitalism). In keeping with the spirit of discourse ethics, I propose a model of market socialism and workplace democracy as a more sustainable alternative (Economic Democracy).

IMPERIAL POWER AND INTERNATIONAL RELATIONS: THE LOGIC OF UNDERDEVELOPMENT AND UNSUSTAINABLE ECONOMIES

Coercion describes several aspects of the global economy. Aggregate choices produce unintended market fluctuations in global supply and demand as well as externalities that limit opportunities for action.

Bargaining leverages negative as well as positive incentives for cooperation. Anchoring these economic mechanisms is a coercive legal system,
shaped by the imperial power of the United States and to a lesser extent
other developed nations that work in tandem with it, whose economic and
geopolitical interests are partly advanced by maintaining the dependency
and underdevelopment of poorer countries.

The United States has resorted to military intervention in pursuit of its
economic and geopolitical aims more than any other nation since the end
of World War II. It has sponsored corrupt military regimes and pursued
violent policies that have contributed to the deaths of millions of civilians.
These actions contradicted the high-minded aims US officials announced
to the public in their support, which typically portrayed them as benevolent attempts to protect the people of foreign governments from being
oppressed by their own leaders or by other foreign powers. But the
foreseeable loss of American economic assets in the face of nationalization
threats posed by Mossadegh in Iran (1953), Arbenz in Guatemala (1954),
Lumumba in the Congo (1960), and Allende in Chile (1968) did not justify
the US–backed overthrow of democratic governments and subsequent
launching of brutal dictatorships in those countries. Nor did the loss of
geopolitical influence in Vietnam, Central America, and Angola in the face
of Communist threats justify US support for wars that left millions dead
and homeless. And the need for American security in the face of terrorist
threats certainly did not justify the bloody invasions of Iraq or
Afghanistan.

My aim here, however, is not to indict American foreign policy makers
for deceiving the public and perpetrating humanitarian crimes in tandem
with client regimes. Instead I want to examine a less violent form of
imperial power which coerces nations within the orbit of American *economic influence* to conform to US aims, regardless of whether doing so
advances the economic interests of those nations' inhabitants. As Richard
Miller notes, even if the "American empire" is not a colonial empire in the
same way that the British empire was, it shares the latter's reliance on
domineering influence rather than simple persuasion to advance imperial
interests (Miller 2010: 120). The US not only exercises asymmetrical
power in its dealings with other sovereign nations, but it also projects
more power than any other nation in influencing international institutions
that shape economic development throughout the world.

Miller cites two important ways in which the United States projects
global dominion: through its near global monopoly over financial and
coordination *prerogatives* and its leveraging of *threats* in its disbursement

of aid, loans, and trade opportunities. US prerogatives impose costs on other countries as the price that must be paid in order to engage in most global economic transactions, especially those involving US–based entities. Regarded as one of the most stable currencies in the world because of its sheer volume and therefore as a hedge against local currency devaluations, the US dollar comprises almost 63 percent of all reserves held by foreign central banks and is involved in about 85 percent of all currency transactions (IMF Report 2015). Another reason why foreign exchange reserves are held in dollars is because the US economy accounts for nearly a quarter of global Gross Domestic Product (GDP), and thus represents an important venue for global investment. The US currency prerogative enables US businesses, banks, and government entities to save billions of dollars in currency exchange fees that are borne by their foreign counterparts.[2]

The US government also enjoys a significant borrowing prerogative. Because of their reliability and liquidity, US Treasury bills are a desirable investment for private investors, with nearly 34 percent of current US government debt ($6.176 trillion) owned by foreign governments and foreign private investors.[3] The scale and ease of US government borrowing enables the US government to amass large deficits in flexibly managing its own domestic and foreign crises, helping it to finance a military that is larger than the next eight largest militaries combined. Aside from rendering the rest of the world vulnerable to US military intervention, the currency and finance prerogatives enjoyed by the US government render other nations vulnerable to fluctuations in the American economy and to Federal Reserve decisions regarding currency depreciation and interest rates. The recent tightening of monetary policy in the US was expected to divert $540 billion in investment capital from the fifteen largest emerging economies that from 2009 to June 2014 had received a positive flow of $2.2 trillion in foreign purchases of stocks and bonds (Goldin 2016: 132).[4] The 2008 Recession that reverberated throughout the world had its origins in the American housing and financial markets. The entanglement of US banks and insurance corporations and the use of "toxic assets"

---

[2] Between 40 and 60 percent of global financial exchanges are transacted in US dollars. This percentage is declining as emerging economies' share of the global market increases.

[3] Treasury Department. http://ticdata.treasury.gov/Publish/mfh.txt.

[4] One contributing cause behind this diversion of capital was the strengthening of US bond markets; higher yield bonds, pegged to the Federal Reserve Bank's increase in prime interest rate, made US bonds a more attractive investment for investors in emerging economies.

in transactions with foreign banks were largely responsible for triggering a global crisis, with European banks holding three-quarters of the $441 billion in "toxic" credit-default swaps involving AIG. In 1979, the Federal Reserve's decision to tame inflation by raising interest rates instigated a global debt crisis that lowered the share of developing countries in world trade from 28 percent in 1980 to just 19 percent in 1986 and lowered per capita GDP in Latin American countries from an average growth rate of 2.9 percent during the period from 1960–78 to a rate of .09 percent from 1978–98 (George 1988: 73; Milanović 2002). Ironically, it was the United States and American banks that encouraged developing countries to take out dollar-denominated loans rather than accept development aid. At the time, this might have made sense because interest rates, tied to Federal Reserve bank rates, had been at historic lows. Again, in the mid-1990s the Federal Reserve's decision to raise interest rates and strengthen the value of the dollar helped trigger the East Asian financial crisis of 1997 by diverting investment away from financially unstable Asian economies.[5]

A large presence in the global economy also bestows coordination prerogatives on US transactions involving other countries. Foreign governments and businesses must adjust their business and financial practices to conform to American standards, licensing credentials, and regulations. The imposition of a standard set of global norms conforming to American requirements guarantees a reserve pool of foreign intellectual labor that is schooled in dominant American technological methods and technocratic ideology. The resulting integration of local elites into the American techno-bureaucratic establishment imposes additional costs on developing countries, ranging from loss of professionals to emigration ("brain drain") to the added expense of training elites in the US and other developed countries, often in accordance with high-tech methods that find little application in developing countries.

US threat potential manifests itself in the workings of the IMF, WB, WTO, and US foreign aid. Thanks to its financial prerogatives, the US government can afford to use the allure of foreign aid (military and economic) as carrot and stick in molding the policies of foreign governments to conform to American interests.[6] Bilateral aid (which constitutes

---

[5] East Asian countries whose currencies were pegged to the dollar (such as Thailand) lost revenue when their exports were priced out of the global market.
[6] President Obama's 2010 Presidential Policy Directive on Global Development urged increasing development assistance as a core pillar of American power in pursuit of national security interests.

70 percent of all US government foreign aid) became a prominent geopolitical weapon during the Cold War, constituting almost 0.6 percent of US GDP (it has since declined by 83 percent to 0.1 percent). Economic aid still tracks strategic interests, with almost a quarter of all aid funding military-related (peace and security) projects. Accordingly, Israel, ranked fifth among high income nations, is targeted to receive the largest amount of US economic aid in 2016 ($3.1 billion) out of a projected total amount of $37.9 billion; followed by Afghanistan ($1.5 billion) and Egypt ($1.45 billion).[7] Only a third of bilateral aid that is specifically earmarked for official developmental assistance (ODA) under the auspices of the US Agency for International Development (USAID) benefits low income countries, and 70 percent of that aid is tied to purchasing US goods and services.[8] Steep reductions in and eventual elimination of direct bilateral US ODA to Haiti following Aristide's refusal to implement Haiti's IMF/ WB loan conditions in 1995 destabilized the country, contributing to the resurgence of right-wing death squads and Aristide's overthrow in 2004.

US threat potential underlies the workings of global financial institutions. Voting in the IMF and WB is weighted by contribution, with the US possessing virtual veto power despite its declining share of the total contribution – which, under 17 percent of IMF reserves, is still three times greater than the contribution of any other member state. By informal agreement, the president of the WB is a US citizen. We should therefore not be surprised if the IMF and the WB (which have become increasingly integrated) pursue agendas that align closely with US interests.

Because the IMF and WB are so dependent on the US for funding, the US Treasury Department is allowed to exercise considerable oversight regarding the issuance and structuration of loans. In 1984 and in 1991, the US Treasury Department threatened to hold back WB funding in opposing loans to nonprivate ventures in developing countries (Gwen 1994: 56, 64, 75; cited by Miller 2010: 135). From the 1960s to the 1980s the Treasury Department's threat to withhold WB funding, often against strong resistance from other WB members, forced the WB to deny loan requests made on behalf of Allende's Chile, Sandanista Nicaragua, and Communist Vietnam, even while acceding to similar requests by such notoriously corrupt, authoritarian regimes as Marcos' Philippines, Somoza's Nicaragua, and Mobutu's Zaire (Miller 2010: 136). Such

---

[7] Figures cited for 2016–2017 are taken from the homepage of *Foreignassistance.gov*.
[8] World Bank *World Development Indicators 2003*, Table 6.9. Citing this report Miller (2010: 289 n62) notes that other donors tied only 20 percent of their aid.

blatant coercion of the WB by the United States in pursuit of its geopoli-
tical interests was expected and demanded from the earliest days of the
WB. The WB's program authorizing low interest, deferred payment loans
to developing countries, the International Development Association
(IDA), was created at the urging of the US as an alternative to a similar
UN fund, the Special United Nations Fund for Economic Development,
which was not subject to US control. In general, countries that run afoul of
US foreign policy objectives do not receive loans.[9]

The "Washington Consensus" represents a relatively new foreign policy initiative that has impacted IMF, WB, and WTO policy. The Bretton
Woods Conference (1944) that led to the establishment of the IMF, WB,
and GATT (forerunner of the WTO) as engines for global development
was dominated by the Keynesian economic thinking of the time, which
held that economic development would require government regulation of
markets and, more importantly, government economic stimulation involving guaranteed income supports, low taxes, low interest loans, and the
like (Kapur, et al. 1997: 155).[10] According to former Senior Vice President
and Chief Economist of the World Bank, Joseph Stiglitz (2002a), this
expansionary economic vision gave way to a very different neo-liberal
perspective in the 1980s, chiefly under pressure from the United States and
its G-7 allies in Europe. The justification for the new policy was that the
old regime of unconditional financial assistance under the auspices of local
government economic intervention in Latin America and elsewhere had
not stimulated sufficient development, and indeed had protected inefficient state-supported monopolies that benefited a very small group of
political insiders. Corruption and excess spending by authoritarian governments, along with the oil crisis of the late seventies, contributed to a
combination of indebtedness, inflation, and economic instability. The
antidote to this malaise, according to Anne Kruger, World Bank Chief
Economist at the time, was a dose of neoclassical economic fundamentalism: ending price controls for agricultural products in order to stimulate
food production and rural development; reducing the power of unions
and ending minimum wage laws; eliminating artificially low interest rates

---

[9] Kapur, et. al., *World Bank*, i. History, p. 155.
[10] The apparent success of the New Deal inspired a generation of economists, most notably
Paul Rosenstein-Rodan, Ragnar Nurkse, W. Arthur Lewis, Walt Rostow, and Albert
Hirschman, to advocate a "big push" of government-stimulated economic "take-off" as a
move away from traditional subsistence farming to surplus-generating manufacturing
and industry (dual sector model), capital accumulation, higher investment, and consumption (Goldin 2016: 23–27).

so as to encourage more savings and more efficient investments; reducing government economic intervention, coupled with market deregulation; and encouraging government downsizing and privatization of public services. Imposing this new market-driven model of development on borrowing nations led to the issuance of conditional loans attached to good governance (movement toward respecting human rights, establishing accountable government, and eliminating corruption) and structural adjustments, including devaluation of local currency to enhance exports, the elimination of subsidies and tariffs to encourage imports and penetration of foreign investment, and the integration of local financial institutions with the global banking system to guarantee financial stability.[11]

Properly designed and equitably enforced, "good government" loan conditions – had they been taken seriously by the WB – might have provided some ethical balance to the more rigorously enforced neo-liberal conditions. These latter conditions, especially those requiring the elimination of protective tariffs and quotas, proved to be more profitable for American businesses, whose technological superiority and, in the case of agribusiness especially, reliance on government subsidies, enabled them to quickly dominate the newly opened markets, sometimes to the point of driving local producers out of business. Surprisingly, the economic contraction experienced by developing nations that were forced to endure these policies did not lead to significant changes in IMF/WB policy.[12]

---

[11] Beginning in the 1990s the WB's use of a Country Policy Institutional Assessment (CPIA) in developing a Poverty Reduction Strategy Paper (PRSP) in tandem with NGOs and governments of low-income countries relied on a multidimensional index that referenced low corruption and good governance as well as adherence to structural policies as conditions of well-being vital to assessing loan applications. (Such conditions are unilaterally imposed by the IMF prior to developing a PRSP.) A study for the WB (Bedoya 2005: 187, 192) found that 45 percent of all legally binding loan conditions focused on structural policies in comparison to 25 percent for anticorruption and rule of law policies related to good government and public sector management. The study found that what mattered most was adherence to structural conditions.

[12] By 1995 thirty-seven sub-Saharan countries had received structural adjustment loans. GNI per capita in the region bottomed out at $482 in 2002, the year the programs were terminated, from $668 in 1980 (Goldin 2016: 34). According to a comparative study of IMF-adjusted versus non-IMF-adjusted countries (Przeworski and Vreeland 2000: 399–402), IMF structural adjustment programs lowered annual GDP by an average of 1.53 percentage points. Another study of ninety-eight IMF-adjusted countries that were in full compliance with all loan conditions replicated this finding (Dreher 2006: 779). According to William Easterly (2001: 5), "the effect of structural adjustment loans on the number of poor [falling below the threshold of $2 per day] was an increase in 14 million." This fact explains the "IMF" riots that have occurred in half of IMF-adjusted countries. For further discussion of these points, see Miller (2010: 138–40).

Although staying the course was justified on the grounds that it would take time for economic reforms to work as expected, Stiglitz himself offers a different explanation why staying the course seemed logical (Stiglitz 2002b: 244): the IMF and WB report to finance ministers and banking elites from the US, the EU, and other industrialized countries. They reflect their thinking and the interests of the developed world, not the thinking and interests of their clients. The interest of developing nations to become equal partners in the global arena – an interest officially endorsed by all parties to the new global contract – does not converge with the interest of developed countries to maintain neo-colonial relationships of economic dependency.[13] Although developed nations would stand to benefit from the growth of emerging markets (as they have in the case of China and India), they also depend on exploiting cheap resources and cheap labor in the developing world for the maintenance of their own economies. This contradiction is projected onto international relations. The professed desire of the US government for peace among free and equal nations finds its limit in that government's desire to project its geopolitical power over countries whose weakness and dependency render them easily malleable to US interests in maintaining its unchallenged global supremacy.[14]

The WTO is another institution that has, until recently, reflected the dominant business interests shaping US trade policy.[15] All countries

---

[13] Raul Prebisch, along with Hans Singer, pioneered the "structuralist" critique of the neoclassical view of comparative advantage. This critique argued that developing countries were at a structural disadvantage in trading with developed countries, such that they would be locked into a spiral of decline and dependency. Because developing countries were relegated to the periphery as suppliers of primary resources to the industrial center, Prebisch – who was later appointed as Secretary General of the newly created United Nations Conference on Trade and Development – recommended a developmental policy of import substitution (Goldin 2016: 27–29).

[14] Despite the multilateralism that has marked President Obama's foreign policy, few would dispute the imperial pretensions embedded in a September 30, 2001 Quadrennial Defense Review Report (Washington DC: DoD) that includes among the enduring national interests to be secured by military force the "vitality and productivity of the global economy" and "access to key markets and strategic resources." President George Bush later reminded an audience in attendance at a 2002 West Point graduation ceremony that "America has, and intends to keep, military strengths beyond challenge."

[15] Most decisions in the WTO, with the exception of those made by the Appellate Body involving suit resolution, are made by consensus, but the democratic equality among member states obscures the powerful veto wielded by the United States in decisions that it disagrees with. Not surprisingly, the Uruguay Round of GATT negotiations (1986–1994) that culminated in the creation of the WTO reflected a US preference for trade liberalization and intellectual property protection. A more development-centered approach to

depend on trade, and few countries can afford to forgo favored trade status with countries that have signed on to agreements under the auspices of the WTO, which reflects a general US orientation toward free trade linked to strong protection of intellectual property rights.[16] As I noted above, market deregulation coupled with export production was a key condition of IMF/WB lending which paralleled the dominant philosophy within the US backed WTO regime. The removal of protective tariffs and government subsidies as a condition for trade, however, has not been evenly demanded in all cases, and this has especially hurt developing countries. The opening up of developing markets in these countries to foreign competition from large-scale, high-tech businesses has on the whole been devastating to them.

US support for trade-related policies that were eventually adopted by the WTO, such as the Agreement on Trade-Related Aspects of Intellectual Property Rights (TRIPS), has enabled American-based pharmaceuticals and businesses to retain exclusive monopolies over both products and processes, which in turn has inflated the cost of drugs and other vital technologies, much to the detriment of poor countries. Thanks in part to the enormous value added to high tech commodities in comparison to raw resources – not to mention licensing fees for foreign production and distribution and the huge markups in artificially inflated pricing sustained by monopoly patents – trade between industrial countries and the developing world has caused global wealth to flow from South to North, thus perpetuating colonial dependency under a less imperial veneer.[17]

trade, which has met resistance from US pharmaceutical and agricultural interests, forms the basis of the Doha Round of WTO Ministerial Conferences initiated in 2001 (see note 47).

[16] For example, in 2005 India was forced by its 1994 agreement with the WTO to abandon its production of generic pharmaceuticals, which India's patent protection of processes but not products had served to promote. The WTO's patent extension to products as well as processes cannot be justified on simple utilitarian grounds as advancing risky investments in costly research that enhances the life of the poor, since research is overwhelmingly skewed toward developing products that are desired by and affordable to affluent consumers. As for the standard argument that patents protect property rights, Pogge (2008: 226–28) deftly refutes the "natural rights" argument supporting ownership of "types" (similar products made by different processes) as distinct from "tokens" (identical products made by identical processes) that some have given in support of extending patents to product types.

[17] Thanks to TRIPS, developing countries have been forced to pay $60 billion in licensing fees for the use of technologies and pharmaceuticals. This figure – almost half the $136 billion in aid poor countries receive from rich donor countries each year – is dwarfed by the more than $1 trillion (as estimated in 2013 by Global Financial Integrity) developing countries lose each year in tax revenue to illicit capital flows (including tax avoidance

Given the advantages in trade enjoyed by all industrialized countries in their dealings with the developing world, it might be more accurate to portray the WTO regime as less an instrument of US foreign policy than a regime of multinational corporate rule that benefits rich nations – and mainly rich people, no matter their nationality – at the expense of their poorer trading partners. Indeed, the economies of developed nations (such as those within the EU) that make up the bulk of US trading partners do not depend on US trade as such. Nor, for that matter, do the economies of many developing countries. However, this is not the case for the smaller economies of Central America and the Caribbean basin. For example, the $3.4 billion in goods Nicaragua exported to the United States in 2015 constituted a third of its entire GDP. Given its dependence on US trade, the second-poorest country in the Western Hemisphere had little choice but to accept the CAFTA-DR trade agreement that was put into force in 2006. Although the US had already eliminated duties on goods imported from Nicaragua in compliance with the Caribbean Basin Initiative, CAFTA-DR required Nicaragua to lift duties on 80 percent of US industrial and consumer goods. Since 2015, duties and quotas on US apparel and fabric have been eliminated and duties that were levied on fifty percent of US agricultural goods are scheduled to be phased out by 2025. Altogether, CAFTA-DR has increased bilateral trade between the US and Nicaragua by nearly 70 percent without lowering Nicaragua's poverty. Nicaraguan farmers have been displaced by the introduction of subsidized US agricultural goods, job-growth in free trade zones has been counterbalanced by low wages and sub-standard working conditions in the predominantly US–based textile manufacturing sector, and CAFTA-DR's Investor-State Dispute Settlement Resolution provision has enabled private corporations to sue the Nicaraguan government for loss of profits stemming from environmental regulations, with the result that 30 percent of Nicaraguan territory is legally zoned for largely unregulated mining (Perez-Rocha and Paley 2014).

In sum, the global economy is a coercive system in which the United States and its partners in the developed world leverage their power in imposing costs on poorer, less powerful nations while extracting advantages for themselves. Although there has been resistance to the Washington

schemes that benefit multinational corporations), 55 percent of which ends up in developed countries and another 45 percent of which ends up in offshore financial centers. Finally, poor countries pay rich countries $600 billion a year to service their debt (Hickel 2017).

Consensus on the part of Andean nations, which in the 1960s formed their own bank, the Development Bank of Latin America (Corporacíon Andina de Fomento [CAF]), to bypass stringent WB rules on infrastructure loans, and even more impressively, by a new bloc of powerful nations – the so-called BRICS alliance composed of Brazil, Russia, China, India, and South Africa – there has not been a decisive challenge to it. The BRICS agreement in 2014 to establish a New Development Bank (NDB) as an alternative to the IMF and WB, whose lending conditions for building infrastructure and other urgently needed development projects in the developing world (emergency assistance, funding for basic social services, funding to conflict-ridden countries, etc.) they deemed to be too strict and insensitive to social costs, reflect their growing share in the global economy: they comprise over one fifth of the global economy but only eleven percent of IMF votes. The NDB is a potentially important development given the fact that South-South trade now exceeds North-South trade by $2.2 trillion. However, it is too early to tell how successful the NDB will be in counteracting IMF/WB hegemony. China's astonishing success in reducing poverty speaks to its rising global leadership but its dominant role in the BRICS alliance is problematic – its economy is larger than the combined economies of its partners – and its undervalued yuan has been criticized by Brazilian and Indian central bankers (Desai and Vreeland 2014).

Aside from possible challenges to its hegemony, it might be argued that the IMF/WB/WTO regime cannot be coercive because it is embraced by the leaders and economic elites in many developing countries. But the question arises whether the economic benefits from neoliberal policy that flow to elites in developing countries outweigh the costs imposed on the vast majority of the world's poor, who often have little say in their government's policies and feel constrained to leave family and community in search of any opportunities they can find. Even if by recent WB calculations there are fewer people living in extreme poverty today than there were ten years ago, the Washington Consensus has arguably not hastened the reduction of poverty faster than other proposed alternatives.

CONTRACTARIAN DUTIES AND THE MORAL BURDENS OF EMPIRE

Realists infer from the self-aggrandizing behavior exhibited in international relations that the global injustices I have laid out above are (and perhaps should be) irrelevant to leaders of states exclusively seeking to maximize their nation's wealth and power vis-à-vis other states. This image of the world as a zero-sum game contradicts the stated desire of government officials, acting on the moral demands of their subjects, to cooperate for mutual advantage in securing lasting peace, if nothing more. The demand for peaceful, fair, and fully voluntary cooperation explains why a social contract account of global justice appears so attractive in comparison to realist accounts that reduce economic and interstate relations to self-contained systems of strategic interaction. When seen from this moral perspective, my summary description of the global economy as a *political* economy elevates the political duty to create just international relations wherein domination and coercion are minimized. It may be, as Rawls says (1999a: 6–7), that eliminating the "great evils of human history" including "starvation and poverty" will have to begin with eliminating war, civil strife, and political oppression. But it is equally true, as the 1968 Medellín Conference of Latin American Bishops concluded, that "underdevelopment . . . is an unjust situation which promotes tensions [including those between classes and arising from internal colonialism] that conspire against peace."[18]

The nexus between imperial dominion and "internal colonialism" specifically redirects our attention away from global duties associated with beneficence. It also, however, directs our attention beyond the contractarian political duties associated with human rights and norms of economic fairness outlined by Rawls.[19] As Richard Miller persuasively

---

[18] The subsection entitled "Peace" of the Bishop's report links tensions arising from internal colonialism to "international tensions and external neo-colonialism." The bishops include among the economic facts pertaining to the latter developing countries' loss of control over their own domestic economies, the growing distortion of international commerce reflected in the depreciation of raw resources in relation to manufactured goods, the rapid flight of economic and human capital, the use of corporate tax evasion strategies, the increasing debt owed to international lending institutions that is borne by developing countries, and the power exercised by international monopolies and the "international imperialism of money."

[19] Rawls (1999a: 41–43) underscores the importance of fair trade and the justice of "larger and smaller peoples [making] larger and smaller contributions and [accepting] proportionately larger and smaller returns" in the global economy as a whole. Such inequalities, Rawls adds, are unjust if they do not advance "the many ends that peoples share," including protecting a human right to subsistence and, more importantly, ensuring that all nations do not fall below a threshold of economic development sufficient to sustain a vibrant political culture. Accordingly, Rawls endorses the fairness of a "free competitive trading scheme [that] is to everyone's mutual advantage" only on the condition that "wealthier nations will not try to monopolize the market, or aspire to form a cartel, or act as an oligopoly." He follows this assertion with the recommendation that "[s]hould these cooperative organizations have unjustified distributive effects between peoples, these

argues, imperial dominion imposes special duties on the citizens of the United States and other developed countries to not only repair the damage inflicted on developing countries under their imperial domination but to care for the most vulnerable inhabitants in those countries by improving their lives, in much the same way that any fully just government, pursuant to Rawls's difference principle, has a duty to improve the lives of its most vulnerable citizens before improving the lives of its other citizens.

would have to be corrected and taken into account by the duty of assistance" (42–43). So, besides duties to respect and protect human rights and "ensure fair trade" – the accumulated results of which, over the course of time, may produce oligopolies and other unfair and coercive trade conditions – Rawls also stipulates a stringent duty on the part of developed countries to assist burdened societies that lack the economic means and political culture to become "well-ordered." The aim of this duty is to help burdened societies achieve a level of good government (noncorrupt, accountable, human rights respecting, but not necessarily liberal democratic in the Western sense of the term) and economic well-being proportional to local standards but higher than subsistence, capable of supporting and sustaining a modestly educated citizenry composed of men and women. The duty to assist burdened nations ends once a threshold of well-orderedness is achieved. Rawls contrasts this limited duty with a duty to continually raise the consumption levels of poor nations to offset growing inequalities between rich and poor countries, a duty that would follow from extending his domestic principle of economic justice (the difference principle), applicable to the internal economies of liberal democratic societies, to the international arena. Criticism of Rawls's hesitance to extend his difference principle globally (or to propose a stronger principle of global distributive justice) by Beitz, Pogge, and others focuses on Rawls's methodological presumption of self-contained, sovereign nations, his neglect of imperialism and neocolonial dependency in shaping a global "basic structure" comprising a quasi-political-legal system of global governance, and his underestimation of the negative side effects that attend large global inequalities between countries. Although concerns about Rawls's failure to address the impact of global economic inequality on the unequal distribution of global political power are sound (and actually repeat Rawls's own concerns about the nexus between economic and political inequality in liberal democracies) they do not refute Rawls's central insight, especially pertinent in an age of global warming and diminished resources, that elevating all nations to the production and consumption capabilities of Europe, Japan, Canada, and the United States through redistribution of global GDP is not necessary to achieve a just and peaceful world. See Beitz (1999: 144–45, 149, 152) for his argument that the global economy comprises a nonvoluntary basic structure to which the difference principle is applicable, albeit to representative individuals rather than to states; and Pogge (2008: 285 note 168), where Rawls (1999a: 108, 117–18) is criticized for endorsing "explanatory nationalism," or blaming poverty on domestic factors such as poor political culture, government disrespect for human rights, patriarchal discrimination against women, absence of industry, and failed population policy instead of unjust global institutions. Elsewhere Pogge (2008: 110–114) criticizes Rawls's "double standard" in failing to see that the domestic context in which liberal democratic standards of justice (such as the difference principle) apply is not essentially different from a global context in which similar principles ought to apply.

This quasi-cosmopolitan method of moral reasoning is undoubtedly counterintuitive. All things being equal, the duties American citizens have toward compatriots have priority over their duties to foreigners, but all things are not equal. Duties to compatriots do not outweigh duties to respect human rights and they do not outweigh duties to compensate for harms done to others for American benefit.[20] Even less do they outweigh duties to vulnerable foreigners who fall within the purview of the American empire. Because of their political – and not merely economic – relationship to American citizens, the global poor who are subjected to US governance and who contribute, willingly or not, to the political and economic processes that sustain it, have a right to demand roughly the same treatment from that government that it extends (or should extend) to its own citizens. This suggests that US citizens (especially the least vulnerable among them) have a duty to refrain from improving their own lives without improving the lives of vulnerable foreigners with whom they are economically and politically related. Given the economics of global warming and global migration, they might even be obligated (going beyond Rawls's difference principle) to sacrifice some of their affluent standard of living for the sake of improving the lives of these others, so long as the latter – assuming they are fortunate enough to live in approximately uncorrupt liberal democracies – take political responsibility for improving their own lives as well, which might include extending full rights and opportunities to women, making available contraception and family planning, lobbying for higher wages and better working conditions, and promoting less destructive and globally sustainable economies.

[20] In addition to a positive duty to help those in poverty, Pogge defends a negative duty, which can be understood in contractarian or consequentialist terms, to refrain from imposing the current global economic regime and to replace it with one that nullifies three harmful effects on the poor: the imposition of a disadvantageous starting point stemming from a common and violent history of colonialism, the denial of a proportionate share of the world's natural resources requisite for leading a minimally flourishing life, and the coercive imposition of rules to which the poor could not have freely and rationally accepted as being in their best interest. Pogge's statement of this argument seems somewhat unclear, at times suggesting that any one of the three conditions noted above suffices to justify the negative duty in question (Pogge 2008: 205) while at other times (215) implying that all three conditions must be met, so that no harm is caused if either the current regime came about fairly, the poor have access to a proportional share of resources, or they could have rationally consented to it as in their best interest. In my opinion, however, the rational consent of the poor is both necessary and sufficient to justify the current regime, while neither of the other conditions is necessary or sufficient in this regard.

Miller does not address the responsibilities of the global poor, who are not, after all, merely passive victims of imperial domination but who partly contribute, through their own choices, to perpetuating practices that worsen their own lives (and the lives of others). Instead, he notes that the special duties that citizens of the US and other European have toward the global poor who are subjected to their governments' imperial dominion last as long as empire exists. Should empire and its quasi-political coercion cease to exist, these special duties would cease to exist as well.[21]

Given Miller's apparent acceptance of the realist approach to international relations, which sees global politics as a power struggle among sovereign states, he seems uncertain whether the US empire will (or should) be replaced by another (perhaps more benevolent) empire (China, say) or allow itself to evolve into a "global social democracy" wherein sovereign states will cooperate with one another in a nondomineering spirit of "civic friendship."[22]

Miller's global social democracy, like his analysis of global empire, raises serious questions about the normative salience of political borders and nationalism in general. After all, if the global poor are subjected to life-altering policies made in Washington, should they not (following the principle of discourse ethics) have a right to democratic representation in formulating, discussing, and ratifying those policies? But Miller never develops this argument. He never asserts that the very political framework in which issues of global justice arise – the Westphalian system of sovereign nation states – is illegitimate on its face, when seen from a quasi-

---

[21] Duties of repair owed by inhabitants of former colonial powers in Europe and North American to the descendants of slaves and colonial peoples inhabiting their former colonies would remain as before. Leaving aside the difficult question regarding the determination of appropriate compensatory remedies, it is at least clear that innocent beneficiaries of past harms have a minimal duty to refrain from exploiting their ill-gotten historical advantages in wealth, social standing, and bargaining power in extracting concessions from the descendants of slaves and colonial subjects whose bargaining disadvantage stems in part from this colonial legacy. For, it is unlikely that the history of slavery and colonialism benefited the descendants of slaves and colonial subjects more than any other conceivable counterfactual history of European discovery (or nondiscovery) might have. Indeed, even if we assume that the real history of European contact with non-Europeans produced the best possible outcome for the descendants of slaves and colonial peoples, it remains the case that this legacy and its outcome would still be stained with the mark of profound (and by today's standards, criminal), injustice calling for some kind of reparation (or forward-looking reform). See Introduction, note 26.

[22] A Chinese empire might be more benevolent than an American empire. With the possible exception of Tibet, China has not occupied a foreign territory and it has not used its economic power to exploit other countries.

cosmopolitan standpoint of moral impartiality, be it a Rawlsian veil of ignorance or a Habermasian ideal speech situation.[23] Nor does he strengthen his argument for global social democracy by appeal to the fact that the global environment is a global public good to which all have an equal stake in preserving. For this reason, he does not take his defense of global social democracy beyond moral platitudes about civic friendship among sovereign states, and he does not argue for stronger forms of global governance that subordinate "sovereign states" to an already existing *institutional* equivalent of global social democracy, as I propose to do in Chapter 6.

FREE VERSUS FAIR TRADE

In what follows I propose to divide the two considerations raised by the expression "political economy" and train our thoughts on economic justice, specifically as this term applies to global trade. That said, global trade remains political insofar as what appears to be free and fair trade from a neoliberal perspective is experienced as coercive and unfair from the perspective of the global poor.

By "coercive" and "unfair," then, I do not mean legally imposed by an imperial hegemon in order to advance its interests to the detriment of other nations' interests. As I argued above, this sense of "coercive" and "unfair" does apply to the current global trade regime with the qualification that the line separating agreements that are self-serving and unilaterally imposed from agreements that are reciprocal and voluntarily accepted is often very fine. That said, we can imagine that the current global trade regime could have originated innocently and maintained its political neutrality over time, as Locke imagined the emergence of a monetized commercial economy, by "tacit consent" and for the sake of mutual benefit, with or without foreknowledge of its stratifying tendencies.

According to Iris Young, this *prepolitical* understanding of social structuration as an unplanned outcome of actions spanning centuries relieves the global economy of much of its colonial legacy and imperial

---

[23] Miller frequently invokes a global application of the veil of ignorance in discussing how global duties (especially sacrifices) are to be apportioned among developed and developing countries without noticing that this "quasi-cosmopolitan" extension of Rawls's argument is virtually indistinguishable from the full-blown cosmopolitanism he and Rawls reject.

distortion. Duties to compensate for structural injustices that place some persons in disadvantageous positions of birth make little sense when no discrete agent can be blamed for the harm.[24] Nonetheless, there remain forward-looking duties based on *social connectedness* alone, which makes Locke's prepolitical understanding of the social contract particularly applicable to global economic structures that have yet to fully evolve centralized forms of international legal regulation and enforcement. The global economy connects persons through relations of global interdependence and mutual effect, so that all share responsibility for structural injustice in differing degrees and respects. Consequently, all have duties to mitigate this injustice, which "put[s] large categories of persons under a systematic threat of domination or deprivation of means to develop and exercise their capacities" (Young 2006: 170).

In this apolitical scenario, the question still arises whether, left to its own devices and freed from the distorting effects of political domination, a system of unregulated "free trade" would likely produce, more than any other feasible alternative, unequal or inefficient distributions that would endanger the agency and basic well-being of some persons. If, following Pogge, we accept a baseline of agential development as essential to a morally acceptable respect for dignified life, then not improving the lives of fellow participants in the global social contract who fall well below that level when it is feasible to do so without imposing significant costs on ourselves amounts to not fully respecting their human right to a decent life. Not only do we harm the global poor (and violate their right to life) by not improving their situation, but we do so even when we improve their situation less than what is fully demanded of us. Moreover, as Miller and Honneth note, a free-trade regime that fully guarantees the enjoyment of everyone's human right to life is still unjust if, more than other feasible alternatives, it engenders social inequalities that facilitate exploitation, domination, and coercion of some by others.

Does a free trade regime most efficiently mitigate these human rights and social justice shortfalls? The reductive neoliberal response to this question is that such a regime should not be judged on whether it meets these moral desiderata but solely on whether it maximizes global wealth. A less reductive neoliberal response is that, in principle, when left to its own devices, a free trade regime is the most efficient system for mitigating

---

[24] However, models of alternative liability based on market share (or some measure of benefit resulting from a discernible harm) that dispense with precise determinations of agent causation do often suffice to assess compensatory remedies.

these injustices *in the long run.*[25] If we assume that poverty, economic inequality, and the production of negative externalities (specifically, environmental costs that are not directly calculated in production and consumption) diminish the agency of the poor and render them more vulnerable to economic and political coercion, then (following neoliberal ideology) we must also assume that a system of free trade will more likely reduce poverty, inequality, and negative externalities better than any other system. Notice that the simple neoliberal response,[26] that reduction of poverty is all that matters, although highlighting what is arguably the most urgent agency-threatening injustice, ignores the fact that poverty is deeply interwoven with economic and political inequality, gender and racial discrimination, and global climate change. Thus, a simple reduction in poverty unaccompanied by reductions in the other injustices will be difficult to achieve, and to the extent that it is achievable, will at most enhance welfare agency at the expense of empowerment agency.

In the final analysis, poverty reduction will depend on radical democratic reforms that only tangentially touch on the issue of free trade, including the eventual replacement of corrupt authoritarian governments that trade their nation's patrimony for goods that exclusively benefit themselves (such as the military hardware requisite to maintain their dictatorial rule).[27] However, to simplify my discussion of trade justice, let me begin by focusing on poverty reduction. Rawls, Miller, Beitz, and Pogge all criticize the current trade regime for contributing to poverty, or at least not mitigating it as quickly and thoroughly as it could if it were suitably reformed. They blame the injustice of a regime that permits powerful countries to subsidize domestic producers while at the same time imposing quotas and tariffs on imports from poorer countries. They accordingly assume that a trade regime that eliminated subsidies,

---

[25] Whether it is right to implement such a regime if doing so necessarily exacerbates such injustices in the short term is an important question I shall leave aside.

[26] Jagdish Bhagwati (2010: 54, 67), for instance, argues that the only decisive factor in reducing poverty is growth, which he believes free trade will best promote, and that the WB's measurement of inter-and intrastate inequality is misplaced.

[27] See Pogge's proposals (2008: chapter 6) for democratizing governments, including his proposals for eliminating the borrowing and resource extraction privileges enjoyed by corrupt regimes. Pogge has no illusions regarding how difficult it would be to implement these necessary reforms – especially in comparison to the relatively costless Global Resources Dividend tax that he proposes to levy on the extraction of nonrenewable and otherwise environmentally costly resources. Wealthy nations depend on strategic resources extracted in the developing world and will be loath to jeopardize their access to them by boycotting or otherwise penalizing corrupt, authoritarian client states.

tariffs, and quotas for *all* trading partners would not only be fairer but would result in considerable exchange flowing back to developing countries, perhaps twice the amount necessary to eliminate extreme global poverty (Pogge 2008: 22).[28]

Leaving aside how much of this added exchange would actually trickle down to the poor, is their assumption correct? Empirical evidence shows that developing countries that drastically reduce their tariffs and quotas from very high levels to moderately low levels have recorded higher rates of *growth*.[29]Some of this growth has trickled down to those poor who benefit from more cheaply priced imports *and* are able to find employment in an export industry. Research shows, however, that a major obstacle to overall poverty reduction is loss of jobs in globally uncompetitive sectors, coupled with the high cost – financial as well as human – in relocating in high growth regions and healthy economic sectors (Topalova 2007: 291–336). Minimum income supports that might cushion the costs of relocating would not affect the human cost associated with being uprooted from community, family, and way of life.

I think that these human costs, unavoidable as they are under the present economic order, could be significantly reduced under a different economic order (see below). That said, my present concern is not to

[28] As Goldin wryly remarks (Goldin 2016: 134), "the average Swiss cow benefits from subsidies which are much greater than the daily income of over 300 million Africans." Exporters in developing countries face double the tariffs that their counterparts in developing countries face. Successful implementation of the Doha Round of Trade Negotiations, which proposes lifting trade barriers, would yield $160 billion in global income gains with more than a quarter going to developing nations (Goldin 2016: 136). Leveling the playing field would save the average consumer in the EU and US over $1000 a year and would reduce the concentration of farm land ownership geared toward environmentally unsustainable monocropping. That said, leveling the playing field might not be fair to developing countries. Developing countries rely on tariffs more than developed countries do to protect their vulnerable economies and generate tax revenue in economies dominated by underground commercial transactions. Therefore Stiglitz and Miller, for instance, qualify their support for free trade by urging developed countries to eliminate tariffs and quotas with respect to imports from undeveloped countries while allowing the latter to retain tariffs and quotas vis-à-vis developed countries, until their domestic industries can compete freely and fairly in the international marketplace (Stiglitz and Charleton 2007: 76–78, 188–89).
[29] Over the past thirty years, countries like India, which reduced its import tariffs from 80 percent to 30 percent in the 1990s, experienced greater growth than countries that did not, much of it caused by importing cheaper production inputs that were used to restructure inefficient industries. Protectionism, however, is on the rise and some developing countries are threatening to raise tariffs higher than the permissible WTO limit for developing member countries (India has threatened to raise its current average tariff 15 percent) (Estevadeordal and Taylor 2008).

defend protectionism and refute free trade but to question a single neo-liberal shibboleth: Absolute freedom of trade mutually benefits all trading partners. To expose this assumption for what it is – an ideology that is not supported by the facts – we need to bear in mind that economic science as it classically evolved in the nineteenth and twentieth centuries was based on rational (largely mathematical) abstractions and oversimplifications. The classical defense of free trade begins with the defense of markets: responsiveness to supply and demand provides the most efficient mechanism for establishing the costs (prices) and quantities of commodities. If we assume that producers and consumers are rational value maximizers, free exchanges are at least Pareto efficient, in that no one is hurt and someone is benefited in every exchange. However, in order to explain the supreme value of international trade for *mutual benefit* economists appeal to the principle of comparative advantage.[30]

If countries A and B each produce commodities a and b, but A produces a at half the cost that B does, and B produces b at have the cost that A does, then it will be mutually advantageous for both countries to specialize in what each produces most efficiently (a in the case of A, b in the case of B) and trade with the other country to obtain what it produces less efficiently (b in the case of A and a in the case of B). Furthermore, for trade to occur between A and B, it is not necessary that each has an absolute advantage in producing something more cheaply than the other. It suffices that each has comparative advantages in different areas of production within their respective domestic economies that make it feasible for each to specialize in advantageous forms of production and trade for things produced less advantageously. Free trade thus allows countries to exploit comparative advantages for achieving greater mutual benefits than if they had not traded at all.[31]

---

[30] See Aaron Crowe (*International Trade: A Justice Approach.* Dissertation. Loyola University Chicago, 2014).

[31] Using David Ricardo's famous example (Ricardo 2007: 818), suppose that Portugal spends 90 hours of labor to produce a unit of cloth and 80 hours of labor to produce a unit of wine, while England spends 100 hours and 120 hours making the same quantities of these goods, respectively. Portugal has an absolute advantage over England in producing both wine and cloth, so it has no obvious incentive to buy either of these products from England. However, the situation is different once we note that England has a comparative advantage over Portugal in its production of cloth (which, in Portugal, is relatively costly to produce in comparison to wine) and Portugal has a comparative advantage over England in its production of wine (which in England is relatively costly to produce in comparison to cloth). Given these comparative advantages, England could import wine from Portugal profitably by exchanging 8/9 unit of cloth for one unit of wine (the exchange rate of cloth for wine in Portugal), because in England that unit of wine is

The principle of comparative advantage has been qualified to take into account multilateral trade involving more complex factors of production. Although the existence of intraindustry trade stands as an exception to the principle, which in any case does not predict actual trade relations in any specific instance, the principle does seem to explain, in theory at least, why it is advantageous for countries to consume less and export more of those products which they are comparatively more efficient in producing. It also explains why the IMF encourages developing countries, whose technological inefficiencies render them at an absolute disadvantage in producing almost any product, to exploit comparative advantages they have in certain sectors of production, such as agriculture and mining that, if undertaken more extensively (and cheaply) by developed countries using more efficient, high-tech methods of production, would divert too much capital away from other investment opportunities that are more lucrative to developed countries (such as pharmaceuticals).

Combining the principle of comparative advantage with the concept of opportunity costs (what a country loses when it invests in one opportunity rather than another) explains how global trade is possible between inefficient developing countries and efficient developed countries. However, in its static Ricardian formulation, the principle has limited explanatory power because it presupposes the immobility of labor and capital across borders as well as full employment and constant rates of return in growing specialized economies. More pertinent to our present concerns, the principle is of questionable value in recommending free trade as the best way to increase domestic consumption in all instances. Even in those instances in which the principle proves valuable for this purpose in the short run, it

---

worth 6/5 units of cloth (it could not profitably import cloth from Portugal, because it would have to exchange 9/8 unit of wine for one unit of cloth, which in England is worth only 5/6 units of wine). Now, given the comparative advantage that each country has with respect to the production of a single product, Portugal and England could choose to specialize in the product possessing that advantage; Instead of spending 100 hours of labor producing just 5/6 unit of wine, England could use all of its 220 hours of labor to make 2.2 units of cloth. Meanwhile, by spending 90 units of labor to produce 9/8 unit of wine, Portugal could use all of its 170 hours of labor to make 2.125 units of wine. If England trades a unit of its cloth for 5/6 to 9/8 unit of Portugal's wine – anything above 5/6 representing a net gain for England and anything below 9/8 representing a net gain for Portugal – then each country can negotiate a rate of exchange between 5/6 and 9/8 unit of wine per unit of cloth that will guarantee that each country can consume at least one unit each of wine and cloth – the rate of consumption before these countries embarked on a course of specialization and trade – and still have a surplus of cloth and wine (less than 0.2 units of cloth for England, less than 0.125 units of wine for Portugal) that it can sell for additional exchange.

does so only by encouraging developing countries to specialize in ways that render them vulnerable to coercion, dependency, market depreciation, resource depletion, environmental degradation, and human resource *underdevelopment* (especially in unskilled labor-driven economies geared toward manufacturing and resource extraction). By contrast, the principle of *competitive advantage*, which presumes labor and capital mobility, does not recommend specialization based on advantage in a single factor of production (say, a raw resource) but instead encourages productivity growth through cost saving strategies (such as efficient exploitation of cheap labor) and market expansion through flexible product innovation (differentiation) (Warf and Stutz 2007). Nevertheless, even this principle, which explains how resource-poor countries like Japan and Taiwan developed their economies by exploiting a relatively cheap but highly skilled labor force in manufacturing, does not recommend itself as an exclusive strategy for developing countries, for some of the very reasons that explain why the principle of comparative advantage fails in this regard.

Historically, virtually every developed country today relied on some form of restricted trade – mercantilism, economic nationalism, etc. – to protect its infant industries from foreign competition and expand domestic production and consumption.[32] Classical economic theory from Smith to the present day, however, touts free trade not only as an ideal to be striven for under more felicitous conditions but as a preferred policy for increasing domestic conception under all conditions. The principle of comparative advantage ostensibly explains why this is so.

In light of economic history, it bears repeating that empirical support for the free-trade development hypothesis is hardly conclusive: growth (if it occurs) does not equal development across *all* regions and sectors.[33]

---

[32] 19th Century US policy, like the policies of its continental European counterparts, was staunchly protectionist, opposing British support for free trade. More recently, South Korea and Taiwan, benefiting from their geopolitical alliance with the US during the Cold War, protected their infant manufacturing sector while simultaneously pursuing an aggressive export policy. Similar policies in other Southeast Asian countries, which relied on authoritarian suppression of labor unions to increase savings and investment, explain why Malaysia saw average incomes rise 3.5 faster than incomes in the US and the G10 economies from 1970–2010. China's rise in average income was even more impressive – 7.6 times faster than comparable growth in the US (Goldin 2016: 42; Chang, 2002: 127–28).

[33] Stiglitz (2002a) notes that economic growth for Latin America during the heyday of its import-substitution policies from 1950–1960 was generally no worse and was sometimes better than economic growth following its embrace of more free-trade friendly policies.

Furthermore, thanks to the enormous comparative advantage that China has with respect to labor costs, which were once anywhere between 10 to 100 times less than labor costs in the US, it is unlikely that the higher productivity of US labor is high enough to give the US a comparative advantage in producing any product that might be exported to China.[34]

The competitive labor advantage enjoyed by China, coupled with the free mobility of capital,[35] leads Stiglitz and others to argue that in today's global economy the principle of comparative advantage is less relevant than the principle of absolute advantage. Although I have been discussing free trade in goods, it is worthwhile to reflect for a moment on the impact that the free mobility of capital has on the developing world. Because capital will flow to where the most cost-effective producers are, capital predominantly flows toward the developed world, which has an absolute advantage in technology, education, and infrastructure.[36] This may explain why some regions of the developing world, such as sub-Saharan Africa, until recently have received relatively little foreign investment.[37] Herman Daly, former senior environmental economist at the World Bank from 1988 to 1994, believes that this hypothesis explains why, from 1994 (the year the WTO regime was instituted) until 2003 eight of the world's twenty poorest countries experienced a net loss in real per capita income, while the twenty wealthiest countries experienced a net increase of 17.6 percent.

---

[34] Between 1991 and 2007, the US lost about 5.5 million manufacturing jobs, 1.5 million of them to China. However, rising labor costs in China – at $3.60/hour in the manufacturing sector–coupled with a need for less costly and more timely delivery chains has resulted in some manufacturing jobs returning to the US (Gomory 2009).

[35] The Trade Related Investment Measures Agreement (TRIMS) in force within the WTO regime resulted in the absorption of developing countries' national banks into the global banking system, which then deprived governments in these countries of much of their control over investing in local development. Furthermore, decisions to rapidly move capital destabilize smaller and weaker economies.

[36] Today Chinese imports are essentially purchased with credit in the form of US Treasury bills, which can be redeemed for US real estate, high-yield assets, and other US resources rather than US goods.

[37] Over the last decade sub-Saharan Africa, with the exception of such distressed countries as Zimbabwe, the Democratic Republic of the Congo, and the Republic of the Congo, has matched or surpassed the average global rate of growth. Driven significantly by increased global trade (especially with China) rather than intraregional trade, this growth (averaging between 4 and 6 percent on average) reflects the region's growing population, political stability, and educated workforce. That said, growth and global investment continued to be concentrated in South Africa, Nigeria, Kenya, and a few other countries, with sub-Saharan Africa accounting for a very small percentage of global trade and investment as a whole (Luce 2016).

But then how does one explain the absolute trade advantage China enjoys, with its relatively inefficient industries, in comparison to the US? According to Daly, the absolute advantage that developing countries like China enjoy vis-à-vis developed countries resides in their cheaper labor costs and cheaper factors of production overall. These factors include lax enforcement of workplace and environmental regulations that are undoubtedly costly to the workers and the people of China as a whole. But these social costs, which the Chinese government is now addressing, are negative externalities that do not figure in calculations of absolute advantage based on efficient productivity. In effect, the people of China – especially farmers who until recently had to sell their product for below market value[38] – were subsidizing inefficient industries to make them more competitive, thereby negating much of the foreign exchange they received because of them.

In sum, thanks to the greater mobility of capital over labor and goods, developing countries like China, which offer the most cost-effective (if not most efficient) conditions of production, have come to possess an absolute advantage in almost all economic sectors in comparison to their more developed counterparts.[39] The result is a "rush to the bottom," where developing countries seek to maximize their competitive advantage in offering cheap labor and unregulated resource extraction by lowering the costs associated with these factors of production relative to the costs proffered by other developing countries. The supply side economic thinking behind this strategy holds that attracting foreign investment and exchange will generate new jobs, but the result, at least when seen from a Keynesian perspective, is overall decline in wages, working conditions, and living environments among developing nations, and among wage earners in all countries. Stagnating global consumption at the bottom of the global economy threatens a global recession just as surely as environmental degradation threatens environmental and ecological crisis (Stiglitz 2009).

MARKETS AND NEGATIVE EXTERNALITIES: DEPENDENCY, ENVIRONMENTAL DEGRADATION, AND GLOBAL WARMING

I have discussed the logic of comparative advantage that undergirds belief that free trade benefits all parties, increasing national consumption and, therewith, decreasing poverty. Granting that free trade often does increase national consumption, it sometimes does so without decreasing poverty,

[38] See note 31 of the Introduction.
[39] For qualification of this claim, see note 34.

let alone inequality. I have also alluded to the hidden costs of free trade. These include transportation and transaction costs, but also costs associated with specialization: the human and material costs of abandoned ways of life, wasted human resources, and economic disempowerment vis-à-vis shifting demand from developed nations. To say that conversion to an export economy is not coerced by elites in thrall to the logic of comparative advantage and does not entail an element of agential deformation is simply wrong.

In addition to these costs, I have discussed other hidden costs associated with the negative externalities of free trade. In comparison to these externalities, the positive externalities often associated with free trade, such as expanded consumer choice and the fostering of peaceful international cooperation for mutual benefit, seem less certain and less salubrious. Environmental and ecological concerns now occupy a central place in discussions concerning the relationship between trade and development. Environmental economics is concerned with the impact that trade has on resource depletion and environmental degradation. The logic of comparative advantage has led many developing countries to specialize in the extraction of minerals and non-renewable energy resources. Reinforced by escalating tariffs in developing countries that tax refined imports, such specialization locks the domestic labor force into an economy of low-paying manual labor and underdeveloped capacitation, even as it raises concerns about the special vulnerability of these countries to resource depletion and environmental degradation.

Worries about resource depletion recall neo-Malthusian concerns about population growth (consumption) outstripping production. Malthus himself may have exaggerated the risks posed by population growth, which shows signs of leveling off, but belief that economic growth – and specifically, unlimited economic growth – is key to development and the eradication of poverty raises questions about what, if any, are the limits of growth. Today's neo-Malthusians fear that the increasing exploitation of limited or otherwise nonrenewable resources will inevitably result in diminishing marginal returns relative to costs of production.

Are they right? The absolute limit on arable land and non-renewable resources such as petroleum did not, contrary to the neo-Malthusian hypothesis, appear to cause an increase in the global price of food and nonrenewable resources, such as petroleum and industrial metals. In fact, these commodities have generally declined in price, thanks to the development of more efficient modes of high-yield agriculture, mining, etc. and the opening up of alternative energy sources.

What's good news for the world, however, is not necessarily good for developing countries. Developing countries that were encouraged by the IMF to exploit their comparative advantage in producing and exporting primary resources subsequently experienced a double loss in both non-renewable resources and foreign exchange. Having not developed other sectors of their economy, they found themselves locked into a downward spiral.[40]

Technological development and resource substitution allay some of the neo-Malthusian concerns about global resource depletion and the limits of growth, even if they do not allay concerns about the differential impact of resource depletion and declining resource prices in developing countries. Daly, for one, considers resource depletion as itself a cost charged against what is typically described as income. If "income [is] the amount you can consume in one period without affecting your ability to consume in subsequent periods [then] revenue from non-renewable natural resource extraction cannot be counted entirely as income, and the situation of these poorest countries is even worse than it appears" (Daley and Farley 2011: 382). The costs – $33 trillion annually in ecosystem services, almost half of global income (Goldin 2016: 125) – are especially high given that the excessive depletion of the world's resources to satisfy the extravagant needs of people living in affluent countries denies future generations the opportunity to achieve even modest standards of living essential to developing their agency.

Daly concedes that resource depletion can be mitigated through resource diversification and more efficient methods of consumption. However, he rejects the view that there are no natural limits to resource consumption (and economic growth): "[T]he notion that we can save the 'growth forever' paradigm by dematerializing the economy, or 'decoupling' it from resources, or substituting information for resources, is fantasy" (Daley 1996: 28). The questionable assumption in the infinite

---

[40] The 1987 UN Report of the World Commission on the Environment and Development: Our Common Future noted that developed nations' high tariffs on manufactured goods from developing countries had forced the latter to rely increasingly on their mineral and energy resources for foreign exchange. As demand for comparatively cheaper foreign imports of minerals and nonrenewable energy resources increases in the developed world, so too increases resource depletion and environmental degradation in the developing world (section 3.1). Conversely, as industrial nations develop more energy efficient forms of production lower demand for imported energy has severely decreased the foreign exchange flowing into developing countries that specialize in the energy sector. As of 2016, the collapse in the price of petroleum has had a severe impact on developing countries that are heavily dependent on petroleum exports for their foreign exchange.

substitution paradigm is that production and consumption form a neat cycle in which (high entropic, low energy) products of production – including wastes – can be recycled back into (low entropic, high energy) factors of production, without loss of low entropic resources.[41]

The problem is the same with respect to environmental degradation. Negative externalities such as pollution that are not factored into the market cost of production might not be indefinitely absorbable into earth's limited holding capacities. These externalities impose special costs on developing countries and their inhabitants, who are exposed to higher risks of disease caused by contaminated air, water, and soil. A similar "tragedy of the commons" is replicated on a global scale when considering the effects of industrial and agricultural production in generating greenhouse gas emissions. However costly it might be for the planet, climate change portends greater suffering for the world's poorest nations and poorest people, who are more adversely affected by coastal flooding, desertification, and the spread of mosquito-borne diseases. Furthermore, because they rely much more heavily on relatively cheap carbon-generated energy than their developed counterparts, developing countries bear the brunt of moving toward more eco-friendly systems of production.

TOWARD AN EFFICIENT AND JUST REDUCTION OF NEGATIVE EXTERNALITIES: MARKET STRATEGIES VERSUS GOVERNMENT REGULATION

Now, economics offers two strategies for internalizing negative environmental and ecological externalities into costs of production. One strategy involves government regulation of the production process itself, including banning harmful processes. The other relies heavily on market transactions, including paying for rights to engage in harmful processes. The former strategy appears to be a more direct and more efficient way to

---

[41] Low entropic energy resources such oil and coal contain complex hydrocarbon molecules that the production process breaks down into less complex compounds (such as CO_2 and H_2O) that become simple waste and cannot be recycled back as energy without the addition of more low-entropic energy. Low entropic raw materials such as wood, metals, and minerals do not lose their chemical structure in the production process, but are disassembled and reassembled, thereby making them non-reusable without additional disassembly and reassembly. In general, most forms of recycling are not economically or ecologically efficient. Wind, water, and solar energy are obviously exempt from this cycle. I thank Aaron Crowe for this explanation.

stop harmful processes. However, because every process – benign or
harmful – produces both social costs and social benefits, banning harmful
practices will produce new costs (such as loss of jobs). Weighing costs and
benefits of any production process is something that the market – not the
government – normally does best. Applying the market strategy, it seems
reasonable to allow producers to purchase the right to engage in harmful
activities from those who are harmed, assuming that the added cost of
purchasing the right does not make the activity less profitable than the
next best investment opportunity they could engage in; conversely, if the
producer is assigned a right to engage in harmful activity, those who are
harmed by the activity will purchase the right from the producer to
suppress that activity, so long as the cost is worth it to them. Regardless
of who is assigned the initial right, a cost-beneficial agreement satisfactory
to all sides can in principle be worked out.[42]

In cases of harmful production processes affecting third parties and
future generations – not to mention the secure enjoyment of human
rights[43] – the simple market model for transacting the social cost of
doing business is of limited application.[44] Some combination of government regulation and market transaction is therefore necessary to inter-
nalize negative environmental and ecological externalities while
maximizing flexibility and efficiency. Government can cap the amount
of carbon emissions in a given industry, while at the same time permitting
producers within that industry to purchase carbon credits from producers
who fall below the cap. Government can also impose tariffs and other
kinds of taxes on production processes that are deemed to be environmentally and ecologically unsustainable (the polluter pays principle) in order

---

[42] The argument favoring markets as the most efficient mechanism for distributing social
costs and benefits distills a line of reasoning famously developed by Ronald Coase (Coase
1960).

[43] I discuss the impact of human rights on our reasoning about ecological justice in
Chapter 5.

[44] Coase himself noted (1960: 21) that the market solution for negotiating social costs
presumes that transaction costs (legal fees, etc.) are set at zero – a fact that seldom obtains
in real life. Because of the added costs of transacting with multiple affected parties (as in
the case of industrial pollution), Coase did not deny the higher efficiency of government
imposed blanket solutions (banning polluting industries, for example) that, minus trans-
actional costs, might otherwise generate higher social costs (short-term loss of jobs).
Coase does not discuss the impact of negotiating costs and benefits on future generations,
which is pertinent to our discussion of resource depletion, environmental degradation,
and climate change, but he acknowledges that "[t]he total effect of [different social]
arrangements in all spheres of life should be taken into account in assessing 'the aesthetics
and morals' of welfare economics."

to achieve trade relations that are free of unfair subsidies (which, following Daly's analysis, attach to products produced by producers who avoid paying for the resource depletion, environmental degradation, and carbon emissions their industries produce).

Without delving into the relative efficiencies attached to different combinations of market- and government-based strategies for addressing the social costs of resource depletion, environmental degradation, and ecological change, it is apparent that a system of free trade oriented toward maximizing immediate (short-term) returns and discounting future (long-term) costs must be accompanied by environmental protections counterbalancing the hidden protectionism of production subsidized by discounting social costs (the precautionary principle). To counter the coerciveness of unilaterally conceived government protections, government should be sensitive to the full range of costs and benefits as reflected in negotiations among all affected parties.

I have argued that the political structure underlying global trade, which generates social costs that threaten the essential consumption of public goods, is coercive (and illegitimate) to the extent that it is imposed without the democratic consent of those whose basic rights are affected by it. Democratizing trade agreements requires a fundamental shift in how trade negotiations are undertaken. Stiglitz is emphatic on this point.[45] Just as he had earlier endorsed discussion and consensus-building between the IMF/WB and loan applicants in working out agreements that respected the capacity and good faith of developing nations with "proven track records" to make maximum use of loans based on intimate familiarity with local conditions (Stiglitz 2002a: 49), he and Andrew Charleton now endorse a discourse ethical approach to negotiating trade agreements in which developed nations shift their priorities from maximizing gains to themselves to helping developing countries on *their* terms (Stiglitz and Charleton 2007: 76–78).[46] Commensurate with this position, they have advanced a *market access proposal* for guiding trade negotiations that requires developed nations to open up domestic markets to exports from developing countries with smaller per capita (and smaller overall) GDP while allowing the latter to levy protective tariffs on exports from

[45] For a fuller defense of this claim see my discussion of Miller in Chapter 2.

[46] Stiglitz and Charleton stress that fair trade agreements must not only be geared toward reducing poverty in developing countries but must be fairly negotiated, taking into account historical injustices (colonialism) that render developing countries at an initial disadvantage vis-à-vis the effects of reciprocal trade liberalization and the costs of dispute settlement, technical negotiation, and implementation of trade rules.

developed countries with higher GDP. The recent renewal of the Doha Round of WTO negotiations focusing on development has resulted in several important agreements that endorse a similar agenda proposing preferential treatment for developing countries, including the elimination of escalating tariffs, used by developed countries to protect their value-added products, which forces developing nations to gear their export-driven economies toward production of raw resources and other low-skilled forms of employment (Stiglitz and Charleton 2007: 96–97).[47]

In addition to these fair trade guidelines, they urge that environmental and labor standards that have been used by developed nations to restrict exports from developing countries be excluded from negotiations unless they impinge on human rights violations (including violations of collective bargaining rights) and production processes that have been subsidized

---

[47] Stiglitz and Charleton presented their market access proposal to the WTO in 2005 in conjunction with the development round of ministerial talks that began in Doha, Qatar in 2001. The Doha Development Agenda (DDA) talks collapsed in 2008 when developed countries, headed by the United States, the EU, and Japan, failed to come to terms with developing nations, led by China, India, Brazil, and South Africa, over a host of issues, the most important of which were developed countries' subsidizing of domestic agriculture, use of quotas and tariffs on agricultural imports (farming constitutes about 75 percent of all occupations in the developing world), and the specific interpretation of the Doha Ministerial Declaration endorsing special and differential treatment (SDT) toward developing countries, especially least developed countries (LDCs). In the 2005 Hong Kong summit, ministers agreed to five SDT provisions, including duty-free and quota-free access to LDCs. However, further talks were suspended when India and the United States disagreed at the 2008 Geneva WTO Summit regarding implementation of SDT provisions on a special safeguard mechanism (SSM), or agricultural tariff, that India argued developing countries should be allowed to impose in the event of a global decline in agricultural prices. While developing countries disagree among themselves about which countries merit SDT – rapidly developing China and India have claimed this status for themselves – developed countries accuse each other of unfairly protecting domestic agricultural industries (the dispute between the US and EU over the latter's reluctance to allow the importation of products containing GMOs remains a major point of contention). The 9th WTO Ministerial Conference in Bali (2013) agreed on some proposals related to the DDA, the most important being a Trade Facilitation Agreement that requires ratification from two-thirds of member states. The 10th Ministerial Conference in Nairobi in December 2015 issued a Ministerial Decision on Export Competition, which requires developed countries to eliminate agricultural subsidies immediately but allows developing countries to retain subsidies until 2018 (extended to 2023 for marketing and transportation costs). The ministers also agreed on SSMs permitting LDCs to impose protective tariffs in the event of market failures and to regulate the importation of emergency food. Additionally, developed countries are required to eliminate all duties and quotas on cotton originating in LDCs. The ministers acknowledged the continuation of fundamental disagreements between developed and developing countries as well as the risk that bilateral and regional trade agreements pose when designed to circumvent the DDA.

through environmental waste and destruction (Stiglitz and Charleton 2007: 153–54). These "gag rules" on what can and cannot be negotiated are difficult to enforce and violate the spirit of open-ended discourse. Nor should the beneficial role of trade in promoting development be taken for granted; forms of protectionism – even when proposed by developed countries – should not be excluded from the conversation. More faithful to the spirit of discourse ethics is Stiglitz and Charleton's proposal to eliminate secret, backroom negotiations, especially ones in which ministers representing a few developing countries negotiate a package of terms for all developing countries that do not adequately reflect their differing concerns (167–69). Also in the spirit of discourse-ethics is their desire to lift conditions on membership for least developed countries (LDCs) (160–62), provide LDCs with technical resources for assessing proposals, and defray litigation costs for LDCs involved in WTO dispute settlement (76–78, 83–84).

THE LIMITS OF CAPITALISM

My discussion of free trade reveals the limits of any global market economy in mitigating poverty, inequality, and environmental damage. Promoting fair trade by eliminating tariffs in developed countries – even while allowing them in developing countries – does not eliminate the rush to the bottom created by global wage competition. Some forms of import-substitution and protectionism that decouple development from trade dependency and relink development to the achievement of domestic economic self-sufficiency should not be peremptorily discounted.

Democratizing government as a public forum for deliberating about the social costs and benefits of economic policy and democratizing trade negotiations between ministers who have everyone's best interests at heart, both of which undoubtedly reduce the coercive nature of a global market economy, might also make this economy more efficient in these other respects as well. Certainly, authoritarian governments – the "Asian Tigers" and China immediately come to mind – can achieve impressive economic growth at the expense of civil liberties. However, a global market economy cannot be made to be more efficient or just without being democratized. The question then arises whether the property relations that form the background to market economies also matter in this regard. In what follows, I will argue that market economies that have as their background private ownership of productive assets (capitalism) are on the whole less democratic and less efficient than market economies that have as their background public ownership of productive assets (socialism), all other things being equal. Perhaps some combination of private and public ownership might turn out best. In any case, more democratic forms of capitalism based on a stakeholder model are better than neoliberal models based exclusively on maximizing stockholder share regardless of social costs.

The critical theory tradition has long argued that capitalism, in any form, is inherently unjust, coercive, alienating, and pathological.[48] Their views about socialism – the only alternative to capitalism over the last century – are more complicated, depending on whether the kind of socialism being discussed is democratic or not.[49] One thing is clear, however. Unlike Marx, contemporary critical theorists such as Habermas endorse the efficiencies associated with market economies, so long as they are regulated in such a way as to minimize uneven development and negative externalities. Indeed, Honneth believes (as did Hegel) that even capitalist labor markets can be ethically justified according to norms of social freedom (mutual recognition), once we acknowledge that these norms are intrinsic to their *non-coercive* functioning.[50]

---

[48] Aside from criticizing capitalism's wastefulness, contemporary critical theorists have *not* trained their sights on what, for Marx, was an equally important consideration: the *inefficiency* of capitalism in producing *overall* material prosperity.

[49] From the early 1940s until the late 1960s, first-generation Frankfurt School critical theorists maintained that, because both welfare capitalism and bureaucratic socialism had largely eliminated competitive markets in labor and goods under a regime of government investment and economic planning, these seemingly opposed systems had converged, with both reflecting a form of class domination spearheaded by technically trained administrators. Contrary to this assessment, second generation critical theorists rejected the idea that the capitalist welfare state entirely (or even mainly) succeeded in managing economic class conflicts and systemic crises by eliminating competitive markets. They did, however, believe that the cost of containing economic crises through coercive administrative policies produced social pathologies and political crises (the most important being legitimation crises). By the 1990s, the most famous exponent of this line of thought, Jürgen Habermas, had assimilated the lessons of having lived two decades under a regime of neoliberal globalization, which again placed the economic contradictions of global capitalism – and the failure of the welfare state to manage its own domestic economy in response to them – front and center.

[50] Honneth, more so than Habermas – who endorses a sharp distinction between economic system and ethical lifeworld – emphasizes the way in which market institutions mark an advance over premarket (e.g., feudal) and postmarket (e.g., bureaucratic socialist) economies in realizing social freedom in both consumption and production. This assessment presumes (against Marx) that capitalist labor contracts are not intrinsically exploitative, insofar as technical knowledge (in addition to wage labor) contributes to the creation of surplus value. Nonexploitative contracts, Honneth contends, presuppose roughly equal bargaining leverage between employers and employees and, most importantly, good faith negotiations by all parties in advancing mutual welfare, empowerment, and the

For simplicity's sake, let us begin by reviewing the contemporary Frankfurt School critique of capitalism. Once that critique is in place, we can then ask whether a feasible model of democratic market socialism represents a more just and efficient alternative to a democratically reformed capitalism.

The Frankfurt School deepened Marx's critique of capitalism by extending his understanding of political economy. Marx defined capitalism as a sociopolitical system in which the legal separation of private capital and social labor produces a concentration of wealth among owners of large industry and the banking establishment that inclines toward primary crises of overproduction as well as secondary social and political crises. Writing during the heyday of *laissez faire*, Marx naturally postulated the causal primacy of the economic subsystem over political, social, and cultural subsystems, thereby in retrospect underestimating the reciprocal influence of these subsystems on the economic system. Writing in the wake of the welfare state, later critical theorists observed that government regulation mitigated capitalism's economic crisis but only at the cost of magnifying crises in the other subsystems. Poverty, they concluded, could be eliminated but only under conditions of heightened political domination and social alienation.[51]

development of everyone's capacities (Honneth 2014:194). Despite this commendatory focus on the underlying ethics of economic life, Honneth does not adequately discuss how different types of property ownership (private versus public) might impact our understanding of this ethos. Within the ambit of his analysis of capitalist markets, he does not even ask whether the ethical understanding of classical "moral economists" that he cites extends beyond the West to include the global economy. Indeed, given his concession that this ethos has been steadily eroded by neoliberalism, one wonders whether it still functions as a shared norm of mutual recognition on the basis of which neoliberalism can be judged pathological. Although he devotes separate sections discussing consumer markets and labor markets, his critical references to financial markets are relatively undeveloped. This neglect underscores the weakness of his defense of a sustainable economy; government regulation of private investment arguably clashes with a fundamental principle of capitalism. If unsustainable economic growth is a structural (and not accidental) feature of capitalism, as I argue below, then the question of property ownership – and the alternative of a market socialist economy composed of worker controlled cooperatives – must occupy center stage in any discussion of economic morality.

[51] My discussion of social alienation in the first three chapters of this book mainly relies on the recognition-based analysis put forward by Honneth and does not fully address other agency-threatening social pathologies associated with capitalism (self-commodification and objectification, alienation from one's natural environment, one's working life, one's fellow human beings, and distortion of one's all-around intellectual, spiritual, social, moral, and aesthetic self-development). Many of these pathologies were discussed by British political economists such as Adam Smith but they became central concerns for philosophers working within the German Idealist tradition, such as Friedrich Schiller,

The decline of welfare capitalism under the new neoliberal regime (see below) places this assumption in doubt, thereby making Marx's focus on economic crisis once more relevant. The classical Marxist explanation for endemic poverty revolves around the necessity of unemployment in a capitalist economy. Competitive advantage achieved through cost-cutting reductions in employee wages and benefits – the chief purpose of labor-saving technology – creates a tendency towards unemployment, which in turn functions as the ultimate threat in disciplining workers' wage demands.[52] Moreover modern monetary policy dictates a level of "natural unemployment," which is defined as the lowest sustainable unemploy-ment (and highest sustainable demand) compatible with levels of inflation conducive to steady rates of saving, borrowing, and profitability (returns on investment). The structural entrenchment of unemployment in a capi-talist economy for the above reasons explains why wage income lags behind investment income, thereby over time producing the sorts of busi-ness cycles (overproduction/underconsumption) at the center of Marx's diagnosis of capitalism.[53] The most important way domestic capitalist economies mitigate these crisis tendencies is by expanding their markets abroad into less developed regions of the world;[54] exploiting cheap for-eign labor while driving out foreign competitors, who lack the technolo-gical advantages associated with efficient, large-scale economies. Small producers, shop owners, and subsistence farmers who lose out in this competitive struggle join the ranks of the unemployed, or if they are lucky, find employment in low-paying sweatshops. Again, thanks to a very large and growing number of the world's unemployed in the Southern Hemisphere, multinational retailers at the top of the chain of production can squeeze local subcontractors below them to offer their services for the cheapest price possible, setting one against the other in a desperate rush to the bottom, where the lowliest laborer who is willing to work for less resides.

Hegel (see paragraph 243 of the *Elements of the Philosophy of Right*) and especially Marx (see the *Economic and Philosophic Manuscripts* [1844] and the first volume of *Capital* [1867]). For a more recent discussion of capitalist social pathology, see Habermas (1987b: 332–403), Ingram (2010a: 271–83; Honneth (2014); and (Azmanova 2012b).

[52] Global manufacturing, for example, is witnessing a precipitous decline in jobs due to automation (in China, job growth in this sector has been negative since 2012).

[53] I discuss Piketty's recent study of income inequality in the Introduction, note 7.

[54] This tendency, which would come to dominate late nineteenth-century and early twen-tieth-century debates over imperialism, was already diagnosed by Hegel in paragraphs 246–248 of the *Elements of the Philosophy of Right*.

To be sure, it is in the interest of the investor class to ensure that global consumption keeps pace with global production; just as it is in the interest of each business owner to ensure that other business owners hire enough well-paid workers to buy the commodities he or she produces. But nothing in the history of capitalism (or in its competitive logic) suggests that business owners will solve their "prisoner's dilemma" any more than that a global welfare state will emerge that will ensure that the poor as well as the rich have enough income to press their consumer demand. Even if these miracles in economic crisis management should somehow come to pass, capitalism would still work against poverty reduction in a way Marx did not foresee. The growth dynamic of capitalism, driven by the cost-efficiencies associated with economies of scale, encourages ever greater resource depletion and energy consumption. Absent a technological miracle, the resulting increase in global temperatures will bring in its train more extreme weather events, flooding, and desertification that will disproportionately harm the world's poorest.

Defenders of a green, sustainable capitalism look for salvation in government regulation. Underlying this vision of reformed capitalism is a faith that citizens, elected officials, and business leaders will come to embrace a community-based, stakeholder conception of corporate obligations. Can this ethos curb the greed and fear that motivate private investors to grow their businesses in unsustainable ways?

Despite antitrust legislation and business failure as normal restraints on capital growth, a healthy capitalist economy must be a growing economy in order to encourage private investors to play a relatively risk-free, positive-sum game. But history shows us that any capitalist economy capable of motivating a steady rate of investment necessary for averting long term recession will perforce grow exponentially. A modest 3 percent/year growth rate (the average rate the US economy grew during the twentieth century) doubled consumption every twenty-four years and led to a sixteen-fold increase in consumption over the course of a century. A low annual rate of 1.2 percent – the growth rate Britain's Stern Review's economic analysis of climate change projected would be necessary to avoid "major disruption to economic and social activity ... on a scale similar to those associated with the great wars and economic depression of the first half of the twentieth century"– would still double consumption every 60 years (Stern 2007: ii, cited in Schweickart 2009: 563).[55]

---

[55] Chapter 10 of the review (Macroeconomic Models of Cost) put forth a range of growth projections that might be required to stabilize the current output of CO_2 at 450 parts per

Rebutting the notion of a no-growth capitalist economy doesn't eliminate the possibility of sustainable growth. Heavily taxing gasoline could lower gasoline consumption and provide revenues for capturing carbon emissions without slowing economic growth so long as government stimulated consumer demand by cutting income taxes and compensated for job loss in the petroleum sector by subsidizing growth in other (more eco-friendly) sectors. But as David Schweickart convincingly argues, faith in the capacity of regulated capitalism to *quickly* transform itself into a sustainably growing economy capable of averting scientific predictions of global climate catastrophe is not supported by historical evidence, which rather shows that radical reform only follows on the heels of economic collapse. Capitalist growth has mainly benefited wealthy countries – the average income gap between rich and poor countries has grown from 3 to 1 in 1820 to 70 to 1 in 1990 – and has trickled down very unevenly to the poor, for structural reasons that I mentioned earlier. So, there is no guarantee that sustainable capitalist growth, were it achievable in time to avert an ecological disaster that will profoundly harm the vast majority of the global poor (if no one else), would sufficiently trickle down to the developing world. In the words of Schweickart, defenders of green capitalism urge us to make a bad Pascalian "wager": against all historical evidence, one must assume that the bare possibility of unending incremental gains in "happiness" through eternal growth in consumption is worth the risk of courting a more probable outcome: infernal planetary misery for most everyone (Schweickart 2009: 568–70).

There is another problem with this wager. Defenders of "green" capitalism invoke an older model of state-regulated capitalism that appears to have been rendered increasingly otiose by today's "financialized capitalism" (to use Nancy Fraser's term) (Fraser 2015). As Karl Polanyi observed seventy years ago (Polanyi, 2001), capitalism places the natural and social systems on which it relies at critical risk, but, more important, it places the political system that could lower this risk – through government regulation – at critical risk.[56]

The path dependent, crisis-driven transformation of capitalism from *laissez faire* to welfare state seems to describe the emergence of today's

---

million; business as usual might require a 3.4 percent *decrease* in GDP; rapid transition to green energy, the use of steep carbon taxes to subsidize growth in other sectors, the efficient use of carbon-trading, etc. might comport with and a 3.9 percent *increase* in GDP. Furthermore, the cost of compensating for the damage done by global warming will also cut into GDP.

[56] Honneth (2014: 186–87) also takes up Polanyi's analysis of "embedded markets" and defense of "counter-moves" designed to reverse market deregulation.

financialized capitalism. The crisis of the welfare state that fueled this latter transformation occurred at many levels. Some critical theorists (notably Habermas) explain the crisis in terms of a displacement of economic crisis tendencies "upward" – onto the administrative, political, and cultural subsystems. Forced to respond to competing administrative imperatives – to subsidize growth through government spending (involving tax-cutting, investment stimulus policy, deregulation of finance and industry) and compensate for the structural side effects of growth (un- and underemployment, financial destabilization, uneven development, and environmental damage) – government saddles itself with increasing indebtedness tending toward fiscal crisis, all of which in turn compel it to mortgage the nation's future through borrowing.

Up to now, the welfare state has banked on enhanced revenue pegged to steady economic growth to pay off its creditors. But in today's slow-growth, financialized capitalism, rent income derived from financial trading and speculation – which, comprising 40 percent of all profits, is taxed at historically low rates – now threatens to eclipse wage income derived from real economic productivity (Krugman 2014). Picketty's blunt assessment – "inherited wealth grows faster than output and income" – pithily underscores the link between inequality and indebtedness (Picketty 2014: 26). In a total reversal of what economists once expected, *developing* countries, which borrowed heavily from *developed* countries to finance their *necessary* growth, now finance rich countries' deficit spending as a way of stimulating their *unnecessary* extravagance, subsidizing share buybacks and bloated dividends for rich investors (China, for example, owns $3 trillion of the $13 trillion in US government debt). However, investment and consumption find new limits in today's financialized capitalism.[57] Governments today (with the possible exception of the United

---

[57] According to the McKinsey Global Institute, as of 2016 worldwide government, corporate, and consumer debt stood at $199 trillion, up $57 trillion from 2007 (before the 2008 recession), with growing debt to GDP ratios in most countries, including especially precarious increases in China (78 percent), Japan (67 percent), and Russia (42 percent). Debt is the single most important cause behind economic crashes. The 2008 recession, for instance, had its root in massive consumer debt, caused in large part by declining wages and compensatory borrowing. In the United States, consumers sought to ease their debt burden by taking out low interest, adjustable rate home equity loans on the assumption that their homes would increase in value. When rates went up and the housing market crashed, banks were left with near-worthless mortgage-backed securities, compounding the rapid decline in consumer demand with a liquidity crisis. Today, US consumers are less indebted (by 3.5 percent) than they were in 2007; however, because of inflation-adjusted income declining across all quintiles from 2009–2014 (the bottom quintile declined 5.7 percent, compared to the top quintile's 2.6 percent decline), they are

States) must be mindful of global bond markets and bond ratings that have the power to drastically increase the cost of borrowing as insolvency increases. Today, a new system of global governance based on currency speculation, free trade, financial and fiscal austerity, and other neoliberal policies imposes stringent limits on what governments can do to protect their domestic economies from capital flight and foreign capture. Forced to privatize, outsource, and downsize public services, cash-strapped governments no longer manage their administrative crises in a way that is publicly accountable to their own citizens, rather than to markets and financiers.

Fraser explains how this new political crisis differs from the legitimation crisis that characterized welfare state capitalism. That legitimation crisis was fueled by a failure of the dominant ideology – of agent-as-passive-consumer/welfare-client – to motivate a deferential, apolitical attitude toward government economic planning premised on trickle-down growth benefiting all. Contrary to Habermas's diagnosis (Habermas 1975), it was "not just an abstract disposition to normative justification" that mainly prompted subjects to identify as active citizens who questioned the justice and goodness of government welfare policy but "the concrete way in which that disposition (was) instantiated via common sense assumptions about agency, public power, society, justice, and history" (Fraser 2015). In short, the welfare state depended on a contradictory mix of political ideologies. The dominant ideology defined agents as atomized individuals who sought to develop their capacities through private work and consumption; it defined public power as a provider of welfare whose technical-managerial elites could be held accountable through electoral recall; it defined society as a balance between state-administered public welfare and capital-driven private interest; it defined distributive justice as at once market-based (libertarian) and egalitarian; and it defined historical possibility against the background of a bipolar struggle pitting

---

spending less, thereby slowing economic recovery. Corporate debt also declined by 2 percent because US corporations have moved their investments abroad where tax rates are lower. However, corporate borrowing has actually increased, most of it being used to boost dividends and increase share buybacks rather than to grow jobs. Meanwhile, federal, state, and municipal governments, confronted with rising pension and entitlement liabilities, have taken on more debt (counting social security liabilities, US federal debt now stands at 104 percent of GDP). The downgrading of government bonds increases future liability dramatically, but the ability of government to stave off the next impending recession (some predict as early as 2017) through stimulus spending has been severely diminished (McKenna and Tung 2015; Mian and Sufi 2014; and Foroohar 2016: 94–101).

a free and democratic capitalism against totalitarian communism. In antithesis to this ideology the emancipatory rhetoric of the New Left defined agents as citizens engaged in collective action, public power as inclusive democratic participation in public deliberation and decision-making, society as space for public empowerment as well as private initiative, justice as simultaneously distributive, recognitive, and representative in a political sense, and history as site for open-ended, experimental learning.

The legitimation crisis confronting the welfare state thus highlighted popular democratic resistance to coercive, top-down bureaucratic planning that drew from both concrete civic republican ideals and abstract discourse ethical ideals stressing rational accountability and participation. Democratic resistance, however, proved to be quixotic, as the old crisis of the welfare state morphed into a new crisis under financialized capitalism. The new crisis reflected the migration of public power from the sovereign state to global economic multilaterals (GEMs)and transnational corporations (TNCs). Along with this hollowing out of democracy came the weakening of unions and the colonization of politics by moneyed interests. While the legitimacy of a supranational regime of trade and finance is challenged on the Left, the legitimacy of a besieged welfare state is challenged on the Right in the name of a new ideology that combines elements of the earlier oppositional ideologies. Here agency is defined in terms of individual entrepreneurial initiative, public power and society in terms of its oppressive coercion. Justice is accordingly defined in terms of market success and failure, where those with initiative always succeed and failure becomes a mark of personal shortcoming, while history recounts the final triumph of capitalism over any conceivable alternative.

As Fraser remarks, the split between Left and Right, far from coalescing into a legitimation crisis, has instead issued in the decline of state-centered politics.[58] This should not surprise us. Anarchism on the Left and entrepreneurialism on the Right both reflect a deepening skepticism toward the

---

[58] Public choice economists, inspired by Nobel laureate James McGill Buchanan, equate democratic politics with "rent seeking" on the part of politicians and interest groups whose "tax and spend" policies coercively restrain the economic freedom of the business class (MacLean 2017). Despite their success in convincing libertarian-minded legislators in the US to curb the power of popular majorities through restrictive voting laws and other procedural changes – thanks in part to the financial backing of the Koch brothers – neoliberal economic policies still meet popular resistance. 2016 witnessed the US presidential election of Donald Trump and the British referendum to exit the EU ("Brexit"), both of which were partly motivated by popular resentment against immigration and free trade.

welfare state. Economic malaise, when not attributed to the welfare state (the standard complaint of the American Right) or to central regional and global banks (the standard complaint of the European Left) is blamed on immigrants, welfare "parasites," and racial minorities. Meanwhile the political system of global capitalism – specifically, its undemocratic political economy – remains largely immune to organized transformational reform.

The absence of a mass political movement challenging the crisis tendencies of global capitalism reflects a fatalistic resignation to what is misperceived as simply a natural economic system. But the potential of capitalism to avert a crisis in any of its economic, environmental, and social subsystems has always depended on the viability of its political system, which, beginning with Bretton Woods, has consisted of an administrative state apparatus and a global organization of trade and finance. Under welfare capitalism, these two pillars of governance were mutually supportive, with the former, chiefly under the sway of the United States as *primus inter pares*, exercising control over the latter. While the welfare state did indeed suffer a political crisis affecting its own democratic legitimacy, there was little doubt that it could bureaucratically manage economic crises emerging within its own territorially bounded subsystems. Today's political crisis, which restores the older subordination of the political system to the (now global) economic system, shows how little faith can now be placed in capitalism's historically privileged crisis management system.

ECONOMIC DEMOCRACY

I began this chapter by asking whether a market economy premised on free trade could live up to the demanding moral expectations underlying a voluntary social contract between nations and persons. Leaving aside the coercive imperial power exercised by the United States and its allies in shaping global trade and finance, I argued that a system of free trade, operating free of imperial constraint, could not be expected to benefit all parties, let alone benefit them equally. Neither comparative advantage nor competitive advantage predicts real world economic distributions, and neither, therefore, provides a reliable norm for guiding global economic policy. Because these principles abstract from the environmental, ecological, social, and political costs of market exchange, they underestimate the extent to which weaker bargaining units suffer a net decline in benefits for themselves and their progeny. To the extent that markets work to the advantage of all, it is because they are regulated by those who participate in them.

But not all regulated markets are equally beneficial. Capitalist markets, I have argued, have structural defects that make it unlikely that both global poverty and global environmental/ecological damage can be significantly reduced *at the same time*. The promise of green capitalism depends on the capacity of government to use a combination of positive and negative incentives to steer the greed and fear of private investors toward sustainable forms of growth that will benefit all. Financialized capitalism undermines the fiscal capacity of government to do this. In any case, investors can simply avoid taxes or refuse subsidies by moving their capital to other countries whose package of negative and positive incentives they deem to be more profitable, if not necessarily greener.

Nothing I have said is meant to suggest that capitalism will succumb to its crisis tendencies. It has proven resilient, thanks to political and legal "reform." Progressive forms of populism can garner further political support for green policies that better facilitate the growth of underdeveloped economies. These political pressures need to be accompanied by private initiatives. Private-public partnerships guided by a stakeholder ethos play a vital role here, as do broad-based consumer advocacy and class action litigation.[59] That the new era of financialized capitalism has cast such a pall on the possibility of averting an impending catastrophe through immediate reform and transformed ethos does not refute the possibility (even likelihood) of future reform, post-apocalypse.

The question then arises: Reform towards what end? Is there an alternative model of market economy that, in theory at least, would more likely reduce poverty, environmental/ecological damage, and social and political inequality better than the most reformed capitalism? Recall the fundamental root of capitalism's crisis tendency: the separation of privately owned capital from socially exploited labor and publicly shared resources (political power and nature). Because class domination is built into the relationship between capital and labor, coercion and exploitation combine to create a system which thwarts long term public freedom and welfare. By releasing capital from this relationship – in effect, transferring it from private to public stewardship – it becomes possible to use it more efficiently, for the good of all, and by the democratic consent of all.

---

[59] Alessandro Ferrara, "Political Liberalism, Indigenous Unreasonability, and Post-Liberal Democracy" (unpublished MS).

The comparative advantages of democratic socialism over democratically reformed capitalism in achieving a more just and sustainable world have been thoroughly detailed by David Schweickart (Schweickart, 2011). The economy in question (what Schweickart calls Economic Democracy) retains many features of a capitalist economy: markets in goods and services, companies,[60] family-owned businesses, and entrepreneurs; even larger capitalist firms that employ wage earners might be permitted under certain circumstances.[61] In Schweickart's model, however, all investment funds and most capital assets are publicly owned and democratically managed. A public investment fund is generated by a flat-rate use tax on capital assets that have already been granted using this fund. National, regional, and local legislatures decide what portion of this money is spent on public services and what portion is spent on economic investment. Each region receives national funding proportional to its population (on a *per capita* basis). National, regional, and local banks[62] then dispense economic funds depending on an investment's likelihood of generating jobs, furthering development, and succeeding in the marketplace (Schweickart 2002: 50–54).[63]

By combining the virtues – while mitigating the vices – of both central planning and market allocation mechanisms of investment, Schweickart's model of socialism eliminates the uneven development that plagues

---

[60] With few exceptions, companies would compete in relatively unregulated markets and workers would be free to leave for better employment opportunities elsewhere. Companies that fail to generate a minimum per capita income (the equivalent of a minimum wage) would be forced to declare bankruptcy, pay back their creditors (mainly other publicly-funded businesses and public banks), and release their workforce (who would be required to seek employment elsewhere) (Schweickart 2011: 50).

[61] As a general rule, small family-owned businesses and publicly-owned cooperatives do not create technological innovation necessary to compete in markets. Schweickart recommends that local communities set up entrepreneurial agencies or hire independent entrepreneurs to solve this problem. Entrepreneurs would be financially rewarded for planning businesses and recruiting workers. In some cases, a group of individuals might be permitted to pool their private savings in setting up a privately-owned business employing wage laborers. These capitalists would only be allowed to sell their enterprise to the community, which would purchase the enterprise at market value upon the death of the founder(s) (Schweickart 2011: 79). Also publicly-owned cooperatives might fund some of their business through foreign investment; in return, foreign investors would receive a share of profits but would have no voting rights over managerial decisions.

[62] Under Economic Democracy, private savings banks might be permitted to charge interest for consumer credit; investment funds, however, would be dispensed only by public banks in the form of taxable grants rather than interest-bearing loans (which require payment on balance) (Schweickart 2011: 76–80).

[63] Like Keynesian – and unlike neoclassical – economic reasoning, Schweickart's model regards unemployment as an inefficiency (or wasted resource).

capitalism and forces poor, unemployed workers to uproot themselves from family and community in search of sustainable employment elsewhere. Two "ethical sociological" principles of fairness that recall my earlier discussion of social recognition-based freedom support the human development right of communities not to be coerced into competing with each other for scarce investment capital:

Societal health requires that individuals develop intergenerational commitments and a sense of place, these being facilitated by regional and community stability. Although individuals should be free to move to other regions or communities if they so desire, they should not be compelled to do so (Schweickart 2002: 51–52).[64]

The second ethical advantage that Economic Democracy has over its capitalist counterpart is its reduction (if not elimination) of domination and exploitation. Workers in public cooperatives manage their own firms democratically and divide company earnings among themselves according to their own democratically chosen criteria. [65] Wage labor in these firms is abolished.[66]

The most intriguing feature of Schweickart's model is its sustainability. Like their capitalist counterparts, businesses in a market socialist economy compete to maintain or increase their market share. But unlike capitalist firms, which maximize profits by replacing costly workers with labor saving technologies, worker-managed firms are generally loath to fire one of their own, unless doing so is necessary to stay in business. In any case, structural unemployment is no longer required in an economy where rents and interest have been abolished and inflation can be controlled by expanding production to meet growing demand. Furthermore, whereas capitalist firms have an incentive to grow – greater productivity means greater profits – worker-managed firms do not (Schweickart 2011: 89). Because profits are shared, adding more workers normally does not

[64] After noting that "guaranteeing each region and community a steady supply of investment funds each year mitigates the *coercion* that a purely market-determined allocation of investment funds is likely to produce" (Schweickart 2002: 52 – my stress), Schweickart adds that "if *large* efficiency gains can be had by pressuring people to relocate [that offset the real costs of labor migration], then the argument for per capita allocation of investment funds is less compelling."

[65] Profits are not necessarily divided equally; workers decide democratically how skill level, seniority, and managerial responsibility factor into levels of remuneration.

[66] Economic democracy would not exist in the few capitalist enterprises that might be allowed to operate for a very limited duration (of about a generation). However, domination would be mitigated within these enterprises insofar as workers would have the option of joining a cooperative enterprise (the threat of unemployment would also be less coercive under a system of near full employment).

translate into larger shares, unless a greater economy of scale results in significant efficiency and cost saving. In sum, businesses operating in Economic Democracy will generally be smaller, less competitive, and less prone to monopolistic tendencies than their capitalist counterparts (Schweickart 2011: 89).

But how would firms in a local democratic socialist economy protect themselves from the kind of cut-throat competition that currently reigns supreme in our global capitalist economy?[67] Here Schweickart recommends a radical alternative to the free and fair trade policies currently in vogue: the adoption of import substitution with a twist. First, tariffs would be imposed on all imports, including imports that do not compete with domestic product as well as highly discounted imports from developing countries that do. The rationale behind this tariff is social: "A 'social tariff' will be imposed on imported goods, designed to compensate for low wages and/or a lack of commitment to social goals regarding the environment, worker health and safety, and social welfare" (Schweickart 2011: 82).

"Socialist protectionism" is guided by the fair trade principle that "one should not, in general, profit from, or be hurt by, the cheap labor of others" (Schweickart 2002: 79). Socialist protectionism does not eliminate wage inequality as such, for doing that would suppress "socially useful kinds of competition – those fostering efficient production and satisfaction of consumer desires." However, it refrains from penalizing technologically inefficient, labor-intensive industry in developing countries. Imports from these countries would be assessed lower tariffs to compensate for their competitive disadvantage, thereby enabling them to sell their product in developed countries.

Second, revenue generated from these tariffs would be remanded back to poor countries for use in developing their economies. Although protective tariffs will lower consumption of imports from poor countries, "which will adversely affect certain workers in those countries during the transition period," rebates will encourage those countries to "devote fewer of their resources to producing for rich-country consumption, and

---

[67] The following discussion focuses on trade. In Schweickart's model, capital, and labor flows across national borders would be prohibited (in the case of capital migrating abroad) or tightly regulated (in the case of labor migrating in). Presumably ordinary immigration for purposes of family reunification (for example) would be unaffected under his scheme and employment of foreign guest workers would be permitted only if genuinely needed to replace workers or provide needed skills (Schweickart 2002: 147–48).

thus to have more available for local use" (Schweickart 2002: 80). As wages and production standards rise in these countries, the need for protective tariffs diminishes, and import substitution can be relaxed. Because democratic socialist economies are protected from cut-throat foreign competition, they can afford to share their technical expertise with the developing world for mutual benefit. (This latter point is especially crucial given that developing countries will need to base their sustainable development on the most advanced Green technologies developing countries have to offer).[68]

The greatest contrast between capitalism and the socialist model I have outlined above is worker democracy. Capitalism is a system of class domination in which those who own controlling shares of businesses dictate terms of investment, production, and employment to the rest of us. The spill-over from this aspect of our work-a-day lives to our civic and political relationships cannot be healthy: Persons who spend their lives taking orders from those who employ them develop deferential attitudes to those higher up in the chain of command while kicking those below them. For this reason, it is hardly conceivable how public power can be politically democratized without democratizing our economic lives.

Legitimate questions remain about the feasibility of Economic Democracy and the possibility of transiting toward it from capitalism.[69]

---

[68] Schweickart adds this qualification: As developing countries increase their consumption developed cou.ntries must lower theirs, so that all countries converge toward a just parity point. To cite Daly (Daly 1996: 106, quoted in Schweickart 2002: 119), "An overdeveloped country is one whose per capita level of resource consumption is such that if generalized to all countries could not be sustained indefinitely." However, the proper aim of a sustainable global economy is to reduce work and consumption in favor of time spent in leisure activity, where people are more focused on living well (Schweickart 2002: 143).

[69] Schweickart cites overwhelming evidence supporting the higher (or at least, equivalent) productivity gains in worker-controlled cooperatives (such as the Mondragon Corporación Cooperativa [MCC] headquartered in the Basque region of Spain) in comparison to privately owned businesses. In general, workers take greater pride and satisfaction in what they have a stake in, recording higher productivity, lower turnover and absenteeism, and have shown themselves to be quite capable of making sound management decisions. That said, Schweickart concedes (citing surveys conducted of MCC workers and managers) that democratic worker management does not eliminate alienated labor and labor-management tensions (Schweickart 2002: 60–70). As for the transition problem, Schweickart lays out several realistic scenarios for solving it. Bureaucratic socialist countries such as China could transition easily. The most realistic transition for rich capitalist countries would involve a popular mandate to bail out and nationalize large companies and banks during an extended crisis, with government buying depreciated stocks and pension portfolios, converting them to publicly financed, term-limited annuities for the expropriated, and recovering the cost via a steeply progressive annuity tax that would leave most average pensioners as well off as they

Needless to say, eliminating coercion from our economic lives and encouraging everyone to participate in decisions regarding investment, production, and employment would make for a more just and efficient economy. Infusing stakeholder business ethics with discourse ethics might not solve all problems associated with a market economy but it would mitigate them better than reformed capitalism. A just distribution of the burdens and benefits attached to the creation of a sustainable global economy will require that all parties to the social contract shift from a one-sided focus on maximizing personal gains – which, when considered apart from its legitimating ethos, appears to be the natural law underwriting any market system, capitalist or socialist – to a broader focus on the common good, with a preference for solutions that maximize the condition of the worst off (and possibly require sacrifices on the part of the better off).[70]

Social democracy as I have here described it composes an essential part of a just global order wherein all have equal opportunities to develop their agential capabilities. Mutual recognition of each person's contribution to a cooperative scheme of mutual freedom enhancement, however, is an increasingly disrespected economic norm in today's financialized, neoliberal capitalism. More essential still in protecting the economic basis of social freedom are human rights. Without these side constraints on negotiating the costs and benefits of global economic policy, there is no guarantee that the most vulnerable and marginalized of the world's inhabitants will have their agency respected. Yet, however plainly human rights function to constrain the excesses of *states* in their behavior toward their own subjects, it is questionable whether they function to constrain *all* agents responsible for endangering the economic well-being of the world's inhabitants. Chapter 5 argues that they should.

were before the "crash." The expropriated rich would still be subsidized – as they are now – but at a lower rate and for a limited period of time, so that they could continue to buffer consumer demand during the transition period (Schweickart 2002: 167–77). This scenario would likely be preceded by a period of reform in which private investment and finance would be heavily regulated and more progressive tax schemes implemented.

[70] Endorsing the Netherland's Environmental Assessment Agency's Framework to Assess International Regimes For Differentiation of Commitment (FAIR), Richard Miller observes that it is just to expect that nations that have per capita contributed more to (and have been benefited more by) the production of global greenhouse emissions be morally required to carry a proportionate share of the costs for achieving at least a moderate level of 450 ppm CO_2 by 2100 to safely avoid a potentially catastrophic 3–4 C. degree increase. Although he believes it is wrong to penalize generations born after 1990 for the sins of their forefathers, he rightly holds that it would be more unjust to require developing countries to scale back development to meet CO_2 reduction targets (Miller 2010: 93–117).

PART III

HUMAN RIGHTS

5

Human Rights and Global Injustice: Institutionalizing the Moral Claims of Agency

I have framed the injustice of the global economic order as a violation of a social duty to refrain from imposing economic structures on persons to which they could not reasonably consent. Economic coercion and domination, not to mention exploitation borne of extreme power differentials, contradict the social contractarian grounds underlying fair economic cooperation. However, duties owed to those who are bound together by mutual cooperation or mutual participation within a political legal regime – even one as geographically unbounded as the imperial regime imposed by the United States with the support of its allies – are not, strictly speaking, universal in scope; they apply specifically to those with whom the duty holder should show special concern, based on sharing a common social-political connection. Such special duties owed to conationals and, to a lesser extent, foreigners who participate in, or find themselves subjected to, sociopolitical relationships of trade, finance, and imperial domination, must be distinguished from the truly universal, cosmopolitan duties owed to all human beings with whom we might have a lesser degree of contact. The question I shall address in this chapter is whether such universal duties, specifically as they flow from human rights, provide a different set of reasons for condemning the economic injustices noted above.

As bad as they are, these injustices do not obviously amount to a human rights violation. If we restrict the scope of human rights to those that are justiciable in courts of law, a government's allowing — but not officially intending – the starvation of some portion of its population need not rise to the level of a criminal human rights violation. This would be true even if the government in question were not overly burdened, incompetent, corrupt, or negligent. Likewise, if we restrict the scope of human rights to just those moral claims that impose duties on others to respect an individual's personhood, agency, or basic interest to lead a life of her choosing, a society that allows a person to starve while otherwise respecting her freedom to think, choose, and do as she wishes does her no harm.

Only if we adopt an understanding of human rights broader than these narrow interpretations can we understand why a government's or society's permitting a person to starve might violate human rights. Such a broader understanding, in fact, finds ample support in both legal and moral interpretations of human rights. Legally binding human rights treaties and soft human rights law of the sort exemplified by the UDHR and the Right to Development, for instance, impose a duty on signatory states – and arguably *all* states – to safeguard their subjects' freedom, through institutional provision of their security, health, education, welfare, and political empowerment. They may also require global economic multilaterals (GEMs) to refrain from imposing conditions of finance and trade on states that prevent them from domestically implementing these social duties. Indeed, they may impose duties on all parties who are responsible for international rules that prevent vulnerable persons from securely accessing the goods legally guaranteed to them as a matter of human right.

Thus, to recall our earlier example of negative trade externalities (resource depletion, pollution, and global warming), it might be wrong to treat these harms as problems that can be resolved through simple negotiation – for instance, through a market-regulatory system of "cap and trade." Treating these harms as matters that can be justly resolved through negotiation presumes that a state's or industry's right to deplete or pollute is equal in moral weight to the right of individuals to an integral environment, so that balancing costs to both parties is morally acceptable. Things look very different, however, if the right to an integral environment is a human right that carries much greater weight than the right to do business; for a human right is not the kind of right that can be bargained away or even compromised for the sake of respecting some lesser right.

Furthermore, the unjust exploitation of others premised on great asymmetries in bargaining power that I cited above as a violation of norms of noncoercive cooperation can also involve a human rights violation even if it does not deprive persons of basic subsistence. Subsistence alone falls short of satisfying the robust developmental and democratic participatory requirements demanded by human rights law. In fact, if human rights are claims on society to guarantee reasonably secure and equal access to a range of goods, resources, and capabilities for all persons, then much of the legally supported global economic system in fact violates human rights, simply by denying persons the opportunity to freely, securely, and equally access these goods.

Moral conceptions of human rights abstractly framed as individual claims to a life of dignity also require securing individuals' social freedom in democratic and economic institutions. Respecting a person's dignity goes well beyond respecting their moral freedom of conscience to reflect and act upon their rationally informed conceptions of what counts as a good life. Although many of the classical "rights of man and of citizen" enshrined in liberal constitutions beginning in the late eighteenth century may have been morally motivated out of respect for the dignity of the individual understood primarily as a free legal and moral agent in this narrower sense, the much older moral right to have one's basic needs met attests to a richer understanding of the meaning of human dignity that finds expression in the preambular language contained in the UDHR and other human rights documents. Philosophical reconstructions of agency of the sort I propose in this book further underscore the empirical (and even conceptual) complementarity of welfare, freedom, empowerment, recognition, and equality. Inserted into the language of the Right to Development (1986) and Vienna Declaration (1993), this conceptual constellation anticipates its own realization in the form of institutionally safeguarded social freedom. Societies that allow severe poverty to afflict some of their members thus stand justly accused of failing to respect (and protect)[1] the dignity of individuals vouchsafed by human rights.

That said, defenders of narrower interpretations of human rights argue that the robust moral and legal interpretations of human rights recounted above cannot be justified or practically implemented. The "inflationary" expansion of human rights beyond those that are justiciable in criminal courts, they note, has the unfortunate consequence of reducing respect for all human rights, as if they were nothing more than "manifesto rights" or arbitrary declarations of wishful fantasy. Furthermore, they note that appeal to human rights is not necessary in order to condemn the economic injustices with which I began this chapter, insofar as the particular rights

---

[1] The UN's 2005 adoption of the responsibility to protect (R2P) rule extends the duty to protect human rights to the entire world community. When originally formulated by the International Commission on Intervention and State Sovereignty (ICISS) in 2001 (see Chapter 6, notes 5 and 6) R2P targeted severe environmental threats to welfare as well as gross threats to human rights centering on criminal atrocities.

and duties of sociopolitical association can fill this social freedom-enhancing function just as well. Finally, they observe that the inflation of very general human rights duties in the absence of a centralized system for legislating, adjudicating, and enforcing human rights only exacerbates an abuse apparent in current human rights practice, where a powerful state, such as the United States, can unilaterally interpret and enforce human rights to its own liking.

These objections are powerful but defeasible. In Chapter 6, I defend the advantages of a more centralized international human rights regime over an international order that makes the legislation, interpretation, and enforcement of rights depend entirely on states. In the present chapter I address the problem of human rights inflation. Following an argument developed recently by Allen Buchanan, I argue that the problem of rights inflation, while real, is partly a figment of philosophical imagination, specifically, of the idea that there is only one justification for human rights and that that justification must appeal to the principle of moral respect for an individual's autonomous agency. While this abstract moral ground may have motivated the legal practice of human rights as it has evolved over the past two hundred years, and may justify certain aspects of that practice today, it is wrong to think that current human rights law "mirrors" moral human rights in this restrictive sense. Once we drop this Mirroring View (as Buchanan refers to it) we are free to think of human rights as having multiple ethical grounds, compatible with collectivist moralities, group rights, and instrumental human rights norms, including duties to provide strong democratic and social welfare institutions. So understood, human rights not only straddle moral and legal domains of freedom, they also constitute, in the words of Honneth, frameworks of institutional solidarity in which each person recognizes his own freedom in the freedom of the other. This institutional understanding of human rights grounds a global duty on the part of all people to treat environmental degradation and climate change as harms meriting legal action.

I develop these points in seven parts. The Ambiguous Status of Human Rights examines the ambiguous moral-legal status of human rights in official human rights documents and practices. The next two sections, Political Theories of Human Rights: Rawls and the Law of Peoples and Legal Theories of Human Rights: Habermas and Constitutional Law, discuss several iconic political and legal theories of human rights that have been advanced by John Rawls and Jürgen Habermas. Such theories mainly highlight the function of human rights in facilitating just and efficient cooperation between states and/or members of a single legal community. Hence, they can be described as *expanding* social contractarian duties beyond legal protection of individuals' negative freedom and *extending* them in a universal (if not necessarily cosmopolitan) direction. Despite their rejection of moral conceptions of human rights that single out only some agential capabilities for protection, these theories fail to explain the full range of human rights. Drawing mainly from James Griffin, Martha Nussbaum, and Habermas, Moral Approaches to Human Rights shows how moral theories recognize a broader range of individual capabilities beyond those associated with the exercise of negative (legal) freedom and positive (moral) self-determination. Hence I argue in Understanding Human Rights Contextually: Pluralism Reconsidered that moral and legal theories of human rights must be embedded within an institutional conception of social freedom; so understood, human rights fulfill multiple complementary functions: legal, political, and moral. Having defended this general thesis, Institutional and Interactional Human Rights: Do Global Economic Structures Violate Human Rights? argues that an institutional understanding of human rights is essential, *if* we are to grasp the full range of justiciable human rights claims (both criminal and civil), specifically as they touch on structurally caused underdevelopment. This section also explains why the current human rights regime should focus on global economic harms, including climate change, that also implicate nonstate institutions. Legitimating Human Rights: Discourse Theory and Democracy concludes by addressing the discourse theoretic features of agency that argue for a human right to democratic participation.

THE AMBIGUOUS STATUS OF HUMAN RIGHTS

The Preamble to the Universal Declaration of Human Rights (1948) describes human rights in a variety of ways that are by no means harmonious. They are described as "the highest aspiration of the common people" and "a common standard of achievement for all peoples and all nations," the universal and effective recognition of which should be spread through "teaching and education." Such recognition is further tied to the "dignity and worth of the human person and in the equal rights of men and women" that have promoted "social progress and better standards of life in larger freedom." So construed, human rights are *moral aspirations* in two senses. First, they progressively interpret freedom in terms of "better standards of life"; second, they progressively extend to all persons equally, solely in virtue of their "inherent dignity and worth." Consonant with this second aspiration, Article 2 asserts that "everyone is entitled to all the rights and freedoms set forth in this Declaration, without distinction of any kind, such as race, color, sex, language, religion, political or other opinion, national or social origin, property, birth or other status."

Belying this moral interpretation of human rights, with its emphasis on the equal dignity of the individual and social progress in living conditions, is a juridical interpretation that describes human rights as legal claims that "should be protected by the rule of law." This clause is immediately followed by another clause that adds: "whereas it is essential to promote the development of friendly relations between nations ..." Here the aim of human rights is political: the facilitation of international peace and cooperation.

Much ink has been spilled contrasting this last aim, with its recognition of the legal sovereignty of nations (as set forth in Article 2.7 of the UN Charter), and the legal protection of individuals' human rights, if need be, by contravening national sovereignty (as permitted under Chapter VII, Articles 41 and 42). The problem of reconciling these aims is an important one that will be addressed in Chapters 6 and 7.[2] My problem here concerns the conceptual tension between moral and legal interpretations of human rights. To the extent that government officials view human rights as setting forth legal limits demarcating tolerable conduct between persons and states, they acknowledge a limited responsibility to protect (R2P) essential liberties from severe criminal predations by providing benchmarks for sanctions and military intervention.[3] Conversely, by conceiving human rights as evolving moral standards and utopian aspirations

[2] See note 1. As Buchanan notes, human rights and state sovereignty can also reinforce each other. Enforcing human rights by compelling global economic multilaterals (GEMs) such as the WTO to modify patent provisions of the TRIPS agreement that currently prevent states from cheaply producing lifesaving pharmaceuticals for their citizens could strengthen the sovereign power of states to carry out their human right responsibilities to not only respect and protect human rights but to promote them domestically (Lafont, 2014). See notes 9, 46–48.

[3] Perhaps one reason for this is that the most powerful government in the world, the United States, signed but has yet to ratify, the International Covenant on Economic, Social, and Cultural Rights (ICESCR). Also, violations of civil and political rights, understood as violations of negative duties to refrain from harming others, are often thought (mistakenly, in my opinion) to be worse than neglect of economic, social, and cultural rights, which usually involves omissions in the performance of positive duties to provide assistance. The International Covenant on Civil and Political Rights (ICCPR), which the United States ratified in 1992, thus reiterates the ICESCR's declaration (Art. I.2) that "[i]n no case may a people be deprived of its own means of subsistence" while remaining silent on the positive

demarcating a life of human dignity, ethicists run the risk of succumbing to human rights inflation; endorsing manifesto rights that do not refer to basic human needs meriting institutional protection.

In truth, the tension between moral and legal interpretations of human rights is subtler than the above description suggests. A narrow moral interpretation, focusing on minimal or selective protection of individual core interests, runs the risk of rights truncation. Likewise, a broad legal interpretation, expanding protection to include superfluous social and political functions, runs the risk of rights inflation. To correct tendencies toward truncation and inflation, it is advisable to develop a comprehensive account of human rights that takes into consideration the multiple and complementary functions that both legal and moral human rights serve.[4]

But how? Bottom-up accounts that hew more or less closely to actual human rights documents and their practical implementation have the advantage of reflecting a working compromise between many different moral standpoints and legal aims. Nonetheless they suffer, as we have just seen, from lack of theoretical coherence. To mitigate this problem, the UDHR, which is not a legally binding treaty, was selectively codified by subsequent human rights covenants and treaties. The interpretation and enforcement of these treaties, which bind only signatory states, have been marked by disagreement and political expediency from the beginning. In practice, only gross violations of civil and political rights – genocide,

duty to provide subsistence. One of the first philosophers to criticize this view of human rights, Henry Shue (1996), defended the equal importance and complementarity of different categories of human rights – specifically, to liberty, security, and subsistence – and observed that none of them could be secured apart from implementing rights in both of the above covenants. At the same time, he observed that some of the rights contained in these covenants were more basic than others, providing necessary conditions for the exercise of any rights whatsoever. In particular, he doubted whether political rights – e.g., to participation in democratic elections – or cultural rights (aside from the right to education) were as basic as other rights – a position that I and others (Kymlicka, 1989; Ingram 2000) have criticized at length. Importantly, the distinction between basic and nonbasic rights corresponds to neither the distinction between legally enforceable and unenforceable rights nor the distinction between rights whose violation counts as a humanitarian crime under international law (subject to international intervention pursuant to the R2P) and rights whose violation does not so count. For further discussion of these distinctions, see note 13.

[4] James Nickel (2006: 270) lists fourteen of these functions, ranging from standards of criminal prosecution and adjudication used by courts, standards of assessment used by NGOs, UN committees, governments, and global lending institutions (such as the IMF) in determining progress along some dimension of welfare; standards of government conduct for criticizing, sanctioning, or militarily intervening, and guides for education, constitution-building, political action, and aspirational reform.

228   *World Crisis and Underdevelopment*

ethnic cleansing, and the like – are targeted under the current responsibility to protect (R2P) rule, and such violations have elicited only occasional international humanitarian intervention and criminal prosecution. Severe deprivations of economic welfare have not inspired similar responses.[5] Judging from historical practice, one might conclude that the right to welfare does not merit the same level of protection as that enjoyed by other human rights (such as the right not to be forcibly removed from one's homeland because of one's membership in an ethnic community). But in that case one should expect an institutional justification for not protecting this right as vigorously as other human rights.[6] That would require higher order theoretical reflection on the meaning and function of human rights in general.

In response to this objection, a defender of the practical approach can object that no higher order theoretical reflection is needed to determine whether a right to welfare is a human right and what degree of international protection it merits. That such a right is a human right, albeit not one whose protection warrants international intervention, is indisputable. Not only does the UDHR assert a person's right to "a standard of living adequate for . . . . the well-being [of a person] and his family" (Art. 25.1), but also the ICESCR asserts the same right as a legally binding right (A.3.5). Furthermore, if international law does not currently contain a complete list of rights that should be universally recognized, it nonetheless prescribes procedures for adding more rights. A group lobbying to add a hitherto unrecognized right to a healthy environment can persuade the United Nations Human Rights Council (UNHRC) to draft a set of principles to that effect, assuming that there is growing international consensus (as reflected in local charters and conventions) to do so. An endorsement of the draft principles by the General Assembly would further strengthen the case that a human right to a healthy environment exists, which would then become conclusive upon the widespread ratification of legally binding treaties asserting this fact.[7]

Of course, the formal positing of a right in international law cannot tell us whether it should have been posited in the first place. More importantly, human rights courts must appeal to norms that are not expressly stated in treaties in applying human rights law. For example, despite the fact that a human rights framework was not incorporated into the 1992 United Nations Framework Convention on Climate Change (UNFCCC)

---

[5] See note 3.
[6] See Chapter 6, note 5.
[7] I draw this example from Griffin (2008: 203–04).

or the Kyoto Protocol (1997), the Chair of the Inuit Circumpolar Conference submitted a petition in 2005 to the Inter-American Commission on Human Rights on behalf of the Inuit of the Arctic regions of the United States and Canada arguing that the impact of global climate change caused by the "acts and omissions" of the United States violated the fundamental human rights of the Inuit peoples. Subsequent petitions by the Maldives and Small Island Developing States sought to incorporate a human rights framework in the negotiating process of UNFCCC. A report entitled "Climate Change and Human Rights" (2008) that was developed by the International Council on Human Rights notes the advantage of shifting from aggregate cost-benefit analysis (emissions rights) to analysis of climate impact on individual human lives (human rights) in setting minimally acceptable outcomes and procedures for legal implementation. Should plaintiffs' petitions and supporting documents reach international courts a difficult decision will have to be made whether a right to a healthy environment merits a level of protection comparable to that assigned to other human rights.

A legal positivist who sought to completely eschew any reference to normative theory in making this decision would have little reason on which to base her decision. The Statute of the International Court of Justice seems to reject legal positivism as well, stating that, besides treaties and customary international law, its decisions will be based on such 'subsidiary means' as general principles of law recognized by all nations, past judicial decisions, and most importantly, the teachings of highly qualified publicists (i.e., experts) (Article 38.1). The use of such subsidiary means seems to require, as some legal scholars note, further appeal to legitimate interests, *jus cogens* norms, and most importantly the normative idea of humanity and the dignity of the human person as discussed in both binding and nonbinding conventions.[8]

So, not just theoretical reflection, but theoretical *moral* reflection, unavoidably enters into the legal practice of human rights (Ingram 2014c: 2014d). Legal positivists worry that such top-down theorizing about human rights will subordinate practical considerations to theoretical reflection in ways that misinterpret or undermine doctrinal human rights legal practice.[9] If our best philosophical reasoning concludes that

---

[8] See my discussion in Chapter 6 of Judge Elihu Lauterpacht's separate opinion delivered to the ICJ in the *Genocide* case (1993) which affirms the supremacy of *jus cogens* norms over both UNSC decisions and treaty law.

[9] In justly criticizing what he calls the "Mirroring View," which holds that international human rights law is justified only insofar as it mirrors, specifies, realizes, applies, or

human dignity is intrinsically bound up with living integrally with one's community and environment, a human rights court could conclude that a government's decision to invest in job-creating industry violates the hitherto uncodified individual human right of its (and other nations') citizens to an unpolluted habitat. Conversely, after reading Rawls, a human rights court could decide that the very concept of human dignity as it appears in the UDHR reflects a Western bias in favor of individualism, so that a government's decision to advance the common good of its citizens in the long run through temporary investments in destructive,

---

enforces moral human rights, Buchanan (Buchanan 2013: 14–23) notes that the UDHR and other human rights covenants limit the conduct of states vis-à-vis their individual subjects rather than merely specify moral rights that individuals can demand from each other and from society in protecting their personal humanity. Humanitarian law imposes an extensive range of duties on states to not only forbear from harming their subjects but also provide them with a minimum level of well-being in a way that does not discriminate on the basis of race, gender, ethnicity, or religion (32). Fulfilling these welfare and nondiscrimination duties need not require investing subjects with legal claim rights but when it does, the rights claimed are often rights to goods of a public nature, such as physical security, health, free speech, and democracy, that protect the social conditions necessary for each individual's equal welfare. These conditions transcend personal interests and impose costs (such as mandatory health and safety regimens, taxes for essential government services, military conscription, derogation of human rights during national emergencies, etc.) that cannot be sufficiently justified by the moral duty to respect any individual person's humanity. Buchanan insists that the moral aims served by the provision of social welfare, such as the facilitation of peaceful social cooperation, possess more than utilitarian justification; they are for the sake of each individual. However, unlike the moral individualism presumed by the Mirroring View, this legal human rights individualism comports with collectivist moralities and group rights, thereby circumventing what Rawls and to a certain extent Buchanan perceive to be a Western liberal bias in favor of moral individualism inherent in some references to the innate (metaphysical) freedom and equality of individuals contained in the UDHR and other human rights documents (314). According to Buchanan, the only way to square the extensive humanitarian legal duties owed to indigenous peoples, ethnic minorities, and other groups is to reconstruct concepts such as individual human dignity in a way that avoids appealing to the Mirroring View. That said, Buchanan's embrace of legal *status egalitarianism* (28) and humanitarian moral individualism (40) suggests a closer link between humanitarian legal duties and moral human rights than Buchanan acknowledges (Letsas 2014). This link is strongest in that area of humanitarian law dealing with gross criminal conduct involving the violation of *justiciable* human rights not to be tortured, kidnapped, murdered, and arbitrarily imprisoned (as Buchanan notes [314], it is weaker in that area of humanitarian law addressing humanitarian crimes against groups, such as genocide). In addition to these points, I would argue that moral norms pertaining to customary human rights law, such as the peremptory and compelling norms of *jus cogens* prohibiting slavery and torture, and the "requirements of public conscience" and "laws of humanity" mentioned in the Martens Clause that was inserted into the 1899 Hague Convention II (Regulations on the Laws and Customs of War on Land) reflect a genealogy motivated by moral human rights. I discuss this possibility below and in Chapter 6.

polluting industry – even by denying them the right to veto this decision through some form of electoral recall – is *not* a violation of an individual human right.

Such disputed theories about what the legal/doctrinal practice of human rights ought to be often single out a primary function that human rights properly fulfill. As we shall see, some of the most frequently mentioned functions that human rights are said to serve are founding constitutional liberties (Habermas 1996, 1998a, 2001), setting benchmarks for nonintervention and egalitarian cooperation between states (Rawls 1999a), selecting high-priority moral duties enjoining the protection of human beings from grave harm to their individual agency, however this is defined (Griffin 2008; Habermas 2010), and articulating moral aspirations enjoining the creation of a just society wherein each may achieve a flourishing and fulfilling life (Pogge 2008). Besides defending an exclusive core function that aims to critically broaden or restrict official lists of human rights, theoretical approaches tend to downplay or even dismiss the importance – of central concern to critical theorists – of historical experience, practical limitations, and political domination in shaping human rights traditions.

No doubt most accounts of human rights fall somewhere in between the extremes of pure theoretical reconstruction and practical interpretation (Griffin 2008; Buchanan 2013; Habermas 2010). However, I contend that theoretical and practical accounts of human rights, even when suitably conjoined, retain residues of elitism unless they are submitted to dialogical criticism and emendation that cuts across cultures and permits local flexibility in application and interpretation. This view resonates with the spirit of Habermas's democratic, or discourse theoretic, account of human rights, an approach, I argue below, that has much to recommend once it is suitably qualified.

Although a discourse theoretic account of human rights represents a top-down account of human rights – and as such poses the risk of theoretically misrepresenting legal and moral human rights practice – it is unique in its theoretical aim, which is to transfer the discourse of human rights from elite philosophical theory to democratic practice. However, before discussing the limits and possibilities of Habermas's discourse theory for moral and legal practice, it behooves us to first examine the political theory of human rights famously developed by Rawls, whose practical limitations Habermas himself singles out for criticism.

POLITICAL THEORIES OF HUMAN RIGHTS:
RAWLS ON THE LAW OF PEOPLES

Social contract theories view human rights as part of a subset of moral
norms that exclusively underwrite just cooperation between legal subjects,
as distinct from moral norms that articulate the dignity of the individual qua
human being (what I call the moral approach to human rights).
Paradigmatic examples of this view may be found in the theories of Rawls
and Habermas. Leaving aside their disagreement over the proper way to
justify and interpret human rights,[10] both philosophers reject the Mirroring
View noted earlier. In particular, both agree that deducing human rights
from a list of universal human interests and capabilities, which such rights
ostensibly serve to protect and promote, wrongly presumes consensus on
what these goods and capabilities are. By contrast, they believe that ascer-
taining features of legal agency, exercised between states or between subjects
of a single state, that require human rights protection is less controversial.[11]

I begin with Rawls's political approach to human rights as laid out in
The Law of Peoples because of its profound influence on a number of
thinkers who have expressly distanced themselves from the Mirroring
View and other moral approaches to human rights, including aspects of
the UDHR.[12] Rawls develops his approach with the intention of guiding

[10] There now exists a vast literature comparing Rawls's and Habermas's respective political
theories (Hedrick 2010; Finlayson and Freyenhagen 2011), much of it addressing their
contrasting theories of human rights (Ingram 2003; Baynes, 2009; Forst 2011, Flynn
2014). Their debate in the 1990s (Rawls 1999c; Habermas 1995, 1998c) already highlighted differences between their respective grounding of basic constitutional rights, with
Habermas favoring a conceptual understanding of civil and political rights as deontological trumps and Rawls interpreting these same rights as primary goods enjoying conditional priority over economic goods. In my opinion, social contract theory should not
prioritize categories of rights (or other values) but should underwrite thinner norms for
democratically negotiating the (multicultural) meaning and ranking of such substantive
goods. I find missing in the Rawls-Habermas literature any discussion of how this
democratic procedure can be integrated into courts (including, ideally, international
constitutional courts) that are delegated the task of adjudicating basic rights. See
Ingram (2014c) and Chapter 6.

[11] As Martha Nussbaum and Charles Taylor persuasively argue, the assumption that a
strictly procedural (or contractarian) account of human rights norms can (and indeed
must) dispense with substantive reasoning regarding human agency is unsustainable. The
desire to avoid philosophically contentious reasoning, however laudable, cannot (nor
should not) be the default standard for political philosophy, given the essential role, much
emphasized by critical theorists working within the Hegelian-Marxist framework, that
historical path dependency plays in legitimating institutions.

[12] Besides Buchanan, Charles Beitz (2009) and Thomas Pogge (2008) develop political or
institutional approaches to human rights that deviate from the Mirroring View.

the foreign policy of liberal democracies in their dealings with each other and with a variety of nonliberal, undemocratic regimes. This *state-centric* approach is justified on the grounds that peoples organized as states are (and will likely remain) the primary agents for enforcing human rights, so that what counts as a human right must be a right that all nations recognize. The aim of securing cooperation with illiberal and undemocratic peoples whose common good conceptions of legal justice meet an acceptable threshold of moral decency, dictates a contractarian method of reasoning that Rawls developed in *Political Liberalism* (1999b), which sought to show how incommensurable comprehensive systems of belief within liberal democracies that meet a threshold of reasonableness converge or overlap in supporting strictly free-standing liberal democratic values. In the *Law of Peoples*, a similar contractarian method is used to defend the stability of a "realistic utopia" composed of peace-loving and justice-seeking peoples that overlap in their agreement on eight principles of international cooperation.

Rawls maintains that all decent and liberal democratic peoples would agree to enforce a special class of urgent rights, "such as freedom from slavery and serfdom, liberty (but not equal liberty) of conscience, and security of ethnic groups from mass murder and genocide" (1999a: 79). Most striking in this formulation is the qualification that human rights need not be exercised by all persons in the same way, if they happen to belong to associationist societies that tailor that exercise to accord with the specific cultural roles and interests of different religious and gendered subgroups within society. Rawls explains that decent societies must permit individual members of such groups to be represented by one of their own in a consultation body to which government leaders are to be held accountable. However, individuals would not have an equal vote to express their personal preferences *qua individuals* in electing representatives.

In addition to nonaggression, Rawls also presents these rights as conditions authoritarian and outlaw regimes that fall below the moral threshold of decency must secure for their peoples if they are to remain immune from sanctions and external military intervention. Last but not least, Rawls says that such universal human rights "set the limit to the pluralism among peoples" (1999a: 80). Rawls is emphatic that these three functions – to specify, respectively, a necessary condition for recognizing the decency of a society's political and legal institutions, a sufficient condition for excluding justified and forceful intervention by other peoples, and a limit to the pluralism among peoples – serve to distinguish human rights from "constitutional rights or from rights of liberal democratic citizenship, or from other rights that belong to certain kinds of political institutions, both individualist or associationist" (1999a: 79–80). Thus, while he accepts Articles 3 through 18 of the Universal Declaration of Human Rights (1948) – which he says characterizes human rights proper – as well as their secondary implications, such as the human rights covered in special conventions on genocide (1948) and apartheid (1973), he expressly rejects as a parochial Western interpretation Article 1's assertion that "All human beings are born free and equal in dignity and rights" and that they "are endowed with reason and conscience and should act towards one another in a spirit of brotherhood" (1999a: 80 n.23). He rejects other rights stated in the UDHR, such as Article 22's right to social security and Article 23's right to equal pay for equal work, not because they reflect a Western liberal bias, but because they presuppose specific types of economic and legal institutions that are best characterized as one among many possible means for securing basic human rights, such as the right to subsistence.

Because Rawls understands the function of human rights doctrine in a law of peoples as setting forth conditions for the conduct of war and stipulating a threshold of domestic conduct sufficient to warrant legal immunity from foreign intervention, he endorses a short list of human rights whose violations are widely accepted to be the most serious, a controversial approach to human rights that Joshua Cohen and others (Cohen 2004; MacLeod 2006) have designated "enforcement minimalism." But the other two functions Rawls mentions, which fall under the different heading of "justificatory minimalism," require that he endorse a short list for other reasons. This list must be minimal, Rawls argues, because liberal democracies should voluntarily cooperate with some non-liberal, nondemocratic nations in upholding these rights. They should do so precisely because these other nations base their legal and political systems on a decent, common good, conception of justice that merits equal respect, even if it is not fully reasonable or just by Western, liberal democratic standards. To constrain these regimes to adopt liberal democratic institutions using even soft forms of government persuasion and diplomacy would violate liberal principles of toleration and reciprocity essential to peace.

Does Rawls's minimalist approach commit him to a partial or incomplete account of human rights?[13] Rawls endorses Article 3 of the UDHR

---

[13] By restricting sanctions and military intervention to the most severe human rights violations, enforcement minimalism acknowledges the detrimental impact these remedies have

which says that "everyone shall have the right to life, liberty, and security of person." But he excludes Article 21 of the UDHR, which asserts that "everyone has the right to take part in the government of his country ... through freely chosen representatives" and that these representatives will be chosen through "periodic and genuine elections" based on "universal and equal suffrage." Rawls's enforcement provision also excludes a more modest human right to have one's interests represented by means of a decent consultation hierarchy. The reason for excluding a robust human right to political participation, however, is empirical, for Rawls concedes that "[s]hould the facts of history, supported by the reasoning of political and social thought, show that hierarchical regimes are always, or nearly always, oppressive and deny human rights, the case for liberal democracy is made" (1999a: 79).

Contractarian theory need not be so minimalist, of course, and less truncated applications of it to problems of international justice and human rights could warrant a more cosmopolitan, liberal democratic theory. Thomas Pogge (2006), for instance, criticizes Rawls for having abandoned the contractarian approach he developed in *A Theory of Justice* (1971) and *Political Liberalism* (1993)(Rawls 1999b). According to Pogge, the two-stage method of reasoning developed in the early theory, which first justifies general principles of justice and then shows how these are to be applied contextually in subsequent stages of constitutional and institutional embodiment, is abandoned in working out a law

on the secure enjoyment of many institutional human rights that outlaw states otherwise promote. Enforcement minimalism that focuses exclusively on remedying mass extermination, expulsion, ethnic cleansing, and enslavement (the proposal advanced by Jean Cohen 2004) conforms to the UN's narrow interpretation of the responsibility to protect (R2P) but, as I argue in Chapter 6, it regresses behind current UN thinking about the deadly impact of poverty, climate change, health pandemics, and financial crises on global security (Lafont 2014), which involve the kinds of human rights deficits that the original ICISS version of R2P targeted. Recommendations to divide human rights into two tiers (enforceable and unenforceable) also regress behind the "indivisibility" doctrine of the Vienna Declaration (1993). Accommodating this objection, Nickel (2006: 274–75) sensibly argues that dividing human rights into two tiers – high priority/universally accepted and low priority/less universally accepted – allows us to retain a *full* complement of human rights whose ranking for purposes of adjudication and enforcement can be adjusted over time. Some difficulties with such a view are that high priority rights might not be universally accepted; the scale of a rights violation, rather than its priority, might matter most in decisions regarding enforcement; massive violations of low priority rights may effectively impede the enjoyment of high priority rights; and the interconnectedness of rights makes distinguishing higher – and lower-level rights difficult (Nickel 2006: 274–75). Too, the question of enforceability must address not only states but also GEMs and transnational corporations (TNCs). See notes 3, 39, and 46–48; Lafont (2014).

of peoples. Instead, Rawls deploys the device of the original position to show that his law of peoples comports, first, with an impartial consensus among liberal democratic peoples and, second, with an impartial consensus among decent peoples. No deeper justification of his eight principles is given to support their superiority in comparison to other alternatives. When Rawls does defend his list of human rights and his proposed duty to assist burdened peoples against cosmopolitan alternatives that seek to extend the principles of justice worked out for liberal-democratic society globally, he appeals to the absence of a global basic structure and disagreement on liberal democratic values, assumptions that have been questioned by Pogge and others.

Allen Buchanan (2006), for instance, questions Rawls's presumption of extreme value pluralism. Rawls's presumption seems to depend on the mistaken view that persons inhabiting associationist societies are incapable of rationally abstracting a concept of individual identity and individual right from a concept of the collective good.[14] If the presumption depends on the moral claim that it is unreasonable to expect them to do so, then that presumption has not been convincingly justified. Rawls compares our respect for decent hierarchical peoples to our respect for decent hierarchical institutions such as the Catholic Church, but membership in the latter is voluntary and does not comprehensively determine public rights and duties, a point he himself makes elsewhere in explaining why consensual patriarchal families must respect equal rights of citizenship. As Buchanan elsewhere notes, the status egalitarianism of human rights need not conflict with collectivist moralities and group rights so long as the insistence on nondiscriminatory treatment is not grounded in a comprehensive subject-centered individualistic ethic. In fact, both he and Habermas ground this status in (to use Buchanan's words) "the capacity for responsiveness to reasons," or rational accountability (Buchanan 2013: 137). Construed as a threshold rather than a scalar concept, this capacity could "presumptively accord severely cognitively impaired individuals the same basic legal status as the rest of us but permit exceptional treatment of them, either as a matter of law or of less formal social practice, under certain extreme conditions" (Buchanan 2013: 139).

Rawls defends decent hierarchical societies on the grounds that they count as genuinely voluntary cooperative associations that merit equal respect (1999a: 84). But are they? Buchanan (2006) and Habermas

---

[14] In this connection, see Habermas's earlier objection to Rawls's political liberalism (Habermas 1995, 1998c), and Rawls's reply (1999c) to Habermas.

(2001: 125) question whether societies that equate public accountability with responsiveness to dissent without permitting a full and equal freedom of speech and association (as specified in Articles 18–20 of the UDHR) even qualify as voluntary associations. Indeed, Habermas goes so far as to insist that valid consent is only possible in liberal democracies, in which in theory, if not in practice, consent is presumed to meet high thresholds of rationality and reasonableness, pursuant to demanding expectations regarding publicity, openness and inclusion, equal freedom to question accepted opinion and propose alternatives — preferably unconstrained by social and legal power.

According to Habermas, free and rational consent follows from internal critical reflection on fundamental values and interests that has been provoked and informed by public argumentation, argumentation whose standards of rational conviction presuppose an orientation to reaching agreement, compelled only by mutually convincing (i.e., shareable) reasons. Using this demanding ideal of rational consent, Habermas challenges the less demanding model of consent implicit in Rawls's contractarian approach (Habermas 1998c). He charges that the bare fact of an overlapping consensus, in which different parties agree to norms for different (and possibly incommensurable) reasons, begs the deeper question about whether this consensus is fully rational.[15]

Rawls's counter – that if only one of several incommensurable rationales supporting an overlapping consensus is true, the consensus in question is valid – doesn't meet Habermas's objection because it provides no *independent* reason for believing that at least one of the overlapping rationales *is* true. Rawls never submits his law of peoples to critical discussion involving competing principles (as Pogge notes). Indeed, when he addresses the difficult question of whether strands of Islamic social and legal thinking might be compatible with liberal and Western democratic ideals, he leaves the question open, which suggests that his default presumption of the reasonableness of extreme value pluralism may be premature (Rawls 1999a: 110 note 39, 151 note 46). Equally premature is his intention to "leave aside the many difficulties in interpreting ... rights and limits, and take their general meaning and tendency clear enough" (1999a: 27). That the "general meaning and tendency" of human rights is *not* clear enough is evidenced by the United States and the forty signatory countries to the 1993 Bangkok Declaration disagreeing rather

---

[15] I qualify this criticism of Rawls's contractarian approach in Chapter 2, note 13.

vehemently over whether social, cultural, and economic rights are human rights at all, and, if so, whether they trump civil and political rights.[16]

In sum, the contractarian political approach Rawls deploys in rejecting the liberal democratic interpretation of human rights contained in the UDHR arguably exaggerates the degree of global value pluralism between peoples. Furthermore, there is no reason to think that an overlapping consensus between peoples is stable for the right reasons. Finally, if voluntary cooperation depends on strong notions of reciprocity in which the terms of the social contract are presumed to respect the equal dignity of each and every individual – a condition dependent on individual rational consent to, or absence of dissent from, these terms – then Rawls must exclude any reference to the equal dignity of persons as a reason why decent hierarchical peoples respect human rights. Decent peoples must guarantee individuals equal protection under the law and must treat like cases alike, but they need not regard individuals as having equal rights to plan their lives as they see fit, based solely on their inherent dignity.

LEGAL THEORIES OF HUMAN RIGHTS: HABERMAS ON CONSTITUTIONAL LAW

Habermas interprets the contractarian approach to human rights less ecumenically than does Rawls, defending a model of rational consent that presupposes liberal democratic institutions. In this respect Rainer Forst,[17]

---

[16] See note 3. For a critique of Rawls's insensitivity to the colonial legacy and his inability to respond to the postcolonial aftermath by taking seriously a multicultural dialogue on human rights, see Flynn (2014).

[17] Forst grounds human rights in a universal *moral* right to justification that defines valid norms in terms of a principle of *nondissent*: Only those norms are justified to which no affected individual could reasonably dissent. Applying this discourse theoretic principle recursively in light of social facts about typical historical violations of human dignity allows us to construct a basic set of abstract (unsaturated) rights principles. In order for human rights to be fully realized and defined, this stage of *moral* constructivism must be followed by a stage of *political* constructivism in which peoples democratically apply (interpret, or legislate) these principles in the form of concrete prescriptive rights in a manner that is sensitive to their unique historical and cultural context. Following Rawls's mature understanding of his stage-sequential theory of justice, Forst insists that because moral constructivism draws upon pertinent facts about human capabilities, moral psychology and the like, it can yield universal human rights norms that are both procedural *and* substantive, imposing positive duties to provide the economic, social, cultural, and political means for their exercise. In this respect, moral constructivism differs from classical natural law theory in drawing its core content from both historical facts and abstract norms, while leaving the more precise determination of human rights to democratic legislation. (Despite its rejection of natural law theory, Forst's theory here evinces

Seyla Benhabib,[18] K. O. Apel,[19] and many others who follow in Habermas's footsteps agree, however much they differ on other points.[20] Habermas's discourse theoretic qualification of the social contractarian approach also goes beyond its Rawlsian counterpart in defending a conceptual link between human rights and the equal dignity of the individual person. However, in some ways this congenial compatibility with the UDHR is purchased at the expense of abandoning the *equal* importance

the Mirroring View justly criticized by Buchanan.) Although Habermas accepts a genetic link between the moral concept of human dignity and the legal concept of human rights (see below), he denies that human rights are grounded in a common *moral foundation* of the sort proposed by Forst (Habermas 2011: 296–98).

[18] Like Forst (see note 17) and Habermas, Benhabib (2013) defends a reflexive, two-stage approach to mediating (or reconciling) cosmopolitan humanitarian law and locally bounded democratic self-determination. Invoking Hannah Arendt's claim that human rights are "[moral] rights to have [legal] rights," Benhabib derives human rights from a discursive principle of communicative freedom, which recognizes the equal dignity of each person. This general moral right to equal status within a legally secured polity is encapsulated in international humanitarian law in general terms only. The legitimate political actualization of this universal strand of legal normativity in the legal form of concretely prescriptive, contextually sensitive legal rights must await a "democratic iteration" at the level of a bounded polity. Although she endorses a conceptual link between a moral discourse principle and a concept of human rights, it is less clear whether she endorses a conceptual link between the concept of human rights and democracy in the way that Habermas does. Also unclear is whether she agrees with Forst's view that the substantive content of moral human rights can be discursively specified prior to being reflexively constructed at the legal and political stage.

[19] Apel can be credited with having copioneered the concept of discourse ethics. He alone among those who ground human rights in discourse theory insists on interpreting this derivation as an *a priori* (viz., transcendental) moral justification (Apel 2002; Ingram 2010a: 167).

[20] Forst, Apel, and Benhabib derive human rights from principles of discourse that, unlike Habermas's own principle of discourse (D), are put forward as *moral* principles. In general, I find any *monistic* derivation of human rights from principles of communication, justification, or discourse problematic. With Buchanan, I hold that the content of legal human rights is justified relative to the *plural* aims they serve (Buchanan 2013: 312). *Moral* human rights are grounded in human interests basic to living a worthwhile life either directly or indirectly. The right not to be tortured requires just as little justification as the perceptual fact that the ball before me is red. By contrast, the right to life in its more concrete *legal* specification – but not in its general *moral perception* – does require discursive justification, simply because of the many conventional exceptions that attach to its application. Consequently, the principle of human rights is *conceptually* linked to the principle of justice only in the specific juridical sense associated with (the human right to) equal protection under the law. Institutions securing distributive, democratic, and discursive justice are indeed *instrumental* to the equal exercise of legal human rights and so their moral grounds provide additional justification for these rights, quite apart from justifying or realizing moral human rights.

of a human right to subsistence, a feature of the UDHR which Rawls accepts without qualification.

Habermas's theory of rights has undergone a number of changes over the past thirty-five years. Although his earlier efforts derived constitutional rights from morality (Habermas 1988) his most recent and definitive effort bears a positivist inclination. As he puts it: "Human rights are juridical *by their very nature*, what lends them the appearance of moral rights is not their content, and most especially not their structure, but rather their mode of validation, which points beyond the legal systems of nation states" (Habermas 1998a; Ingram 2014d).

In *Between Facts and Norms* (Habermas, 1996) Habermas deduces human rights from the classical civil and political liberties informing Western constitutional law. Such rights are not moral rights; they do not follow from prior moral duties. Instead they follow from two axioms: the abstract form of modern law (the principle of subjective, or private, right), which permits legal subjects freedom to pursue their aims without interference from others and without having to justify them to others; and the principle of discourse (D), which asserts that "just those action norms are valid to which all possibly affected persons could agree as participants in rational discourse" (1996: 107).[21] The intersection of (D), which is not to be confused with a principle of moral universalization, and the legal form yields the simple idea that legal subjects should have *equal* rights.[22] The next important move in this deduction, once we derive equal permissive

---

[21] Forst's monism of morality and law, Habermas argues, neglects the essentially *juridical form* of human rights as specifying "subjective rights," or *permissions to act without need of justification* that can be *enforced* against government and nongovernment agents. Moral rights, by contrast, derive directly from moral *duties*, so that, properly speaking, the moral right to justification follows from a prior moral duty to justify one's actions to others (Habermas 2011: 296–98). By conceiving human rights as permissive rights, Habermas commits himself to interpreting human rights violations as violations of reciprocal *negative* duties to desist from causing harm, specifically by interfering with the freedom of others. Although this interpretation can be used to indict global economic institutions for having denied poor people of their rightful access to the world's resources (see Pogge 2008), it does not explain a government's positive duty to secure their social, economic, and cultural human rights. Forst's monistic view does, despite its apparent endorsement of the Mirroring View justly criticized by Buchanan.

[22] Note that the derivation (or construction) of unsaturated human rights principles is itself an exercise in monological reasoning, much like the kind of reasoning Habermas rejects in criticizing Rawls's method of justifying his two principles of justice. The stage sequential procedure of practical reasoning (from ideal to nonideal social premises), which roughly corresponds to monological and dialogical procedures, respectively, thus finds application in Habermas's as well as Rawl's justification of their political philosophies. For a more detailed discussion of this point, see Chapter 2, note 13.

rights, equal rights to membership in a legal order, and equal rights to legal procedures for processing legal claims, is the derivation of *democratic* political rights. These rights follow from a second application of (D) to the procedure of lawmaking, which explains the voluntary, binding authority (or *legitimacy*) of laws: we are obligated to obey only those coercive laws which we ourselves have contributed to democratically legislating. Thus, in the words of Habermas, there exists "an internal relationship between human rights and popular sovereignty" (1996: 123). The biconditional relationship between human rights and democracy leads, finally, to a third application of (D), the actual democratic legislation of a democratic constitution in an ideally representative constitutional assembly.

Habermas's insistence on a conceptual link between democracy and human rights seems both historically and logically mistaken. Constitutional rights to property, freedom of conscience, freedom of speech, and the like predated the birth of democratic constitutions in the late eighteenth century. Furthermore, only some of these classical rights are really necessary for democracy, understood as an institutionalization of inclusive discursive deliberation (one needn't have a right to property in order to freely deliberate about the scope of one's right to practice one's religion, say). In response to these objections, Habermas insists that his biconditionality thesis does not assert an existential but only a normative link between human rights and democracy, and that some classical rights (to personal freedom, for instance) have a basis in the "grammar of the legal code" rather than in democracy or norms of discourse (Habermas 2001: 117–18).

But the human right to subsistence and other positive social rights do not seem to have a basis in either the positive right to democratic participation or the modern legal form, which structures rights as permissive negative liberties. In fact Habermas adduces a fifth category of social rights that go considerably beyond a minimal human right to subsistence insofar as they function to secure the all-purpose means to realizing liberal and democratic rights. These include "basic rights to the provision of living conditions that are socially, technologically, and ecologically safeguarded" (1996: 123). However, by asserting that the first four categories of basic rights are "absolutely justifiable" while the fifth category "can be justified only in relative terms," Habermas consigns social rights to a status below that of basic (i.e., relatively absolute and unconditional) human rights. The first three categories of equal rights are essential to the very concept of a modern legal code, the fourth category of democratic rights is essential to the concept of legitimacy. By contrast, the fifth category of social rights serves to guarantee the "fair value" of "civil and political rights" (as Rawls puts it). Habermas invokes this phrase against the signatories to the Bangkok Declaration (1993) who seek to reverse the priority of civil and political rights over social, economic, and cultural rights (Habermas 2001: 125).[23] Because the latter rights are instrumental toward realizing civil and political rights, they cannot trump these rights.

The priority of civil and political rights over social rights is retained in Habermas's view that international law must develop along a constitutional path. Habermas here recommends that distinct categories of injustice be dealt with by different legal regimes, with the UN policing human rights violations as agent-caused crimes and transnational organizations negotiating terms of global distributive justice. This priority is reinforced by Habermas's claim that "liberal (in the narrower sense) basic rights make up the core of human rights" and so "acquire the *additional* meaning of liberal *rights against the state*" (Habermas 1996: 174).

In sum, the advantage of Habermas's constitutional interpretation of human rights, which adduces social rights beyond the meager right to subsistence, cannot compensate for its conceptual subordination of this category of rights as instrumental — but not essential – to constitutional rights. But if Habermas is wrong and social rights are full-fledged human rights, then he must either reject his equation of human rights with constitutional rights (as Rawls does) or concede that social rights are essential to constitutional rights, after all. Indeed, Habermas's later insistence that human dignity finds integral protection only with the constitutional institutionalization of cosmopolitan democracy does seem to entail that social rights conceptually complement other human rights within a fully realized constitutional order.[24]

---

[23] For additional discussion of the ranking problem see Chapter 7.
[24] The narrowness of Habermas's constitutional approach contrasts sharply with his objection to neoliberalism's restriction of human rights to the "negative liberties of citizens who acquire an immediate status vis-à-vis the global economy" (2006: 186) and his strong endorsement of Germany's constitutional entrenchment of social rights. Habermas's instrumental understanding of social rights tracks Buchanan's, except for the latter's insistence that civil and political rights possess no greater weight than social rights in securing the equal exercise of human rights (see note 9). This problematic feature of Habermas's constitutional derivation of human rights does not diminish the considerable merits of his proposal for a constitutionalization of human rights (including social rights), as my own discussion of constitutional human rights review (Ingram 2014d) attests. For an exhaustive analysis of the moral and legal aspects of Habermas's theory of human rights, see Moka-Mubelo (2016).

Before examining Habermas's later approach to human rights, let me briefly note a related difficulty with equating human rights with constitutional rights or with any other legal right. One might argue that juridifying human rights is not always essential for their effective implementation (Pogge 2008: 68–69).[25] This is necessarily true if human rights designate mainly moral *standards* for assessing society's success in progressively safeguarding the basic dignity of its members. Although the concept of human dignity entered constitutional and humanitarian law only after the Second World War, it played an important moral role in historically motivating the establishment of constitutional and humanitarian law dating back to the European Enlightenment. So, it would appear that the moral concept of what we today call human rights both historically and conceptually preceded the legal concept. The question then arises: Does this fact alone dictate a Mirroring View approach to understanding legal human rights of the kind I am seeking to avoid?

MORAL APPROACHES TO HUMAN RIGHTS

The Mirroring View exemplifies one iconic way of grounding legal human rights in morality. But this way of grounding legal human rights, whether proceeding from natural law premises or not, hardly exhausts the moral arguments in support of human rights. Rawls and Habermas both emphasize that legal human rights will be supported by some moral reasons, either collectivist or individualist, regardless of whether these reasons appeal to the moral human rights of individual persons. Evan Buchanan concedes that besides the instrumental moral reasons justifying social and political human rights there is the moral principle of equal status itself, which refers back to the inherent dignity of the individual. This "moral individualist" principle, he reminds us, need not be understood in a natural law or moral mirroring manner (Buchanan 2013: 105).

---

[25] Some of the goods morally required to satisfy an acceptable level of human flourishing need not (and in some instances, should not) be legally mandated. As Martha Nussbaum notes (Nussbaum 2000: 295), patriarchal customs, which regulate familial relationships that are otherwise legally constituted, cannot be outlawed without violating consensual rights to familial privacy, even though such customs effectively deny women secure access to education, subsistence, and other goods to which they have legitimate human rights claims. The appropriate remedy to such human rights violations is therefore not legal (or exclusively legal) but pedagogical. Because human rights are generally formulated at a high level of abstraction, they leave open the types of remedies that can bring communities into compliance with them.

In a recent essay, "The Concept of Human Dignity and the Realistic Utopia of Human Rights," Habermas explains how this might be done by clarifying his own juridical approach to human rights with reference to the "moral-legal Janus face of human rights through the mediating role of the concept of human dignity" (Habermas 2010: 464).

I did not originally take into account two things. First, the cumulative experiences of violated dignity constitute a source of moral motivations for entering into historically unprecedented constitution-making practices that arose at the end of the eighteenth century. Second, the status-generating notion of social recognition of the dignity of others provides a conceptual bridge between the moral idea of the equal respect for all and the legal form of human rights (Habermas 2010: 470 note 10).

In contrast to his earlier deduction of basic rights in *Between Facts and Norms*, which derived the idea of equality from a *nonmoral* (or morally neutral) principle of discourse (D), Habermas here pursues a less "deflationary" (and less abstract and formal) derivation of this idea that recalls Honneth's more concrete, historical reconstruction in terms of a substantive moral notion of mutual recognition. This notion of dignity captures the formal idea, expressed in Kant's categorical imperative, of universal equal respect for each person as an absolute end, but its legal significance refers back to a complex ethical genesis.

Once *dignitas* – a strictly legal status that originally grounded the Roman nobleman's particular claim to preferential treatment – became a universal moral status attached to humanity, it opened the "portal" through which moral duties to respect the equal humanity of each individual entered the legal domain of claim rights (Habermas 2010: 469, 473).[26] In short, human

---

[26] Habermas traces the modern concept of dignity from the Stoics' supreme elevation of *dignitas humana* in the cosmic order to Christianity's proclamation of the equal dignity of each individual made in the image of God, and finally to modern secular morality's demand that each be treated with equal respect (473–74). In the Christian natural law tradition, especially beginning with the late Spanish scholastic tradition of Suarez and continuing through Locke, the moral duty to respect others gets linked to the notion of a natural (innate) inalienable claim right. Although this metaphysical linkage of morality and law is retained in the American Declaration of Independence and the French Declaration of the Rights of Man and Citizen, and persists in the language of the UDHR, ICCPR, and ICESCR, which characterize human rights as rights that all persons are "born with," it contravenes the modern, rationalistic conception of law inaugurated by Hobbes. For Hobbes and the liberal political tradition, the authority behind legal rights consists entirely in their having been legislated (posited) by a sovereign; hence the foundational human rights documents also "declare" (or "constitute") human rights (469). Likewise, in the rationalist moral tradition of Kant, the *moral* foundation for basic legal rights cannot be described as a natural (in born) *fact* but must also be described

dignity elevates a moral *duty* to respect others to the political status of a legal *claim* against others that one be respected.[27]

In addition to grounding the universal status of human persons as claimants demanding equal, unconditional respect from others, the concept of human dignity also possesses substantive meaning, simultaneously referencing a past history of suffering, humiliation, and disrespect and anticipating a future beyond indignity (Habermas 2010: 467–68). It is this substantive meaning that links the static formal status of legal equality to a dynamic aspiration, a concrete utopian promise of fully realized dignity possessing "inventive" and "explosive political force," in which it becomes clear, to cite Article 22 of the UDHR, that economic, social, and cultural rights, no less than civil and political rights, are equally "indispensable to [an individual's] dignity and the free development of his personality" (Habermas 2010: 468). Embedded in a long history of suffering, indignity, and disrespect, the substantive concept of dignity helps us to recall that all categories of human rights are logically

as a kind of positing, in this instance, however, one stemming from a purely rational act of self-legislation with reference to an ideal, otherworldly Kingdom of Ends. This attempt to reinvest human rights with moral authority by redescribing that authority in terms of an act of legislation fails insofar as rational moral legislation is conceived of as occurring within an otherworldly, rather than this-worldly, domain – a gap that is overcome once we redescribe moral authority in terms of a rational will that is the outcome of this-worldly practical discourse (474–75). For Habermas, the apparent contradiction between innate moral rights and posited legal rights contained in human rights documents is dissolved once we (a) reinterpret the original authority underlying moral rights in terms of a constitutional practice regulated by the principle of discourse (D) and the principle of universalizability (U) and (b) reinterpret the original authority underlying legal rights in terms of a different constitutional practice regulated by that same principle (D) *and* the concept of human dignity, which bridges the (legal) permission to claim rights and the (moral) duty to respect rights. The great advantage of this complicated conceptual genealogy of human rights is that it captures the subtle conceptual linkage between morality and human rights without obviously reducing legal human rights to moral rights, as the Mirroring View requires. Its disadvantage, at least from the standpoint of legal documentation and practice, is that it does not seem to apply to human rights that attach to groups and corporations. Thus, from Buchanan's perspective, this conceptual genealogy would seem to be too closely allied to the Mirroring View (and the correlative attempt to delegitimize human rights attached to groups and corporations) if it were advanced as the *sole* moral ground of human rights. However, if this conceptual genealogy is offered as an explanation for only human rights that attach to embodied persons, then it can serve the useful task of prioritizing the human rights claims of persons over competing human rights claims of groups and corporations, as I argue below. See Buchanan (2013: 20) and note 9.

[27] Whether Habermas's appeal to human dignity as link between moral duty and legal claim renders grounding of human rights indistinguishable from similar justifications advanced by Forst and other "monists" (see notes 17–21) is a question I cannot pursue here.

interconnected, regardless of their distinctive moral grounds (Habermas 2010: 466).[28]

The heuristic function of human dignity is the key to the logical interconnectedness between [civil, economic, social, and cultural] categories of rights ... Human dignity grounds [their] indivisibility ... Only in collaboration with each other can basic rights fulfill the moral promise to respect the equal dignity of every person *equally* (2010: 468–69).

Affirming the equal status of all categories of human rights pursuant to the Vienna Declaration (1993) corrects a defect in Habermas's earlier constitutional approach. Furthermore, linking two important legal functions demanded by human rights — protection of persons' equal treatment *and* welfare — avoids two problems that arise whenever these functions are separated, or more precisely, whenever one function is subordinated to the other (Buchanan 2013: 28–36, 46). Human rights that only protect a baseline of welfare still allow for its discriminatory provision, the indignity associated with inferior treatment in comparison to others; conversely, human rights that only prohibit discrimination still allow for a common state of undignified existence (Buchanan 2013: 99–101). Habermas's linking of the egalitarian and welfare functions served by human rights in his integral concept of dignity reinforces the idea that human rights are intended to legally safeguard the nondiscriminatory enjoyment of robust civil, political, economic, social, and cultural rights of a kind that can only be enjoyed by an equal citizen inhabiting a fully realized social democracy.[29] So construed, neither welfare nor equality are subordinate to (or merely instrumental for) each other.

Assuming that welfare and equality converge in the dignity vouchsafed by social democracy, it seems advisable to qualify their conceptual convergence in the following way. To begin with, the concept of dignity cannot clarify the human rights of corporations, which claim a right to due process, or groups, such as indigenous peoples and even developing nations, which as I noted earlier claim a right to development. This is not a problem so long as one thinks that current legal documents and practices

---

[28] See my discussion of Buchanan (2013) in note 9 where I qualifiedly endorse his understanding of the plural grounds underlying different types of human rights.

[29] It may be that the current human rights order primarily understands "equal status" to mean *intrasocietal* equality between conationals and not *intersocietal* (or global) equality between cosmopolitan citizens. However, as Habermas and Buchanan note, the order's inclusion of a right to democratic governance that must, *in some sense*, extend to global governance institutions entails a commitment to global equal basic status (Buchanan 2013: 145).

that presume that groups and corporations have such rights are philosophically misguided. But defending that conclusion would likely involve an appeal to some version of the Mirroring View.[30]

Secondly, appealing to the dignity of the democratic citizen cannot easily explain the supreme equal status enjoyed by all embodied persons. Habermas argues that the "infinite dignity" of the individual that Kant imputed to the "inviolability of [his] domain of free will" (Habermas 2010: 474) must be given a more precise, mundane interpretation as determined by the "self-respect and social recognition from a status in space and time – that of democratic citizenship" (479). Linking dignity to liberal democratic citizenship in this way might be questioned for two reasons: it selects a subset of social statuses meriting recognition as dignity-bestowing – specifically those pertaining to democratic citizenship – which persons living in undemocratic societies do not yet possess; and it selects a subset of vital moral capacities that young children and persons with severe mental disabilities lack. Only if Habermas uses "dignity" to mean a possible (as of yet unrealized and utopian) way of life and not a universal formal status that attaches to each person can he equate one dignity-conferring species potentiality – the capability for moral (rational) accountability – with the enjoyment of one concrete historical status: democratic citizenship in both national and cosmopolitan senses of the term (Habermas 2010: 476). In short, Habermas needs to better distinguish the static idea of human dignity qua formal marker of supreme legal status from the dynamic concept of human dignity qua substantive marker of an evolving, utopian idea of human development (welfare) that grounds the indivisibility of historically evolving human rights.

James Griffin's grounding of human rights in a narrower notion of normative agency leads him to explicitly ponder what is only implied in Habermas's genealogy of dignity: Do young children and mentally disabled persons possess human rights at all? But Griffin draws another implication from this grounding strategy that speaks to its limitations. As he notes, possessing human dignity and living a "minimally worthwhile life" do not directly entail democratic citizenship unless we factor in a second ground for human rights: human practicalities.

In this, as in much of Griffin's pluralistic account of human rights constrained by human practicalities, there is much to recommend, including (*pace* Habermas) his denial that human rights always trump other worthwhile ends (Griffin 2008: 20). However, whereas Habermas's

[30] See note 9 and Chapter 7.

appeal to human dignity as an inventive source for human rights that grows out of and unifies the "plethora of human experiences of what it means to get humiliated and be deeply hurt" (Habermas 1996: 467–68) runs the risk of inflating the content of humanitarian law, Griffin's insistence that human rights be narrowly tailored to protecting individual agency runs the opposite risk of truncating that same content.[31]

A strategy that promises to avoid the extremes of inflation and truncation involves settling on a range of important human capabilities, not restricted to human dignity or normative agency narrowly construed,[32]

[31] Griffin criticizes as either superfluous or excessive human rights language in the UDHR and other official human rights documents that cannot be grounded in human normative agency and practicalities. For example, he reasonably notes (2008: 99) that our strong interest in achieving (as the ICESCR puts it) the "maximal attainable health" possible cannot ground a corresponding a human right to maximal health. Elsewhere, this "mirroring view" critique (see note 9) displays a problematic side, as when Griffin (2008: 5, 207–09) criticizes as inflationary the right to work and the right to "periodic holidays with pay" (UDHR, A. 23–24). As Buchanan notes, such institutional legal human rights as these might be justified as advancing other social ends (for instance, the creation of a welfare state) that are instrumental to the exercise of human rights (Buchanan 2013: 18). Again, Griffin's claim that group rights to nationality and to the preservation and protection of subnational minority cultural/religious identity are not human rights, but are legal rights of a different sort, or are moral rights of a different (justice-based) sort, reflects his view that moral group rights, if they are at all justified by human rights, must be reducible to moral human rights of individuals (to religious freedom, liberty, self-determination, etc.) (2008: 266, 275). Joseph Raz's view (Raz 1994) that group rights protect public goods, such as solidarity and democracy, that must be enjoyed collectively speaks against Griffin's instrumentalist view. For Raz, such group rights impose duties that cannot be easily overridden by any individual interest (think of the state's right to military conscription). Griffin's counter – that states can claim their rights only on condition of respecting the individual human rights of their citizens and resident foreigners (2008: 275) – at best establishes that the duties imposed by this (and many other) group rights are conditional, as is the case with all human rights, which may sometimes conflict with other high-end moral values (Ingram 2010; 2011). For more on the conflict between individual human rights and group rights, see Chapter 7.
[32] Amartya Sen (1999) and Nussbaum (2000) have pioneered the capabilities approach to human rights as an alternative to Rawls's primary goods approach. Nussbaum provisionally lists about ten capabilities (paraphrasing, these are life, bodily health, cognition, emotion, practical reason, social affiliation, concern for other living things, play, and control over one's environment). Human rights are claims (and aspirations) grounded in *innate* capability potentials possessed by infants and children (basic capabilities), in *naturally developed* capabilities of mature persons (internal capabilities), and in internal capabilities whose development and exercise is advanced or hindered by *external* (mainly social and institutional) circumstances (combined capabilities). While basic capabilities ground the "worth and dignity of basic human powers" sufficient to justify extending equal human rights to life and bodily integrity to infants, internal and combined capabilities ground higher levels of human functioning whose neglected development suffices to establish a state-condoned human rights deficit (Nussbaum 2000: 78–86). Whether

that human rights are supposed to protect. According to this pluralistic approach, which has been proposed by Martha Nussbaum,[33] a particular human right might protect some capabilities but not others. Supposing that consciousness is one of the important capabilities in virtue of which human life acquires dignity, young children, profoundly mentally disabled adults, and possibly nonhuman beings (Gilabert 2015)[34] could possess some important moral and legal human rights.

Following accepted human rights doctrine and practice recommends being theoretically open-minded about the meaning and extension of the concept of dignity, whether we understand this concept to refer back to normative agency, human capability, or historical experience of diminution, marginalization, cruelty, and insult. Beyond these general features of personhood, and apart from the circumstantial practicalities associated with the just and legitimate legal protection of personhood, dignity grounds the egalitarian status of human rights holders.

This status-designating grounding attaches an additional value to individuals that other human rights claimants, such as groups and corporations, cannot avail themselves of. Ascribing dignity to only individuals functions to prioritize their human rights vis-à-vis the potentially conflicting human rights of groups and corporations (Lafont 2016).[35] Dignity

these latter capabilities are sufficient to justify the full range of human rights in the absence of other practicalities is doubtful, as I indicate in note 33 below and in Chapter 2, note 18.

[33] "Pluralism" in this context refers solely to the plural capabilities and statuses that adhere in personhood and underwrite different human rights. Besides personhood, Griffin (2008: 37) discusses another ground explaining human rights: *human practicalities*, viz., limits of social and legal association, human motivation, and so on. If justice forms a part of the conditions of social and legal association, then equality and democracy must be additional factors explaining, respectively, the status of human rights claimants and the legitimacy of humanitarian law. Beyond these grounds, there are, as Buchanan notes, (see note 9) social and political reasons supporting human rights to specific types of institutional provision that cannot be justified solely in terms of protecting individuals' capabilities and statuses. Finally, "human rights pluralism" can be extended to include the multiple ends (political and nonpolitical) human rights serve in many different contexts and institutions. See Nickel (2006) and notes 3 and 4.

[34] In an unprecedented case initiated by the Nonhuman Rights Project and supported by the Center for Constitutional Rights in an *amicus curiae* letter brief, the New York Supreme Court in April 2015 held that four chimpanzees kept for research at Stony Brook University were legal persons (albeit not bearers of human rights) that had a right not to be held in captivity and a right not to be owned. On July 30 Judge Barbara Jaffe reversed her preliminary ruling that would have granted *habeas corpus* relief, citing conflicts with legal precedent.

[35] The Asian values controversy, which I discuss in Chapter 7, illustrates this conflict with regard to developing nations exercising their human right to development in a manner that subordinates individual rights to duties to the community. With regard to the human

fulfills this formal function regardless of whether those who agree on this status-designating purpose disagree on its substantive moral content. These latter disagreements touch on the definitional problem of dignity. Because defining dignity is a fraught enterprise, its place in humanitarian law instigates rather than mitigates tendencies toward rights truncation or (what is historically the case) rights inflation. Mitigating these tendencies within the current legal framework will remain a difficult but necessary task.[36]

UNDERSTANDING HUMAN RIGHTS CONTEXTUALLY: PLURALISM RECONSIDERED

I began this chapter by arguing that the apparent incoherence of the UDHR regarding the moral, political, and legal status of human rights justifies theoretical reconstruction and clarification. Such clarification must be sensitive to the multiple functions and justificatory grounds of human rights. Political and legal theories should be wary of prematurely dismissing the ecumenical moral content of human rights documents out of hypersensitivity to ethnocentrism or rights inflationism. Part of that content is the idea of human dignity, which seems indispensable for understanding the equal legal status of persons. Dignity highlights the supreme value of one distinctly human capability – rational moral accountability – that elevates the

---

rights of corporations, Article 34 of the European Convention of Human Rights recognizes applications put forth by "any person, nongovernmental organization or group of individuals." Using this definition of human rights agent, the Russian oil company Yukos lodged a complaint with the European Court of Human Rights in 2004, which was accepted in 2009 (after Yukos had been liquidated in 2007), claiming that its human rights to a fair trial (Article 6) and to peaceful enjoyment of its possessions (Article 1), among other human rights, had been violated by the Russian Federation when it denied the company adequate time to prepare its defense on charges of unpaid taxes and subsequently confiscated and auctioned off its primary holdings. In 2011, the court ruled in favor of Yukos on these points but not on others. Although some of the Convention's human rights, such as the right to a fair trial, the right to the peaceful enjoyment of one's possessions, the right to nondiscrimination, and the right to associate freely, apply to corporations, others, such as the right to privacy and the right to freedom of speech do so, if at all, in a more problematic way. Other human rights, such as those protecting the bodily integrity of living persons, do not apply at all (Muijsenbergh and Rezai 2012).

[36] Buchanan (2013: 286–92) mentions seven ways this might be done, emphasizing three especially promising options: introducing institutional filters for proposed treaties, distinguishing rights from administrative directives for their realization, and allowing human rights courts to refuse to hear cases. Less promising, in my opinion, are strategies that encourage states to include reservations in treaties or that prevent judges from expansively interpreting human rights principles.

human rights of individuals above the human rights of groups.[37] This combined capability (invoking Nussbaum's phrase) depends on the development of society without being subordinated to it.[38] It points beyond moral and legal autonomy to the full realization of social freedom within democratic institutions.

Human capabilities, historical indignities, and institutional practicalities together explain the scope and rationale underlying current human rights law. Only by being constitutionally interpreted, statutorily codified, and judicially inserted into a body of case law (Ingram 2003)[39] can human rights protect individuals from predations by governments and other institutions that exercise power over them.[40] As things currently stand, failure to protect persons' human right to welfare can support civil but not criminal actions against states, with GEMs and TNCs enjoying virtual immunity in this regard.[41] As we shall now see, expanding the scope of actionable relief requires reconceptualizing human rights failures as institutional violations of strong, negative duties.

INSTITUTIONAL AND INTERACTIONAL HUMAN RIGHTS: DO GLOBAL ECONOMIC STRUCTURES VIOLATE HUMAN RIGHTS?

Every year 18 million of the earth's six billion inhabitants die from lacking means of subsistence. We who live in developed nations typically blame this catastrophe on drought, overpopulation, resource mismanagement, corrupt government, and other local factors, thereby relieving ourselves of any responsibility for this suffering. At the same time, we do not hesitate to invoke the language of human rights in condemning this state of affairs. Either we do so in the name of moral progress, as when we say, following the UDHR, that the world has fallen short of achieving an aspiration essential to civilized humanity; or we do so in the name of moral offense, as when we condemn selected government officials for having committed acts of genocide, ethnic cleansing, and the like.

---

[37] See note 9 and my discussion of group rights in Chapter 7.
[38] I discuss Nussbaum's capability approach in note 32.
[39] I develop this point further in Chapter 7.
[40] As Johan Karlsson Schaffer notes (Schaffer 2017) courts also allow the hearing of nonjusticiable human rights claims with the intent to publicize a cause, exercise political leverage, or reshape public opinion.
[41] See notes 1 and 3 for a discussion of the contrasting ways in which the responsibility to protect rule has been interpreted.

One might ponder whether either of these two senses of human rights – as *aspirations* and *standards* for measuring moral progress or as justiciable *claims* against government officials for failing to discharge their duties to their citizens – generates a moral discourse sufficient for coming to terms with the injustices of globalization discussed in Chapter 4. In particular, one wonders whether they adequately respond to the fact that impersonal international norms and global institutions prevent the poor from freely accessing their means of subsistence.

There are several difficulties with conceiving a legal human right to subsistence and welfare only as a positive duty in the way that Rawls, Habermas, Buchanan, and Griffin do. First, a positive duty to provide assistance is normally thought to be weaker than a negative duty to refrain from causing harm. But the injustice of a government or economic order that denies persons free access to subsistence indicts the institution in question and, in varying degrees of responsibility, all those who contribute to maintaining it, for failing to fulfill appropriate negative duties towards those persons as well. Second, the strength of positive duties varies in proportion to our solidarity with those with whom we feel duty-bound. Although ties of global friendship might be extended to the point where we feel a positive duty to assist "burdened societies" (as John Rawls argues), Habermas himself notes that our solidarity with strangers is primarily ignited by violations of a negative duty to respect their freedom to procure their living. We feel outrage – and accordingly demand international intervention – when a government deliberately sets out to starve to death some significant portion of its citizenry. We feel only discomfort and resignation when people starve for lack of assistance owing to the seemingly insurmountable costs of providing it.

In order to capture the way in which governments and global economic institutions can be said to violate a negative human rights duty – nearly equivalent in gravity to the criminal violation of persons' most important civil rights to life – we need to show how impersonal institutions can be held liable for criminal negligence in erecting legal barriers to the secure enjoyment of basic welfare.

Following Pogge and Shue, I shall henceforth distinguish human rights claims against institutions from human rights claims against individuals (Pogge 2008: 69–73; Shue 1996: 65). The latter (interactional) claims impose correlative duties on persons to either positively assist or negatively refrain from harming others. At one end of the interactional rights spectrum, a *libertarian* theory of human rights asserts that a public official P is *not* failing in his *negative* duty to person Q who is subject to his control so long as P's official conduct causes Q no harm by intentionally violating Q's human right to access some basic good. If P acts otherwise, then he has failed in his duty by violating Q's right. Suppose a leader of a local Janjaweed militia in Darfur prevents members of a tribe from freely accessing international food relief specifically targeted for them by intentionally stealing it. Both the leader of the militia and Omar al Bashir, President of the Sudanese government that sanctions such behavior, fail in their negative duty toward these people and can be said to violate their right to subsistence. By contrast, if an impersonal economic structure permits the World Bank to loan Bolivia money on the condition that Bolivia sell off its public water rights to private multinationals in ways that threaten to deprive residents of Cochabamba and El Alto of secure access to water, no personal harm has been done to these residents and we cannot say that their right to subsistence has been violated.[42]

According to the libertarian conception of human rights, the economic structure is not responsible for harming these residents because this conception regards responsibility in terms of personal liability.[43] This model

---

[42] Succumbing to pressure from the World Bank to refinance old debt in order to take out new loans, Bolivia sold Bechtel the rights to Cochabamba's water supply and distribution and passed laws that required the purchasing of licenses in order to collect rain water. Bechtel then proceeded to increase water prices by as much as 200 percent (equivalent to 1/5th of the average family income). This action sparked five months of rioting that led to the cancellation of the contract barely six months after it had been ratified in 1999. A new law (Ley # 2878) passed in 2004 recognized traditional water rights, guaranteeing water rights for irrigation and indigenous farming communities. But in that very same year, a second "water war" erupted in El Alto, which had had its water rights sold to the French multinational Suez in 1997. Pegging rates to the dollar, water prices rose 35 percent. Aguas del Illimani, the private consortium owned by Suez, charged households $445 for installing water service and ended up leaving 200,000 people without service. Water service is crucial, however, since lack of clean water is the chief cause of child morbidity and mortality in Bolivia. In 2002, the UN Commission on Economic, Social, and Cultural Rights declared that "The human right to water is indispensable for leading a life of human dignity. Water and water facilities must be affordable to all."

[43] Young (2007: 159–86) illustrates the difference between liability and social connection models of responsibility with reference to the phenomenon of structural injustices, which arise when the unintended and aggregate effect of actions bring about impersonal structures, such as global market systems and their subsidiary institutions, that create unequal opportunities for developing and exercising human capabilities between differently positioned groups of persons. Within the sweatshop institutions emergent in global capitalism, we can distinguish between violations of workers' rights directly caused by individual disregard for minimum wage, workplace safety, and collective bargaining laws – often abetted by government officials – and violations of subsistence rights caused by the lawful and normal operations of a market economy in which sweatshops are forced to operate on a precariously thin margin of profitability in order to meet the demands of multinational retailers and their affluent clients.

of responsibility defines harms as deviations from a normal background of conventionally sanctioned hazards that are causally traceable to the discrete actions of individual wrongdoers. However, in the water privatization case, the harm is not caused by the deviant actions of a discrete class of persons; it is rather caused by the all-too normal hazards generated by global conventions regarding borrowing and resource extraction privileges bestowed on governments, which in turn are constrained to borrow and sell resources by the impersonal (albeit politically supported) laws governing a global capitalist economy.

At the other end of the interactional rights spectrum, a *utilitarian* theory of human rights asserts that a public official P is not failing in his *positive* duty to Q so long as P helps Q gain access to her water up to the point where P sacrifices resources possessing value comparable to the value of Q's accessing her water. If P has ample resources to help Q but does not, he has failed in fulfilling his positive duty and can be subject to civil (but normally not criminal) action. Or suppose that P simply has no resources to help Q access her water because sources of water have been privatized and the government is too poor to purchase said water rights. His positive duty is derogated by circumstances beyond his control and he cannot be held liable for failing to fulfill his duty. When a government cannot provide the resources needed to ensure that its inhabitants enjoy their human right to subsistence, the positive duty to provide subsistence may then fall upon the UN Humanitarian Affairs and Emergency Relief Coordinator or other capable parties (NGOs, wealthy governments, etc.) who are not socially connected to the inhabitants in question but who nonetheless have a responsibility to protect (pursuant to the original ICISS draft of the R2P principle).[44] Failure on the part of these third parties to provide subsistence might merit severe moral condemnation but, falling short of constituting a harmful act or omission, does not merit civil or criminal action.

Libertarian and utilitarian theories of human rights present us with opposed visions of our moral and legal responsibilities with respect to upholding human rights. The libertarian theory presents a *minimalist* view, which holds public officials only liable for actively preventing persons (their own or another government's legal subjects) from freely exercising their human rights. The utilitarian theory represents a *maximalist* view, which also holds public officials – primarily government leaders charged with the welfare of their subjects, and secondarily persons in

---

[44] See note 1 for further clarification of the ICISS draft.

charge of global social welfare organizations and leaders of wealthy countries – liable for not helping persons (their own or another government's legal subjects) to exercise their rights, where the amount of help to be provided, though indeterminate, is costly.

Despite their differences, both libertarian and utilitarian versions of the interactional theory of human rights share certain features. First, they see the failure to uphold human rights as stemming directly from *personal* acts or omissions to act. Second, they see this failure as either a rights violation; i.e., as an actual deprivation of some basic good to some person, or as a legally culpable act of official negligence in protecting rights whose provisions are immediately threatened. These two features indicate the fundamental weakness of the interactional approach. Far from being personally intended, deprivation of basic resources might be the unintended (if foreseeable) side effect of normal institutional functioning. Furthermore, what is important is not that a person has actually been deprived of (or has been threatened with the loss of) a basic good as a side effect of normal institutional functioning but that her access to it has been rendered *insecure* (Shue 1996: 13). In the water privatization case, we might want to say that Q's access to her water – her human right to water – was not regarded as a socially recognized legal claim. Privatization may not have directly deprived Q of water. Perhaps she was one of the lucky ones who could afford – at least for the time being – to pay the higher rates. Nonetheless, Q's right to subsistence was no longer securely exercised; it may not have been violated but it was also not legally protected.

Who was responsible for this human rights deficit? It is tempting – using an interactional model of human rights – to say that Bolivia's leaders and the CEOs of Bechtel and Suez were. But these persons were acting lawfully, in accordance with institutional procedures and mandates. The real agents responsible for this deficit are institutions: the Bolivian government, the WB, and the institutions that constitute global capitalism: trade agreements and international lending institutions that reflect the unfair bargaining leverage of wealthy multinationals, banks, and nations; unjust monopolies over resources; and structural constraints that force – and conventions that allow – government officials to sell their nation's resources.[45]

---

[45] The motives for selling off a nation's resources are often not benign, or intended for the country's good. Resource-rich countries such as Nigeria seem destined to have corrupt rulers who find willing buyers of discounted resources in developed countries who, in turn, are willing to bankroll loans to these same rulers so that they can buy the arms that keep them in power.

Again, it is tempting to think that an institutional human right to subsistence should take the form of a claim against a government for failing in its positive duty to provide its subjects with a decent standard of living; under the ICISS draft of the R2P framework, such a claim would have been addressed to other governments as backups in the event of domestic failure. Instead, current human rights practice recognizes such justiciable claims only under the category of civil complaints. Individuals can file formal complaints with human rights compliance bodies when their own (or some other) government has failed to fulfill its positive duty to provide adequate welfare as mandated by a treaty to which they are signatory.[46] More relevant to my argument, governments of developing countries have declared that actions undertaken by the WTO violate a *negative* duty to refrain from imposing conditions of trade that impede their performance of their treaty-mandated human rights duties.[47] The claim that WTO policies impose conditions of trade that harm poor persons (threaten their lives) amounts to charging the WTO with criminal negligence. There is no reason why corporations like Bechtel and Suez should be excused from respecting human rights, either.[48] Complying

---

[46] Seven of the nine core international human rights treaties have instituted individual complaint mechanisms for addressing the failures of states to adhere to the three pillars of human rights responsibilities (to respect, protect, and promote human rights); The Optional Protocol of the ICESCR (in force since May 2013) specifically allows the UN Committee on Economic, Social, and Cultural Rights to hear complaints from individuals or groups who claim their rights under the ICESCR have been violated and it also allows the Committee to investigate, report upon, and make recommendations regarding "grave or systematic violations" of the Convention (Lafont 2014: 9).

[47] Less formal complaint mechanisms have been adopted by states to protest rights-infringing policies of GEMs. After the UN committee exercising oversight of the ICESCR issued a statement in December 2001 asserting that global agreements on trade and property rights (such as TRIPS) could not conflict with states' human rights obligations – including the duty not to adopt "retrogressive measures" – the WTO ratified a declaration, put forth by twenty developing nations, that affirmed "the WTO members' right to protect public health and, in particular, to promote access to medicines for all" (WTO, Doha Declaration on the TRIPS Agreement and Public Health). To be sure, neither the WTO nor the IMF/WB has entrenched international human rights law in their operational mechanisms.

[48] The Special Rapporteurs commissioned by the UNHRC and OHCHR have proposed operational human rights standards that could be applicable to both GEMs and TNCs in line with John Ruggie's 2009 Report to the UNHRC. This report enjoins TNCs to exercise "human rights due diligence" by (a) adopting a human rights policy, (b) undertaking and acting upon a human rights impact assessment, (c) integrating human rights policy throughout all company divisions and functions, and (d) tracking human rights performance to ensure continuous improvement." (See "Report to the Human Rights Council of the Special Representative of the Secretary General On the Issue of Human Rights and

with the letter of trade law, after all, is perfectly compatible with acting in ways that prevent people from securely accessing vital resources vouchsafed to them by human right.

The line of reasoning I am pushing has far-reaching ramifications for how we address the harms of global climate change and environmental degradation. Perhaps habitat destruction as a side effect of doing business should not be regarded as a social cost to be balanced against benefits of economic growth. Perhaps the International Council on Human Rights properly noted in the report I cited earlier that the right to emit greenhouse gases into the atmosphere could no longer be justified by its presumed benefits, regardless of its negative impact on the human rights of vulnerable peoples to basic resources. Governments, GEMs, and TNCs that significantly contribute to rising sea levels and desertification prevent people from accessing the very land their country and culture is built upon. No gain in global wealth can compensate for this loss of self-determination.

In sum, I have argued that there are two sorts of justiciable human rights claims: interactional and institutional. According to the *interactional* model, a justiciable human right is a claim against a discrete individual who wields official or unofficial police and administrative power over a rights claimant. Here, failure to respect the claimant's right entails a straightforward human rights *violation*, typically involving the commission of a serious humanitarian *crime* on a massive scale (such as genocide) which issues in criminal prosecution conducted under the auspices of a national or international criminal court.

The second, *institutional* model of justiciable human rights responds to a weakness in the first model, namely a failure to conceptualize as criminal or legally culpable human rights negligence for which personal

Transnational Corporations and Other Business Enterprises" adopted by the HRC on July 2011 and the more recent "United Nations Guiding Principles on Business and Human Rights" [2013]. Both documents are discussed by Lafont [2014: 16]). Currently, TNCs can only be held accountable for human rights violations that count as international crimes as defined by the Rome Statute of the ICC. TNCs domiciled in Europe can be sued for civil human rights violations only in European Courts. The sole country that has provided recourse to plaintiffs who wish to seek extraterritorial relief is the United States. Recently the Seventh, Ninth, Eleventh, and D.C. Circuit Courts have upheld corporate liability under the Alien Tort Statute (1789), which allows aliens to file civil suit against TNCs for violations of the customary "law of nations" or a treaty entered into by the US government. However, the 2013 US Supreme Court's dismissal of the *Kiobel* case, involving a suit brought by twelve plaintiffs against Royal Dutch Shell alleging collusion with the Nigerian government's sponsorship of torture and murder, held that the ATS does not provide relief for extraterritorial civil harms.

causal responsibility cannot be ascertained. These infractions can take two forms: failure to perform positive duties in implementing reasonable measures to reduce standard threats to life and failure to perform negative duties to refrain from imposing conditions that impede the performance of these positive duties. Importantly, both types of infractions can be caused by the normal, legal functioning of domestic or international institutions. With respect to the former kind of infraction, Pogge has in mind international trade agreements, lending practices, and resource extraction privileges that prevent the poor from gaining secure access to their fair share of the world's resources, including potable water, uncontaminated land, adequate food and shelter, etc. According to this model, a failure by a government, GEM, or TNC to respect the claimant's right entails a human rights deficit, whose severity is proportional to the number of those (discriminately) harmed as well as to the foreseeability of the harm inflicted.

Both models for understanding how human rights are justiciable bring into play the vital interests of specific individuals. However, in cases where plaintiffs seek to enjoin harmful institutional conduct, judges are often required to balance the harm done to an individual's vital interests (protection of which is guaranteed by human right) against competing rights of other agents (states, corporations, GEMs, TNCS, and other subgroups). Human rights are not unconditional – they do sometimes conflict with each other and with other important institutional values. But the dignity accorded individual persons endows their human rights claims with presumptive priority over the human rights of corporate persons and groups.

LEGITIMATING HUMAN RIGHTS: DISCOURSE THEORY AND DEMOCRACY

Let me conclude by briefly noting the relevance of discourse theory to what I have said above. The juridical construction of human rights law through official declaration, binding treaty, or judicial interpretation raises concerns about that law's legitimacy. The law succeeds in coordinating interaction legitimately to the extent that those affected by it converge in believing that the benefits of coercion outweigh the costs, which is to say that the law functions in a reasonably just and efficient manner in procuring a generally desired social good. This general *standard* of legitimacy comports with different *criteria* of legitimacy depending on institutional context (Buchanan 2013: 178–96).

Within the context of constitutional law, the moral idea of equal human dignity finds expression in the idea that each should enjoy equal protection under the law in such a way that securing that protection requires holding those who make the law accountable for the content of that law. Therefore, in this context, a *prima facie* moral argument can be made for democracy. Because judges who serve on constitutional courts where basic rights are adjudicated are not elected, a question arises how proceedings at this level can be made democratically accountable.

I have argued elsewhere (Ingram 2014c, 2014d) that this legitimation problem can be theoretically and practically mitigated. But does a similar problem of democratic legitimacy arise at the level of international law? Should procedures for making and applying humanitarian law be subject to the same criteria of democratic legitimacy that apply to the constitutional state?

There are plausible reasons for thinking not. An "ecological" account of legitimacy of the sort proposed by Buchanan appeals instead to a symbiotic division of labor whereby states and international organizations derive their legitimacy from each other: the international humanitarian regime outsources functions of legislating, adjudicating, and enforcing human rights to states (most of them constitutional democracies) whose own legitimacy (and the legitimacy of the international state system) in turn depends on submission to human rights law. So understood, "the lack of representative legislative institutions and a developed, independent judiciary operating within a context of constitutional constraints on legislation" at the international level does not imply a legitimacy/democracy deficit (Buchanan 2013: 316).

As Buchanan rightly remarks, this justification of the international order's legitimacy does not eliminate the tension between constitutional and international law, especially insofar as the latter requires constitutional incorporation of treaties imposing robust welfare duties and sometimes even changes in constitutional law itself. When treaties change the character of the polity by altering constitutional terms of collective self-determination, they must be constitutionally incorporated through some form of "robust democratic authorization" (Buchanan 2013: 48).

This qualification, and Buchanan's own concern that dependence of human rights law on voluntarily assumed treaty obligations weakens the universal scope of human rights, recommends that we consider a more centralized institutionalization of that law in which criteria of democratic legitimacy apply. If, for instance, a supermajority of ratifying states is legally empowered to unilaterally impose a treaty on all nations (Buchanan's recommendation [Buchanan 2013: 27]), then problems of majoritarian tyranny arise that require constitutional solutions – at the international level.

I shall address in Chapter 6 the long-term project of constitutionalizing international law that Habermas and others have pursued to deal with the issues raised by Buchanan (including the weakness of treaty law in dealing with global economic injustices that impact the exercise of human rights). Suffice to say, the problem noted above regarding the democratic legitimation of constitutional review resurfaces at this level. Without going into detail regarding the solution to this problem, it is clear that the appointment of large, representative panels of judges who are publicly accountable to one another and to global public opinion marks an important step toward realizing discourse theoretic values at this elite level of technical-ethical theorizing (Ingram 2014c, 2014d).

But the heart of a discourse theory of law remains political democracy. Few would dispute that the modern, liberal idea of democracy presupposes the constitutional entrenchment of some human rights, most notably those that protect individuals' freedom of (political) association and freedom of (political) speech. Less clear is whether human rights presuppose democracy. Must there be included among the many human rights that are universally recognized by all peoples a human right to participate as an equal in the periodic election of lawmakers and executive officers and, if so, why?

Rawls's worry about the apparent ethnocentrism of this legacy of Western individualism underestimates how widespread personal indignation to global threats posed by modern administrative apparatuses and market economies has become. But although democracy might be the best (and only) empirically effective remedy to these threats, there does not appear to be any *conceptual* necessity for its being the sole institutional form that a legitimate human rights regime must assume. There is no logical connection between freely deciding upon and carrying out a worthwhile plan of life – which I take to be the central (if not exhaustive) unifying idea underlying the capabilities and interests earmarked for protection by human rights – and casting an equally weighted (albeit insignificantly influential) ballot in electing government officials. Even under the best of circumstances, democratic majoritarian government can threaten individual interests. Furthermore, combining the moral idea of equal individual dignity with practicalities does not justify the logical necessity of liberal democracy. Supposing that the Habermasian school is correct in its assumption that one of the relevant human practicalities that bears on the specification of human rights is a deep-seated (transcendentally unavoidable) connection between rational suasion and moral consent, it would seem to follow that the practical inclusion of democracy among those goods that ought to be protected by human rights is conceptually necessary. Democracy so conceived would not necessarily require an exercise of legislative self-determination mediated by liberal, one-person, one-vote procedures for deciding policies and electing representatives. But it would require institutional guarantees securing nondomination: publicly accountable government protecting a right to individual dissent, unrestricted participation in the formation of public opinion, and freedom of political association. Only by expanding our pool of reasons to include empirically contingent practicalities referring, for instance, to the superior historical track records of modern-day liberal democracies in protecting human rights can we make a fully compelling case for including among our universally recognized legally binding human rights a right to a distinctly liberal democracy.

So, if Buchanan is right, a human right to democracy, like many other human rights, might be justified, apart from serving the vital moral interests of individuals, as the best means for procuring social justice and political peace – perhaps the most important factor conditioning the secure and stable enjoyment of all human rights. Indeed, how else should one understand the UDHR's admonition (A.1) that "All human beings ... should act towards one another in a spirit of brotherhood," if not as a call to global solidarity in assuming democratic responsibility for progressively realizing the demanding moral aspirations for a minimally humane world?[49]

---

[49] While institutional authorities can be held liable in courts of law for authorizing human rights violations and deficits, a global capitalist economy, whose growth dynamics disparately harm the vital interests of the poor, is in important respects *authorless*. This economic system arose not through treaty but through the unintended aggregate effects of billions of market transactions spanning over half a millennium. Although no person or institution is causally responsible for its creation, everyone contributes to its maintenance – from exploited sweatshop workers in the developing world to affluent consumers in the developed world. The fact that everyone is indirectly connected to everyone else through the global economy implies shared responsibility for its structural injustices. In the absence of shared *liability*, where juridical notions of agent causation no longer apply, shared *responsibility* can only be forward-looking, oriented toward fostering grass-roots social movements that have as their aim democratic reform of global institutions.

6

Making Humanitarian Law Legitimate: The Constitutionalization of Global Governance

Human rights impose duties on government to respect and safeguard the capabilities essential to dignity. The failure of states to discharge this function explains why human rights were embedded in international law. But the current international human rights order has also failed in this regard, raising the question: Is the current humanitarian regime justifiable?

From the critical theory standpoint adopted in this book, the current humanitarian regime was justified as a necessary response to problems inherent in the regime it replaced.[1] The League of Nations did not recognize the human rights of individuals but only the rights of ethnic minorities. The United Nations was created to protect these rights but its failure to intervene in preventing or effectively mitigating genocidal conflicts in Rwanda, the former Yugoslavia, the Middle East, and countless other places – and its failure to adequately respond to the life-threatening global crises I recounted earlier – suggest that its continued existence might no longer be justified.

---

[1] See Hauke Brunkhorst's (2014) evolutionary account of international human rights law. Other critical theoretic approaches, both within and without the Frankfurt School tradition, take a more critical view of international human rights law and law in general. Thus, while Walter Benjamin (1996) and Giorgio Agamben (2005) equate law with violence and positively assess its future disappearance, Jacques Derrida (1990) recommends a more reform-minded "deconstruction" of law. Michel Foucault's genealogy of modern legal institutions (2008), by contrast, unmasks the complicity of modern law with liberalism and utilitarianism in grounding the political economy of modern subjectivity and governmentality. Foucault's and Agamben's writings are especially pertinent to understanding international law as a locus of power relations (Foucault) and arbitrary exceptions (Agamben) that render legal status ambiguous and subject to arbitrary disciplinary action.

Similar doubts appear in a 2004 report of the UN High-Level Panel on Threats, Challenge, and Change, *A More Secure World: Our Shared Responsibility*.[2] The report observes that human rights are at risk of becoming empty manifesto rights, subject to self-serving interpretation and selective enforcement by governments and beholden to the foreign policy agendas of the most powerful members of the UN Security Council (UNSC).[3] The lack of democratic accountability plaguing that body seems to be characteristic of the entire process of originating and interpreting human rights.[4] Finally, the report's expanded definition of security risks that threaten human rights takes aim at global economic multilaterals (GEMs) and transnational corporations (TNCs) whose conduct threatens the capacity of states to protect their subjects from economic and environmental harm.[5] Given the ineffective

---

[2] The Report invoked a "new security consensus" that extends the concept of security risk beyond interstate conflict, civil war, terrorism, possession of WMDs, and organized crime to "any event or process that leads to large-scale death or lessening of life chances and undermines States as the basic units of the international system" (Report 2). Poverty, disease, social marginalization, and environmental degradation are mentioned as examples of such security risks, but the Report takes special aim at the UNSC, focusing on its unjustified selectivity in militarily intervening on behalf of civilian populations endangered by terrorism and ethnic cleansing: "Too often, the United Nations and its Member States have discriminated in responding to threats to international security. Contrast the swiftness with which the United Nations responded to the attacks on September 11, 2001 with its actions when confronted with a far more-deadly event: from April to mid-July 1994, Rwanda experienced the equivalent of three 11 September attacks every day for 100 days, all in a country whose population was one thirty-sixth of that of the United States" (Report 19).

[3] Military actions, sanctions, and other coercive measures deigned to mitigate gross human rights violations must be approved by the UNSC without veto from any of its permanent (P-5) members. Even criminal prosecutions of human rights violations undertaken by the International Criminal Court (ICC) must be referred to that court by the UNSC or a signatory country in which the violation occurred. Today, the inaction of the UNSC in response to the Syrian government's continued violation of its citizens' human rights and the current immunity of Syrian president Bashar Assad from criminal prosecution stems from Russia's threat to veto any UNSC action that might weaken its strongest ally in the Middle East.

[4] The creation of human rights law lacks democratic accountability if this is understood to presuppose a legal procedure for originating and ratifying law through popular plebiscite or parliamentary legislation. To be sure, global public opinion can press governments to collaborate in drawing up human rights treaties. But treaties are binding only on signatory governments, some of which are not democratically accountable. The statutory specification and legislative ratification (if required) of human rights treaties at the national level is often undertaken in a way that may be democratically accountable. The process of translating vague treaties into enforceable laws still allows governments to interpret their human rights duties in ways that serve their own interests.

[5] In 2001, the International Commission on Intervention and State Sovereignty (ICISS) formulated the function of state sovereignty to include a "responsibility to protect"

and unaccountable enforcement of human rights at the highest level, it is hardly surprising that many critics of the current human rights regime claim that its costs outweigh its benefits and that its very existence violates the right of states to sovereign self-determination.⁶

(R2P), which was later endorsed by the General Assembly of the UN at the World Summit of 2005. In its original formulation, the ICISS defined R2P to cover a broad range of security threats, including "overwhelming natural or environmental catastrophe, where the state concerned is either unwilling or unable to cope or call for assistance and significant loss of life is occurring or threatened." The World Summit Outcome Report rejected this broad definition of life threats as too controversial and too practically open-ended, and restricted the list of threats to include war crimes, crimes against humanity, genocide, ethnic cleansing, and serious human rights violations. As I noted in Chapter 5, under ICISS's broader definition states (such as Brazil) were entitled to bring human rights complaints against the WTO.

⁶ This charge has been leveled against the R2P principle (see note 5). The First Pillar of the R2P principle asserts the hitherto unprecedented international legal doctrine that sovereign states have a duty to protect their subjects. In cases where they are unable to do so, they may call on other states and international civil society organizations for assistance (Second Pillar). Finally, all states are tasked with the responsibility to prevent criminal atrocities from occurring by using timely and decisive action, principally of a peaceful nature (Third Pillar). Unlike the ICISS proposal, the World Summit Outcome Report does not list six criteria for nonpeaceful intervention. The ICISS report carefully distinguished R2P from humanitarian military intervention (which, despite limiting sovereignty, does so in the name of states' right to intervene rather than in pursuit of their responsibility to protect). The ICISS noted that military intervention would have to meet the following six conditions: 1. *just cause* (permissible only in cases in which serious and irreparable harm to human life was immanent); 2. *right intention* (permissible only for the sake of preventing human suffering); 3. *last resort* (permissible only when all other preventive measures have failed or would likely fail); 4. *proportional means* (permissible only to the extent necessary for achieving the objective); 5. *reasonable prospect of success* (permissible only if the consequences of non-intervention are likely to be worse); and 6. *right authority* (permissible only when authorized by the UN Security Council). So construed, R2P does not weaken sovereignty so much as redefine it, tailoring its function in the international legal order as principally one of cosmopolitan duty holder rather than of communitarian rights-bearer. Nevertheless, because the World Summit Outcome Report deleted the six criteria for military intervention contained in the ICISS report, it has been criticized for allowing interventions that may have violated state sovereignty or failed to uphold state sovereignty. For example, it has been criticized for allowing ulterior political motives to pervert the principle of a just cause (the 2011 NATO intervention in Libya under the pretext of R2P morphed into a regime change intervention). It has also been criticized for its selective "double standard" enforcement, in which Palestinians living in Gaza were not protected from Israeli Defense Force tactics targeting civilians and Syrians were not protected from war crimes inflicted on them by their own government and those seeking to topple it. Most serious, as the Saudi R2P intervention in Yemen illustrates, the current R2P regime prescribes no international panel of experts to authorize, regulate and monitor R2P interventions in order to reduce civilian suffering to a minimum. Finally, current applications of R2P do not require that military interventions be followed by peaceful interventions aimed at securing the long-term safety of civilian populations.

If the very thought of abolishing an international human rights regime is unconscionable to those who justifiably find the moral costs associated with the state system rationally unacceptable, the current practice of allowing powerful states to determine when a human rights violation has occurred and what should be done about it is not less so. The world's only democratic hegemon, the United States, will not risk lives and capital in protecting foreigners abroad unless doing so serves to advance its own strategic interests[7]. The creation of a world state that would remedy these defects is not only practically unrealistic at this point in time but also threatens the concentration of power in a distant tyrannical bureaucracy.[8] That the UN Charter's recognition of national sovereignty prohibits this from occurring merely confirms a plausible assumption that any democratic alternative to tyranny implies territorially bounded governance, however susceptible to popular revision the boundaries of such governance should be.

Conceding the infeasibility of a world state, I submit that mitigating the abuses permitted under our current human rights regime will nonetheless require strengthening that regime's coordinating capacity by implementing a constitutional separation of powers similar to what we observe in a liberal democracy.[9] On one hand, a more representative General Assembly could be empowered to pass enforceable resolutions regulating the content and conduct of international trade and security-related agreements pertaining to the resettlement of refugees, the treatment of immigrants and guest workers, and the equitable distribution of burdens associated with climate change and environmental degradation. On the

---

[7] The High-Level Panel's report, however, emphasized that "there is little evident international acceptance of the idea of a security best preserved by a balance of power, or by any single – even benignly motivated – superpower" (Report 62).

[8] Hobbesians who identify legal systems with state apparatuses possessing centralized legislative and enforcement capabilities argue that international law is at best a primitive anticipation of a world state and at worst a contradiction in terms (Rabkin 2005). Allen Buchanan (2013: 226–44) provides a compelling rebuttal of this position in his defense of international law as an ecological system that relies heavily on states for statutory interpretation and enforcement of international law. I argue that an ecologically structured system of international law does not go far enough in allaying Hobbesian concerns about uncertainty in enforcement and interpretation. My proposal for creating an independent international human rights court speaks to this concern.

[9] In this chapter, I discuss the objections that an international human rights order violates national sovereignty, inevitably serves the interests of the most powerful nations, and lacks institutional legitimacy. I discuss in Chapter 7 the objection that such an order imposes an egalitarian individualism that is incompatible with collectivist moralities embedded in some world religions.

other hand, instituting an international court empowered to review UNSC decisions and universally enforce human rights treaties would protect individuals and states from unchecked abuses of power.

I submit that a human rights regime reformed in this way would be more effective and democratically accountable. But is reform really necessary to accomplish these ends? Does it not also risk the threat of domination?

Answering these questions will require examining the meaning of legitimate governance and democracy as well as their relationship. Governance that is regulative rather than legislative might require little more than transparency for its legitimacy, which can be achieved without instituting democracy. If international human rights are understood as softly regulating states' domestic policies, then their democratic origination and ratification in a reconstituted General Assembly might not be necessary. Conversely, empowering democratically unaccountable international courts to review human rights agreements and executive decisions of the General Assembly, the UNSC, the WTO, and individual states, might be unnecessary and raise the risk of adding a new source of domination.

My response to these objections is simply this: Once we insist that human rights should bind *all* nations their origination and ratification will require a more centralized mechanism beyond that afforded by international treaty. Even if this transnational mechanism is not strictly legislative, its legitimation will still have to accord with minimal democratic criteria of transparency, accountability, and susceptibility to reform instigated by popular initiative. Furthermore, whatever system is chosen for implementing review of this regulatory mechanism's decisions will require for its own democratic legitimacy a layered (and perhaps distributed) procedure permitting individuals, states, and civil society associations a right to initiate complaints.[10]

My argument for this complicated proposal is divided into seven parts. Justifying the International Human Rights Regime takes up the challenge of justifying the current human rights regime against those who claim that it is illegitimate or serves no useful purpose. My discussion of this matter closely follows Allen Buchanan's comprehensive analysis. Buchanan's qualified justification of the current regime poses a serious challenge to

---

[10] I offer no easy formula for remedying the countless ways in which governments and powerful agents can skirt their human rights duties by appeal to security threats and alternative legal venues and jurisdictions ("forum shopping"). I offer instead the principle that such problems can be mitigated only by instituting a higher order coordinating mechanism of some kind, such as an international constitutional court.

my thesis insofar as he understands the regime's legitimacy as sufficiently established by its modular composition and dependence on sovereign democratic states. Although I agree that this ecological (as Buchanan calls it) understanding of the relationship between international human rights law and sovereign states is basically correct and allows for potential reform of the human rights system in ways that will increase its overall legitimacy, I submit that it does not go far enough in addressing concerns that Buchanan himself raises regarding human rights treaty law and the persistence of free-riding governments in avoiding sacrifices attendant on equitably combatting global crises.

Modern International Law and Constitutional Legitimacy: Some Preliminary Remarks argues that these and other deficiencies in the current humanitarian regime can be better addressed by implementing constitutional changes in the regime itself. These changes, in turn, require rethinking what democratic legitimation might mean at the transnational level once that level is structured more hierarchically. In preparation for conducting these discussions, I begin by defending the claim that international law over the past two hundred years has increasingly embodied a legitimating principle that is social contractarian and liberal democratic, or constitutional in a distinctly modern sense. Most important for our concerns, the international legal system evinces a federal distribution of overlapping units of governance as well as a separation of legislative, executive, and judicial powers. What it lacks is the hierarchical centralization and correlative interbranch checks and balances associated with constitutional democracies.

The UN and Global Constitutional Order explores the feasibility of further reforming the international order along this constitutional path by defending the idea that the UN, in both its charter and in its practical functioning, understands itself as the unique and supreme constitutional foundation of international law. This defense shows that the charter's recognition of national sovereignty and of compulsory customary law under the auspices of the International Court of Justice (ICJ) comports with its supreme constitutional authority. However, it does not show how other international constitutional regimes, such as the WTO, can be subsumed under that authority. Along with this challenge to its authority, the UN Charter does not delegate to the General Assembly (UNGA) regulatory power vis-à-vis human rights legislation and matters of global security[11] and does not empower the ICJ or any other court to exercise

---

[11] The UNGA's powers include voting on the election, admission, suspension, and expulsion of members and on binding UN budgetary concerns. The UNGA is also empowered

review of UNSC decisions.[12] In addition to this absence of constitutional structure, the UN Charter delegates to governments of member states responsibility for appointing representatives to the UNGA, which raises concerns about that body's democratic accountability.

The UN Charter as Constitution of a Single Legal Order examines each of these three challenges to the UN's global constitutionality, beginning with the supremacy challenge. This challenge can be met with an argument, first advanced by Hans Kelsen, establishing a case for legal monism, in which national law is understood to be normatively binding only if authorized by international law. Although Kelsen's Hobbesian identification of law and state implies a world state as corollary to international law, his views about how subsidiary legislative, judicial, and executive organs produce determinate law in applying higher law suggests otherwise.

The second challenge to UN constitutional reform – how to make the UNGA more democratically accountable – addresses doubts about the extension of democracy beyond states. The example of the European Union (EU) illustrates the plausibility of such an extension. Two concerns arise with regard to its quasi-federal, power-sharing structure and internal separation of functions that also crop up in the case of a similarly organized UN: Does its power sharing arrangement comprise a hierarchy or heterarchy of governing units and does either of these descriptions comport with a plausible ideal of transnational democratic legitimation?

My own response to this question in Toward a More Legitimate and Democratic International Order draws from Habermas's much debated description of the current constitutional regime as a hierarchically

---

to vote on nonbinding resolutions and recommendations on any matter within its scope, including those pertaining to human rights. It may also pass a resolution concerning any security issue that is not under UNSC consideration, except in the event of a UNSC deadlock. Most matters calling for resolution require a two-thirds majority, with each nation receiving one vote.

[12] The ICJ is empowered to settle disputes submitted to it by states according to international law and to issue advisory opinions on legal questions, including questions touching on human rights, submitted to it by other bodies within the UN. It is composed of fifteen judges elected by the UNGA and UNSC to serve nine-year appointments. The International Criminal Court (ICC) was established in 1998 by a separate multilateral treaty (the Rome Statute) and has jurisdiction to prosecute individuals for international crimes of genocide, crimes against humanity, and war crimes. Its oversight is contingent on those individuals falling within the territorial jurisdiction of signatory states, unless the UNSC refers cases under an expanded jurisdiction. The ICC is empowered to adjudicate cases that national courts are unable or unwilling to process. Neither the ICJ nor the ICC exercises strict review over decisions made by the UNSC, the UNGA, or national courts.

structured human rights order that regulates a nonhierarchically structured system of international law. Habermas suggests that this description makes plausible amendments to the Charter reconstituting the UNGA as a democratically accountable deliberative body representing a variety of cosmopolitan and international concerns bearing upon the regulation of human rights legislation, global security arrangements, international trade agreements, refugee resettlement, and global climate change. Although this ideal of global constitutional order properly links human rights and global distributive justice, it does not satisfy standard criteria of democratic legitimation. I suggest instead that it invites us to revise our thinking about what democratic legitimation might mean at the transnational level in terms of the republican principle of nondomination.

Subjecting the UNSC to Judicial Review: A Step toward Democratic Constitutionalization takes up the third challenge to global constitutional order: the creation of an international court empowered to safeguard against domination. Rather than arbitrate international disputes (the function of the ICJ) or try individuals accused of humanitarian crimes (the function of the ICC) this new court would be empowered to review UNSC decisions, UNGA regulations, and transnational agreements to ensure their compliance with human rights law. To support the feasibility of this proposal, I examine the *Kadi* case in which judicial review has already been effectively exercised by the European Court of Justice (ECJ) with respect to the UNSC 's unconstitutional listing of individuals suspected of terrorist activity in apparent disregard for their human right to due process.

Because the ECJ's ruling involved a regional body overruling an ostensibly superior international body, it might seem that this case illustrates not only the questionable legitimacy of the UN as the supreme organ of international law but also the classical problem of subordinating a more democratically representative body (in this case, the ECJ) to an organ that is less so (the UNSC). This problem recalls the familiar dilemma of reconciling democracy and judicial review, a problem that would continue to plague international appellate and constitution courts, even in the absence of an international legislative body.

Democratizing Global Constitutional Review in a Fragmented Legal Universe surveys various constitutional arrangements by means of which this dilemma has been mitigated in different liberal democracies and argues that similar arrangements might be extended to international law as well. On one hand, the case for locating judicial review in a hierarchical system of international courts is made stronger by the ever-present threat of legal fragmentation. A high court could provide a forum whereby individuals could redirect legal conflicts back to human rights and away from excessive preoccupation with commercial and national security rights. On the other hand, the technical adjudication of legal claims by judges delegated the task of applying a complex system of legal rules to specific cases often does not permit a robust consideration of the moral principles underlying these rules and may even result in the premature subordination of human rights enforcement to the exigencies of commerce and national security. In this respect, not only legal fragmentation but also legal consolidation endangers the larger mission of achieving global justice and both do so by circumventing democratically accountable institutions in which one would expect issues of global justice to stand front and center. Pursuant to a democratic principle of nondomination, I propose distributing formal review procedures throughout multiple judicial and legislative institutions, supplemented by the oversight and advocacy of NGOs and global public opinion.

JUSTIFYING THE INTERNATIONAL HUMAN RIGHTS REGIME

Justifying an international human rights regime raises a number of questions that can be approached from different angles. One can take the system as it is and ask whether it excludes some rights that ought to be protected as human rights or includes some rights that ought not to be so protected. Because I have addressed this question in Chapter 5 in a provisional way, I will not take up this justificatory problem here. Instead, I will ask whether the *kind* of human rights regime we currently have in place is justifiable and legitimate.[13]

Following Buchanan, I shall address this question in two stages. The first stage defends the regime as necessary for justifying the state system *as a whole*; the second stage defends the regime as necessary for justifying

[13] I here address only one of the four objections against an international human rights order (see note 9). I take it as settled that an international regime that fulfills the welfare and egalitarian status functions that I discussed in Chapter 5 should specify at least some of the duties it imposes on states in terms of legal human rights. Enabling individuals to demand the performance of such duties as a matter of right protects against paternalism, respects agential autonomy, and most efficiently secures equal treatment (Buchanan 2013: 132–34). I also take as settled that legal human rights to health, education, democratic government, economic liberty, and so on cannot be guaranteed to individuals equally unless the government fulfills additional duties to coordinate the provision of these mutually sustaining public goods that are irreducible to the moral duty to protect any individual's personal well-being (159–72).

(legitimating) each state *taken separately*. The regime also provides additional benefits to states such that these two considerations taken together generate a duty on the part of states to create and participate in the regime.

To begin with, prior to the current human rights regime, states were accorded a sovereign right to criminally mistreat their subjects and engage in imperial aggression. Today national sovereignty still entitles a government to steal its people's resources, drive them into debt to finance its oppressive corruption, enforce draconian border controls that violate the rights of refugees, and exercise asymmetrical power in shaping international relations to the extreme detriment of the world's most vulnerable populations. The sovereign prerogatives that entitle governments to harm people both inside and outside their borders could not be justified on discourse ethical principles unless they were reined in by international human rights laws that compelled governments to collectively protect the basic interests of humanity above all else (Buchanan 2013: 121–30).

Because states enjoy prerogatives of sovereignty, they have a duty to ensure that they create and participate in a system of international law that renders the exercise of sovereignty morally tolerable and legitimate (Buchanan 2013: 130–32, 152–58).[14] This duty is strengthened in view of additional benefits that flow to states from this system, ranging from the provision of a mechanism for coordinating international efforts in dealing with global security risks to the establishment of a backup system in the event that a government fails to protect the domestic rights of its subjects (Buchanan 2013: 107–21).[15]

The latter benefit touches on the second stage of Buchanan's justificatory strategy, which underscores the necessity of the international human rights regime in procuring the democratic legitimacy of individual states.

[14] "In signing the Charter of the United Nations, States not only benefit from the privileges of sovereignty but also accept its responsibilities. Whatever perceptions may have prevailed when the Westphalian system first gave rise to the notion of State sovereignty, today it clearly carries with it the obligation of a State to protect the welfare of its own peoples and meet its obligations to the wider international community" (Report 17). The R2P principle, which I discuss in notes 5 and 6, is the latest and perhaps most profound attempt to specify the legal obligations of states towards protecting their own and other nations' subjects.

[15] Additional benefits include: encouraging the creation of domestic bills of rights; providing independent adjudication of disputes between citizens and their governments; modeling less parochial and less discriminatory constitutional rights; supplying resources for incorporating humanitarian law (governing the conduct of interstate armed conflict) into human rights law; and correcting for the tendency of democratic states to pursue the interests of their citizens at the expense of the rights of foreigners (Buchanan 2013: 108).

Most striking about Buchanan's argument is his provocative assertion that the legitimacy of that regime does not depend upon its possessing a democratic constitutional structure.

His reasoning here is premised on three assumptions: the international human rights regime need only minimally satisfy general standards of legitimacy (imperfect justice being no hindrance to legitimacy); not all institutions that compose the regime need to satisfy these standards fully in order for the regime as a whole to be judged legitimate; and the regime can be judged legitimate without being democratic, so long as it partly derives its legitimacy from states that are.

To begin with, the general criteria of legitimacy (what Buchanan calls the Meta-Coordination View) require that an institutionalized coordinating system, regardless of whether or not it exercises legal rule, meet only a minimum threshold of effective and just functioning (Buchanan 2013: 174, 178). The argument for this general concept of legitimacy is social contractarian: In contexts where institutional coordination is deemed overall to be mutually beneficial for participating parties, participation in the institution is less costly to the degree that it is voluntary, motivated as much by duty as by self-interest (Buchanan 2013: 180–88). Buchanan mentions several other factors that bear on positively assessing an institution's legitimacy: having an untainted origin, reliably providing the goods the institution is designed to deliver, possessing integrity (reasonable match of institutional goals with institutional performance), avoiding serious unfairness, and being accountable (in situations where lay persons lack sufficient expertise to hold institutions accountable, public transparency in institutional decision making becomes the decisive factor) (Buchanan 2013: 189). Finally, Buchanan remarks that criteria of legitimacy become more demanding depending on whether the institution in question exercises a ruling (coercive) function, claims exclusive authority in its domain of operation, or performs coordinating functions that are deemed to be less necessary (in contrast to vital functions whose performance ought not to be jeopardized by having to satisfy democratic and other more stringent criteria) (Buchanan 2013: 188–89).

These criteria entail that states, to the extent that they are judged to be legitimate, must be democratic on account of their territorial rule in a way that noncoercive international organizations need not be. International human rights law is mainly regulatory and becomes coercive law only by incorporation into domestic legal systems. International human rights need only derive their democratic legitimation from these systems. In essence, the boundaries separating international and domestic institutions are porous, with both outsourcing legitimating tasks to each other.

Buchanan's *ecological* model of legitimation comports well with the discourse theoretic questioning of political boundaries I have been defending in this book. By delegating the prerequisites for legitimate international institutions to local legislatures we have in effect expanded democracy beyond borders. Global democracy is simply the sum of concurring local democracies. Admittedly, this summative view requires that all nations implement democracy locally. It also requires that global democracy impact local democracy by way of a feedback loop. As global democracy increases with the progressive democratization of the world's nations, it builds support for multiple global public spheres wherein global human rights movements and other global civil society agents leverage global public opinion to pressure recalcitrant governments to become more democratic and respectful of human rights.

Whether this understanding of global democracy satisfies criteria of democratic legitimation depends on what we mean by democratic accountability. Does global public opinion alone suffice to render national governments accountable to humanity? Are those governments accountable to all their inhabitants, including immigrants, refugees, and so-called stateless persons? If the answer to these questions is "no," then a stronger notion of democratic accountability analogous to what we find institutionalized in local democracy might be necessary at the global level.[16]

I will explore this possibility later. Related to this question, however, is Buchanan's view that the legitimacy of an international human rights regime taken as a whole need not depend on the full legitimacy of each of its subsidiary institutions. According to this *modular* account of legitimacy, international human rights institutions are less ecologically interconnected in sharing legitimation functions than is the regime as a whole vis-à-vis democratic states. Indeed, the functional interdependency between the regime and democratic states resembles to a higher degree the kind of functional interdependency we find in constitutionally separated institutions that mutually check and balance each other. Just as a

---

[16] Buchanan himself seems agnostic regarding whether the democratic constitutionalization of the international order might enhance the legitimacy it already possess: "If, under modern conditions, exclusion from meaningful participation in domestic governance institutions is incompatible with equal basic moral status, then it is hard to see how similar exclusion from global governance institutions is morally acceptable" (Buchanan 2013: 145). Buchanan's rejection of democracy as a necessary condition for the legitimacy of "international institutions generally at this point in time" (222) allows that democratizing these institutions might become necessary for their future legitimacy should they increase in power and scope in the direction he thinks is desirable (145).

domestic legislature's legitimacy depends on its laws meeting approval by a constitutional court (with the latter's legitimacy in turn depending on adherence to established law), so too the legitimacy of a state depends on its laws meeting approval by an international human rights regime (with the latter's legitimacy in turn depending on the democratic approval of state legislatures).

According to Buchanan, the fact that some of the regime's subsidiary institutions fall very short of satisfying reasonable expectations for legitimation that would otherwise have to be met even on a very modest ecological account does not mean that the system as a whole lacks legitimacy, so long as other institutions are assessed more positively. For example, the UNSC scores low in satisfying the criterion of integrity; it repeatedly fails to authorize interventions to stanch genocide and other mass killings that states have a responsibility to protect against (Buchanan 2013: 197) while at the same time authorizing sanctions that sometimes cause intolerable levels of civilian suffering. The UN High-Panel Report I cited earlier proposes some changes in the way the UNSC deploys sanctions and military force.[17] However, the UNSC scores low on accountability as well, since a P-5 veto need not be accompanied by a principled justification. Its decision-making process also lacks transparency (although some secrecy may be necessary for its effective functioning) (Buchanan 2013: 200–02). According to Buchanan these deviations from democratic accountability do not by themselves render the UNSC illegitimate since great powers might be unwilling to assume the overwhelming cost of humanitarian military interventions if they were not protected from having to engage in less worthy interventions desired by a simple majority of their UNSC copartners (Buchanan 2013: 199).

Even if the P-5 veto privilege were justified for reasons noted above, one could argue that inclusion within the P-5 should be subject to review, since the power of some members of the P-5 club has declined over the years and neither Africa nor Latin America has representation in it.[18] However, amending the UN Charter to grant robust review of the UNSC's P-5

---

[17] These include: doing a better job of fine-tuning and monitoring sanctions so as to avoid civilian suffering; distinguishing peace-keeping and peace-enforcing missions; focusing more resources on postconflict peace-building; and using proportional means, proper assessment of risks and consequences, etc. (Report 65–66). Similar suggestions have been made with respect to applying the R2P principle (see notes 5 and 6).

[18] Since the 1990s many countries, especially in Africa and Latin America, have been pushing for the elimination or restriction of the P-5 veto power along with making membership in the UNSC more democratic (Gordon 2012).

membership and UNSC actions is extremely unlikely, since such an amendment would require a UNSC resolution subject to a potential P-5 veto. Furthermore, even if Buchanan is right that the UNSC's failure can be compensated for by multilateral humanitarian intervention on the part of a "concert of democracies," it is wrong to dismiss the UNSC as an inessential part of a legitimate human rights organization. As Buchanan himself notes, multilateral human rights enforcement by NATO forces or some other coalition would have to be "effectively designed to reduce the risk of blundering or opportunistic intervention" (Buchanan 2013: 203). However, given that this risk already exists with the UNSC, why not constitutionally incorporate into the UN Charter an alternative procedure for authorizing intervention, with full right of appeal and review?

I will advocate for just this possibility below. Buchanan himself concludes that the international human rights regime is legitimate, despite the low legitimacy of the UNSC and the questionable legitimacy of the ICC (whose prosecution of alleged human rights violators often requires UNSC approval).[19] Presumably, the process of originating human rights law compensates for this legitimacy-deficit by providing an inclusive – albeit, with the decline of the International law Commission (ILC) in drafting treaties, *ad hoc* – procedure for originating humanitarian law. The decline of a uniform institutionalized process for drafting treaties raises concerns about the democratic accountability of drafting groups, but Buchanan parries these concerns by noting that institutionalization often comes at the expense of inclusivity and that the domestic ratification and statutory implementation of treaties – which are not formulated as coercive laws – typically satisfies stringent standards of democratic accountability (Buchanan 2013: 206).

---

[19] Since its operations began in 2002, the ICC has convicted only four persons of war crimes and crimes against humanity (involving the use of child soldiers and sexual violence), three from the Congo and one from Mali. It failed to gain a conviction against Kenyan President Uhuru Kenyatta and was unable to have Sudanese President Omar al-Bashir arrested after his indictment. It currently has ten investigations in process, all but one involving African cases. The 124 signatories to the Rome statute do not include the United States, Russia, or China; Gambia and Burundi, whose rulers have been accused of gross human rights violations, announced their intention to revoke their memberships in 2016, along with South Africa, alleging an anti-African bias (despite the fact that that six cases were initiated at the request of African nations). In May 2014, China and Russia vetoed a UNSC resolution to indict Syrian President Bashar al-Assad for war crimes (Syria is not a signatory to the Rome Treaty). The court, however, is expanding investigations of crimes in Afghanistan, Ukraine, Colombia, and the Palestinian territories, along with crimes that were allegedly committed by British forces in Iraq. The Hague court employs 800 staff members at a cost of around $164 million (estimate for 2017) (Copper 2016).

I am doubtful whether the current practice of originating human rights law is sufficiently inclusive as things presently stand. If Buchanan's proposal to make all human rights treaties that find support among a supermajority of nations binding on all nations were adopted, a procedure for insuring greater inclusivity among all concerned parties – nations as well as cosmopolitan bodies representing, for instance, stateless refugees – would have to be adopted as well. Such a procedure, I shall argue, should take the form of a fully representative UNGA, reconstituted as a quasi-legislative body.

As for the Human Rights Council (UNHRC) and other commissions whose task it is to monitor treaty compliance, Buchanan notes that their legitimacy remains intact despite their inability to effectively enforce human rights on their own.[20] Their task is not to enforce treaties, since this function, too, is properly delegated to domestic and regional courts. States can pressure other states to adopt and enforce human rights provisions through a vast array of incentives and disincentives (loans, credits, alliances, sanctions, etc.). NGOs play their part by leveraging the power of global public opinion and acting as "external epistemic agents" that monitor performance (Buchanan, 2013, 218).[21] In this respect the international human rights regime is just as effective as the WTO in enforcing norms through the retaliatory sanctions of its respective member states and other subsidiary institutions.

Despite the effective use of retaliatory threat and collaborative encouragement in enforcing human rights, the enactment of human rights solely by means of voluntarily assumed treaty obligations leads Buchanan to endorse an amendment whereby a treaty would become universally binding on all states so long as a supermajority of legitimate states ratified it (Buchanan 2013: 27). One wonders how a supermajoritarian act of coercion of the sort proposed here, which anticipates the disappearance of any legal dualism separating international and domestic law (see below), could be made legitimate without undertaking a constitutional restructuring of international law. The legitimacy of majority (or even

[20] The UNHRC replaced the UN Commission on Human Rights in 2006, which was criticized for including representatives from countries with poor human rights records. However, the forty-seven governments currently occupying three-year terms on the council, many of them from the Middle East and Africa, have been criticized by the U.S and other countries for focusing too much attention on the Israeli-Palestinian conflict and protecting themselves, as well as China and Russia, from criticism.
[21] The High-Level Panel report also recommends closer collaboration between NGOs and the General Assembly (Report 109).

supermajority) rule depends on a constitutional system of checks and balances in which a dissenting minority, whose rights may have been violated by a decision, has a right to appeal the decision. Given that Buchanan himself holds up the constitutional separation of powers with its checks and balances as exemplifying the kind of ecological legitimacy that obtains between international human rights law and sovereign democratic states (Buchanan 2013: 217), it is surprising that he doesn't see that implementing supermajority rule as a procedure for universally imposing human rights duties requires for its legitimacy a corresponding constitutional court of appeal, possessing *binding* authority, rather than the *advisory* authority currently exercised by the International Court of Justice.[22]

The case for Buchanan's amendment proposal and concomitant international constitutional reform becomes stronger if, following Buchanan, a supermajority of democratic states happened to agree on a just resettlement of "stateless" refugees or a just distribution of burdens in reducing greenhouse gases and global poverty (Buchanan 2013: 118). Buchanan correctly diagnoses the legitimation crisis besetting the international humanitarian order. What he fails to see is that his proposed solution to the crisis would generate new legitimation problems unless accompanied by a constitutionalization of that very same order.

MODERN INTERNATIONAL LAW AND CONSTITUTIONAL LEGITIMACY: PRELIMINARY REMARKS

Before examining the extent to which the modern system of international law exhibits features that are amenable to constitutionalization, it behooves us to recall that the general ethical worldview underlying that system evinces what might be broadly characterized as a distinctly modern set of constitutional priorities. Christian Reus-Smit has recently observed that all regimes of international law reflect the dominant domestic

---

[22] Buchanan's Principle (M) (see note 56) proposes a federal rather than a functional solution to the problem. For its part, the ICJ can issue nonenforceable advisory opinions about the legality of UNSC decisions if requested to do so by the UNSC itself, the UNGA or an official body of the UN, such as the WHO. It can also rule on the legality of particular actions in conflicts involving states, including UNSC decisions, when asked to do so by one of the parties. This occurred when Libya brought suit before the ICJ against the US and UK for UNSC sanctions they obtained for Libya's refusal to extradite bombing suspects in the 1971 Lockerbie plane bombing (with the ICJ upholding the legality of the sanctions in 1998) (Gordon 2012).

constitutions of their time. By "constitution" Reus-Smit has in mind an organizing principle of sovereignty that possesses a moral core specifying "a systemic norm of procedural justice and shapes" and "shapes institutional design and action, defining institutional rationality in a distinctive way leading states to adopt certain institutional practices and not others" (Reus-Smit 1999: 6).

A backward glance at the evolution of international law over the last four hundred years suffices to illustrate Reus-Smit's point. The natural law paradigm that prevailed during the time when the modern state system took shape following the Peace of Westphalia (1648) aimed at preserving a divinely ordained hierarchical social order anchored in absolute sovereignty, as reflected in a legitimating procedure of dynastic succession and unquestioned obedience to monarchic authority. The Westphalian system recognized the monarch's absolute dominion over his or her own domestic territory and allowed sovereign states to pursue their interests through means peaceful or bellicose, constrained by principles of just war.[23] By contrast, the contractarian constitutional order that gradually replaced this system in the nineteenth century embodied a liberal ethos that valued individual self-determination and nondomination. The rights-based legal order that corresponds to this moral paradigm accordingly displaces sovereignty onto the will of the people. Institutionalized in democratic procedures, this legitimating principle takes shape through a separation of mutually checking and balancing powers.

The evolution of the liberal democratic paradigm in response to limitations and inefficiencies inherent in the older feudal economic-administrative system laid the legal foundation for a new capitalist economy premised on individual property rights. At the same time, its revolutionary moral progression toward greater equal democratic inclusion was propelled by growing economic inequalities generated by that very same system (Brunkhorst 2005, 2014). This dialectical interplay of evolutionary and revolutionary

---

[23] The law of peoples (*ius gentium*), descended from Ciceronian Stoicism and articulated in the writings of Hugo Grotius (Grotius 1925: 17, 20) in the 17th Century and by Emer de Vattel (Vattel 1916: 113, 131, 135) in the 18th century also specify cosmopolitan duties to humanity, in a way that anticipates modern humanitarian law. In Vattel's writing, these duties include a weak duty of beneficence charged to nations to intervene in the internal affairs of another state in defending the just side in a civil war or to guarantee the "safety of the human race." The difficulty these theorists encounter in extending to states universal duties of natural morality that properly attach to individual human beings in their relationships to one another explains why the natural law approach to grounding international law and human rights gave way to the social contractarian approach favored today by such notable contemporary thinkers as Rawls and Buchanan.

change transformed the international order as well. Thanks to the global spread of capitalism and European colonialism, the limitation of national sovereignty for the sake of protecting individual freedom became the hegemonic constitutional paradigm underlying the postcolonial period of nation building. From the standpoint of international law, the contractarian aim of seeking mutually beneficial cooperation through voluntary consent is achieved by outlawing aggressive war, protecting weak states from domination by more powerful states, protecting the human rights of individuals against abuse by their own governments, promoting equitable commercial relationships, and uniting together to solve global problems (Reus-Smit 1999: 38, 122, 131–34).

The new international constitutional regime does not entirely efface the values and institutions of its predecessor. The right of states to pursue their self-interest in the international arena is still recognized under the new order. But sovereignty is now limited by higher universal moral values, such as cosmopolitan solidarity and responsibility to protect the human rights of all people (R2P principle). It is this latter cosmopolitan trend that suggests that the new international regime has entered upon an unprecedented era of constitutionalization.

Before examining this hypothesis further we need to recall some of the elements that distinguish modern processes of constitutionalization from juridification simpliciter. These elements include the rule of law, the entrenchment of higher over lower law, the democratic structuration of political power, and the scheduling of basic (human) rights (Zurn 2007: 84–103). The *rule of law* denotes regulation of government to promote its stable and predictable intervention in human affairs. When viewed from an evolutionary perspective (relative to the enhancement of economic and administrative efficiency), the rule of law creates a stable environment within which economic and administrative calculations can be made with a reliable degree of certainty. When viewed from a revolutionary (or moral) vantage point, the rule of law enables those who are subject to government coercion to pursue their interests freely and rationally (what Lon Fuller famously characterized as the "internal morality of law"). In sum, the rule of law requires that laws be publicly promulgated, prospectively and consistently applied, and imposed in a manner that is reasonable.

The *entrenchment of higher law* advances the rule of law by immunizing basic rights and laws structuring legislation, adjudication, execution and interbranch dispute settlement against capricious nullification by majoritarian decisions. When viewed from an evolutionary standpoint, entrenchment serves a conservative function; when viewed from a revolutionary standpoint, this function serves the progressive aim of preserving moral achievements against threats to freedom and equality generated by a growing economic-administrative system. Included among these achievements are *basic rights* to freedom, security, democratic political participation, and social welfare.

Finally, constitutions *structure the democratic process and strengthen institutional legitimacy* by separating and balancing mutually checking governmental powers. Structuration typically consists of two forms of power sharing: federal and functional. Federal structure incorporates local political units into larger ones in which competencies are typically assigned according to a principle of subsidiarity. Along with assigning different competencies to different levels of government, federal structure typically (but not necessarily or in all instances) subordinates local law-making competencies to legal requirements imposed by a more inclusive federal government. Functional structure within each unit (or level) of governance separates different competencies (e.g., legislative, executive, and judicial) and, as noted above, enhances the legitimate operation of each by instituting a system of interbranch checks and balances.

How far can this state-centered model of constitutionalization be extended to the current international order? Clearly, rule of law, legal entrenchment, and protection of individual rights are elements intrinsic to this order. Humanitarian law predictably limits the external and internal conduct of states according to institutional procedures entrenched in the UN Charter in a manner that protects the human rights of individuals. Other governing bodies such as the WTO regime that regulates international trade have charters that institutionalize similar features. Less evident, however, is the fourth element of modern constitutionalization: democratic structuration.

The UN Charter exhibits *some* federal and functional structure. For example, it possesses peacekeeping and international security competencies that member states do not, such as the power to authorize military interventions and international sanctions in order to preserve global peace and security, and mitigate gross human rights violations and other humanitarian disasters. Member states, by contrast, are delegated primary responsibility for legislating, adjudicating, and enforcing human rights. Furthermore, the UN Charter internally differentiates executive, quasi-legislative, and judicial functions.

Other institutions of international governance besides the UN also exhibit constitutional structure of a sort. This is most evident in the case of regional governing bodies, such as the EU; it is least evident in the case of specialized bodies such as the WTO or the International Labor Organization (ILO). The WTO, for instance, is mainly designed to facilitate trade agreements and adjudicate trade disputes; regulation and enforcement is delegated to member states. The ILO is designed to regulate global labor practices; adjudication and enforcement is delegated to individual governments.

If we grant that the UN and other global governance institutions exhibit varying degrees of internal constitutional structure, the question remains whether their structures make possible levels of institutional functioning that satisfy appropriate criteria of legitimacy. To recall my discussion of Buchanan, democratic accountability is not a necessary criterion for legitimating institutional decisions that are only regulative or adjudicative. In appropriate circumstances, democratic accountability can be instituted ecologically. Furthermore, institutional modularity is not inherently inimical to institutional legitimacy, democratic or otherwise. Federal structure can consist of modular political units that are delegated highly specialized competencies (military defense versus domestic policy) that need not overlap, and each can function legitimately according to criteria appropriate to it. Functional structure can also consist of nonhierarchically (heterarchically) ordered institutions that need not substantially interact.

However, as I noted in my discussion of Buchanan, federal and functional constitutional structures that are too modular typically encounter both coordination and legitimation problems that they cannot solve. A human rights regime that delegates the creation of universal human rights law to independent states pursuant to voluntary treaties binding and coordinating only signatory governments undermines the legitimate authority of human rights to bind all governments universally. A human rights regime that entitles any member of the P-5 to veto humanitarian and peacekeeping/security interventions or to join with nine of the fifteen UNSC members in authorizing such interventions without the counterweight of judicial appeal both obstructs and misauthorizes coordinating powers. Last but not least, an international order that modularly distributes the governance of trade, international finance, international labor, refugee resettlement, and the global environment with little or no regard for the human rights of individuals fails as a legitimate means of international coordination.

In summation, I have argued that the current international order is too heterarchical in constitutional structure to legitimately coordinate international efforts to respect, protect, and promote human rights. The first step toward remedying this defect involves placing the human rights regime at the regulative pinnacle of a new global hierarchy. The governing institution most appropriate for overseeing the operations of this now expanded regime is the UN. Making a convincing case for this proposal will require showing three things. First, we need to examine whether and to what extent the UN can be *described* as *already* founding a new global political community claiming supremacy over its constituent parts. Second, we need to provide a separate *normative* (or conceptual) argument in support of this claim; in other words, we need to establish the fact that there is but one (international) legal order authorizing all other orders. Finally, we need to see whether a UN human rights regime can legitimately authorize all other legal orders; in short, we need to see how much democratic constitutional structure it must incorporate before it can legitimately exercise more coercive powers.

THE UN AND GLOBAL CONSTITUTIONAL ORDER

There are three ways in which one might describe the UN's constitutional role in the global order. The first way, which is mainly descriptive, views the UN as one among many – and not necessarily the most important and powerful – organization constituting global legal order. To the extent that this realistic assessment of the UN is normative, it emphasizes the supreme authority of sovereign states within a global community populated by overlapping, horizontally related (heterarchical) legal regimes, including regional regimes such as the EU and sectorial regimes such as the WTO and UN, which are delegated limited regulatory competencies with respect to trade, security, human rights, or some other sector of concern. Such regulatory competencies are solely authorized by state governments, each signatory government reserving final authority to recognize and implement treaty provisions as it sees fit.

The second way to describe the UN's constitutional role in the international community qualifies the authoritative role of sovereign governments in constituting global governance. Qualification is necessary in the first place because states have ceded much of their control over their own internal affairs to events beyond their borders. To cite Habermas,

[N]ation states have in fact lost a considerable portion of their controlling and steering abilities in the functional domains in which they were in a position to make more or less independent decisions until the most recent major phase of globalization (during the final quarter of the twentieth century). This holds for all of the classical functions of the state, from safeguarding peace and physical security to guaranteeing freedom, the rule of law, and democratic legitimation. Since the demise of embedded capitalism and the associated shift in the relation between politics and the economy in favor of globalized markets, the state has also been affected, perhaps most deeply of all, in its role as an intervention state that is liable for the social security of its citizens (Habermas 2008b: 444).

It may be that *transnational* economic and legal *systems* – not governments – are the supreme independent "agents" now driving the global order. Or it may be that governments (loosely defined) are still the primary agents controlling this order, but that their sovereignty is shared *across borders* (as in the case of the EU) and that the legitimate exercise of shared sovereignty depends on its accountability to nonstate communities (including the UN). This description may or may not accord legal supremacy to the UN.

The third way to describe the UN's constitutional role in global governance regards the UN as the sole anchor of a monistic, hierarchical legal order. Appeal to conceptual as well as factual grounds sometimes undergirds this view; among the factual reasons given in support of this view (and the second view as well) is the evolutionary decline in state sovereignty, or at least diminution of state-centered governmental capacity, in the face of global economic challenges. In short, national governments have lost control over many parameters affecting their domestic economies and much else. The need to strengthen the coordinating powers of the UN to ensure that governments share equal (or proportional) burdens in jointly managing their overlapping and increasingly integrated environments for the benefit of humankind requires as well rethinking the very concept of global democratic legitimation.

This latter view permits a more optimistic assessment of the constitutional potential of a UN-*centered* global legal order than do the other alternatives, even though all three descriptions of a UN-*mediated* order can be characterized as advancing different accounts of how global governance evinces constitutional order. The first description conceives the UN's role as constituting a federation of sovereign states; the third conceives it as constituting a single federal government that devolves (in Buchanan's sense of ecological outsourcing) considerable powers to semi-sovereign states; and the second conceives it as an overlapping network of states and nonstate institutions that fits either a centralized or decentralized scheme of federation.

The first approach is exemplified in the writings of the English School. Robert Jackson cites Articles 2(4) and 2(7) of the UN Charter that establish, respectively, the territorial integrity and independence of states and the sovereign right to noninterference. Article 51 of the Charter permits the use of military force only for the sake of national defense, while the provision of the P-5 veto power for the UNSC (Article 27.3) acknowledges the basic principle that "international responsibility must be commensurate with political power." Jackson thus concludes that the UN Charter and other important treaties that both predate and postdate its inception establish a "global covenant" for peaceable cooperation based on voluntary consent that privileges both state sovereignty and political power over coercive human rights enforcement. And it does so in recognition of an "anti-paternalistic ethics" that is conscious of potential abuse of centralized political institutions by hegemonic powers. Skeptical realism thus counsels legal pluralism in international affairs (Jackson 2003: 17–19).

Recent events, such as the UN's adoption of the Responsibility to Protect (R2P) doctrine in 2005, challenge Jackson's view that rights of sovereignty supersede human rights enforcement.[24] Indeed Chapter VII of the Charter authorizing the UNSC to intervene in stanching aggression and breaches of or threats to peace would be meaningless if state sovereignty were supreme. The second view, which finds support among a wide range of scholars, extending from deliberative democrats to systems theorists, recognizes these and other legal challenges to state sovereignty. Many systems theorists, for instance, view institutions regulating economic and legal systems (such as the WTO trade regime and the UN human rights regime) as exercising near-autonomous control over their respective environments, which cross state boundaries. Although such systems are partly constituted and regulated by states, they come to take on a life of their own, much as a market economy takes on a life of its own vis-à-vis the individual agents whose actions constitute and regulate it. In both instances there exists a kind of feedback loop whereby the aggregate effects of individual actions function to constrain these same actions.

A striking feature of much systems theory literature is the emphasis placed on the plural and largely parallel environments in which systems

---

[24] See notes 5 and 6. Unlike humanitarian intervention, R2P is more firmly entrenched in international law, given that its imposition of cosmopolitan duties on states expressly refers to Chapters VI and VIII of the UN Charter outlawing mass atrocities and the Rome Statute founding the ICC, which criminalizes genocide, war crimes, and crimes against humanity (but not ethnic cleansing).

function. Legal scholars working within this tradition, for instance, are fond of pointing out the self-referential nature of differently coded legal systems that "interfere" (or interface) with one another without really communicating. As for the diverse legal systems that make up international law, many of these scholars note the impotence of public regulatory law, be it national or international, in the face of emergent global economic forces that create their own unsurpassable power through a new transnational system of private law (Teubner and Korth 2010). The current legitimation crisis besetting the welfare state that I discussed in Chapter 4 is symptomatic of this tendency toward legal autonomy. Instigated by the ascendance of what I (following Fraser) earlier referred to as financialized capitalism, the new international regime of commercial law effectively imposes treaty obligations on all states, willing or unwilling. As I noted in Chapter 5, these legal obligations conflict with human rights law, thereby lending the appearance of a fragmented legal terrain contested by competing legal regimes.

The High-Level Panel's report specifically highlights the above tendency as a major obstacle to tackling "problems of sustainable development." Because countries "have to negotiate across different sectors and issues, including foreign aid, technology, trade, financial stability and development policy," the absence of any high-level leadership on the part of economic powerhouses renders concerted action nearly impossible (Report 26).[25] The neoliberal subordination of public power to private law raises a deeper question about legitimation. The technocrats and managerial elites that run the WTO, WB, and IMF are hardly democratically accountable, and their goal of compelling states to permanently cede domains of government control to private sectors and market mechanisms deprives (in Habermas's words) "future generations of the very means they would require for future course correction" (Habermas 2008a: 351). Ironically, the neoliberal rejection of the supremacy of public law in all matters economic – its celebration of market freedom and consumer

---

[25] This is not to deny that the insularity of national legal and political systems also exacerbates the fragmentation of supranational legal and political systems. As UN Secretary General Ban Ki-Moon observed in an Associated Press news conference (September 14, 2016), the UN lacks a "reasonable decision-making process" – not one requiring near-consensus on UNGA and UNSC decisions – that prevents it from carrying out its own policy initiatives rather than the policy initiatives of powerful member states. Casual meetings of the G-8 and other similar summit meetings hardly begin to address this problem, because leaders must think about what is most politically expedient given what their respective electorates will accept. *Chicago Tribune* (September 15, 2016), Sec. 1, p. 14.

pluralism – requires coercing states that have embedded capitalism according to their own religious customs and collective cultures to accept the hegemonic regime imposed by Washington or suffer the consequences.

Deliberative democrats, who wish to retain the benefits of transnational legal pluralism for facilitating global cooperation in a way that also meets a threshold of cosmopolitan human rights protection and democratic accountability, abandon the uncompromising reduction of local, sectorial, and supranational legal regimes to self-enclosed (self-referential) systems. In its stead, they propose a *political* analysis of *communication networks* linking distinct but overlapping communities of deliberation and decision. The analysis put forward by James Bohman (Bohman 2007), for example, "is not nationalist or internationalist to the extent that it argues for the feasibility of democracy outside of states and the delegated authority of states; it is not cosmopolitan and does not require a form of political organization at the apex of a hierarchy" (Bohman 2010: 1).

By "democracy" Bohman has in mind a normative (specifically republican) principle of *nondomination*. This principle does not specifically require that the people are "authors and subjects of laws" but that they "exercise their creative powers to reshape democracy according to the demands of justice" (Bohman 2010: 2).[26] What is minimally required for this exercise is a capacity to deliberate and hold institutions accountable by introducing demands and claims. Also required is the power to initiate changes in the very boundaries and constitutional ground rules of political association. This "reflexive" constitutional power cannot be exercised at the cosmopolitan level of a world state or a centralized constitutional order at whose apex sits the UN because the UN and the communities it claims to represent – humanity and international society – are not bounded polities (*demoi*) that provide localizable sites for deliberation and political initiative. However, according to Bohman, as members of the UN, states can be held democratically accountable to other states and to social justice associations (or social movements) for failing to protect the

---

[26] Bohman deploys an "exhaustive" typology of transnational schemes divided by four axes (or binary possibilities): social or political; institutional or noninstitutional; democratic or nondemocratic; transnational or cosmopolitan. He defines his view as political, institutional, democratic, and transnational, in contrast to the alternatives advanced by Rawls, David Held, and Dryzek, which (respectively) are nondemocratic, cosmopolitan, or noninstitutional. Cosmopolitan (centralized and top-down) and noninstitutional (decentralized, bottom-up) schemes exclude precisely that robust *deliberative* (and not merely contestatory) interaction between civil society organizations that inhabit global overlapping public spheres, on one hand, and decision-making institutions, on the other, that is necessary for *transformational* political action (Bohman 2007: 44).

human rights of their own subjects as well as the subjects of other states. Acting collectively under the auspices of the UN Charter they can satisfy this accountability requirement without being beholden to a singular cosmopolitan *demos* or "the unified will of the people expressed in self-legislation" as would be expected if the UNGA were reconstituted as a quasi-legislative body.

Bohman's account of how democracy can be exercised beyond the state adds a welcome supplement to Buchanan's focus on states as the exclusive loci for democratically legitimating human rights law. By distributing the cosmopolitan referent of humanitarian law – humanity – across plural polities, including nonstate associations that advocate on behalf of stateless refugees, indigenous peoples, women, minorities, and the global poor – Bohman's model of global governance as a form of polyarchy locates global democracy at precisely the point where otherwise marginalized groups are empowered to press their claims against institutionalized domination. This view is in keeping with the cosmopolitan spirit of the R2P doctrine, which in some of its earlier formulations covered a broader range of security threats (including natural and environmental catastrophes) and hinted at the right of threatened populations to protect themselves using armed resistance, if necessary.[27] His discussion of the EU as in some respects an exemplary model of what a nonhierarchical federation of mutually coordinated states looks like is instructive for illustrating the dangers of hierarchical domination.[28] That said, skeptics will question the practicality of

---

[27] See notes 5 and 6 above.

[28] Bohman (2007) and John McCormick (2007) cite the EU's open method of coordination in which transnational committees facilitate communication between communities (or polities) whose members are chiefly concerned about local or sectorial matters that affect them directly. In the case of national communities, EU member states can opt out of some agreements (e.g., common currency, defense policy) and opt into other agreements (trade, labor mobility, etc.). The heterarchical autonomy (openness) of the EU model of federation contrasts sharply with the hierarchical domination of (say) American federalism, in which incorporated cities are beholden to states and the federal government for much of their government powers and funding. Furthermore, under the EU system local and sectorial communities of interest have a more effective impact on EU policy than does the European Parliament, which is less representative of local interests. According to Bohman and McCormick's analysis of the EU's neocorporatist method of democratic power-sharing, individuals' participation in supranational governance is *indirect*, mediated by the various communities to which they claim membership, rather than *direct*, as would be the case if they were members of a single European public sphere that actually influenced EU parliamentary decision-making in the few areas of budget, immigration, crime, trade, and agricultural policy delegated to that body. The loss of broad public accountability at the level of a unified legislative body is compensated for by the gain in local autonomy and direct popular control. As Bohman himself notes, the accuracy of this

Bohman's extension of deliberative public spheres and civil society organizations beyond the nation state.[29] Others (myself included) will question whether the democratic minimum Bohman proposes for judging the legitimacy of the UN and other human rights organizations goes far enough. Democracy must no doubt take a different form in these latter institutions than what it assumes in state governments. But how different? If the UN must function as the apex of a more centralized human rights regime in order to fully protect human rights, then will it not also need to incorporate institutional designs more closely resembling those found in liberal democracies?

The third approach to describing the UN's role in the global order affirms the antecedent condition contained in this question. It takes up the High-Level Panel's description of the UN as well as its reform agenda but goes beyond it in highlighting the supremacy of the UN in the global order. It chiefly finds support among cosmopolitan globalists like Bardo Fassbender. Fassbender argues that the Charter is the constitution of the entire international legal order, not just the UN.[30] Furthermore, he

---

explanation as a general description of EU functioning must be severely qualified in light of the hegemonic domination the EU Commission, the Central Bank, and its principal contributor, Germany, exercise over the rest of the European monetary union.

[29] In his review of Bohman's book Thomas Cristiano (2010: 595–99) notes that the knowledge required to participate in deliberative democracy far exceeds the capacity of average citizens and must be compensated for by political parties and other civil society organizations that are largely absent at the level of a regional body, such as the EU, not to mention at the level of global society. He also shares my concern about the effectiveness of Bohman's nonhierarchical model of global democracy as a coordinating mechanism. The recent failure of the EU to coordinate refugee resettlement only reinforces this concern.

[30] The High-Level Report I cited earlier emphasizes four ways in which the UN Charter marked an innovative advance beyond the League of Nations, understood merely as a super-treaty: Following Kant's proposal as expressed in *On Perpetual Peace* (1795) the Charter links the achievement of international peace with global protection of human rights; outlaws and penalizes war, while insisting on sanctions and military interventions as permissible means for securing humanitarian goals; subordinates sovereignty to the overarching goal of procuring peace and collective security, and admits all nations into the UN. However, the Report also noted unresolved tensions that undermine the Charter's innovative status as a supreme and universal constitution setting forth compulsory duties on the part of all states, chief among them being: the contradiction between Art 2.7, which prohibits interventions "in matters which are essentially within the jurisdiction of the state" and the duty to protect human rights from state-sponsored "mass atrocities" (Report 65), and the contradictory composition of the Human Rights Council, some of whose elected member states have not shown "a demonstrated commitment to the ... protection and promotion [of human rights]" (Report 89). The UN adoption of the R2P doctrine in 2005 has not resolved these practical problems, which call for further institutional reform (see notes 5 and 6).

disagrees with those, such as Christian Tomuschat and Jackson, who regard the Charter as nothing more than a "world order treaty" alongside other treaties that codify and concretize earlier agreements and customs.

Fassbender's objection to their social contractarian grounding of international legal authority recalls a similar objection famously put forward by the great Austrian constitutional theorist, Hans Kelsen, a century ago, to wit: because it makes no sense to say that sovereign states voluntarily treating with each other generate a higher authority that supersedes their consent, there must be a higher authority representing less conditional moral duties that precedes and binds their consent. I will examine this argument below. For my present purpose it suffices to note that, for Fassbender, this higher authority can only be the UN, which has largely supplanted customary law in this regard (Fassbender 1998: 550, 585–88). Fassbender designates the UN, rather than customary law, as the highest treaty-authorizing institution because it embodies eight constitutional features:

1. The Charter's Preamble declares the intention of its authors to constitute a new world community;
2. The Charter establishes procedures for creating, applying, adjudicating, and executing law;
3. The Charter specifies states (later extended beyond states) as members of the world community (Chapter II);
4. The Charter establishes the primacy of its provisions whenever they conflict with ordinary treaty obligations of member states (Article 103);
5. The Charter makes no provision for termination and amendments to it made in accordance with Articles 108 and 109 are binding on dissenting states;
6. The Charter declares its own special legal supremacy by declaring itself a charter rather than an ordinary treaty;
7. The Charter has functioned since its inception as a global forum for the discussion of all concerns of international import;
8. The Charter's membership is virtually universal and its provisions possess sovereign authority (573–82).

For the sake of simplicity I will focus on the three most important ideas listed above: the UN Charter is the supreme constitution of the international order (points 1 and 8); its authority is higher than any other law (point 4); and it establishes a complete set of constitutional powers (point 2).

Let me begin with the last idea (point two). The Charter provides for the creation of the UNSC, the UNGA, and the ICJ. These institutions perform executive, legislative, and judicial functions, respectively, which combined constitute the minimum "rule of recognition" required for a fully functioning rule of law (Hart 1991: 212–21).[31] But these functions, I have argued, are not fully developed (UNGA resolutions, for example, are not binding laws). More important, they pertain to only those international legal sectors bearing on peace, security, and human rights (R2P). The fact that they constitute a more complete set of governing institutions than (say) the WTO, the charter of which provides only a mechanism for adjudicating trade disputes, does not render their jurisdiction any less sectorial. Nor does their constitutional status necessarily render them superior to customary law and treaty law, as I argue below.

The second idea – that the Charter supersedes all treaty law in cases of conflict – comes closer to establishing the Charter's potential universal scope and supremacy. But this is not as obvious as it may at first appear. Citing Judge Elihu Lauterpacht's separate opinion delivered to the International Court of Justice in the *Genocide* case (1993), Anne Peters notes that "acts privileged by Article 103 of the Charter [asserting the Charter's constitutional supremacy as a super-treaty] still rank below *jus cogens* and would have to give way in case of conflict" (Peters 2006: 598). As we know, the broad powers granted to the UNSC (especially the P-5) by the Charter have indeed been exercised in ways that conflict with human rights, if not the peremptory and compelling norms of *jus cogens*.[32] Given the UNSC's lack of accountability – which in the absence

---

[31] Without such institutions – which Hart himself finds absent at the international level – there is no way to ascertain the specific legal, as opposed to moral, force (or identity) of customary international norms and duties. Following Kelsen, customary law remains at best "primitive" law until it has been posited by legislative or judicial agents.

[32] To cite Lauterpacht: "The concept of *jus cogens* operates as a concept superior to both customary international law and treaty. The relief, which Article 103 of the Charter may give the Security Council in cases of conflict between one of its decisions and an operative treaty obligation cannot – as a simple hierarchy of norms – extend to a conflict between a Security Council resolution and *jus cogens*. Indeed, one only has to state the opposite proposition thus – that a Security Council resolution may even require participation in genocide – for its unacceptability to be apparent" (*Separate Opinion of Judge Lauterpacht* in *Case Concerning Application of the Convention on the Prevention and Punishment of the Crime of Genocide (Bosnia and Herzegovinia v. Yugoslavia)*, at paragraph 100). Lauterpacht's opinion was in response to a UNSC embargo of arms imposed on belligerent parties in the Yugoslavian civil war that enabled Serbia, with its superior military, to engage in genocide.

of a procedure for decisional review is glaring – the claim that the current UN regime is a constitutionally supreme order appears dubious at best.

In the event of a conflict between *jus cogens* norms and UNSC decisions, individual states could stand on higher legal ground – higher even than the Charter – in disobeying those decisions. But this inference is too hasty. It presumes that *jus cogens* norms impose external rather than internal limits on the Charter's sovereignty. In fact, *jus cogens* prohibitions against genocide and slavery have been incorporated into the Charter.[33] International conventions that were later incorporated into the Charter go further by expressly including the unwritten "laws of humanity" and "requirements of public conscience" as "peremptory grounds of international law."[34] So UNSC decisions that violate *jus cogens* norms are better described as *unconstitutional*. As I argue below, that such an internal conflict appears to render the supremacy of the UN Charter suspect reflects the Charter's failure to provide for an internal procedure for reviewing UNSC decisions, leaving regional and national courts to declare the inapplicability (if not unconstitutionality) of those decisions. In particular, the refusal of the European Court of Justice to enforce a UNSC sanction in the *Kadi* case (2012) places in jeopardy Fassbender's earlier belief that Article 103 subordinates treaty obligations to UNSC decisions.

The third idea – that the UN Charter is the supreme and universal constitution regulating all actions whatsoever – goes beyond the second idea in positing the Charter as the constitution of a single legal order encompassing all regional, sectorial, and national orders. It certainly goes beyond the way the UN is commonly perceived, judging by its actual power and authority as a global coordinating mechanism. Many international legal scholars concede the centrality of the UN as *primus inter pares* in a looser system of Post-Second World War international law that emerged in conjunction with and sometimes alongside of it. Membership in the

---

[33] Jurists debate about what these norms are, and whether their status is closer to that of customary law (the dominant view) or natural law, which seems to be Judge Lauterpacht's view, as stated in the opinion quoted in the preceding footnote. As for their content, *jus cogens* norms overlap human rights prohibiting slavery and genocide and possibly torture. As a general rule, human rights do not enjoy the absolutely compelling and peremptory status accorded *jus cogens* norms, as is apparent whenever they come into conflict with countervailing national security interests (which in cases of national emergency can justifiably require suspension of the right to *habeas corpus*).

[34] See, for example, the Martens Clause that was inserted into the preamble to the 1899 Hague Convention II: Regulations on the Laws and Customs of War on Land (Egede and Sutch 2013: 71–72).

international community is not coextensive with membership in the UN: regional bodies (such as the EU), sectorial organizations (such as the WTO), and even regional human rights regimes have their own independent bases of authority. So the UN may be supreme in its sectorial jurisdiction over security and criminal violations of human rights but is not supreme over matters pertaining to trade, for instance. In any case, it remains to be seen whether the R2P doctrine, which in its earlier formulation was applied by states against WTO policies that were deemed to cause a severe threat to the secure enjoyment of their subjects' subsistence rights, can be reformulated once again to extend UN regulatory power over global economic affairs, such as trade and global climate change.

Even if, as things currently stand, the global constitutional order extends beyond the UN, the latter still provides (In the words of Erika de Wet) "a structural linkage of the different [regional, national, and sectorial] communities through universal state membership [and] inspires those norms that articulate the fundamental values of the international community" (De Wet 2007: 57). It is considerations such as these that now compel us to re-examine the possibility that this structural linkage, or coordinating function, is itself constitutionally required and authorized by the UN Charter.

THE UN CHARTER AS CONSTITUTION OF A SINGLE LEGAL ORDER

Constitutional reform of the UN as the supreme authority underlying all law whatsoever – what I shall call *strong legal monism* – appears utopian in light of the three plausible descriptions of its role in international law that I sketched above. Even Fassbinder's description of the UN Charter as founding a fully functional constitution incorporating legislative, judicial, and executive organs capable of serving as a rule for recognizing what is and is not international law seems overly optimistic in light of international disagreement on human rights and the R2P principle, the relative weights and meanings to be accorded to various treaties, and jurisdictional authority. Perhaps we have not reached the stage in legal evolution where Fassbinder's description is fully accurate. We might still defend the supremacy of international law as a "primitive" legal order consisting of widely recognized norms and other forms of soft law.

The grounds for that defense are conceptual, and were powerfully advanced a century ago by Hans Kelsen: No state, defined as a territorially bounded legal hierarchy, exists until it has been legally recognized by other states. Recognition requires some act of official declaration on the part of a significant portion of the interstate community, which normally involves an exchange of diplomats and the signing of treaties. According to Kelsen, the binding authority behind any treaty – what obligates each party to fulfill its treaty obligations – can only be the customary international law that treaties must be respected (*pacta sunt servanda*).[35] It matters not that this law is customary; in the absence of any international constitution providing for higher order legislative, judicial, and executive functions, it suffices as a "quasi-constitutional" rule for recognizing the legality of any treaty.

Leaving aside difficulties associated with Kelsen's view that respect for treaties is the basic and highest law (*Grundnorm*) regulating the international order,[36] his argument that no state can be recognized as a state without legal recognition from other states provides a compelling argument for the supremacy of international law. The argument hinges on demonstrating the absurdity of the contrary proposition: the idea that each state is solely capable of authorizing its own legal sovereignty.[37]

---

[35] Kelsen (Kelsen 1989: 216) later reformulated this principle accordingly: "Coercion of state against state ought to be exercised, under conditions and in a manner that conforms to the customs constituted by the actual behavior of states." This formulation extends the scope of the norm beyond the authorization of treaties to include the authorization of the UN Charter and *jus cogens* norms.

[36] Hart, for one, criticized the norm that states ought to do what they've obligated themselves to do as vacuous (Hart 1991: 230). However, he noted additional problems with this norm (somewhat mitigated in Kelsen's later formulations of it; see note 35): Treaty law must be subordinated to legal decisions authorized by the UN Charter, whose own authority does not depend on the voluntary consent of member states. Even if the Charter were nothing more than a super-treaty, decisions authorized by it would have to conform to the higher authority of *jus cogens* norms. However, a second difficulty – raised by Fassbender and Hart – concerns the legal (specifically constitutional) status of these latter norms. This difficulty arises If we regard the binding authority of these norms as merely *customary* – a status that also attaches to states' duty to fulfill their treaty obligations. Contrary to Hobbesians, the difficulty here does not stem from a lack of centralized state agency for enforcing treaties; for Kelsen and Hart (Hart 1991: 221), in a primitive legal system aggrieved parties can resort to the convention of "self-help," or retributive sanction and war, in seeking compensation for harms suffered from broken treaties. Rather, the difficulty stems from the fact that customary norms are generally not distinguishable from (noncoercive) moral norms. For legal positivists like Kelsen and Hart, this is a defect that can only be remedied by replacing a primitive "legal" order with a constitutional legal order consisting of secondary rules for legislating, adjudicating, and enforcing law (Hart 1991: 245n).

[37] Kelsen's monism, in both its domestic and international applications, has come under attack by pluralists such as Joseph Raz (1979: 122–45), who raises two main counter-examples to the thesis: the presence of distinct customary and statutory sources (basic norms) of law within the same legal system and, in the case of former colonies being

Because a legal system would then be absolutely sovereign over its jurisdiction in all matters that affect it, internal as well as external, it logically follows that only one truly sovereign (self-authorizing) legal system could exist.

But which system? Does the system of international law function as the one and only supremely sovereign system delegating rights to state organs; or does each of these state organs, understanding itself to be supremely sovereign, delegate rights to international law? The conventional answer affirms the second alternative. But this alternative is improperly stated. If state law were absolutely sovereign, the state would not be legally bound by international treaties whenever these conflicted with its domestic laws. In that case a truly supreme system of international law would be impossible (Kelsen 1920: 45). But a state of nature composed of multiple sovereign states and multiple legal systems would also be impossible – at least if we adopted the standpoint of an absolutely sovereign state towards its legal relationships with other states. Because each state would interpret the legality of any action affecting it from the standpoint of its own system, what counts as the proper interpretation of any treaty or lawful interstate relation would vary depending on the standpoint of each self-referential legal monad. From a standpoint independent of these self-referential standpoints, the legality of any contestable action affecting multiple states would not be decidable (Kelsen 1920: 206).

Factually speaking, any impartial observer of international relations might justifiably conclude that what international law requires or permits in this or that instance of interstate conflict *is* undecidable. One might then be justified in concluding that international law does not exist except as an

granted independence, the authorization of a new state constitutional order (basic norm) by another state constitutional order, in which both orders (basic norms) are considered distinct yet equally authoritative. For Kelsen, the first counter-example is not compelling because any legal system will designate a higher (constitutional) authority as a common source specifying how conflicts between customary and statutory law are to be resolved (usually in favor of the latter). The second counter-example fails because it can be interpreted in two ways that comport with Kelsenian monism: If a former colony sees itself as breaking with the mother country in a revolutionary manner, it will not regard its constitution as standing in a relationship of continuity with the constitution of the mother country, in which case its constitution will be seen as grounding an entirely separate order. If it does not see itself as breaking with the mother country (as perhaps exists in the case of British Commonwealth countries today), then by definition it recognizes its order as in some sense coextensive with the basic norm of the mother country (some British Commonwealth countries may recognize the British monarch as the titular if symbolic authority behind their law). For a detailed comparison of Kelsen and Habermas on international law, monism, democracy and human rights, see Ingram (2014d, 2016).

illusion, or subterfuge for power politics.[38] But of course individual governments do not view interstate conflict that way because they are parties to the conflict and have no other alternative but to decide the conflict in a manner conformable to their own domestic legal orders. In order to be true to its legal standpoint, each government in a legal conflict must deny the legality of the other state's legal standpoint; it must regard its own law as globally supreme. Although Kelsen concedes the coherence of this kind of legal monism (Kelsen 1920: 120, 134), he notes that it, too, would logically entail an imperialistic power politics at odds with the rule of law. Indeed, the destruction of an objective legal order would unleash a solipsistic will to power incompatible with normativity as such (Kelsen 1920: 37).

Perhaps international relations *is* at bottom a lawless domain of power politics. But if it is lawful, then that is because states have intentionally subordinated their legal authority to the authority of international law. They have in fact done so, whether voluntarily (through treaty) or not: Respect for humanitarian law and *jus-cogens* norms is legally required of all states, pursuant to the UN Charter; respect for human rights – now reformulated as responsibility to protect human rights (R2P) – is legally required of states that are party to corresponding human rights treaties. The voluntary nature of such treaties need not render them less supreme with respect to domestic law, so long as they contain provision for self-execution.[39]

Their supremacy notwithstanding, the fact that human rights treaties are binding only on signatory states belies their implicit claim to universal legal validity. For a legal monist such as Kelsen, allowing governments that refuse to ratify human rights treaties to violate the human rights of

---

[38] See Carl Schmitt (1996: 54). Even after the horrors of WWII this former Nazi did not alter his view that "humanitarian wars" were pretexts for wars of aggression against enemies. Having transferred his former belief in the absolute sovereignty of nations to a new belief in the absolute sovereignty of postnational imperial regimes, he now rejected the justice of aggressive war in favor of the noninterventionist international order that emerged during the Cold War. This change of heart, however, was premised on the assumption that the new order was really founded on a balance of power between hemispherical spheres of territorial and ideological influence of the sort first proclaimed by the Monroe Doctrine of 1823 (Schmitt 2006) rather than on "some substantive notion of justice, or in an international legal consciousness" (Schmitt 1991: 34).

[39] Self-executing treaties stipulate specific rights and duties that do not require subsequent domestic legislation in order to become enforceable. Nonself-executing treaties, by contrast, consist of general principles that do not have the force of law and thus depend on domestic legislation for their enforceability. For a positivist such as Hart, only self-executing treaties constitute genuine law.

their subjects without suffering legal sanction is contrary to the very spirit of an international rule of law that is cosmopolitan in scope, assigning rights to individuals as well as to states. He himself could conceive no remedy to this defect short of establishing a single world state (Kelsen 1920: 319).

Conceptually speaking this makes sense: If "state" is synonymous with "legal order" and not "popular power" (Kelsen's identity thesis), then it follows that the creation of fully functional and universally binding human rights implies the existence of a federal world state, however ecologically distributed to subsidiary units its functions might be. To be sure, a world state possessing the exact same constitutional structure as a nation state might not be attainable or desirable. And perhaps such a state is not even necessary to secure a monistic human rights regime within a pluralistic global order.

In my opinion, Kelsen's legal philosophy allows for both of these possibilities, despite the hierarchical logic of its monism. The first possibility denies the feasibility and desirability of a hierarchical state that would impose uniform human rights laws constraining nation-states possessing different cultural traditions and facing different historical circumstances. The second possibility makes the same point in a different way, by denying that the universal legislation, adjudication, and execution of human rights needs to be centrally located in a single (highest) governing unit. So long as nation states are obligated by a supreme governing unit to incorporate the human rights principles into their own domestic laws, they can (and must) specify the content of these principles conformable to their own constitutional traditions and historical circumstances.

Kelsen's legal theory belies its own hierarchical monism in practice by authorizing lawmaking competencies to agents who are obligated to apply higher law. That states should make the very law that constrains and authorizes them may suggest a vicious circle. In fact, it denotes a *reflexive* structure that is inherent in any legal system, as becomes apparent when we consider the parallel between international and domestic law. Besides formally delegating lawmaking competencies to a legislature, the general and abstract substantive constraints contained in higher (constitutional) law, which are often stated as principles rather than as enforceable rules, require progressive realization at descending orders of application: legislation, adjudication, and execution – all the way down to their most humble exercise by an individual rights-bearer.

In conclusion, we can draw an important corollary from the aforementioned parallel between international and national law: Contrary to

H. L. A. Hart, the fact that human rights treaties require ancillary legislation in order to become legally enforceable renders them no less legally binding than constitutional law in this regard. From a Kelsenian perspective, states have a legal obligation to incorporate the human rights treaty principles they have agreed upon into their enforceable domestic laws.[40] *That* obligation, however, presupposes widespread acceptance of the moral legitimacy of the system that generates these principles.

As I noted in my discussion of Buchanan's ecological description of the human rights regime, democracy is only one among many (less stringent) criteria of legitimacy that explains that regime's moral authority. Having made an empirical and conceptual case for the supremacy of international law with a UN-centered human rights government at its apex, it is now incumbent on me to address in more detail that regime's potential for democratic legitimation in light of needed constitutional reform. If we accept that human rights should be universally binding on all states, which

---

[40] This obligation clearly applies in cases in which international treaties do not conflict with domestic constitutions (see note 56). Article 94 of the Netherlands' Constitution (1983) upholds the supremacy of human rights law even when it conflicts with domestic law, requiring approval by two-thirds of both chambers of Parliament only in cases in which a treaty conflicts with the constitution. Austria and Finland have similar super-majoritarian procedures for executing treaties in cases of constitutional conflict. Other countries, including France, Spain, Portugal, and Greece, elevate treaty law above normal federal legislation (some countries, such as Russia, Romania, and the Czech Republic do so only with respect to human rights treaties). Other countries, including the United States (Art. II.2 of the US Constitution), regard *all* treaty law as equivalent in status to ordinary federal legislation, so that conflicts between treaties and statutes are resolved through temporal postponement of treaty enforcement. The US Supreme Court ruled in *Paquette Habana* [1900] that international *customary* law is a part of federal law; but in *Sei Fujii v. California* [1952] it later ruled that the UN Charter and other human rights treaties are not self-executing, lacking the quality and certainty requisite for justiciable rights, so that they remain subordinate to domestic law until expressly executed in federal legislation. Chief Justice Roberts' majority ruling in *Medellín* (2008) regarding the legally binding status of the Vienna Convention on Consular Relations (VCCR) (footnote 2) as it applies to the duty to inform a diplomatic consul of any legal action pending against a legally detained citizen of that consul's nation follows *Sei Fujii* in asserting that only *self-executing* treaties are binding federal law. Roberts' opinion arguably contradicts the Supremacy Clause stating that all treaties, *including nonself-executing treaties*, are binding law. Contrary to Roberts' opinion, nonself-executing treaties might be regarded as positively enforceable through a federal statute, such as the Federal Habeas Corpus Act (1867), which provides jurisdiction and a cause for action of a claim by a detainee that "he is in custody in violation of the Constitution or laws or treaties of the United States" (Vladeck 2008). In my opinion, Roberts' opinion opens up a hornets nest regarding the legally binding authority of human rights treaties, the subsequent execution of which consenting parties must have intended, and contradicts the Constitution's assertion that "all treaties ... shall be the supreme Law of the Land."

in turn have a responsibility to ensure their protection for all cosmopolitan citizens, then their origination will have to follow a different procedure than the present one. Buchanan himself proposes treaty ratification by a supermajority of states as an alternative procedure suitable for this purpose. The legitimacy of this constitutional amendment would remain in doubt unless the organ most likely to resolve on its adoption – the UNGA – was itself more democratically structured than it presently is. We will now see whether this constitutional reform is feasible.

TOWARD A MORE LEGITIMATE AND DEMOCRATIC INTERNATIONAL ORDER

Defending "a [global] monistic constitutional political order" *un*buttressed by a world state (Habermas 2008b: 449) Habermas observes that "[t]he classical meaning of sovereignty has already shifted in a direction anticipated by Hans Kelsen. Today the sovereign state is supposed to function as a fallible agent of the world community; under the threat of sanctions, it performs the role of guaranteeing human rights in the form of basic legal rights to all citizens equally within its national borders" (453).

There are many ways in which one might parse this last sentence. The weak interpretation merely reiterates the compulsory supremacy of international human rights over domestic law pursuant to the R2P framework (weak monism). The strong interpretation asserts, in addition to this interpretation, the need for a constitutional reform that would transform the UN human rights regime into a quasi-governmental order (strong monism). There have been numerous attempts to defend and articulate such a reform, beginning with Kelsen's (1950).[41] For the sake of convenience, I shall focus on Habermas's own evolving thoughts on this matter.

Habermas proposes a *tri-level* model for understanding the current system of global governance that, in its initial formulation, resembles the ecological model advanced by Buchanan. Like Buchanan, Habermas affirms the necessity of (democratic) states as sanctioning agents within a

---

[41] As early as the 1930s, Kelsen had argued that "The democratic type (of government) has a definite inclination towards an ideal of pacifism, the autocratic, towards one of imperialism ... The aim of [a] war [may be the] final establishment of peace through a world organization which bears all the marks of democracy: a community of states having equal rights under a mutually agreed tribunal for the settlement of disputes, if possible a world court, as a first step to the evolution towards a world state" (Kelsen 1973: 106–107). For further discussion of Kelsen's critique of the UN Charter and the League of Nations, see Ingram (2016).

global system regulated by human rights.⁴² However, given the current lack of civic solidarity (or patriotism) at the global level approximating that found within democratic states, Habermas believes that it would be unreasonable to expect states to actively promote human rights to subsistence and development outside their borders. Governments of rich nations are loath to sacrifice the high standard of living of their own citizens for the sake of helping the global poor. To state the matter bluntly, the international community lacks a united will when it comes to redistributing wealth and developmental opportunities for the sake of the common good of the planet, and therefore cannot legitimately empower the UN or any other quasi-global government to solve global problems of this nature. At best, there exists a common will among the peoples of the world to sanction the worst humanitarian crimes and to promote the most urgent human rights. Below this highest level of UN-centered governance, global civic solidarity wanes. Even at the intermediate level of transnational governance, states, GEMs, and regional institutions unavoidably negotiate treaties on trade, finance, and global warming from a partisan perspective. However diligently they respect cultural and historical differences and distribute global burdens and benefits proportionally, treaties invariably give greater weight to the priorities and interests of the most powerful parties.

Habermas himself somewhat reluctantly endorses this imperfect but functional distribution of *supranational, transnational, and national* competencies when discussing the limited role of the UN in global governance: A UN that is "specialized in securing peace and implementing human rights" should not "shoulder the immense burden of a global domestic policy designed to overcome the extreme disparities in wealth within the stratified world society, reverse ecological imbalances, and avert collective threats, on the one hand, while endeavoring to promote an intercultural discourse on, and recognition of, the equal rights of the major civilizations, on the other" (Habermas 2008b: 445). Because there is no "institutional framework for legislative competencies and corresponding processes of political will formation" in dealing with these problems in a way that could *directly* satisfy democratic demands for legitimation, such problems must instead be treated in heterarchically structured "transnational negotiation systems"

---

⁴² "Whereas the political constitution ... can also extend across national borders, the substance of the state – the decision-making and administrative power of a hierarchically organized authority enjoying a monopoly of violence – is ultimately dependent on a state infrastructure" (Habermas 2008b: 445).

uniting governmental actors (powerful, regionally extensive states, such as the United States, China, and Russia, as well as regional governing bodies, such as the EU) and nongovernmental bodies (Habermas 2008b: 446).[43]

It bears repeating that the above model of global governance deprives the UN of any competency to regulate the global distribution of wealth and the negative by-products that accompany its creation. But delegating responsibility for negotiating treaties on trade, greenhouse emissions, and other matters of global domestic policy to partisan governments and their corporate clients leaves the poorest and least well-represented segments of the world's population vulnerable to economic and climate insecurities that threaten their human rights (Schmalz-Bruns 2007: 269–93; Habermas 2008b: 348). This was the conclusion reached by the UN High-Level Panel as well as the ICISS in its original draft of the R2P policy.[44] Indeed, the connection between universal human rights, global security, and global economic justice alone justifies submitting transnational-negotiations over global domestic policy to supranational regulation by the UN, regardless of whether or not the R2P doctrine is interpreted expansively.[45] This explains Habermas's recent change in his

[43] Nongovernmental bodies here include entities that specifically address political issues, such as NGOs and GEMs (the World Trade Organization, the World Bank, the International Monetary Fund, etc.) as well as entities that address technical coordination problems concerning international health, energy, and telecommunications. Owing to the dearth of democratic institutions at this level, states with elected representative bodies must retain a vital legitimating role at the bottom rung of global governance.

[44] See notes 2, 5, and 6.

[45] The three functions of the UN in securing the objectives of international cooperation – promoting and protecting universal moral standards such as human rights, managing interdependence among nations through exercise of responsible sovereignty and collective provision of global public goods (peace, global financial stability, healthy environment, etc.), and reducing inequalities in development between and within states – are interconnected. Key to achieving the coordination of the entire system is the UN Economic and Social Council (ECOSOC), which along with the UNGA provides the most open forum for discussing matters pertaining to the intersection of human rights, security and development. The 2012 UN Conference on Sustainable Development endowed ECOSOC with a mandate to monitor, balance, and coordinate economic, social, and environmental dimensions of sustainable development that later entered into the 2030 Agenda. That said, ECOSOC lacks the political representation possessed by the UNGA and its decisions are not binding on the subordinate agencies and member states whose policies it seeks to coordinate. Furthermore, developing and developed states prefer to work directly with the Bretton Woods Institutions. Despite these political handicaps, ECOSOC is respected as an impartial forum by all states and civil society entities. Besides sharing policy creation and implementation functions with the UNGA, ECOSOC is the principal follow-up to global conferences and summits, remains the chief coordinator of the UN system, and continues in a more limited capacity to coordinate humanitarian interventions in emergency situations. In tandem with replacing the G-20

thinking about the limited role of the UN in global governance, a change that portends a shift from a state-centered, ecological model of global governance to a model based on a cosmopolitan "world state." As he explains,

Only in a world state would the global political order be founded upon the will of its citizens. Only within such a framework could the democratic opinion- and will-formation of the citizens be organized both in a *monistic* way, as proceeding from the unity of world citizenry, and *effectively*, and hence have binding force for the implementation of decisions and laws (Habermas 2008b: 448).

Habermas immediately follows this striking reference to a familiar Kelsenian trope with an important qualification: The logical and moral exigencies pressing for global constitutional democracy may appear to require the creation of a cosmopolitan world state. However, because democratic self-determination is exercised most effectively by geographically bounded polities that already have well-founded human rights traditions, we need a middle alternative between a cosmopolitan world state and an ecologically constituted international order that delegates human rights legislation and enforcement to states and regional federations.

Many models of transnational governance recommend themselves as candidates for such a middle alternative. Not surprisingly, deliberative democrats like Bohman and Habermas look to the EU as perhaps the most promising among them. But they emphasize different democratic virtues in their respective descriptions of this federal union; where Bohman sees a decentralized and heterarchically structured coordinating mechanism facilitating communication across independent, self-governing polities, Habermas sees a more centralized, *dually constituted* legislative hierarchy with wide-ranging powers vis-à-vis its constituent elements (Habermas 2015).[46] And where Bohman sees overlapping and convergent spheres of

as an apex body with a more globally representative Global Economic Coordination Council composed of developing as well as developed countries as was proposed by the Stiglitz Commission (2009), ECOSOC has the potential to further multilateral cooperation on human rights and development between all stakeholders (Ocampo, 2016: 3–31).

[46] Habermas proposes a hypothetical democratic reconstitution of the EU "as if its constitution had been brought into existence by a double sovereign" composed of all the citizens of the EU taken individually and the same persons taken as citizens of EU member states. Habermas imagines that such a reconstitution would empower the European parliament (representing citizens of the EU) to introduce legislative proposals over all areas of policy, while ratification of bills would have to pass through that chamber as well as the European Council of Ministers (representing member states). Executive decisions made by the European Commission would be answerable to both the Council and the Parliament (Habermas 2015: 40–41). Importantly, Habermas conceives the relationship

deliberation, Habermas sees an inclusive transnational (European) sphere
of deliberation encompassing these other local and sectorial public spaces.

I have expressed my doubts about whether Bohman's description of the
EU as anticipating a new concept of democratic coordination based on the
principle of nondomination is fully adequate to the tasks it sets for itself. If
the EU must also aspire to a more unified constitution based on the
principle of self-determination in order to legitimate its coordinating
actions, then the same is likely to be true of a "world state."

It is in this context that Habermas proposes to extend his thinking about
the EU to global governance. Any "thought experiment" about the possibility of constituting such a system of governance out of a "second state of
nature" composed of legitimately recognized nation states, he submits,
must serve three major ends. First, the tension between cosmopolitan and
national interests "must be defused in a monistic constitutional world
order." Second, this order should not constitute a world republic that
would require sacrificing "the loyalty of citizens to their respective
nations." Finally, "consideration of the distinctive national character of
states... must not, in turn, weaken the effectiveness and the binding implementation of supra- and transnational decisions" (Habermas 2008b: 449).

Pursuant to these conditions, Habermas proposes the following constitutional reform of the UN:

A General Assembly, composed of representatives of cosmopolitan citizens, on the
one side, and delegates from the democratically elected parliaments of member
states, on the other (or alternatively, of one chamber for the representatives of the
cosmopolitan citizens and one for the representatives of states) would initially
convene as a Constituent Assembly and subsequently assume a permanent form –
within the established framework of a functionally specialized world organization –
as a World Parliament, although its legislative function would be confined to the
interpretation and elaboration of the Charter (Habermas 2008b: 449).

Leaving aside details about how representatives would be elected to a
world parliament, it is apparent from the last sentence in this passage that
such a parliament would not be responsible for legislating human rights or

between Parliament and Council as heterarchical. The relationship between national and
supranational government, by contrast, is neither hierarchical (as would be appropriate
in the case of a federal union) nor heterarchical (lacking any supranational regulation). It
is not hierarchical because states would have a "right of review," exercised through their
national courts, to "prevent European law from falling below the level achieved in
member states;" and they would retain "strong competencies... in implementing
European decisions," which in any case would be "justified only in functional terms
and not by the general priority of federal over national competencies" (41–42.)

world domestic policy in the fullest sense of that term. It would, however, be responsible for elaborating "the meaning of human rights" and resolving on "principles of transnational justice from which a global domestic politics should take its orientation." These principles would aim to secure the "equal value" of political and civil rights as well as the performance of "duties that citizens of privileged nations have towards the citizens of disadvantaged nations, where both are considered *in their role as cosmopolitan citizens.*" This would mean that

Power politics would no longer have the last word within the normative framework of the international community. The balancing of interests would take place in the transnational negotiation system under the proviso of compliance with the parameters of justice subject to continual adjustment in the General Assembly. From a normative point of view, the power-driven process of compromise formation can also be understood as an application of the principles of transnational justice negotiated at the supranational level. *However, "application" should not be understood in the judicial sense of an interpretation of law. For the principles of justice are formulated at such a high level of abstraction that the scope for discretion they leave open would have to be made good at the political level* (Habermas 2008b: 452 – my stress).

In sum, Habermas proposes to mitigate the legitimation deficit plaguing transnational bargaining by transforming the UN Assembly into a democratic body exercising regulatory oversight but not plenary legislative power (which would still reside with states in their capacity as interpreters and enforcers of human rights and global domestic policy). The success of this proposal depends on two factors: the possibility of extending democratic civic solidarity beyond national borders to encompass cosmopolitan solidarity; and the possibility of popular initiation of constitutional change itself.

I will address the former possibility in Chapter 7. In addressing the latter possibility, it suffices to note that popular initiation of constitutional change at the global level, while more difficult to achieve than at the national level, is not impossible. In response to Bohman's concern that constitutional structure in a "world state" would be fundamentally resistant to such reflexive change, my argument that even hierarchical constitutional structure requires reflexive lawmaking at descending levels of application permits (indeed requires) individual initiative in adapting that structure to local circumstances. The last sentence in the passage quoted above makes this abundantly clear: *"Application" should not be understood in the judicial sense of an interpretation of law. For the principles of justice are formulated at such a high level of abstraction that the scope for discretion they leave open would have to be made good at the political level.*

Having stressed the reflexivity (or circularity) of lawmaking competencies in a way that clearly evokes Kelsen's thinking on this matter, Habermas must now discuss how other "legislative" organs within the UN – specifically the ICJ and the UNSC – would have to be constitutionally reformed in order to balance democratic initiative and rule of law (specifically, as this pertains to the entrenchment of human rights). It is in this context that he observes that UN governance "would be *more judicial than political*," with courts and executive bodies assuming an authoritative role in interpreting and applying humanitarian law in cases of potential abuse.

Although potential for abuse abundantly manifests itself at the level of the nation state, its presence at the highest level of global governance cannot be discounted. The ever-present danger of discriminating against stateless refugees, undocumented migrants, ethnic minorities, aboriginal peoples, immigrants, and ostracized castes that haunts every democracy can vitiate deliberative decision-making even in a "cosmopolitan" world parliament. Checking this threat recalls a familiar constitutional remedy: a supreme court of appeal or a constitutional court. Unlike the current ICJ, such a court would do more than exercise advisory rulings on UNSC actions. Pursuant to republican nondomination, it would allow individuals as well as states to initiate claims against the organs of the UN itself.

SUBJECTING THE UNSC TO JUDICIAL REVIEW: A STEP TOWARD DEMOCRATIC CONSTITUTIONALIZATION

One remedy Habermas recommends for combatting UN abuse of power would grant the General Assembly veto rights over resolutions of the UNSC.[47] Another remedy would recognize "rights of appeal of parties subject to Security Council sanctions before an International Criminal Court equipped with corresponding authority" (Habermas 2008b: 451).

Thanks to the unprecedented review exercised by the European Court of Justice (ECJ) over EU implementation of UNSC sanctions, UNSC sanctions have been lifted and individual challenges to the UNSC's 1267 sanctions regime are now procedurally facilitated by an ombudsman.[48] At this juncture it behooves us to once again recall the extraordinary power granted to

---

[47] The UNGA Uniting for Peace Resolution [377 (1950)] allows for a special emergency session in cases where the UNSC fails to act in securing peace and security, enabling the UNGA itself to authorize collective action.

[48] UNSC Resolution 1904 (adopted December 1, 2009 and most recently extended by Resolution 2161 in 2014).

the UNSC and how the abuse of that power has led to reforms that can only be described as constitutional in nature. Perhaps the greatest need for constitutional review at the global level concerns the virtually unlimited exercise of power enjoyed by the members of the UNSC, especially the P-5. Chapter VII, Article 41 permits the UNSC to command member states to use measures (not involving armed force) necessary to "give effect to its decisions." Should these actions fail, Article 42 permits the UNSC to impose blockades and other demonstrations using sea, air, and land forces. The only limitations to UNSC Chapter VII are contained in Article 24(2), which provides that in discharging its duties the UNSC shall act in accordance with "the Purposes and Principles" of the United Nations as set forth in Article 1, which advocates cooperation in solving international humanitarian problems and promoting respect for human rights (1.3).

Interpreting these limits has been left to the discretion of the UNSC. Thus, invoking Article 103, the ICJ ruled that UNSC sanctions against Libya for refusing to extradite suspected terrorists in the Lockerbie plane bombing to the UK were legal, despite Libya's justified claim that its action accorded with its treaty obligations under the 1971 Montreal Convention (Gordon 2012). Not long afterward, the UNSC imposed an arms ban on the belligerent parties in the Yugoslavian conflict with genocidal consequences.[49] During this period, acting unilaterally under the auspices of the 661 Committee, the US persuaded the UNSC to impose harsh sanctions on Iraq for thirteen years that killed 500,000 Iraqi children (Gordon 2010). Although US officials knew the consequences of their actions, they could not be held accountable in international law for their criminal liability, partly because neither the ICC nor the ICJ is empowered to issue binding rulings involving the UN and its executive organs.

However, the ECJ's recent decision on July 18, 2013 to uphold the European General Court's (EGC) earlier removal of Yassin Abdullah Kadi from a UNSC-imposed EU sanction list targeting suspected terrorists (*Kadi I* and *Kadi II*) shows that courts have asserted their prerogative to subject EU sanctions in compliance with UNSC decisions to substantive as well as procedural review.[50] The ECJ did not directly rule against the UN 1267 sanction in its opinion, but it expressly ordered the EU to effectively disobey that sanction. This, in turn, created a ripple effect that eventually led to the 1267 Committee delisting Kadi in October 2012. Most

---

[49] See note 32.
[50] Kadi was a shareholder in a bank in which it was alleged that planning sessions for an attack on the US had taken place.

important, the ECJ ruled on substantive grounds in the Kadi case, arguing that Kadi's right to defense, effective judicial protection, and to property (proportionally balanced against security interests) had been violated by the EU, when it obeyed the 1267 (now 1989) regime.[51]

Whether in fact the EU was effectively required by the ECJ to disobey the UNSC's decree is open to debate (the UNSC listing may have given the EU discretion to withhold sanctions in particular instances). In any case, when the ECJ stated that it was acting in the name of peremptory standards of "effective judicial protection" (*Kadi II* at para 133) the UNSC understood that its own authority to impose sanctions over the better judgment of a regional court had been placed on notice. By subsequently removing Kadi from its listing, it could be argued that the UNSC tacitly acknowledged the power of the ECJ and other courts to issue advisory decisions that could not simply be ignored. In any case, as of 2009 challenges to these decisions could be processed by an independent ombudsperson. But the end result may be a constitutional challenge to the Charter's immunization of the UNSC from judicial review. Such a challenge – perhaps issued by far-seeing judges on the ICJ (or ICC, as Habermas suggests) – would be one way to compel the General Assembly (with the concurrence of the UNSC) to amend the Charter to conform to its own peremptory human rights principles.

DEMOCRATIZING GLOBAL CONSTITUTIONAL REVIEW IN A FRAGMENTED LEGAL UNIVERSE

The resolution of the *Kadi* case hardly stands as an unambiguous testament to centralized judicial review. It could just as easily be understood as a repudiation of UN legal authority by the EU; a subordination of the

---

[51] In order to avoid the appearance that it was acting outside of its authority by nullifying the higher dictates of international law, the ECJ justified its substantive review on procedural grounds. It noted that the UN Charter "leaves the Members of the United Nations a free choice among the various possible models for transposing [Security Council] resolutions into their domestic legal order" (*Kadi I* at paragraph 298). Clearly, this weaker, procedural standard of review did not nullify the UNSC's decision to place Kadi on the sanctions list. However, because the 1373 regime adopted by the UNSC allows member states the discretion to determine *who* is to be listed, the EGC analogously interpreted its discretionary power in the Kadi case accordingly, and so reviewed the substantive grounds for Kadi's listing. Because the EU only had the vague and unsubstantiated evidence provided it by the UNSC to justify its listing of Kadi, the EGC and the ECJ ruled that the EU should remove Kadi from the EU list with the understanding that doing so did not nullify the UNSC's sanction.

UN's executive branch to the judiciary; or simply as the solitary act of a rogue court acting outside of international law. However, seen from the vantage point of Habermas's understanding of the EU and the UN as constituting quasi-hierarchical, nonfederal forms of transnational union,[52] the ECJ's review of the UNSC listing can best be understood as evincing a proper balance between local and individualized powers, on one side, and a central power, on the other.

The fact that national and regional courts should be empowered to exercise constitutional review over supranational law does not eliminate the need for constitutional review at the supranational level (although whether the ICJ or the ICC should assume that function is technically debatable).[53] More worrisome for defenders of an international constitutional court is conceptualizing its legitimate authority: Do we want to invest so much power in the judiciary – especially one that is so centralized – given the democratically unaccountable way that power is typically exercised?

Here is not the place to rehash a long-standing debate about whether constitutional review is compatible with democracy. Suffice to say, simply ensuring that international judicial panels comprise a diversity of judges elected or appointed for specific terms, which to a certain extent is already the case with respect to the ICJ and ICC, would go a long way toward rendering them more democratically representative and accountable. However, given that international humanitarian law contains *jus cogens* norms and other types of customary law that invite moral interpretation, it may be demanding too much to expect international courts to refrain from legislating humanitarian law from the bench.

The question about whether courts should exercise supreme authority in a constitutional democracy is moot. Constitutional review serves multiple functions that seem all but unavoidable within any modern constitutional regime. These generally involve resolving legal conflicts: conflicts between basic rights, interbranch conflicts at the federal level, conflicts between federal and local laws, conflicts between federal acts (legislative and executive) and constitutional rights and democratic procedures, and conflicts between federal courts. Similar conflicts occur at the international level. Conflicts between competing human rights – for instance, between the rights of individuals and the rights of groups and corporations, which I discuss in Chapters 5 and 7 – require both technical and

---

[52] See note 46.
[53] For a defense of a world court, see Kozma, et al. (2010); for an argument against using the ICJ or ICC for this purpose, see De Wet (2004).

ethical resolution (vis-à-vis human dignity and other prioritizing norms). Likewise, at the international level court conflicts can occur when two courts having overlapping jurisdictions exercise their discretion to try a case under competing legal perspectives (human rights, national security, etc.). This latter kind of lower-court conflict is better described as a form of legal fragmentation that, in the opinion of some jurists, threatens the constitutional entrenchment – if not the systemic coherence – of international law as a whole.[54]

Citing numerous cases in which international courts were forced to choose between competing legal perspectives from which to interpret a conflict, Martti Koskenniemi notes that the shift from the old power politics of state sovereignty to the new rule of law has not led to a corresponding constitutional privileging of human rights over power politics.[55] If anything, it has obscured the politics of "forum shopping" and global influence

[54] For a view that defends legal universalism outside the framework of constitutional structuration, see Simma (2009).

[55] For example, in opposition to the Israeli government's insistence that building the Palestine Wall flowed from its right to defend against terrorist attacks, the *Palestine Wall Advisory Opinion of the ICJ* (2004) interpreted this act as a violation of Palestinian's right to self-determination as well as a violation of their human rights to liberty of movement (as specified under Article 12 of the International Covenant on Civil and Political Rights [ICCPR]) and to work, to health, to education, and to an adequate standard of living (as specified by the International Covenant on Economic, Social, and Cultural Rights [ICESCR]). In the *Al Jedda* case (2005), by contrast, the High Court of Justice of Britain appealed to the law of security in denying relief under the British Human Rights Act of 1998 to the plaintiff – a dual Iraqi-British citizen, who had been detained for ten months without charge. In another case, *Legality of the Threat or Use of Nuclear Weapons* (1996), the ICJ observed that both the law of armed conflict and the ICCPR applied equally to the strategic use of nuclear weapons. In deciding that the law of armed conflict was more directly relevant to the use of nuclear weapons (applying the principle of *lex specialis*) it favored a narrow interpretation of ICCPR Article 6's clause concerning the "arbitrary deprivation of life." Critics of this interpretation argued that the ICJ had made an error in its judgment about which legal regime was more relevant to the "arbitrary deprivation of life" inasmuch as nuclear weapons are weapons of mass destruction that technically have no strategic military use. Finally, the case involving the environmental impact of the MOX Plant nuclear facility at Sellafield, UK illustrates how different legal institutions, each with its own jurisdiction, frame the issue of impact from their own perspective. Is the issue to be decided by the Arbitral Tribunal responsible for adjudicating matters that pertain to the United Nations Convention on the Law of the Sea (UNCLOS), the tribunal established by the Convention on the Protection of the Marine Environment of the North-East Atlantic (OSPAR Convention), or the European Court of Justice (ECJ) under the European Community and Eurotom Treaties? As the Arbitral Tribunal for UNCLOS) observed, even if the other two tribunals applied rights and obligations that were similar or identical to those of UNCLOS, they would do so relative to their own peculiar context, objective, purpose, case law, and historical experience. Cited by Koskenneimi (2007: 7).

peddling behind the façade of institutional expertise, as if law were the "technical production of pre-determined decisions by some anonymous logic" (Koskenniemi 2007: 29).

Koskenniemi places hope in the democratization of international law ("giving voice to those not represented in the regime's institutions"). However, he remains dubious about whether instituting a legal hierarchy of the sort proposed by human rights monists such as Habermas would circumvent the twin evils of elitism and politicization. Unfortunately, there are no simple remedies for avoiding this dilemma: instituting judicial review within the legislature or executive administration threatens politicization; instituting it within the judiciary threatens elitism.

A dispersal of judicial review in different institutional settings therefore recommends itself, if it can be done without replicating or exacerbating tendencies toward legal fragmentation. Before discussing how this might be done, it behooves us to enumerate the advantages and disadvantages of institutionalizing constitutional review in the judiciary. Three types of arguments favor this solution (Zurn 2007: 275–85). First, a nonelected judiciary is structurally independent from politics. Following Kelsen's recommendation, the danger of "legislating from the bench" can be avoided by limiting the power of a constitutional court to statutory nullification. Second, the judiciary is uniquely competent to use techniques of formal and analogical reasoning that ensure systemic coherence in the law as a whole. Courts possess a long memory of case law and other precedents. Third, judicial reasoning is often more elevated and principled than the narrow, interest-driven bargaining that occurs within a legislature. Apart from defending the inclusion of constitutional review as a permanent fixture in a global judiciary, this argument has the practical merit of showing how such a review, even if adopted temporarily, might ease the transition toward global democracy in the face of recalcitrant resistance by the world's only superpower. Despite the reluctance of the Bush and Obama administrations to seek formal recognition of the International Criminal Court (ICC) for fear that American soldiers and diplomats might be tried for war crimes and crimes against humanity, the establishment of an independent international constitutional court that can review the decisions of lower international courts as well as the resolutions of a world parliament whose representatives mainly come from poor or developing nations is probably necessary if the United States is to give up its exceptional power (which extends well beyond its P-5 veto power) and submit to democratic world government (Tännsjo 2007: 91, 115).

Speaking against these arguments are the following: First, courts cannot simply nullify statutes without interpreting the constitution. Unlike ordinary application, in which the specification of a concrete case typically refers to a determinate legal rule, constitutional provisions are abstract, open-textured, and suffused with moral principles whose evolving meanings are open to dispute (Ingram 2006). Second, insofar as the analogy with case law breaks down in the case of constitutional review, the reliance on technical reasoning is as likely to interfere with the aims of moral justice, and in two senses. To begin with, as noted above, treating a human rights dispute as a technical legal issue whose resolution is specific to a particular case, encourages litigants to subordinate their claims to the technical resolution of some other issue (e.g., security) raised by the case in question. Furthermore, by encouraging legal fragmentation, it also opens the door to the distorting influence of lawyers representing powerful clients. A more abstract review that considers the justice of a law on its own merits, however, appears to usurp a role that rightly devolves upon the people, here understood in Habermas's sense as the dual constituent authority behind the moral meaning of the constitution. Third, as noted above, when the court's reasoning is morally elevated and not merely impartial in a technical sense, it is more likely than not to reflect only a narrow range of public opinion (Zurn 2007: 290).

Considerations such as the above recommend that the judiciary not be the sole repository of constitutional review. Following Chris Zurn's recommendation (2007: 301–11), I propose that the judiciary share this role with other branches of government. A reformed General Assembly could undertake an internal review of the constitutionality of its own general pronouncements regarding human rights and distributive justice prior to final ratification of its resolutions. In keeping with Kelsen's idea, it could allow any dissenting minority to enjoin final ratification pending further review. As noted above, a reformed UNSC now has an ombudsperson to conduct internal review of its sanctions regime, and Erika de Wet (2004) has suggested that states be permitted to reject illegal UNSC decisions as a "right of last resort." As for inter-branch dialogue, a constitutional court could provide *a priori* clearance of pending legislation (as in the French model). Or, in a manner analogous to the UK's Human Rights Act of 1998, which allows courts to declare the incompatibility of a parliamentary or administrative act with the European Court of Human Rights without nullifying it, it might permit the General Assembly breathing space to reconsider its decision. Conversely, a constitutional court could adopt something like the "Notwithstanding Clause" embedded in Section 33 of the Canadian Charter, which allows unconstitutional federal or provincial statutes that do not impinge on political rights to stand for five years until being withdrawn or reinstated.

Constitutional courts, too, would be well advised to incorporate the best of Continental and Anglo-American procedures of review. Like many Continental courts, they could delegate appellate functions to other courts, so that they can focus more squarely on the abstract justice of particular laws rather than get bogged down in legal technicalia. But the Anglo-American system has a unique advantage that shouldn't be ignored. Because concrete review applied to particular cases is more sensitive to the effects of law on individual persons and empowers individuals to initiate constitutional changes pursuant to a republican principle of nondomination, appellate courts at national and supranational levels should be delegated authority to make referrals to the constitutional court (in Spain, an impartial ombudsperson refers cases to the constitutional court).

Regardless of whether we adopt a decentralized or centralized procedure of review, dispersed or not across different government branches and jurisdictions, the final authority for global constitutional review should be the people, who exercise ultimate (if dual) constituent powers. The people in their dual national and cosmopolitan capacities properly contribute to the democratic formation of global public opinion. Thus, it is they who should initiate amendments to the UN Charter and choose whether to incorporate international laws that "can be reasonably expected to result in significant alterations in constitutional structures or in significant diminutions in political self-determination" (Buchanan 2013: 244).[56]

---

[56] Buchanan sensibly proposes a metaconstitutional principle (M) to justify constitutional convention, constitutional amendment, popular referendum or other super-majoritarian procedures for ratifying "Robust international law (with a capital R)," which has the potential to "derange" the constitutional separation of powers and alter the terms and scope of democratic self-determination (242). Thus, in the United States Senate treaty approval bypasses full legislative enactment, thereby creating potential conflicts between domestic and international law (with the Supreme Court resolving in favor of the former). Appealing to "the ultimate source of political authority, the people" – in cases involving secession, accession to a federation, or devolution from a centralized state to federalism – protects against nonconsensual constitutional changes through a "process of accretion," a process that constitutes the normal procedure through which international law is incorporated into domestic (constitutional, statutory, and common) law. The concern here is that constitutionalizing international governance through implementing global democracy does not address the tension, typically overlooked by liberal cosmopolitans, between constitutional democracy and international law. These legal values are not intrinsically incompatible. The idea that any (international) legal authority that has been delegated by a constitutional democracy must be *exclusively* accountable to that

To conclude, I have argued that continued support for the international legal order in the face of emergent humanitarian crises will require making that order a more effective, just, and democratically accountable system for securing human rights. The impact of self-serving political power on negotiating global policy and enforcing human rights renders that reform imperative. The proposal I defend recommends strengthening and extending the global regulatory power of the UN as the supreme governmental institution authorizing all international (and by extension, domestic) law. The authority of the UN to wield consolidated plenary power, I have maintained, depends less on its capacity to function as a world state than on its incorporation of democratic constitutional structure, pursuant to both principles of nondomination and self-determination. For without that structure, its legitimacy (or authoritative standing) will remain impaired and the voluntary compliance of states and other global institutions in enforcing its resolutions will be diminished.

Although the assumption of democratic accountability stands as the UN's most urgent desideratum, that reform – involving the reconstitution of the General Assembly as a quasi-parliamentary body representing cosmopolitan as well as national interests – will remain incomplete without its indispensable complement: a high court charged with reviewing the constitutionality of parliamentary resolutions and executive decisions. The legitimacy of that institution, in turn, can be strengthened by distributing the power of review among other, more democratically representative and responsive institutions at both national and supranational levels.

In sum, constitutional reform of the UN must reflect the discourse theoretical norms that I have insisted underwrite non-coercive, domination-free deliberation and decision-making. The importance of breaking through political and institutional boundaries that discourse theory entails in its cosmopolitan mandate harkens back to the UDHR's admonition with which I concluded in Chapter 5: "all human beings ... should act towards one another in a spirit of brotherhood." Global civic solidarity thus becomes the ultimate prerequisite for reforming the global order. Can it be achieved?

constitutional democracy, thereby ruling out international dispute arbitration by independent international courts, is repugnant to the very idea of peaceful cooperation under international rule of law. However, acceding to impartial rule of international law must also be done in a way that respects the ultimate constitutional authority of liberal democratic peoples (229–30; 246–48).

7

Nationalism, Religion, and Deliberative Democracy: Networking Cosmopolitan Solidarity

A democratic human rights order depends on the possibility of fostering cosmopolitan good will. The imperative to regulate social relations fairly, in a manner acceptable to all affected – that is to say, for the equal and universal benefit of everyone – must be motivated by genuine concern and caring. The discourse ethical imperative to transform one's understanding of what properly lies within one's self-interest in light of the interests of others implies even more: a willingness to make sacrifices for a cause greater than oneself, what we typically mean by *solidarity*.

Although solidarity is not reducible to justice (or moral duty), it remains dependent on it. For, as solidarity extends beyond feelings of devotion to those to whom we feel closest, it engages more complex forms of social cooperation premised on the pursuit of common interests, of which social justice is one. At the very least, cosmopolitan solidarity presupposes that the world's peoples can agree on what their cosmopolitan interests are. But it remains an open question whether they can agree on whether human rights even occupy a central place among these interests. So the future of human agency hinges, first of all, on whether multicultural differences do not eviscerate agreement on human rights; and secondly, on whether the well-being of distant foreigners can become a matter of general concern.

I propose to examine these twin challenges in two steps. Step one examines different senses of solidarity – descriptive and normative, internal and external, affective and partisan. One sense in particular appears promising for my project: social struggle on behalf of a common existential threat. I conclude, however, that our duty to struggle in solidarity on behalf of humanity remains too vague unless it is linked to partisan struggles on behalf of specific injustices and threats. These struggles will remain impotent and disconnected unless they find integral support within a democratic public sphere. Partisan solidarity must extend its cause to include the internal solidarity of the larger political sphere in which it operates (Solidarity: A Preliminary Analysis). In light of this conclusion I proceed to examine whether one conception of internal solidarity might prove especially fruitful in this regard. Drawing on the two paradigms of internal solidarity famously elaborated by Émile Durkheim, mechanical and organic, I argue that modern societies have evolved a type of democratic civic solidarity whose mechanical and organic features have the potential to reconcile different life plans and cooperative endeavors within the ambit of universal humanism (Mechanical and Organic Solidarity). However, this potential appears incapable of realization. Although mechanical features, such as agreement on universal human rights, point beyond the nation-state to a global community, organic features, such as cooperation for mutual benefit within a shared economic and political structure, do not. As Rawls notes, only a structure of mutual dependency, governed by a democratic state, generates a duty to distribute wealth to the benefit of the least well off in recognition of their estimable contributions. Although I agree that global civic solidarity cannot exist in the absence of a global democratic state, I submit that the reform I proposed in Chapter 6 for a democratic constitutionalization of global governance could go far in promoting it (Civic Solidarity).

The potential for realizing civic solidarity at the global level provides a partial response to the second objection listed above, that there could be no moral or psychological motivation for peoples of the world to make reasonable sacrifices for the sake of improving the lives of the more vulnerable. I also maintain, however, that, even in the absence of a global structure of democratic governance, international cooperation between peoples according to social contractarian principles of justice alone might suffice to motivate such sacrifices.

The second step of my argument defends the concept of global civic solidarity against the first objection. This objection has two parts. The first part asserts that the very concept of democratic civic solidarity is incoherent: human rights conflict with democracy and with group rights attached to nations and subnationalities. The gravity of this indictment becomes apparent once we realize that the right to development attaches principally to developing nations and not to individuals. How do we balance the human rights of individuals against their duties toward realizing the development of their communities?

A related objection argues that deliberative democracy requires the radical critique and transformation of cultural identities, thereby under-mining group solidarities and promoting atomistic individualism. Deliberative democracy has an ambivalent relationship to cultural groups, being dependent on their integral worldviews for sources of meaning, purpose, and motivation while subjecting them to transformative critique (Civic Solidarity: An Incoherent Concept). I argue that the transformation of a cultural group's identity need not weaken its internal solidarity. In any case cross-cultural dialogue can foster a more inclusive and cosmo-politan kind of solidarity.

The second part of the objection – what I call the multiculturalism challenge – asserts that human rights and democracy contradict central tenets of some major non-Western confessions, especially variants of Islam. This objection is damaging insofar as world religions comprise the most original form of transnational solidarity, one that has shown much promise in motivating the faithful to risk their lives for the sake of realizing democracy and human rights. Proponents of the objection main-tain that this linkage of world religion and human rights is entirely fortuitous and obscures a deeper conflict between these two grounds of moral authority.

This objection, I submit, exaggerates the conflict between secular and religious forms of solidarity; likewise, it underestimates the degree to which religion strengthens civic solidarity in its care for universal justice and the common good (Religion and Civic Solidarity). Drawing from empirical research and philosophical debates about religion in political life, I submit that civil engagement by religion in the public sphere in pursuit of partisan aims often promotes the ancillary aim of revitalizing democracy. The confluence of secular democracy and faith tradition brings in its wake the potential cosmopolitan transformation of each (From Religion to Cosmopolitan Solidarity).

I conclude that civil engagement by religion in democratic politics illustrates the potential for a new kind of cosmopolitan solidarity, what Carol Gould calls network solidarity (Building Cosmopolitan Solidarity Out of Solidarity Networks). Given the unlikelihood of persons' feeling solidarity with humanity as a whole or fighting for justice on its behalf, we would be well advised to reimagine cosmopolitan solidarity as a secondary expression of our primary solidarity on behalf of regional or sectorial struggles. Such struggles form a cosmopolitan network to the degree that the injustices they combat are linked by a single global threat: capitalism.

SOLIDARITY: A PRELIMINARY ANALYSIS

Any discussion of cosmopolitan solidarity must begin by addressing the oddity of that concept in light of the standard ways in which "solidarity" has been used.[1]

Prescriptive Uses of Solidarity

Solidarity can be prescribed and the assertion of its existence can implicitly have the force of a prescription. Solidarity can be prescribed when, for instance, many persons who face a common challenge mistakenly believe that each person acting alone can surmount that challenge. The force of this prescription may be prudential or moral, depending on whether or not the challenge in question poses a moral risk.

When we ascribe solidarity to a group we sometimes mean that its members ought to feel and act a certain way. It would be wrong for a person who claimed to stand in solidarity with other persons not to care about or identify with them. In most instances willingness to act on their behalf – sometimes to the point of sacrificing something of importance – is also demanded. If inhabitants of the world stood in solidarity with one another it would follow that they should care about each other and perhaps act accordingly; but it is not clear what this means.

Prescribing solidarity and prescribing feelings and actions that accord with solidarity can just be shorthand for clarifying duties that attach to specific types of social relationships. Duties of reciprocity, ranging from duties of mutual cooperation to duties of mutual aid, are a case in point. My solidarity with my fellow citizens – my empathetic identification with them and my corresponding sense of duty toward them – is prescribed by my need to cooperate with them in achieving my life goals and warding off external threats. Because my fellow compatriots assume burdens and make sacrifices for my benefit, I should do the same for them.

---

[1] My discussion of solidarity closely tracks the taxonomy set forth by Kurt Bayertz (1999: 3–28). Bayertz distinguishes humanitarian, internal, partisan, and bureaucratic forms of solidarity. Most useful for my defense of cosmopolitan solidarity is Bayertz's discussion of "project-related solidarity." Feminist philosophers (Sandra Bartky, Carol Gould, Fiona Robinson, Diana Meyers, and Virginia Held) further highlight the importance of care and empathy in sustaining this kind of solidarity. Finally, Jodi Dean, Craig Calhoun, Max Pensky, and others influenced by Habermas stress the importance of communication in linking together diverse solidaristic projects across national borders. For a good summary of these positions as the relate to transnational solidarity, see Carol Gould (2007: 148–64).

The prescriptive sense of solidarity recounted above normally attaches to duties that members of a bounded community have to each other. But duties of mutual aid extend beyond duties of mutual cooperation, which in turn extend across communities. Feelings of solidarity on behalf of distant strangers who are suffering political oppression or grievous human rights violations sometimes accompany our sense of being duty-bound to relieve their suffering with the expectation (however unlikely) that they should help us if we were to suffer similarly. Furthermore, duties to aid humanity as distinct from duties of personal care become meaningful to the degree that potential duty holders believe that their shared life as a species united by feelings of mutual respect is threatened. In keeping with this line of thought, Habermas once provocatively proclaimed that "justice conceived deontologically requires solidarity as its reverse side (Habermas 1989: 49).² Solidarity with suffering humanity can evoke a cosmopolitan duty to ameliorate global poverty, environmental degradation, and climate change. Linking otherwise disparate social movements, this kind of network solidarity demands strengthening democratic global governance and cosmopolitan civic solidarity.

Descriptive Uses of Solidarity

Civic solidarity highlights an important descriptive category. Solidarity can describe the *internal cohesion* of a group (internal solidarity) or it can describe *support for* a group or a cause (external solidarity). Expressing

---

² "Morality brings to bear the inviolability of socialized individuals by requiring equal treatment and thereby equal respect for the dignity of each one; and it protects *intersubjective relationships of mutual recognition requiring solidarity of individual members of a community*, in which they have been socialized. Justice concerns the equal freedoms of unique and self-determining individuals, while solidarity concerns the welfare of consociates who are intimately linked in an intersubjectively shared form of life – and thus also to the maintenance of the integrity of this form of life itself. Moral norms cannot protect one without the other" (my stress). Writing almost thirty years later Habermas today rejects this linkage of universal morality and solidarity, preferring instead a narrower definition linking solidarity to bounded forms of social cooperation aimed at achieving common goals (Habermas 2009: 187). According to this definition the civic solidarity of a democratic state premised on securing common defense and mutual welfare marks the outermost boundary of genuine solidarity (with the exception of religious and ideological loyalties). I think Habermas underestimates the extent to which civic solidarity can become cosmopolitan, aimed at preserving the integrity of a global public sphere against fragmentation and colonization (Ingram 2015). His speculation regarding a "species ethic" that resists biotechnological engineering and other threats to a communicatively-structured human nature reinforces my opinion (Habermas 2003a). See also Pierce (2017) and my discussion of Bohman in Chapter 6.

solidarity with a group or cause typically entails having empathy (or caring) for members of that group.[3] It also typically involves identifying with its struggle for justice.[4] Sometimes external solidarity explains internal solidarity. The internal cohesion of a group may consist in nothing more than its members supporting each other in their struggle against some external threat.

If the above analysis is correct, external solidarity can be directed toward humanity in a metaphorical sense only.[5] One might identify with humanity but not empathize with its struggles.[6] Nor is cosmopolitan concern about the future of humanity equivalent to being in solidarity with the persons that make up that community. Partisanship on behalf of humanity is meaningless.

MECHANICAL AND ORGANIC SOLIDARITY

Functional descriptions of group cohesion seem equally uncongenial to describing the global community. Émile Durkheim's famous distinction between *mechanical* and *organic* solidarity seems to apply to bounded communities exclusively (Heyd 2007: 119).[7] Communities exhibiting mechanical solidarity depend on "collective consciousness." Cohesion is achieved by each member possessing identical desires, feelings, and patterns of behavior. Members conduct their parallel lives independently of each other (as self-sufficient familial segments) while at the same time living in a state of ritual conformity. Durkheim ascribed this kind of solidarity to tribal societies that suffuse a common culture. He ascribed

[3] Empathy for the oppressed differs from personal empathy in the same degree that caring for humanity differs from personal caring. Feminist care ethicists, however, rightly insist that interpersonal empathy is essential for appreciating oppression and injustice (Gould 2007: 148; Held 2004: 141–55).
[4] In this respect solidarity differs from loyalty to family and friends (Heyd 2007: 118, 128 n10).
[5] A common refrain urges the world's inhabitants to join in solidarity in fighting global warming, but on further reflection this exhortation seems misplaced. Solidarity builds on affective attachments which evolve into cognitive identifications as the scope of interpersonal solidarity expands. It remains to be seen whether cognitive identification with suffering humanity suffices to ground cosmopolitan solidarity in the absence of any affective attachment to humanity.
[6] Rorty (1989: 189–98) speculates that we can feel solidarity for "all humanity," by which he means that we can feel empathy for any human being who is suffering and oppressed.
[7] As Honneth notes (Honneth 2014: 193), Durkheim (Durkheim 1964: 127–29, 319) was the last thinker after Hegel to propose that labor and capital could meet as solidaristic occupational groups conjoined by nonantagonistic contractual relationships.

a very different institutional form of solidarity to complex societies built upon an advanced division of labor. This organic form of solidarity arises out of cooperation between economic agents who possess different (indeed, unique) desires, beliefs, and skills.

Durkheim appeals to self-imposed duties of a contractual nature to explain how organic solidarity functions. However, his insistence on the importance of voluntary consent in stabilizing self-interested cooperation shows that a precontractual residue of mechanical solidarity remains. A form of civil religion based on common respect for the rights and welfare of each citizen stands as a counterpoise to anomic individualism.

Both functional and normative features of Durkheim's account of modern solidarity suggest potential for cosmopolitan expansion. The evolution of modern solidarity, which parallels the evolution of the con-tractarian legal paradigm I discussed in Chapter 6, is driven by the global spread of a capitalist system that dissolves solidaristic communities into differentiated, stratified social orders. The emergence of class conflict and religious schism challenges the social integration capacities of the feudal administrative state, which can no longer legitimate oppressive class hierarchies by appeal to the mechanical solidarity afforded by religion. Synthesizing earlier models of solidarity – the civic friendship model informing the ancient Greek city-state and the universal brotherhood model informing Christianity – the revolutionary movements of the late eighteenth-century propel the adoption of a novel solution to the state's legitimation crisis – a democratic form of national civic solidarity – *fraternité* (Brunkhorst 2005).

Subsuming religious, ethnic, regional, and class-based loyalties, nation-alism marks the high point of an affective type of mechanical solidarity based on *conventional* morality. Revolutionary nationalist movements fused this idea of solidarity with a rational *postconventional* ideal based on identification with humanity and its interests.[8] These interests find their quintessential articulation in the universal rights of man and of

---

[8] Lawrence Wilde (2013: chapter 2) mentions three cosmopolitan variants of postconven-tional solidarity that emerge alongside liberal-democratic civic solidarity: the *ethico-inclusive* ideal, which has its roots in Pierre Leroux's peaceful, humanitarian vision of egalitarian democratic worker cooperatives; the *redemptive* ideal, which Mikhail Bakunin invoked in calling for an anarchic annihilation of the state and all forms of legal domina-tion; and Marx's *class struggle, or internationalist working class* ideal, which entrusts the urban proletariat with the task of creating a classless communist society out of the ruins of capitalism. In my opinion, any movement espousing global solidarity today will likely borrow elements from all three of these (suitably updated) variants.

citizen: respect for the inherent dignity of the individual coupled with a commitment to regulate public life in accordance with an egalitarian democratic procedure. Democratic patriotism now designates an ambivalent loyalty: to universal constitutional ideals *and* to a particular national identity.[9]

CIVIC SOLIDARITY

Let us assume that these twin pillars of civic solidarity coexist harmoniously. The question then arises whether civic solidarity can provide a plausible model for cosmopolitan solidarity.

At first glance, neither communitarian nor social contractarian accounts of national civic solidarity appear promising in this regard. Hegel's description of the noncontractarian (recognitive) ethos underwriting economic cooperation and political cohesion only explains the willingness of citizens to sacrifice their commercial activities and lives for the sake of defending the state.[10] Honneth's Hegel-inspired notion of social freedom fares little better in demonstrating cosmopolitan potential.[11] As he understands it, liberal

---

[9] Collapsing these two identities threatens imperialism; sundering them threatens totalitarianism. The Napoleonic wars and American western expansionism (Manifest Destiny) exemplify the former pathology; fascism, which aims to solidify a disintegrated mass society of atomized individuals, exemplifies the latter. To refine this taxonomy, one should distinguish between fascist imperialism, whose expansionism aims at claiming space for a mythically favored race of people (not specifically tied to a particular nation state) and Communist imperialism, whose expansionism aims at realizing a specific variant of the Enlightenment's ideal of rational emancipation: a cosmopolitan dictatorship of the proletariat. J. -F. Lyotard (2002: 235–39).

[10] Hegel's understanding of this ethos (*Sittichkeit*) specifies both a particular and a universal referent; the particular referent designates a historical community, the universal referent designates institutionalized forms of mutual recognition common to all modern societies, such as familial relationships based on romantic love, economic relationships based on market conceptions of mutual need satisfaction, and political relationships based on mutual deliberation and decision-making. Hegel's understanding of the disintegrative tendencies of a capitalist market system and the dehumanizing effects of mechanized industry led him to endorse solidaristic occupational groups (corporations) and government intervention (the police) in stabilizing prices, ensuring production and provision of necessities, controlling for quality, and guarding against unemployment and poverty (Hegel, *Elements of the Philosophy of Right*, paras 195, 198, 236).

[11] For Honneth (2014: 53–54), legal (negative) and moral (positive) conceptions of freedom draw their meaning and purpose from a richer notion of social freedom. In principle, legal and moral spheres of action are only partly detached from sociocultural and political spheres of action. Although all spheres of action function as media for realizing noncoercive relationships, only sociocultural and political spheres of action institutionalize a form of mutual recognition that makes possible social freedom based on the harmonious

democracy designates a concrete way of life, not an abstract system of rights and constitutional norms.[12]

Of course, a democratic ethos might be extended globally if we reimagined it as a communication network linking solidarity groups whose particular identities have been expanded to encompass each others' struggles. Before we explore that possibility, let us first examine how far a social contractarian understanding of global society can generate cosmopolitan solidarity.

Rawls, for instance, recognizes a natural duty to assist burdened societies. But whatever sacrifices this duty entails pale in comparison to the stronger social contractarian duties of distributive justice that citizens – whose lives are structurally interwoven by a single government and a single domestic economy – are required to make on a permanent basis to ensure that the least well off among them meet a threshold of material prosperity requisite for participating in political life. By contrast, the contractarian duties of distributive justice that obtain at the international level are of an *ad hoc* nature, generated by treaties between self-selected groups of nations for the sake of equitably distributing burdens associated with military defense, trade, and other forms of cooperation mainly benefiting their respective peoples. Treaties aimed at providing a cosmopolitan benefit, such as carbon reduction, also claim to distribute burdens proportionally. But such treaties seldom impose significant burdens; when they do, legal enforcement is not automatically stipulated. This speaks to

pursuit of common goals. I discuss Honneth's appropriation of Hegel's theory of recognition in developing an account of social freedom in Chapter 1.

[12] Honneth maintains that notions of humanitarian solidarity that presume a common goal beyond that of recognizing "equal cultural differences" are "abstractly utopian." Abstract moral and legal norms mandating respect for human rights and cultural toleration are too thin (formal or procedural) to sustain mutual recognition based on liberal democratic interdependency. Although Habermas has urged a more formal or procedural understanding of liberal democratic solidarity in terms of legal (or constitutional) patriotism, he now appears to endorse a view similar to Honneth's. Rejecting his earlier view that solidarity is the reverse side of justice (see note 2), Habermas distinguishes our *negative* solidarity for victims of gross human rights violations from our *positive* solidarity to cooperate with co-nationals in pursuing common goals. In my opinion (see note 3), once we dismiss global solidarity as an impossible chimera, the international project of collaborating on global domestic policy becomes inexplicable (Honneth 2007: 123–24; 254–62; Habermas 2014: 9–11). More recently, Habermas has emphasized the dual constituent role of persons as citizens of both states and supranational polities without resolving the tension between these divided loyalties. My discussion of network solidarity shows how this tension can be mitigated (Habermas 2012: 335–48).

the relatively weak solidarity people in wealthy countries profess in relating to their poorer counterparts (Heyd 2007: 127).

In sum, the civic solidarity characteristic of those liberal democracies – in which wealthier citizens (in principle at least) as a matter of justice surrender a portion of their income in order to improve the lives of their less well-off compatriots – appears to be almost nonexistent in today's global society. True forms of cosmopolitan solidarity – most notably those expressed on behalf of the victims of gross humanitarian crimes – certainly exist and even compel interventions that require sacrifice from intervening nations. But the sacrifice they motivate is small in comparison to what is willingly assumed in the name of national self-defense. Cosmopolitan duties of compensatory justice impose sacrifices as well; they may be done willingly, as a matter of justice, but are seldom done out of solidarity with those who are owed compensation.

None of the above speaks against extending civic solidarity transnationally. My own proposal to reform the human rights order by strengthening its democratic constitutional structure presupposes such an extension. However, three objections to that reform stand in the way of its realization. First, if cosmopolitan solidarity must already exist in order to motivate reform, then we will need to imagine a concept of cosmopolitan civic solidarity different than the institutional one I have just outlined. The more pressing objections are those which I stated at the outset of this chapter: Is the concept of civic solidarity coherent? Can cosmopolitan respect for human rights coexist with duties to the community? Can communal solidarity flourish within democracy? And, can those two elements of civic solidarity be defended against multicultural challenge?

CIVIC SOLIDARITY: AN INCOHERENT CONCEPT?

Civic solidarity means loyalty to a community of individual rights holders. As the guarantor of their rights, the community claims rights of its own. This explains why the human right to development (RTD) was formulated as a right of a national community to develop in cooperation with other peoples. The RTD is therefore more readily interpreted as laying out duties of states toward each other and duties of persons toward their own community.

The idea that entities besides individual human beings can be the bearer of human rights reverses a standard assumption. Claimed by individuals *against* the community, human rights seem to elevate the good of the individual above the good of the community. This is clearly problematic, if, as Article 29 of the Universal Declaration of Human Rights (1948) puts it: "Everyone has duties to the community in which alone the free and full development of his personality is possible." In the words of Nigerian political scientist Claude Ake (Ake 1987: 5).

> The idea of human rights, or legal rights in general, presupposes a society that is atomized and individualistic, a society of endemic conflict ... We [Africans] assume harmony, not divergence of interests, competition, and conflict; we are more inclined to think of our obligations to other members of our society rather than our claims against them.

The conflict between human rights and duties to the community came to a head during the so-called "Asian values" debate that surfaced prior to the 1993 Vienna Conference on Human Rights. The Bangkok Declaration signed by ministers of many Asian countries proclaimed that Asian cultures, such as those influenced by Confucianism, do not rigidly separate legal rights from traditional ethical duties to family, community, and state. Appealing to the RTD, the Declaration echoed Ake's concern about the corrosive effect that a Western, individual-centered understanding of human rights has on social solidarity – however engineered it might be by authoritarian government – underpinning economic development.

We should be cautious not to infer too much from these communitarian challenges to human rights. Suppose the community in question is an indigenous tribe whose way of life is threatened by the state. Developing such a microcommunity may depend on the members of that community exercising their individual human rights to freely associate, organize, and speak out on behalf of their human right to practice their way of life – without interference from outsiders who want to impose their model of "development" on them.[13]

Human rights that protect individuals *and* groups from state-sanctioned predations — even those undertaken in the name of development—do not unconditionally elevate human rights over duties to the state.[14] Human

---

[13] Assigning rights to individual members of a group might be the *only* way to protect the group if it lacks organizational leadership necessary to lobby for protection *as a group* (Buchanan 2013: 264–65).

[14] The list of international conventions, treaties, and declarations dealing with issues that touch on group rights is too long to discuss in detail. Notable documents include UNESCO's *San Jose Declaration* (1989) condemning "ethnocide" or denial of a cultural group's "right to enjoy, develop or transmit its own culture and its own language, whether collectively or individually," and the Universal Declaration on Cultural Diversity (2001). Other notable documents are: the ILO's Convention Concerning Indigenous and Tribal Peoples in Independent Countries (1989); and the Declaration on the Rights of Persons Belonging to National or Ethnic, Religious and Linguistic Minorities (1992). Many other documents prohibit discrimination against women, racial

rights law permits the derogation of some human rights for the sake of national security and other duties to the community during times of national emergency. Indeed, as the RTD reminds us, human rights imply corresponding communitarian duties (How else is one to make sense of the human right to nationality?). Human rights entitle individuals to the communal provision of education, health, welfare and social security, which in turn obligates them to protect and maintain the provider.

Human Rights and Duties to the Community

This is not to deny that human rights sometimes conflict with duties to the community. Israel's identity as a Jewish nation compels its government to defend policies in the name of national security that arguably violate the human rights of its citizens and permanent residents of Palestinian descent. The right of indigenous peoples inhabiting tribal lands to preserve their native religion may conflict with the human rights of individual tribal members to practice a nonnative religion.[15]

The fact that the twin principles of civic solidarity (democratic self-determination and human rights) sometimes clash with each other suggests a standard solution: subordinate one principle to the other. The primacy of human rights in the international order ordinarily limits what national majorities are entitled to do. In most instances, the rights of groups do not trump human rights. For James Griffin and others, the (sometimes correct) impression that they do comes from wrongly classifying them as a species of human right in the first place.

One way to demonstrate this misclassification is to argue, as Griffin does, that the only group rights that are legitimately listed as human rights are not group rights at all, but are at bottom individual rights. It might be argued that group rights belong to a subcategory of instrumental human rights, or secondary human rights that are means to protecting the primary human rights of individuals .[16] A right's being instrumental for the

groups, and disabled persons; others mandate giving special rights to migrants and their families, refugees, children, and workers. Finally, as I observed in Chapter 5, The European Convention of Human Rights recognizes the human rights of corporations.

[15] As I argue in the case involving the New Mexico Pueblo tribe's suppression of Christian converts (*Santa Clara Pueblo v. Martinez* [1978]), the option of exiting a community is limited and very often imposes an unconscionable burden on the dissident who chooses that option (Ingram 2000: 116–18).

[16] Kymlicka (1989) and Taylor (1994), for example, note that acculturation into values that shape personal identity and agential capability invariably involve participation in thick traditions passed down by groups. Axel Honneth makes a similar point regarding the

protection of some other right does not preclude it from also being a human right; indeed, Griffin himself gives examples of legitimate instrumental human rights (such as freedom of press) and, as Allen Buchanan rightly notes, many if not most legal human rights are instrumental in this sense.

However convincing the instrumentalist defense of group rights might appear to be, it only goes to prove Griffin's point that "group rights . . . can be dissolved by reduction" Griffin 2008: 273). This would seem to be the case, at least, with respect to those group rights that Griffin himself regards as legitimate, such as the rights of states and peoples to sovereign self-determination. For, according to Griffin, the right to sovereignty is conditional on a prior respect for individual human rights.

We must be cautious not to infer too much from this simple truth. Griffin himself concedes that the UN Declaration of 1970 asserts something nearly opposed, namely, that "No state or group of states has the right to intervene . . . *for any reason whatsoever* in the internal or external affairs of any state(my stress)."[17] Drawing the obvious inference from this statement, he concludes that "if this once common understanding [of the right to sovereignty] is correct, then [this] group right is not reducible to these individual rights" (Griffin 2008: 274). Because Griffin himself believes that this "once common understanding" is no longer correct *unqualifiedly*, he draws the opposite conclusion: The Declaration's prohibition against humanitarian intervention in the internal affairs of a state *only* applies to interventions that carry grave moral risks of their own, such as posing serious threat to civilian lives. But merely conceding this latter qualification, which acknowledges that even rights-violating states typically continue to secure many social goods for their subjects, weakens Griffin's argument. For in the vast majority of cases involving human rights violations, delinquent states continue to legitimately exercise a sovereign group right that in practice trumps some of the human rights of some of their individual members.

---

importance of social recognition to the performance of social roles vital to the maintenance of family, religious community, and nation. As Joseph Raz remarks (Raz 1986: 207–09), the personal good derived from feelings of solidarity and self-esteem is itself a public good that depends on others within the group both sharing and recognizing the same social experiences.

[17] Declaration of Principles of International Law Concerning Friendly Relations and Cooperation among States in accordance with the Charter of the United Nations, adopted by the United Nations General Assembly, October 24, 1970, Section on the sovereign equality of states.

The fact that group rights are listed as human rights, combined with the fact that they can conflict with the human rights of individuals, suggests either that they are wrongfully included as legitimate human rights – Griffin's preferred way of resolving the conflict – or that official human rights doctrine is incoherent, deploying the concept of "human right" inconsistently. Both of these possibilities may be true of course. But there remains a third possibility: group rights are legitimate *and* nonreducible human rights. Following the logic underlying this possibility, we can render group-ascribed human rights conceptually coherent pursuant to Buchanan's critique of the Mirroring View (which holds that human rights are identical to moral rights that only protect aspects of *individual* agency). The fact that they potentially conflict with other human rights is not unique to them. Nor should it occasion wonder that in some cases of conflict group-ascribed human rights should prevail over individual-ascribed human rights. So, it would seem that our divided loyalties to nation and humanity are unavoidable after all.

Deliberative Democracy and the Destabilization of Group Solidarity

The above discussion has not resolved the tension between national and cosmopolitan forms of solidarity. It has, however, shown that the tension is internal to the cosmopolitan human rights order itself. Thus, affirming our primary solidarity with that order commits us to the possibility that in some cases the different rights and duties it prescribes (or permits) will conflict with each other. Far from endangering the coherence of a cosmopolitan order, this result confirms one of the conclusions drawn in Chapter 6, that citizens' divided loyalties to *polis* and *cosmopolis* must both be represented in constituting a new democratic global order. Furthermore, as I argued in Chapter 5, the importance of instituting constitutional review within that order attests to the importance of international courts or other well-placed bodies that have been delegated responsibility for review in immunizing what are arguably higher-ranking human rights claims of individuals who possess "human dignity" against lower-ranking human rights claims of groups and corporations.

There remains a second challenge to the conceptual coherence of civic solidarity. This challenge is more serious because it suggests that democracy itself undermines solidarity. This idea seems odd in light of the history of modern democracy in Europe. Advocates for democracy initially appealed to a sovereign national will – metaphysically identified with "the people" – as a placeholder for a unique and continuous ethno-linguistic community extending backwards and forwards in time. This "community" was mythic in several conflicting senses of the term: at once signifying a natural origin *and* a fiction fabricated by propagandists.

The myth of national solidarity suppresses the fact that individuals forge their communal bonds through political debate amongst themselves.[18] What Habermas calls "constitutional patriotism" best describes their solidarity, which depends on culture-transcendent norms of discourse, as these have been adapted to particular legal traditions.

Before he embraced a notion of dual sovereignty, Habermas held that a proper constitutional patriotism should dispense with nationalist solidarity – should become *postnational*. Furthermore, although he insists even today that such a form of patriotism should be justified rationally, that is to say, independently of citizens' nonshareable comprehensive cultural beliefs, he does not think that it should efface them. First, like Rawls and other liberals, Habermas endorses liberal pluralism, toleration, and accommodation as essential conditions for free and robust dialog. Second, like them, he is concerned that a mass of culturally deracinated individuals will lack shared values distilling concrete images of a just and fulfilling life. Without such values democratic deliberation has nothing of substance to deliberate about.

The question arises, however, whether constitutional patriotism doesn't undermine the very cultural resources upon which its own tepid solidarity must partly depend. For liberals like Rawls and Kymlicka, this question need never arise. They take for granted the quasi-natural, self-constituted nature of comprehensive cultures.[19] That these cultures should sustain liberal democracy and give meaning and purpose to its otherwise vacuous norms requires only that they should overlap in endorsing some thin ideas of freedom, equality, toleration, and justice. But a deliberative democracy based on discourse ethical principles demands more than this. Overlapping consensus remains suspect of ideological

---

[18] Habermas's earlier objection (1994: 130) to Charles Taylor's defense of Quebec's signage laws speaks to the futility of preserving cultural traditions by administrative means once those traditions acquire their multicultural recognition through dialog between cultural insiders and outsiders. See Chapter 3 for my discussion of the implications this view has for immigration policy.

[19] Rawls (1999a: 23 note 17) even cites J. S. Mill's outdated – and by modern standards, questionable – opinion, expressed in the opening sentences of chapter XVI of *Consideration on Representative Government* (1862) that among the causes generating a (national) culture of "common sympathies" are "race and descent."

taint; only discursively achieved consensus constructed out of a potentially transformative dialog between comprehensive belief systems meets
minimum standards of rational justification.

Such a dialog by its very nature questions the comprehensive (metaphysical) faith commitments solidifying integral cultures by insisting that
their practitioners disaggregate them into criticizable assertions and moral
judgements. Critical dialog devalues cultural values by diluting their
capacity to distill a sense of objective meaning, purpose, and identity out
of the subjective chaos of momentary desires. Cultures live on in a fragmented state, deprived of their former power to inspire solidarity.
Increasingly beholden to individual appropriation, they become so many
items on a multicultural menu that can be mixed and matched at will.[20]

The very logic of deliberative democracy erodes cultural solidarity and, it
would seem, political (civic) solidarity, leaving in its wake the atomized
individuals that regressive forms of fascism prey on. But this conclusion is
surely premature. Cultural identities are intrinsically constructed and contested from the get-go. Modern democracy, which presumes that all who are
affected by a decision have a right to participate in deliberations impacting
that decision, merely accelerates that process by forcing nationalities and
subnationalities to justify their exclusion of outsiders from domestic policy
disputes using reasons that these outsiders could accept (or not reasonably
reject). Being essentially transnational, cosmopolitan, and multicultural,
democracy does not so much dissolve cultural solidarities as hasten their
dynamic transformation and proliferation. What cultures lose in the form of
fixed and stable identity they gain in flexible adaptability.

Three consequences follow from this analysis that bear on the possibility
of cosmopolitan solidarity. First, civic solidarity relies on both constitutional
patriotism *and* particular cultural attachments to flesh out the meaning of
social freedom that democratic political life seeks to actualize. Second, the
discourse ethical norms underwriting constitutional patriotism mandate cosmopolitan inclusion of different sociocultural perspectives in a way that
renders all cultural and political identities fluid, porous, and open to mutual
(albeit contested) recognition, without necessarily dissolving their capacity to
generate meaning and purpose. Indeed, the possibility of democratically
mediating dual (or multiple) attachments – national, transnational, and
cosmopolitan – at all levels of governance depends on critically reconstituting

---

[20] Max Pensky (2000: 64–79) properly recommends resignation in the face of cultural
identity loss and a willingness to embrace a "cosmopolitan solidarity of remembrance"
of what we have collectively gained in the course of modernization (77).

cultural attachments in this manner. Finally, once rendered fluid, porous, and open to critical recognition from others, these various cultural and regional solidarities can communicate with each other at the global level in jointly promoting justice and the common good.

RELIGION AND CIVIC SOLIDARITY

Because world religion functions as the original and most powerful cosmopolitan form of cultural solidarity, its capacity to motivate liberal democratic reform is of special interest to us. But is religion really an ally of liberal democracy?

Habermas has remarked on more than one occasion that religion has belied sociological predictions of its demise. Contrary to his own earlier prognosis that reflexive cultures must suffer dissolution of their dogmatic core in the course of undergoing modernization (Habermas 2002: 79), he today concedes that this core can be accommodated to modern democratic life.[21] Indeed, he finds hope in the fact that religion's utopian imaginary can be transposed to a more secular key without exposing it to direct questioning. But religion's potential for inspiring liberal democratic reform – which could make it a powerful voice in the struggle for realizing human rights and cosmopolitan justice – seems dubious, to say the least.

Take Islamic theocracies – like Saudi Arabia – that do not give women the same rights as men, do not give non-Muslims the same civil and political rights as Muslims, and even deny the latter civil and political rights enjoyed by citizens of liberal democracies.[22] Does the Saudi government's human rights record reveal a conflict between Islamic values and the current human rights regime?[23] Or does it reveal a conflict between an extreme,

---

[21] Reiterating his earlier claim that the "opaque core of religious experience" remains "abysmally alien to discursive thought," Habermas insists (Habermas 2008: 143, 297, 303–09) that practitioners should relinquish this core's claim *as a comprehensive worldview* whenever it conflicts with civil rights.

[22] Saudi Arabia abstained from ratifying the UDHR in 1948, claiming that it violated *Shari'a* law. This reason for rejecting the UDHR was rejected by Pakistan, which did ratify the UDHR, along with Turkey, Syria, and Egypt. Saudi Arabia has ratified some important human rights conventions, including (in 2000) the Convention on the Elimination of All Forms of Discrimination Against Women.

[23] Iran's representative to the UN dismissed the UDHR as a "secular understanding of the Judeo-Christian tradition." In 1990, the Organization of the Islamic Conference (now the Organization of Islamic Cooperation) voted to support an alternative human rights document, the Cairo Declaration on Human Rights in Islam, which asserts that persons have "freedom and a right to a dignified life in accordance with the Islamic Shari'ah," which forbids discrimination based on "race, colour, language, sex, religious belief,

fundamentalist interpretation of those values and that regime? If the latter is the case, then the conflict is exceptional rather than basic, highlighting the peculiar moral obtuseness of the Saudi interpretation of Islamic law in relation to the rest of the Muslim world.[24] If the former is the case, then the conflict is basic, suggesting that some important features of human rights that the international human rights regime maintains are necessary for global development (e.g., extending equal civil and political rights to both men and women) are not supported by a major world religion.[25]

Religion and Secular Democracy: The Case of Islam

Leaving aside other religious worldviews,[26] the argument that Islam is incompatible with human rights and secular democracy appears to be the

political affiliation, social status, or other consideration." The Declaration, which has been signed by forty-five states, was nonetheless condemned by many human rights organizations, including the International Commission of Jurists, for denying Muslims freedom of conscience (a non-derogable right), endorsing corporal punishment, and reaffirming discrimination against women and non-Muslims (Abiad 2008).

[24] In sharp contrast to the Wahhabist branch of Sunni Islam institutionalized in Saudi Arabia, many Sunni moderates derive a strong commitment to democracy and human rights from the 8th Century Hanafite School, whose interpretation of *shari'a* emphasizes the role of analogical reasoning and rational deliberation about the common good above traditional consensus *(ijma)* and textual literalness. Shiism and branches of Sufism (which emphasizes mystical revelation) also interpret the Qur'an this way. For a detailed discussion of Islamic fundamentalism (especially Wahhabism and the origins of the Hanbali legal school) and its relationship to the Shafi'ite, Malakite, and Hanafi schools, see Ayubi (2006) and Ess (2006).

[25] Alessandro Ferrara (2013: chapter 5) argues that in Muslim society individual rights are typically invoked in a restorative manner, as compensations for torts and damages, rather than as "natural properties" of persons that serve to delimit state power and "trump" duties to the community. Russel Powell (2004) suggests a theological basis for these different human rights practices: The opposing ways in which Christian and Muslim theologians working within a natural law context have traditionally interpreted human nature – divided (sinful) versus undivided – correlates with opposing views of legal authority, with Islam favoring less divided forms of government that would be less amenable to separation of religion and state. Powell further adds that Islam, or Muslim culture broadly construed, is less accepting of social conflict as a necessary and unavoidable – and perhaps even positive – feature of modern political life. Therefore, any rational interpretation of *shari'a* that takes into account its four sources – the Qur'an, hadith, consensus, and analogical reasoning – will privilege the common good over individual rights.

[26] Space limitations prevent me from surveying the full range of world religions. Suffice to say, Eastern religions show little regard for human rights understood as individual legal claims that take precedence over duties to the community. Confucianism interprets human rights *(ch'uan-li)* ethically as conventional norms of proper living intended to facilitate the context-sensitive fulfillment of unequal duties associated with different statuses and social roles in a manner that enables both individual and community to

reverse side of a broader argument, advanced by signatories to the Bangkok Declaration (1993), that liberal democratic rights are not truly universal rights in the way that (say) a right to life is.[27] According to the Declaration, economic development trumps civil and political freedom because it makes possible the civic aptitudes requisite for political participation in the first place. (The counter to this argument is that economic development normatively entails civil and political freedom.)[28] But Islam – so the argument goes – rejects this freedom in principle.

realize their proper natures. Traditional Confucianism emphasizes filial piety, clan loyalty, and respect for wise and virtuous rulers but recent scholarly debates have also shown how Confucian belief in balancing powers and civic education can complement constitutional democracy and a liberal legal understanding of human rights (Dallmayr 2017: 103–20 and note 28 below). The cosmocentric ecologism of Eastern reform Buddhism interprets human rights within the context of a broader compassion for the dignity of each suffering being. In my opinion, nothing in these worldviews contradicts Western conceptions of human rights. See Ingram (2004: 222–28); Taylor (1999: 101–91); Inada (1990); and Ames (1988).

[27] Signatories to the Bangkok Declaration (led by China, Singapore, Malaysia, and India), which was drafted before the Vienna World Conference on Human Rights (1993), endorsed the view that "while human rights are universal in nature, they must be considered in the context of a dynamic and evolving process of international norm setting, bearing in mind the significance of national and regional particularities and various historical, cultural, and religious backgrounds" (Art. 8). In particular, the Declaration's emphasis on the near inviolability of government's sovereign right to maintain social harmony and order reflected a largely one-sided, Confucian understanding of "Asian values." Significantly, the ASEAN Human Rights Declaration of 2012 abandons reference to "regional particularities" that formed the original context for debating the cultural relativity of human rights vis-à-vis "ASEAN values." There are other subtle but notable shifts towards accepting the UN's understanding of human rights. Article 6, for instance, substitutes "balances" for "depends" in its assertion that "the enjoyment of human rights ... must be balanced with the performance of corresponding duties as every person has responsibilities to all other individuals, the community, and the society where one lives." Article 7 reasserts in milder (and potentially uncontroversial) form the importance of applying human rights in a manner that is sensitive to "different regional and national contexts bearing in mind different political, economic, legal, social, cultural, historical, and religious backgrounds." With the exception of including the preservation of "public morality" among the reasons for derogating some human rights, along with national security, public order, public safety, public health, and "the general welfare of peoples in a democratic society," Article 8 approximates the language of Art. 29(2) of the UDHR. The inclusion of "public morality" has been criticized by human rights groups advocating on behalf of women, gays, and others who maintain that standards of public morality are subject to reasonable disagreement (Renshaw 2013).

[28] Habermas, for instance, argues (2001: 120–36) that the path toward economic development undertaken by authoritarian Asian countries commits them to corresponding functional prerequisites. These include the rule of law and a modern legal code that minimally specifies individual property rights associated with modern market systems. Legitimating this legal code implies democracy.

Is this explanation right? It depends. Speaking against it is the fact that many Muslim majority states have liberal democratic constitutions that expressly endorse *some* separation of sectarian Islamic values from the legal administration of justice.[29] Again, depending on how they are interpreted, foundational Islamic texts allow for secular government and robust equal human rights for both men and women.[30] To be sure,

[29] Majority-Muslim governments that have secular constitutions permit Muslims to settle family and property disputes in *shari'a* courts. Others that constitutionally entrench *shari'a* as a system of higher legitimating values and principles (such as Iraq and Pakistan) institute secular forms of democratic governance legitimating legislation and public law adjudication. Again, in the wake of the recent Arab Spring uprising, Tunisia's 2014 Constitution entrenches Islamic values (Article 1) while guaranteeing full and equal religious freedom for all (Article 6). In the case of Indonesia, we find yet another variety of this example of religious legitimation of secular democracy, expressed in the nonsectarian principle of *pancasila*. Turkey also illustrates how complicated state/religion relationships are even in governments that have instituted a rather severe form of state/religion separation. The Turkish Republic's former ban on religious parties and public displays of religious symbolism (dating back to Mustafa Kemal's obsession with combating religious divisiveness in the founding years of the republic) resembles the laïcism of the French Republic, even though the Religious Affairs Directory appoints imams, issues religious decrees (*fatwas*), mandates religious education, and shapes curriculum according to its own flexible and rational adaptation of the Qur'an. The permission granted to the AK (Justice and Development) Party by the military (the official guardians of the Turkish constitution) to form a government in 2002 marked an important step toward liberalization, since the AK's platform, informed as it is by the toleration characteristic of Turkish Sufism, advocates a modestly pluralistic society in which most religious and nonreligious beliefs are permitted public expression, within limits (Tezcür 2007).

[30] Noted political theorist Abdullahi Ahmed An-Na'im (1990: 21; 2008) observes that provisions of *shari'a* based exclusively on a literalist reading of the Qur'an and Hadith are problematic in that they subordinate women to men, deny non-Muslims full civil and political rights and require them to pay a special tax, and condemn Muslims who abandon their faith. These provisions, when legally imposed, appear to violate human rights, at least insofar as these rights are fully understood to apply to all individuals equally, pursuant to Articles 1–3 of the UDHR (1948). However, An-Na'im also remarks that an interpretation of the Qur'an, based on the early Mecca teachings of Mohammad, before the flight to Medina and the establishment of a Muslim state, permits accommodation with liberal human rights, gender equality and democratic ideals, and even requires the religious neutrality of the state (quoting Surah 256 of the Qur'an, which commands that "there shall be no compulsion in religion"). Historically, in fact, the four Caliphs that followed Mohammad were chosen by the community of converts (*umma*) as spiritual interpreters of *shari'a* based on their personal association with him, but they were not administrators of a coercive state apparatus. Concluding that these caliphates did not amount to a fusion of state and religion, Ira Lapidus adds (1975: 64) that later dynastic rulers of the Ummayyad (661–750), Abbasid (750–1258), Mameluke (1250–1517) and Ottoman empires (1299–1922) *were* state administrators. They instituted a divided government along the lines of the doctrine of two swords that prevailed in Medieval Christendom, which conceded distinct domains of legal jurisdiction to secular and religious authorities. The Sultans and Emirs did protect the Muslim faith from internal

political life in Muslim majority states is sometimes dominated by Islamist political parties. However, as I have argued elsewhere, moderate forms of secular liberal democracy do not require the exclusion of religion from law and politics;[31] indeed, religion can sometimes further the cause of liberal democracy (Ingram 2014a, 2014b). This is no less true of Islam today (as evidenced by the Arab Spring uprisings) than it was of Catholicism thirty years ago.[32] No doubt, both religions have at times confronted modern secular institutions such as liberalism and democracy as existential threats,[33]

and external enemies and they sought to institute *shari'a* but, as Olivier Roy observes (1994: 14–15), they derived most of their legitimacy from their political and administrative functions, such as the power to coin money and preserve order.

[31] Islamic thought and practice reveal a spectrum of epistemic, political, and institutional forms of secularism. When speaking of secular democracy political scientists normally focus on the *institutional* separation of religion and state. Equally important, however, is the political *culture*; viz., the degree of democratic toleration and civility religious political parties display in furthering their aims. Closely connected to this *political* secularism is an *epistemic* secularism, or the capacity, as Rawls puts it, for religious parties to accept the "burdens of judgment" in refraining from imposing religious doctrines or appealing to religious rationales whose truth cannot in principle be demonstrated to all. While it may seem that extreme epistemic secularism correlates with political secularism, I argue that religion is sometimes a better stimulus to creating and preserving secular democracy (Ingram 2014b).

[32] Samuel Huntington (1991: 91) observes that the "third wave" of democratization from 1974 to 1990 was "overwhelmingly a Catholic wave," with roughly three-quarters of the thirty countries transitioning to democracy being predominantly Catholic. Samuel P. Huntington, *The Third Wave: Democratization in the Late Twentieth Century* (Norman: University of Oklahoma Press 1991), p. 91. Also see Philpott (2004: 32–46).

[33] Well into the twentieth century the Church defended positions that were hostile to liberalism and democracy. Critics blamed this illiberalism on the Church's highly centralized authoritarian structure and on its intolerance of other faiths, which followed from its state-assured monopoly on moral and religious instruction in many Catholic nations. However, the Church's relationship to liberalism and democracy has also been shaped by its understanding of the threats arrayed against it. Anticlerical legislation spurred on by nationalist republican sentiment in Europe and Mexico during the late nineteenth and early twentieth centuries may have succeeded in forcing the Church to accommodate liberal democracy up to a point, albeit mainly as an expedient in non-Catholic countries in which it did not enjoy a monopoly of influence – a fact which explains its reverse accommodation of anti-Communist governments of a virulent Fascist stripe. Only after the Second World War did the Church desist from seeking hegemony while embracing freedom of religion as an intrinsic value. By the time the Vatican II reform culminated in declaring religious liberty with Pope Paul VI's *Dignitatis Humanae* (1965) – partly under pressure from American Catholics led by John Courtney Murray and partly out of an evolving understanding of its own natural law tradition dating back centuries – the Church was well positioned to become the chief champion of human rights and democracy throughout Latin America and Eastern Europe. By contrast, 20th century Islamist political movements arose in reaction to foreign- imposed secular governments and home-grown nationalist movements. Many of these governments were deemed to be hostile to the moral and social justice precepts of Islam. Some of them, such as Gamar

but both have also embraced them as opportunities for promoting nonsectarian social justice policies.[34]

Religious Solidarity within the Limits of Civic Solidarity

This last point highlights an often overlooked fact: The degree to which a polity constitutionally entrenches liberal democratic principles depends on the willingness of courts to intervene on behalf of vulnerable minorities and women and the willingness of the state to educate its citizens in the subtle art of free and civil debate. In a deliberative democracy, civil debate is entrusted with shaping not only public opinion but also *public reason*, which is tasked with interpreting general human rights principles in accordance with the traditions and historical events specific to that democracy. Key to public reason is a capacity to assume the *burdens of judgment*, which Rawls defines as an acknowledgement of the reasonableness of pluralism, or the impossibility of converting others' moral consciences to one's own way of thinking by means of rational suasion alone.

To reason publicly involves standing back from oneself and adopting the eccentric standpoint of an outside critic. Culminating a moral evolution whose apotheosis is an awareness of universal human rights and humanitarian solidarity, its logic becomes increasingly irresistible in the face of a multicultural politics of recognition. Even religion succumbs to its secularizing allure – or flees into an isolationist cocoon of fundamentalism.

Religion must accommodate public reason if it is to remain a partner in the human rights dialog, but must public reason accommodate religion? Is

Abdel Nasser's in Egypt, were inspired by Arab nationalism and socialism, and so regarded Islamists as a divisive force that needed to be repressed. Similar motivations inspired Kemal's suppression of public religious expression in Turkey as well as Shah Reza Pahlavi's repressive policy in Iran. Indeed, even Pakistan, a regime founded on Islam, has suppressed fundamentalist Islamist groups opposed to its weakly secular form of government.

[34] From a strategic point of view, movements with strong ideological commitments are propelled to moderate their agendas in order to avoid government suppression, win elections, and develop an organizational leadership consisting of professionally trained lawyers, economists, and other professionals capable of proposing and implementing realistic solutions to a wide range of social problems. Once these movements come to appreciate the reciprocal benefits to themselves and other like-minded movements of political liberalism, they come to endorse secular democracy and political liberalism for its intrinsic justice, and converge toward an overlapping consensus in grounding these ideals in the "truth" conveyed by their own incommensurable doctrines (Wickham 2004; Schwedler 2008). For an insightful application of this theory to Muslim reform politics in Iran and Turkey, see Tezcür (2010).

it appropriate for elected representatives to appeal to religion in parliamentary debate? And, is it appropriate for ordinary citizens to do the same when they debate public policy with nonbelievers?

To answer these questions, let us recall why minorities who dissent from majoritarian policies have a *prima facie* duty to abide by them. The usual "you play by the rules, you accept the outcome" response to this query presumes that everyone recognizes the fairness of the rules. In order for the rules governing democratic politics to be fair, it is not enough that they allow everyone an equal vote and an equal right to speak out and associate freely. These safeguards against the worst kind of majoritarian tyranny – the violation of the minority's human rights – do not address a less oppressive form of majoritarian "winner-take-all" tyranny. A fair democracy must also allow the minority an equal chance to be responded to in a way that respects its ethical standpoint (assuming that that standpoint is tolerant of other standpoints). Losers as well as winners in democratic contests have a legitimate expectation that their concerns have been met with arguments whose premises they find to be reasonable – arguments whose reasons respect their own ethical standpoint even if they do not compel their assent. To rephrase this point in the language of deliberative democracy, some effort at rationally achieving a generally acceptable consensus on common interests, free from the constraints of hegemonic ideology and socioeconomic power, must guide the process of public will formation and legislation in order for legal outcomes to merit the presumption of normative legitimacy (worthiness of recognition as prima facie morally binding); and this deliberative effort, whether successful or not in its consensual aim, cannot move forward unless citizens speak to one another in a mutually comprehensible and respectful language.

This is what John Rawls and other defenders of political liberalism have in mind when speaking of a civil duty to hew one's political thinking to *public* reason (Rawls 1999b; Habermas 2008a).[35] Three questions arise as to its exercise: Who falls under the duty? Which political issues activate the duty? What does the duty require? Extreme secularists insist that this duty extends to all citizens, ordinary and official; applies to all political issues regardless of content; and requires that all religious reasons be bracketed. For instance, Robert Audi counsels the complete *privatization* of religious faith as a necessary condition for exercising civic

---

[35] For a more detailed discussion of Habermas and Rawls on religion in the public sphere, see Ingram (2010a: chapter 8).

responsibility and showing solidarity with fellow citizens. He insists that citizens bracket their religious motives – the dogmatic core commitments founding their solidarity with like-minded believers – as well as religious language in deliberating about legislation (Audi 1989: 278–79).[36]

A more moderate secularist might question the extreme requirement that ordinary citizens as well as parliamentarians debate and deliberate in accordance with such a demanding notion of public reason. One might also question applying the requirement to all policy debates regardless of their relevance to human rights. Finally, one might dismiss the need to bracket religious motivations along with religious arguments. Addressing the issue of application, Rawls accepts the civility of religious argumentation in justifying policies that do not touch on constitutional freedoms or that only expand rather than restrict such freedoms. But debates over obscenity and hate speech (not to mention laws prohibiting blasphemy or offensive displays of religion) illustrate that the distinction between constitutional and nonconstitutional, freedom-restricting and freedom-enhancing, policies is hard to draw in practice.[37] Virtually every form of expressive behavior can be interpreted as politically meaningful *or* provocative and harmful. Robust free speech potentially undermines the equal protection of some group(s), but efforts to control for the harmful effects of expressive behavior at least indirectly infringe on constitutional liberties and human rights.

These concerns have been given new life in light of Europe's continuing struggle to assimilate its marginalized Muslim communities. But the difficulty in distinguishing kinds of speech and speech regulation is made even harder in the case before us, which impinges on the unavoidable infiltration of religion into politics. Habermas and Rawls acknowledge that religious speech and thought are particularly recalcitrant to bracketing when it comes to things that matter most to people. Along with other

---

[36] These sentiments are echoed by the Muslim secularist Lahouri Addi (1992: 124): "It is necessary to show how political modernity is incompatible with the public character of religion and how modernity is built on the depoliticization of religion."

[37] Judging from the lively debate over prohibiting Muslim women from wearing the *burqa* in public spaces, the *burqini* at public beaches, and Muslim girls from wearing the *hijab* in public schools, the French government's enforcement of its own aggressively humanistic (and nationalistic) "civil religion" (ensconced in the principle of *laïcité*) arguably runs afoul of its own secular values of freedom, equality, and fraternity. The Stasi Commission's ruling that wearing a less ostentatious sign than the *foulard*, which it interpreted as a sectarian act of hostility toward the republic, would have been acceptable reinforces this impression. For further discussion of the historical and constitutional differences between French and American secularism, (see Ingram 2014b).

relatively unquestioned comprehensive belief commitments, religion provides an authoritative anchor for deep moral convictions that cannot be acquired through science or other forms of practical thinking. These thinkers note the capacity of utopian religious imagery to expand our secular thinking about social justice and the unique dignity of the human person, as exemplified, for instance, in the American movement to abolish slavery. This belief in the importance of faith-based values in anchoring civil society also informs Iranian philosopher Abdolkarim Soroush's notion of "religious democracy," which he opposes to the corrosive libertarianism of neoliberal capitalism. For Soroush, democracy implies "respect for the will of the majority and the rights of others, justice, sympathy, and mutual trust," not to mention "tolerance in the domain of beliefs" and "fallibility in the domain of cognition" (Soroush 2000: 125, 152–53). Democratic societies, he explains, "do not need to wash their hands of religiosity nor turn their backs on revelation" so long as they "absorb an adjudicative understanding of religion" based on "collective reason" and public "common sense" (127–28, 140). He concludes that, "if the pluralism of secularism makes it suitable for democracy, the faithful community is a thousand times more suitable for it" (143–45).

Like Soroush, Habermas and Rawls allow religious rhetoric in debating and deliberating within the public sphere while insisting on its eventual translation into secular argumentation at the level of government. In order to ease the asymmetrical burden that falls on believers in meeting the requirements of public reason, Habermas suggests that even nonbelievers share in the duty to translate religious appeals into secular arguments.

A number of questions are raised by this proposal. To begin with, reconciling religious appeal to the demands of pubic reason might not require much, if any translation. For instance, Martin Luther King's quotation of the Bible in his "I Have a Dream Speech" – "There is neither Jew nor Gentile, neither slave nor free, nor is there female and male, for you are all one in Jesus Christ" (Galatians 3:28) – is readily comprehended by believers and nonbelievers alike as referencing the inherent dignity of the individual and the universal equality of all. Furthermore, secularization brings in its wake the rationalization of religious language. In Christian-majority and Muslim-majority countries, the ethical contents of the Abrahamic religious tradition (recall the Biblical passage quoted above) have already been translated into secular ideas, such as the idea of universal human rights. Finally, as the debates surrounding abortion, gay marriage, euthanasia, cloning, and stem cell research amply attest, advocates of religiously motivated policies have had little difficulty in finding secular arguments supporting their positions. These arguments, to be sure, might not express the main reasons why they advocate a policy. Arguing by conjecture – showing that a position can be justified by appeal to reasons that are convincing to one's opponent but not to oneself – need not be as duplicitous and insincere as it first appears, especially if the arguer announces his or her real motives for supporting her position. Perhaps this is all that Rawls and Habermas have in mind when they talk about translating religious appeals into the secular language of public reason. If that is so, then not just appeals to religion but appeals to any comprehensive worldview, however secular, will require translation into a more broadly shared idiom in order to convince others (Taylor 2011: 50–56).

Contrary to Rawls and Habermas, Taylor simply denies that religion poses a special challenge to secular democracy requiring special vigilance and separation. This challenge would not be so pressing if one could easily separate faith from reason, as Habermas and Rawls admonish us to do. But as the preceding discussion has shown, this cannot be done. What appears reasonable from the standpoint of public reason is invariably shaped by faith-anchored judgments.

Does that mean that there is little distinction to be drawn between religious and nonreligious faith commitments, as Taylor insists? Habermas mentions that purely religious faith commitments differ from nonreligious faith commitments in several important respects. First, they impose themselves on the faithful only through personal revelation and conversion. Second, they command their fulfillment as a necessary condition for eternal salvation. Third, they command their fulfillment as the highest and most unconditional commands (Habermas 2011: 61–62).

The first and third traits mentioned above do not define religious commitments exclusively. Secular humanists also speak of epiphanies, revelations, and conversion experiences that explain their complex journey from believer to nonbeliever. People in general are reluctant to abandon core beliefs that are acquired more or less unconsciously over time and that have become deeply ingrained in their personal identities. Having emerged in ineffable experience, they ineffably color future experience, thereby creating a self-confirming circle of faith informing reason and vice versa. As for the third defining characteristic, secular faith commitments such as the moral duty to protect even strangers from life-threatening mob persecution can also command unconditionally, sometimes at great personal sacrifice.

The second trait, however, may seem to be peculiar to religion. The motivations for hewing to secular commitments appear less powerful than the promise of eternal salvation or the threat of eternal damnation vouch-safed by some religions. It may therefore seem that religiously convicted people have less incentive to compromise and be persuaded by others for mundane reasons. Taken to the extreme of fanaticism, they demonize those who oppose them as emissaries of evil whose arguments must be resisted if not suppressed.

But religion does not have a monopoly on ideological extremism. Fanatics of all stripes have been willing to sacrifice mundane freedom, happiness, and commonsense for the sake of intangible rewards. Such fanatics can still speak the language of public reason; at the very least, they can conjecture how nonbelievers might be persuaded to agree with them. What they cannot do is conform themselves to the spirit of public reason.

So, both Taylor and Habermas are mistaken; *pace* Habermas, the challenge to secular democracy is not that religious appeals resist transla-tion into a secular idiom; *pace* Taylor, the challenge to secular democracy is not that particular creeds will contaminate the ideological neutrality of the state. Rather, the challenge to secular democracy is an unwillingness to be persuaded by others who might tempt us to compromise our deepest faith commitments. This undemocratic disposition is not unique to reli-gion; nor is the disposition to demonize others who disagree with us. Rather, all organized ideological movements whose members display this disposition pose unique challenges to secular democracy.

FROM RELIGION TO COSMOPOLITAN SOLIDARITY

Despite talk of a "clash of civilizations" (Huntington 1996) the real threats to human rights and global solidarity have been authoritarian governments and a rapacious form of global capitalism that has exacer-bated social divisions, threatened stable communities, and weakened the power of popularly elected regimes to care for their neediest citizens. Religion, with its uncompromising commitment to social justice, is well positioned to resist the fundamentalist neoliberal ideology that underpins global capitalism and, by so doing, promote democracy and human rights. Muslims, too, can draw inspiration from their faith in advancing this cause. As Andrew March observes (March 2007), the absence of any concrete declaration of underlying values and principles in Islamic law allows Muslims to reinterpret that law's commandment to observe con-tracts in accordance with liberal democratic social contractarian precepts. Reinterpreting *shari'a* in this manner enables them to expand their bond of solidarity to include all those with whom they are "contractually bound" by ties political, social, and economic. It thereby enables them to view the core social justice values of their own faith as free-standing and faith-transcending – universal, multicultural, and secular.[38]

Religion cannot embrace secular democracy without relinquishing at least some of its identity, even if secular democracy which incorporates *both* liberal and civic republican values turns out to be the best worldly expression of that identity. That the dignity of the individual embodied in liberal human rights can degenerate into a self-centered nihilism unless coupled with a civic republican devotion to justice and the common good has been a mainstay of democratic theory for over three hundred years. Both Weber and Durkheim warn us of this secular danger, as do moderate Muslim secularists like Soroush, who counsel against equating democracy with the tyranny of selfish interests (Soroush 2000: 125). We know from our experience with the secular "political theologies" of the twentieth century – nationalism, fascism, and communism – that this danger can provoke a fundamentalist backlash. A formal democracy that does nothing more than protect against government tyranny by delivering political life over to powerful interests and aggregated preferences is fertile soil for its cultivation.

In sum, although religion is often thought to be a divisive force in national politics opposed to democratic solidarity, I submit that it can become an instrument of public reconciliation when focusing its energy on bringing justice to the world. Empathy toward our copartners in public reasoning, appropriately accompanied by awareness of the fragility and vulnerability of those recognitive relationships that we share in common is the other instrument (Habermas 1989/90: 47).

Both instruments of solidarity-building reinforce each another. The motivation required to risk one's identity by entering public discourse cannot come from public discourse itself. Nor can it come from the

---

[38] This claim found empirical support in Indonesia's 1999 elections, in which Islamic parties (such as the PKB and PAN) that did not focus on single-issue messages based on political Islam fared better than those (such as the Crescent Star Party [PBB]) that did (PKB won 12 percent and PAN 7 percent, while PBB won only 2 percent). The message was clear: pious Muslims who constituted an overwhelming majority of the population were also interested in issues revolving around any emergent market economy: health, welfare, security, jobs, and basic subsistence. Those political Islamist parties (such as the Prosperous Justice Party [PKS]) that abandoned single-issue politics in order to broaden their appeal to moderate and liberal Muslims saw dramatic improvements in their popularity in the elections of 2004 (from 1.7 to 7.4 percent) and 2009. For further discussion of Indonesia's struggle to maintain a secular liberal democracy in the face of Islamic fundamentalism. See Ingram (2014b).

accountability one must assume when coordinating one's actions with others. But if religion (or an equivalent awareness of one's membership in a community of hope) motivates the assumption of existential risk, dialog transforms the solidarity that redeems it.

BUILDING COSMOPOLITAN SOLIDARITY OUT OF SOLIDARITY NETWORKS

Cosmopolitan solidarity enjoins the protection of human rights and the salvation of humanity from apocalyptic destruction and suffering. Discourse ethics and religious experience meet at the intersection of these two commitments. Empathy for the oppressed finds just cause in redeeming a form of life sustained by mutual recognition.

Carol Gould's concept of network solidarity offers a promising model for clarifying how humanitarian movements communicate their distinctive concerns in building solidarity. Pursuing different social justice causes, they become aware that their aims are organically interdependent. Networking in this way enables them to assess the impact of their own strategic pursuits on the pursuits of others; and it enables them to critically modify these pursuits in taking into account the highly contextual and individualized perspectives of those with whom they are joined in solidarity. In this way, the production and application of technical expertise in service to global justice is democratized (Gould 2007: 155–60).

Gould notes several difficulties in translating network solidarity into global solidarity. The theoretical difficulty is a familiar one: Network solidarity is essentially cognitive and rational, rather than affective and empathetic. This difficulty is lessened once we recall that the basis for human rights rests on empathy and utopian imagination as well as rational reflection. (The line dividing "secular and religious reasons," Habermas reminds us, is fluid [Habermas 2003a: 109].) The practical difficulty is related to the theoretical. Altruism depends on transferring our empathy for others to our duty toward humanity (Gould 2007: 161).

Empathy, however, is drawn to the suffering of those who are nearby, often aroused by sensationalistic reportage. News media neglect more distant and global – less fathomable – humanitarian crises. What coverage they provide is selective (Gould 2007: 162). Catering to niche audiences, cable and internet providers have become untethered to reality.[39] Media-induced resentment against women, minorities, and immigrants,

---

[39] For a critical assessment of digital media in politics, see Ingram and Bar-Tura (2014).

fuels reactionary solidarity among groups of white Europeans and North Americans whose belief in their own unjust marginalization is as much a product of misinformation as it is of prejudice. The polarized framing of issues by politicized media largely goes unfiltered. Overexposure to apocalyptic commentary induces cynicism and withdrawal.

There remains another challenge to global solidarity: Economic crises exacerbate social division. They also unite people in solidarity. Labor violence in the United States during the Great Depression fueled the growth of the union movement. The unprecedented migrations and racial tensions of that period set in motion a massive revolution in American constitutional jurisprudence that led to the elevation of new civil, political, and social rights over entrenched economic and racial interests. Today, a similar renewal of purpose is possible to the degree that citizens collectively reclaim their right to self-determination and communal-ecological integrity against the disempowering and disintegrative effects of financialized capitalism.[40]

The question arises whether this kind of civic solidarity can be extended globally in fighting this common nemesis. That it cannot *yet* be extended is proven by the absence of civic solidarity in the very country where possessing solidarity would seem to matter the most: the United States.[41] Habermas's long-standing worry about the democratic deficit plaguing the economic unification of the EU testifies to a similar lack of solidaristic leadership coming from that corner of the world. As of 2016, the EU has managed to increase overall economic and monetary integration without making the bureaucracy in Brussels accountable to the people. Instead, it has managed the current financial crisis in a way that has pitted bureaucrats allied with Germany's neoliberal policies against the interests of Greeks, Spaniards, and other EU citizens living in crisis-ridden states of the Euro Zone.[42] The Lisbon Treaty, with its marginal closure of the

---

[40] With the advent of global financial capitalism civic solidarity has declined in proportion to the weakening of unions. Heightened inequalities have created divisions among the large mass of people whose incomes have stagnated or declined and are now fighting each other for a dwindling portion of the pie.

[41] Scandanavian countries that exhibit a higher degree of civic solidarity than the United States give a much higher percentage of humanitarian aid. Unfortunately, only the United States has the logistical and financial capability to become a cosmopolitan leader for the entire world (Schwartz 2007).

[42] "Under the leadership of the German government, the European Council is adhering to a crisis agenda that insists on ... each individual state's balancing its national budget on its own [thereby] adversely affecting the social security systems, public services and collective goods ... at the expense of the strata of the population that are disadvantaged" (Habermas 2014: 9).

democracy gap, has not made the Brussels bureaucracy more accountable, but has instead allowed this bureaucracy to shatter whatever solidarity once existed between northern and southern member states. It only took the current refugee crisis to compound mistrust with xenophobic withdrawal behind closed borders.

Democratic solidarity cannot thrive on constitutional loyalty alone. It must be cultivated as well in interpersonal and economic relationships (Honneth 2014: 326). These institutional presuppositions depend for their realization on a public space of critical reflection informed by a shared memory of concrete historical struggles for justice and the common good. Progress marked by one nation's exemplary struggles, in turn, must provoke empathetic enthusiasm in other nations (Honneth 2014: 233–35).[43]

Prospects for channeling such transnational narratives of progress, as weak as they are in the EU, appear even bleaker from a global standpoint. Beholden to global forces, citizens must increasingly look beyond their local governments to new forms of global cooperation, without losing their primary ethical roots. With a hope bordering on religious fervor, they must reimagine themselves as *future* cosmopolitan citizens whose civic solidarity is forged alongside a growing planetary solidarity. Living harmoniously with their global environment in a sustainable way will require them to reimagine a world beyond financialized capitalism, a world that combines the ethical virtues of economic markets with the redemptive and reconciling justice of democracy.

---

[43] Honneth here cites Kant's famous observation ("The Contest of Faculties") that disinterested spectators of history during his time would judge the sublimity of the French Revolution for exemplifying a universal idea of freedom (Reiss 1977: 182).

Bibliography

Abbott, C. 2013. "Obama's Food Aid Plan faces Backlash," *Chicago Tribune* (May 3).

Abiad, N. 2008. *Sharia, Muslim States, and International Human Rights Treaty Obligations: A Comparative Study*. London. British Institute of International and Comparative Law.

Aboulafia, M., M. Bookman, and C. Kemp, (eds.). 2002. *Habermas and Pragmatism*. New York. Routledge.

Adams, R.H. and J. Page. 2005. "Do International Migration and Remittances Reduce Poverty in Developing Countries?" World Development 33(10): 1645–69. DOI: 10.1111/ejop.12273

Addi, L. 1992. "Islamist Utopia and Democracy," *The Annals of the American Academy of Political and Social Science* 524: 120–30.

Adorno, T. and M. Horkheimer. 1972. *Dialectic of the Enlightenment*. New York. Herder and Herder.

Agamben, G. 2005. *State of Exception*. Chicago. University of Chicago.

Aizer, A. 2011. "Poverty, Violence and Health: The Impact of Domestic Violence During Pregnancy on Newborn Health," *The Journal of Human Resources* 46(3): 518–38.

Ake, C. 1987. "The African Context in Human Rights," *Africa Today* 34(1): 5–12.

Alampay, E. A. 2012. "Technology, Information, and Development," in P. Haslam, J. Schafer, and P. Beaudet (eds.), *Introduction to International Development*, pp. 471–90.

Allen, A. 2014. "Paradoxes of Development: Rethinking the Right to Development," in D. Meyers (ed.), *Poverty, Agency, and Human Rights*, pp. 249–69.

2016. *The End of Progress*. New York. Columbia University Press.

Alonso, J. 2016. "Beyond Aid: Reshaping the Development Cooperation System," in Ocampo (ed.), pp. 101–35.

Ames, R. 1988. "Rights as Rites: The Confucian Alternative," in L. Rouner (ed.), *Human Rights and the World's Religions*. University of Notre Dame Press.

An-Na'im, A. A. 1990. *Toward an Islamic Reformation: Civil Liberties, Human Rights, and International Law*. Syracuse, NY. Syracuse University Press.

2008. *Islam and the Secular State: Negotiating the Future of Shari'a*. Cambridge, MA. Harvard University Press.

Apel, K.-O. 2002. "Regarding the Relationship of Morality, Law, and Democracy: On Habermas's Philosophy of Law from a Transcendental Pragmatic Point of View," in M. Aboulafia, M. Bookman, and C. Kemp (eds.), pp. 17–30.

Audi, R. 1989. "The Separation of Church and State and the Obligations of Citizenship," *Philosophy and Public Affairs* 18(3): 259–96.

Ayubi, N. 1991. *Political Islam: Religion and Politics in the Arab World*. London. Routledge.

Azmanova, Albena. 2012. *The Scandal of Reason: A Critical Theory of Political Judgment*. New York. Columbia University Press.

2012b. "Social Justice and Varieties of Capitalism: An Immanent Critique," *New Political Economy* 17(4): 445–63.

Bacon, D. 2008. *Illegal People: How Globalization Creates Immigration and Criminalizes Immigrants*. Boston. Beacon Press.

Banerjee, A., E. Duflo, R. Glennester, and C. Kinnan. 2015. "The Miracle of Microfinance? Evidence from a Randomized Evaluation," *American Economics Journal: Applied Economics* 7(1): 22–53.

Barnett, M. 2010. *The International Humanitarian Order*. New York. Routledge.

Bateman, M. 2011. *Micro-Finance as a Development and Poverty Reduction Policy: Is It Everything It's Cracked up to Be?* ODI Background Notes. London. Overseas Development Institute.

Bayertz, K. 1999. "Four Uses of Solidarity," in K. Bayertz (ed.), *Solidarity*. (Dordrecht. Kluwer.), pp. 3–28.

Baynes, K. 2009. "Discourse Ethics and the Political Conception of Human Rights," *Ethics and Global Policy* 2(1): 1–21.

Bedoya, H. 2005. "Conditionality and Country Performance, in H. Bedoya, et. al. (eds.), *Conditionality Revisited*. Washington. World Bank.

Beitz, C. 1999. *Political Theory and International Relations*. Princeton University Press.

2009. *The Idea of Human Rights*. Oxford University Press.

Benhabib, S. 1992. *Situating the Self: Gender, Community, and Postmodernism in Contemporary Ethics*. London. Routledge.

2002. *The Claims of Culture: Equality and Diversity in the Global Era*. Princeton University Press.

2004. *The Rights of Others*. Cambridge University Press.

2013. "Reason-Giving and Rights-Bearing: Constructing the Subject of Rights," *Constellations* 20(1):38–51.

Benjamin, J. 1988. *The Bonds of Love: Psychoanalysis, Feminism, and the Problem of Power*. New York. Pantheon.

Benjamin, W. 1996. "Critique of Violence," in M. Bullock and M. Jennings (eds.), *Walter Benjamin: Selected Writings: 1913–1926*. Harvard University Press.

Bernstein, J. 1996. "Confession and Forgiveness: Hegel's Poetics of Action," in R. Eldridge (ed.), *Beyond Representation: Philosophy and Poetic Imagination*. Cambridge University Press.

Bhagwati, J. 2010. *Defense of Globalization*. Oxford University Press.

Bobo, L. 2009. "Crime, Urban Poverty, and Social Science," *Du Bois Review: Social Science Research on Race* 6 (2): 273–78.

Bohman, J. 2007. *Democracy Across Borders: From Demos to Demoi*. MIT Press.
  2010. "Introducing Democracy Across Borders: From Demos to Demoi," *Ethics and Global Politics* 3 (1).

Brandom, R. 1994. *Making it Explicit: Reasoning, Representing, and Discursive Commitment*. Harvard University Press.
  2000. "Facts, Norms, and Normative Facts: A Reply to Habermas," *European Journal of Philosophy* 8.

Brock, G. 2014. "Global Poverty, Decent Work, and Remedial Responsibilities: What the Developed World Owes to the Developing World and Why," in D. Meyers (ed.), *Poverty, Agency, and Human Rights*, pp. 119–45.

Brodzinsky, S. and E. Pilkington. 2015. "U.S. Government Deporting Central American Migrants," *The Guardian* (October 12).

Brown, L. 2008. *Plan B 3.0 Mobilizing to Save Civilization*. New York. W. W. Norton.

Brunkhorst, H. 2005. *Solidarity: From Civic Friendship to Global Legal Community*. MIT Press.
  2014. *Critical Theory of Legal Revolutions: Evolutionary Perspectives*. London, Bloomsbury Press.

Buchanan, A. 2006. "Taking the Human Out of Human Rights," in Martin, pp. 150–68.
  2013. *The Heart of Human Rights*. Oxford University Press.

Carens, J. 1995. "Aliens and Citizens" in W. Kymlicka, (ed.), *The Rights of Minority Cultures*. Oxford University Press, pp. 331–45.
  2013. *The Ethics of Immigration*. Oxford University Press.

Cattaneo, C. and G. Peri. 2015. "The Migration Response to Increasing Temperatures," National Bureau of Economic Research Working Papers 21622.

Center For Disease Control and Prevention. 2016. "Social Determinants and Eliminating Disparities in Teen Pregnancy," 24/7 (April 29).

Chaloupka, F. 1999. *The Economic Analysis of Substance Use and Abuse: An Integration of Econometrics and Behavioral Economic Research*. University of Chicago Press.

Chang, H. J. 2002. *Kicking Away the Ladder*. New York. Anthem.

Chen, S. and M. Ravallion. 2008. *"The Developing World Is Poorer than We Thought, but No Less Successful in the Fight Against Poverty."* Washington: World Bank.

Cheston, S. and L. Kuhn. 2002. *Empowering Women Through Microfinance*. New York. UNIFEM.

Christman, J. 2014. "Human Rights and Global Wrongs: The Role of Human Rights Discourse in Responses to Trafficking" in D. Meyers, *Poverty, Agency, and Human Rights*, pp. 321–46.

Coase, R. 1960. "The Problem of Social Cost," *Journal of Law and Economics*, 3: 1–44.

Cobham, A. 2005.*Tax Evasion, Tax Avoidance, and Development Finance*. Working Paper 129. Finance and Trade Policy Research Centre, Queen Elizabeth House. Oxford University.

Cohen, Jean. 2004. "Whose Sovereignty? Empire Versus International Law," in *Ethics and International Affairs* 18: 1–24.

Cohen, Joshua. 2004. "Minimalism About Human Rights: The Most We Can Hope For?" in *The Journal of Political Philosophy* 12(2).

Cook, L. and M. Hadjicostis. 2016. "EU, Turkey Strike a Migrant Deal," *Chicago Tribune* (March 19): 6.

Copper, M. 2016. "ICC Foresees Pain in 3 Planed Exits: African States Rue International Court," Associated Press (November 1, 2016).

Cristiano, T. 2010. "Review of James Bohman, *Democracy Across Borders: From Demos to Demoi*," *Philosophical Review*, 119(4): 595–99.

Crowe, A. *International Trade: A Justice Approach*. Dissertation. Loyola University Chicago. 2014.

Cudd, A. 2014. "Agency and Intervention: How (Not) to Fight Global Poverty," in D. Meyers, (ed.), *Poverty, Agency, and Human Rights*, pp. 197–222.

Cushman, T. (ed.). 2012. *Handbook of Human Rights*. New York. Routledge.

Dallmayr, F. 2017. *Democracy to Come: Politics as Relational Praxis*. Oxford. Oxford University Press.

Daly, H. 1996. *Beyond Growth: The Economics of Sustainable Development*. Boston. Beacon Press.

Daly, H. and J. Farley. 2011. *Ecological Economics: Principles and Applications*. Washington D.C. Island Press.

Derrida, J. 1990. "Force of Law: The Mystical Foundations of Authority," *Cardozo Law Review* 11: 919–1045.

Desai, R. 2012. "Theories of Development" in P. Haslam, J. Schafer, and P. Beaudet (eds.), *Introduction to International Development*, pp. 45–67.

Desai, R. and R. Vreeland. 2014. "What the New Bank of BRICS is all about," *The Washington Post* (July 17).

De Wet, E. 2004. *The Chapter VII Powers of the UN Security Council*. Oxford. Hart/Bloomsbury.

   2007. "The International Constitutional Order," *International and Comparative Law Quarterly* 55.

Diamond, J. 1997. *Guns, Germs, and Steel: The Fates of Human Societies*. New York. W. W. Norton.

Dickson, C. 2014. "Private Prisons Rule with Little Oversight on America's Border." www.thedailybeast.com/articles/2014/06/20/private-prisons-rule-with-little-oversight-on-america-s-borders.html.

Dixon, R. 2014. "South Sudan's Violence Leaves Donors Disillusioned," *Los Angeles Times* (March 1). http://articles.latimes.com/2014/mar/01/world/la-fg-south-sudan-governance-20140301.

Dow, M. 2004. *American Gulag: Inside U.S. Immigration Prisons*. University of California Press.

Dreher, A. 2006. "IMF and Economic Growth," *World Development* 34.

Druckman, J. 2004. "Political Preference Formation: Competition, Deliberation, and the (Ir)relevance of Framing Effects," *American Political Science Review* 98: 671–86.

Durkheim, E. 1964. *The Division of Labor in Society*, trans. G. Simpson. New York. Free Press.

Easterly, W. 2001. "The Effect of International Monetary Fund and World Bank Policies on Poverty," *Policy Research Working Paper* 2517. Washington, D. C. World Bank.

   2014. *The Tyranny of Experts: Economists, Dictators, and the Forgotten Rights of the Poor*. New York. Basic Books.

Egede, E. and P. Sutch. 2013. *The Politics of International Law and International Justice*. Edinburgh University Press.

Ellerman, D. 2006. *Helping People to Help Themselves: From the World Bank to an Alternative Philosophy of Development Assistance*. University of Michigan.

Earnest, D. 2009. "Voting Rights for Resident Aliens: A Comparison of 25 Democracies." www.allacademic.com/meta/p89774_index.html.

Escobar, P. 1995. *Encountering Development: The Making and Unmaking of the Third World*. Princeton University Press.

Ess, J. von. 2006. *The Flowering of Muslim Theology*. Harvard University Press.

Estevadeordal. A. and A. Taylor. 2008. "Is the Washington Consensus Dead? Growth, Openness, and the Great Liberalization, 1970s-2000s." Washington, D.C. National Bureau of Economic Research Working Paper 14264.

European Commision. 2016. *Report on the EU and the Refugee Crisis*. Brussels. European Commission.

Faiola, A. 2015. "Europe Struggles with Migrant Surge: Rising Numbers of Asylum Seekers End Up in Germany, Sparking Protests," *Chicago Tribune* (April 30): 1: 15.

Fassbender, B. 1998. "The United Nations Charter as Constitution of the International Community," *Columbia Journal of Transnational Law* 36: 529-619.

Ferrara, A. 2013. *The Democratic Horizon: Hyper-Pluralism and the Renewal of Political Liberalism*. Cambridge University Press.

Feenberg, A. 1999. *Questioning Technology*. London: Routledge Press.

   2017. *Technosystem: The Social Life of Reason*. Harvard University Press.

Finlayson, J. G. and F. Freyenhagen, (eds.). 2011. *Habermas and Rawls: Disputing the Political*. New York. Routledge.

Fishkin, J. 2005. "Experimenting with a Democratic Ideal: Deliberative Polling and Public Opinion," *Acta Politica* 40: 284–98.

Flynn, J. 2014. *Reframing the Intercultural Dialogue on Human Rights*. New York. Routledge Press.

Foroohar, R. 2016. "Bubble Trouble," *Time*, 187(6): 94–101.

Forst, R. 2011. "The Justification of Justice: Rawls and Habermas in Dialogue" in Finlayson and Freyenhagen, pp. 153–180.

   2012. *The Right to Justification: Elements of a Constructivist Theory of Justice*. Columbia University Press.

Foucault, M. 1979. *Discipline and Punish: The Birth of the Prison*, trans. A. Sheridan. New York: Pantheon Press.

1979. *The History of Human Sexuality, Volume I: An Introduction*, trans. R. Hurley. New York. Pantheon Press.

2008. *The Birth of BioPolitics: Lectures at The Collège de France 1978–1979*. New York. Palgrave-Macmillan.

Francis, L. P. and J. G. Francis. 2014. "Trafficking in Human Beings: Partial Compliance Theory, Enforcement Failure, and Obligations to Victims" in Meyers, pp. 146–69.

Fraser, N. 2001. "Recognition without Ethics." *Theory, Culture, and Society*, 18(2).

2010. *Scales of Justice: Reimagining Space in a Globalizing World*. Columbia University Press.

2015. "Legitimation Crisis: On the Political Contradictions of Financialized Capitalism," *Critical Historical Studies* 2(2): 157–89.

Fraser, N. and L. Gordon. 1994. "A Genealogy of Dependency: Tracing a Keyword of the U.S. Welfare State," *Signs* 19: 309–36.

Fraser, N. and A. Honneth. 2003. *Redistribution or Recognition: A Political-Philosophical Exchange*. London. Verso.

George, S. 1988. *A Fate Worse Than Debt*. London. Penguin.

Gheaus, A. 2014. "Children's Rights, Parental Agency, and the Case for Non-Coercive Responses to Care Drain" in Meyers, pp. 299–320.

Gilabert, P. 2015. "Human Rights, Dignity, and Power," in R. Cruft, M. Liao, and M. Renzi (eds.) *Philosophical Foundations of Human Rights*. Oxford University Press, pp. 196–213.

Gillis, J. 2012. "Pace of Ocean Acidification Has No Parallel in 300 Million Years, Paper Says," *The New York Times* (March 2). http://green.blogs.nytimes.com/2012/03/02/pace-of-ocean-acidification-has-no-parallel-in-300-million-years-paper-finds/?_php=true&_type=blogs&_php=true&_type=blogs&_php=true&_type=blogs&_r=2.

Global Humanitarian Forum. 2009. *Human Impact Report: Climate Change: Anatomy of a Silent Crisis*. Geneva: Global Humanitarian Forum. www.ghf-ge.org/human-impact-report.php.

Goldin, I. 2016. *The Pursuit of Development: Economic Growth, Social Change, and Ideas*. Oxford University Press.

Gomberg, P. 2002. "The Fallacy of Philanthropy," *Canadian Journal of Philosophy* 32(1):29–66.

Gomory, R. 2009. "Manufacturing and the Limits of Comparative Advantage," *Huffington Post* (July 8). www.huffingtonpost.com/ralph_gomory/manufacturing-and-the-lim_b_227870.html.

Gordon, J. 2010. *Invisible War: The United States and the Iraq Sanctions*. Harvard University Press.

2012. "The Sword of Damocles: Revisiting the Question Whether the United Nations Security Council is Bound by International Law." *Chicago Journal of Law* (Winter): 605–45.

Gould, C. 2007. "Transnational Solidarities," *Journal of Social Philosophy* 38(1): 148–164.

Green, D. 2008. *From Poverty to Power: How Active Citizens and Effective States Can Change the World*. Oxford. Oxfam International.

Griffin, J. 2008. *On Human Rights*. Oxford University Press.

Grotius, H. 1925. *On the Law of War and Peace* (1625) trans. F. Kelsey. Oxford. Clarendon Press.

Gutmann, A. (ed.). 1994. *Multiculturalism: Examining the Politics of Recognition*. Princeton University Press.

Gwen, C. 1994. *U.S. Relations with the World Bank, 1945–92*. Washington. Brookings Institute.

Habermas, J. 1971. *Knowledge and Human Interests*. Boston. Beacon Press.

   1973. "Labor and Interaction: Remarks on Hegel's Jena Philosophy of Mind," in Habermas, *Theory and Practice*. Boston. Beacon Press.

   1975. *Legitimation Crisis*. trans. T. McCarthy. Boston. Beacon Press.

   1979. *Communication and the Evolution of Society*. Boston. Beacon Press.

   1984. *Vorstudien und Ergänzungen zur Theorie des kommunikativen Handelns*. Frankfurt. Suhrkamp.

   1987a. *The Philosophical Discourse of Modernity: Twelve Lectures*. Cambridge, MA. MIT Press.

   1987b. *The Theory of Communicative Action: Volume Two: System and Lifeworld. A Critique of Functionalist Reason*, trans. T. McCarthy, Boston. Beacon Press.

   1988a. *Law and Morality. The Tanner Lectures on Human Values*, Vol 8. In S. M. McMurrin, (ed.). Salt Lake City, pp. 217–79.

   1988b. *On the Logic of the Social Sciences*, S. W. Nicholsen, and J. Stark, (trans.). Cambridge, MA. MIT Press.

   1989/90. "Justice and Solidarity: On the Discussion Concerning Stage 6," *The Philosophical Forum*, 21(1–2): 32–52.

   1994. "Struggles for Recognition in the Democratic Constitutional State," in A. Gutmann (ed.), *Multiculturalism: Examining the Politics of Recognition*, pp. 107–48.

   1995. "Reconciliation through the Public Use of Reason: Remarks on John Rawls's Political Liberalism," *Journal of Philosophy* 92(3), pp. 109–31.

   1996. *Between Facts and Norms: Contributions to a Discourse Theory of Law and Democracy*, trans. W. Rehg, Cambridge: MA. MIT Press.

   1998a. *The Inclusion of the Other. Studies in Political Theory*. Trans. C. Cronin, and P. De Greiff, Cambridge, MA. MIT Press.

   1998b. *On the Pragmatics of Communication*. Cambridge, MA. MIT Press.

   1998c. "'Reasonable' versus 'True', or the Morality of Worldviews," in Habermas (1998a), pp. 75–101.

   2001. *The Postnational Constellation: Political Essays*. Cambridge, MA. MIT Press.

   2002. *Religion and Rationality: Essays on Religion, Reason, and God*, in E. Mendietta, (ed.), Cambridge, MA. MIT Press.

   2003a. *The Future of Human Nature*. Trans. W. Rehg, Cambridge. Polity Press.

   2003b. *Truth and Justification*. Cambridge, MA. MIT Press.

   2006. *The Divided West*. London. Polity Press.

2008a. *Between Naturalism and Religion: Philosophical Essays*, in C. Cronin (ed.), Cambridge. Politiy Press.

2008b. "The Constitutionalization of International Law and the Legitimation Problems of a Constitution for World Society," *Constellations* 15(4): 444–55.

2009. *Europe: The Faltering Project*. Cambridge. Polity Press.

2010. "The Concept of Human Dignity and the Realistic Utopia of Human Rights," *Metaphilosophy* 41 (4): 464–80.

2011. "Reply to My Critics," in Finlayson, pp. 283–304.

2012. "The Crisis of the European Union in Light of the Constitutionalization of International Law," *EJIL* 23(2): 335–48.

2014. "Plea for a Constitutionalization of International Law," *Philosophy and Social Criticism* 40(1):5–12.

2015. *The Lure of Technocracy*. Cambridge. Polity Press.

Hardin, G. 1974. "Living on a Lifeboat," *BioScience* 24 (10): 561–68.

Harding, J. 2000. *The Uninvited: Refugees at a Rich Man's Gate*. Profile Publishers and London Review of Books.

2012. *Border Vigils: Keeping Migrants Out of the Rich World*. London. Verso.

Hart, H. L. A. 1991. *The Concept of Law*, 2nd Edition. Oxford. Clarendon.

Haslam, P., J. Schafer, and P. Beaudet, (eds.). 2012. *Introduction to International Development: Approaches, Actors, and Issues*, 2nd Edition. Oxford University Press.

Haynes, D. F. 2006. "Used, Abused, Arrested and Deported: Extending Immigration Benefits to Protect the Victims of Trafficking and Secure the Prosecution of Traffickers" in B. Lockwood (ed.), *Women's Rights: A Human Rights Quarterly Reader. Baltimore*. Johns Hopkins Press.

Hedrick, T. 2010. *Rawls and Habermas: Reason, Pluralism, and the Claims of Political Philosophy*. Palo Alto. Stanford University Press.

Hegel, G. W. F. 1975. *Introduction to the Lectures on the Philosophy of World History*, trans. H. B. Nisbet, Cambridge University Press.

1977. *Phenomenology of Spirit*. Trans. A. V. Miller, Oxford University Press.

1991. *Elements of the Philosophy of Right*, in A. Wood (ed.); trans. H. B. Nisbet, Cambridge University Press.

Heidbrink, L. 2013. "Criminal Alien or Humanitarian Refugee: The Social Agency of Migrant Youth," *American Bar Association Children's Legal Rights Journal*, 33(1): 133–90.

Held, V. 2004. "Care and Justice in the Global Context," *Ratio Juris* 17(7): 141–55.

Heyd, D. 2007. "Justice and Solidarity: The Contractarian Case against Global Justice," *Journal of Social Philosophy* 17(7): 112–130.

Hickel, J. 2017. *Aid in Reverse: How Poor Countries Develop Rich Countries, The Guardian (January 14)*.

Hobson, P. 2002. *The Cradle of Thought: Exploring the Origins of Thinking*. Oxford University Press.

Honneth, A. 1996. *The Struggle for Recognition: The Moral Grammar of Social Conflicts*. Cambridge, MA. MIT Press.

2002. "Grounding Recognition: A Rejoinder to Critical Questions," *Inquiry*, 45 (4): 499–519.

2007. *Disrespect: The Normative Foundations for Critical Theory.* Cambridge. Polity Press.

2008. *Reification: A New Look at an Old Idea.* Oxford University Press.

and Fraser, N. 2003. *Redistribution or Recognition: A Political-Philosophical Exchange.* London. Verso.

2012. *The I in We: Studies in the Theory of Recognition.* Trans. J. Ganahal Cambridge. Polity Press.

2014. *Freedom's Right: The Social Foundations of Democratic Life.* Columbia University Press.

2009. *Human Impact Report: Climate Change: Anatomy of a Silent Crisis.* Geneva: Global Humanitarian Forum. www.ghf-ge.org/human-impact-report.php.

Huntington, S. 1991. *The Third Wave: Democratization in the Late Twentieth Century.* University of Oklahoma Press.

1996. *The Clash of Civilizations and the Remaking of World Order.* London. Penguin.

Inada, K. 1990. "A Buddhist Response to the Nature of Human Rights," in C. Welsh and V. Leary (eds.), *Asian Perspectives on Human Rights.* Boulder, CO. Westview.

Ingram, D. 1990. *Critical Theory and Philosophy.* New York: Paragon House.

1995. *Reason, History, and Politics: The Communitarian Grounds of Legitimacy in the Modern Age.* Albany, NY. SUNY Press.

1996. "The Subject of Justice in (Post)Modern Discourse: Aesthetic Rationality and Political Judgment," in S. Benhabib and M. D'Entreves (eds.), *Habermas and the Unfinished Project of Modernity. Essays on the Philosophical Discourse of Modernity.* London. Polity Press.

2000. *Group Rights: Reconciling Equality and Difference.* Lawrence, KS. University Press of Kansas.

2002. "Immigration and Social Justice," *Peace Studies Review* 14(4): 403–14.

2003. "Between Political Liberalism and Postnational Cosmopolitanism: Toward an Alternative Theory of Human Rights," *Political Theory* 31(3): 259–91.

2004. *Rights, Democracy, and Fulfillment in the Era of Identity Politics: Principled Compromises in a Compromised World.* Lanham, MD. Rowman and Littlefield.

2005. "Foucault and Habermas," in G. Gutting (ed.), *The Foucault Companion,* Second and Revised Edition. Cambridge University Press.

2006. *Law: Key Concepts in Philosophy.* London. Bloomsbury Press.

2009. "Exceptional Justice? A Discourse-Ethical Contribution to the Immigrant Question," *Critical Horizons* 10(1): 1–30.

2010a. *Habermas: Introduction and Analysis.* Cornell University Press.

2010b. "Recognition Within the Limits of Reason: Remarks on Pippin's *Hegel's Practical Philosophy,*" *Inquiry,* 53(5): 470–89.

2012. "Group Rights: A Defense," in Cushman, pp. 277–90.

2014a. "Civility and Legitimacy: The Ambivalent Role of Religion in Transitional Democracy," in M. Schuck (ed.), *Democracy, Culture, and Catholicism.* Fordham University Press.

2014b. "How Secular Should Democracy Be? A Cross-Disciplinary Study of Catholicism and Islam in Promoting Public Reason," *Politics, Religion, and Ideology* 15(3): 1–21.

2014c. "Pluralizing Constitutional Review in International Law: A Critical Theory Approach," *Revista Portuguesa de Filosofia. Special Issue: Law and Philosophy: Foundations and Hermeneutics* 70(2–3): 261–86.

2014d. "Reconciling Positivism and Realism: Kelsen and Habermas on Democracy and Human Rights," *Philosophy and Social Criticism*. 40(3): 237–67.

2015. "Habermas on Solidarity and Praxis: Between Institutional Reform and Redemptive Revolution" in S. Giacchetti (ed.), *Critical Theory and the Challenge of Practice: Beyond Reification*. London. Ashgate, pp. 173–88.

2016. "A Morally Enlightened Positivism? Kelsen and Habermas on the Democratic Roots of Validity in Municipal and International Law," in J. Telman (ed.), *Hans Kelsen in America: Selective Affinities and the Mysteries of Academic Influence*. New York. Springer Publishing Company.

Ingram, D. and Bar-Tura, A. 2014. "The Public Sphere as Site of Emancipation and Enlightenment: A Discourse Theoretic Critique of Digital Communication," in D. Boros and J. Glass (eds.), *Re-Imagining Public Space: The Frankfurt School in the 21st Century*. New York. Palgrave.

2013. International Monetary Fund, "Press Release: IMF Calls for Global Reform of Energy Subsidies: Sees Major Gains for Economic Growth and the Environment" (March 27). www.imf.org/external/np/sec/pr/2013/p r1393.htm.

Jackson, R. 2003. *The Global Covenant*. Oxford University Press.

Jaggar, A. 2014. "Are My Hands Clean: Responsibility for Global Gender Disparity," in Meyers, pp. 170–94.

Kabeer, N. 1998. "'Money Can't Buy Me Love'? Re-evaluating Gender, Credit, and Empowerment in Rural Bangladesh." IDS Discussion Paper 363. Sussex: Institute for Development Studies.

2001. "Conflicts Over Credit: Re-evaluating the Empowerment Potential of Loans to Women in Rural Bangladesh," *World Development* 29(1): 63–84.

Kaiman, J. and S. Bengali. 2015. "For Many, Nowhere to Land," *Chicago Tribune* (May 27): 1: 16.

Kapur, D. 1997. "Rough Notes of Staff Loan Committee Meetings" in *The World Bank: Its First Half Century*. Washington, D.C. Brookings Institute.

Kaye, J. 2010. *Moving millions: How Coyote Capitalism Fuels Global Iimmigration*. Hobokin, NJ. Wiley & Sons.

Khader, S. 2014. "Empowerment Through Self-Subordination: Microcredit and Women's Agency," in Meyers, pp. 223–48.

Kelsen, K. 1920. *Das Probleme der Souveränität und die Theorie de Völkerrechts: Beitrag zu einer reinen Rechtslehre*. Tübingen: L. C. Mohr.

1950. *The Law of the United Nations: A Critical Analysis of Its Fundamental Problems*. The London Institute of World Affairs/Frederick A. Praeger.

1973. *Essays in Legal and Moral Philosophy*. Dordrecht. D. Reidel Publishing Company.

1989. *Pure Theory of Law*, 2nd Edition. Gloucester, MA. Peter Smith.

Kim, J. M. 2013. "Ending Poverty Means Tackling Climate Change" (July 10). www.worldbank.org/en/news/opinion/2013/07/10/op-ed-ending-poverty-in cludes-tackling-climate-change.

Kirsch, N. 2012. "Global Governance as Public Authority," *International Journal of Constitutional Law* 10(4): 976–87.

Koskenniemi, M. 2007. "The Fate of Public International Law: Between Technique and Politics," *Modern Law Review* 17: 1–30.

Kozma, J., M. Nowak, and M. Scheinen. 2010. *A World Court of Human Rights: Consolidated Statute and Commentary.* Neuer Wissenschaftlicher Verlag.

Krugman, P. 2014. "Why We're in a New Gilded Age," *The New York Review of Books* (May 8).

Kymlicka, W. 1989. *Liberalism, Community, and Culture.* Oxford University Press.

Lafont, C. 2002. "Is Objectivity Perspectival? Reflexions on Brandom's and Habermas's Pragmatist Conceptions of Objectivity," in Aboulafia, pp. 185–209.

2014. *Human Rights, Sovereignty, and the Right to Protect: Critical Theory in Critical Times.* New York. Columbia University Press.

2016. "Should We Take the 'Human' Out of Human Rights? Human Dignity in a Corporate World," *Ethics and International Affairs* 33(2): 233–52.

Lapidus, I. 1975. "The Separation of State and Religion in the Development of Early Islamic Society," *International Journal of Middle East Studies* 6(4).

Letsas, G. 2014. "Review of Allen Buchanan's The Heart of Human Rights," *Notre Dame Philosophical Reviews* (May 24).

Lewis, O. 1987. *Five Families: Mexican Case Studies in the Culture of Poverty.* New York. Basic Books.

Luce, K. 2016. "Rise of the African Opportunity," *Boston Analytics* (June 22, 2016).

Lyotard, J. -F. 2002. "Memorandum on Legitimation," in D. Ingram (ed.), *The Political.* London. Blackwell, pp. 229–39.

MacLean, N. 2017. *Democracy in Chains: The Deep History of the Radical Right's Stealth Plan for America.* New York. Viking.

Macleod, A. 2006. "Rawls's Narrow Doctrine of Human Rights," in Martin, pp. 134–49.

Main, A. 2014. "The Central American Child Refugee Crisis: Made in U.S.A," *Dissent* (July 30). www.dissentmagazine.org/online_articles/the-central-ame rican-child-refugee-crisis-made-in-u-s-a.

March, A. F., 2007. "Reading Tariq Ramadan: Political Liberalism, Islam, and "Overlapping Consensus," *Ethics & International Affairs* 21(4): 399–413.

Marcuse, H. 1964. *One Dimensional Man: Studies in the Ideology of Advanced Industrial Society.* Boston. Beacon Press.

Markell, P. 2003. *Bound by Recognition.* Princeton University Press.

Martin, R. and D. A. Reidy (eds.). 2006. *Rawls's Law of Peoples: A Realistic Utopia?* Oxford. Blackwell Publishers.

May, L. 2007. "The International Community, Solidarity and the Duty to Aid," in *Journal of Social Philosophy* 38(1).

Bibliography   355

McCarthy, T. 2009. *Race, Empire, and the Idea of Human Development.* Cambridge University Press.

McCormick, J. 2007. *Weber, Habermas, and Transformations of the European State: Constitutional, Social, and Supranational Democracy.* Cambridge. Cambridge University Press.

McKenna, C. and I. Tung. 2015. "Occupational Wage Declines Since the Great Depression," *National Employment Law Project* (September 02).

McNay, L. 2008. *Against Recognition.* London. Polity Press.

Mendieta, E. and J. Vanantwerpen (eds.). 2011. *The Power of Religion in the Public Sphere.* Columbia University Press.

Meyers, D. 1989. *Self-Identity and Personal Choice.* Columbia University Press.
  (ed). 2014a. *Poverty, Agency, and Human Rights.* Oxford University Press.
  2014b. "Rethinking Coercion for a World of Poverty and Transnational Migration" in Meyers, pp. 68–94.

Mian, A. and A. Sufi. 2014. *House of Debt: How They (and You) Caused the Great Recession, and How We Can Prevent It from Happening Again.* University of Chicago Press.

Milanović, B. 2002. "True World Income Distribution, 1988 and 1993: First Calculation Based on Household Surveys Alone," *The Economic Journal* 112: 51–92.
  2002. *The Two Faces of Globalization.* Washington, D.C. World Bank.

Miller, D. 2016. *Strangers in Our Midst: The Political Philosophy of Immigration.* Harvard University Press.

Miller, R. 2010. *Globalizing Justice: The Ethics of Poverty and Power.* Oxford University Press.

Mitchell, T. 2002. *Rule of Experts: Egypt, Techno-Politics, Modernity.* University of California Press.

Moka-Mubelo, W. 2016. *Reconciling Law and Morality in Human Rights Discourse: Beyond the Habermasian Account of Human Rights.* Cham SZ. Springer Publishing.

Mouffe, C. 1995. "Politics, Democratic Action, and Solidarity," *Inquiry* 38: 99–108.

Moynihan, D. 1965. *The Negro Family: The Case for National Action.* Washington, D.C. United States Department of Labor.

Murray, C. 2011. *Coming Apart: The State of White America: 1960–2010.* New York. Crown Publishing Group.

Murray, C. and R. Herrnstein. 1994. *The Bell Curve: Intelligence and Class Structure in American Life.* New York. The Free Press.

Myrdal, G. 1944. *An American Dilemma: The Negro Problem and Modern Democracy.* New York. Harper & Row.

Narayan, D., R. Patel, and K. Schafft. 2000. *Voices of the Poor: Can Anyone Hear Us?* New York. World Bank Group and Oxford University Press.

National Public Radio Podcast. 2013. "How Could Drought Spark a Civil War?" (September 8). www.npr.org/2013/09/08/220438728/how-could-a-drought-spark-a-civil-war.
  2015. "Hungary Steps Up Arrest and Deportation of Migrants" (October 12).

Neblo, M. 2007. "Change for the Better? Linking the Mechanisms of Deliberative Opinion Change to Normative Theory" in *Common Voices: The Problems and Promise of a Deliberative Democracy.* http://polisci.osu.edu/faculty/mne blo/papers/ChangeC4.pdf.

Nickel, J. 2006. "Are Human Rights Mainly Implemented by Intervention?" in Martin, pp. 263–77.

Noble, K. and S. Houston. 2015. "Family Income, Parental Education, and Brain Structure in Children and Adolescents," *Nature and Neuroscience* 18: 773–78.

Nozick, R. 1974. *Anarchy, State, and Utopia.* Oxford. Blackwell.

Nussbaum, M. 2000. *Women and Human Development: The Capabilities Approach.* Cambridge University Press.

Ocampo, J. A. (ed.). 2016. *Global Governance and Development.* Oxford University Press.

O'Connor, A. 2002. *Poverty Knowledge: Social Science, Social Policy, and the Poor in Twentieth Century U.S. History.* Princeton University Press.

Organization for Economic Cooperation and Development Data Website. 2016. www.oecd.org/dataoecd/52/18/37790990.pdf.

Oxfam Website. 2013. "Annual Income of Richest 100 People Enough to End Global Poverty Four Times Over" (13 January).

2017. "An Economy for the 99 Percent" (January 16).

Parfit, D. 1984. *Reasons and Persons.* Oxford University Press.

Parsons, T. 1955. *Family, Socialization and Interaction Process.* Glencoe, IL. The Free Press.

Parsons T. and E. Shils (eds.). 1951. *Toward a General Theory of Action.* Harvard University Press.

Pensky, M. 2000. "Cosmopolitanism and the Solidarity Problem: Habermas on National and Cultural Identities," *Constellations* 7(1): 64–79.

2008. *The Ends of Solidarity.* Albany, NY. SUNY Press.

Perez-Rocha, M. and J. Paley. 2014. "What "Free Trade" Has Done to Central America," *Foreign Policy in Focus* (November 21).

Peri, G., I. Gianmarco, and P. Ottaviano. 2012. "Rethinking the Effect of Immigration on Wages," *Journal of European Economic Association,* 10(1): 152–97.

Peters, A. 2006. "Compensatory Constitutionalism: The Function and Potential of Fundamental Norms and Structures," in *Leiden Journal of International Law* 19 (3): 579–610.

Philpott, D. 2004. "The Catholic Wave," *Journal of Democracy* 15(2): 32–46.

Pierce, A. 2017. "Justice Without Solidarity? Collective Identity and the Fate of the Ethical in Habermas's Recent Political Theory" *European Journal of Philosophy* 25(2): DOI: 10.1111/ejop.12273. http://onlinelibrary.wiley.com/ journal/10.1111/(ISSN)1468-0378/earlyview.

Piketty, T. 2014. *Capital in the Twenty-First Century.* Harvard University Press.

Piperno, F. 2007. "From Care Drain to Care Gain. Migration in Romania and Ukraine and the Rise of Transnational Welfare, *Development* 50(4): 63–68.

Pippin, R. 2008. *Hegel's Practical Philosophy: Rational Agency and Ethical Life.* Cambridge University Press.

2010, "Reply to Critics," *Inquiry* 53(5): 506–21.

Pogge, T. 2002. "Can the Capability Approach Be Justified?" *Philosophical Topics* 10(2): 167–228.

2006. "Do Rawls's Two Theories of Justice Fit Together?" in Martin, pp. 206–25.

2008. *World Poverty and Human Rights*. 2nd Edition. Cambridge. Polity Press.

2010. *Politics as Usual: What Lies Behind the Pro-Poor Rhetoric*. London. Polity Press.

Polanyi, K. 2001. *The Great Transformation: The Political and Economic Origins of our Time*. 2nd Edition. Boston. Beacon Press.

Powell, R. 2004. "Toward Reconciliation in the Middle East: A Framework for Muslim-Christian Dialog Using Natural Law Tradition," *Loyola University Chicago International Law Review*, 2(1).

PricewaterhouseCoopers. 2014. *Two Degrees of Separation: Ambition and Reality: The Low-Carbon Economy Index 2014* (September).

Przeworski, A. and J. Vreeland. 2000. "The Effect of IMF Programs on Economic Growth," *Journal of Development Economics* 62(2): 385–421.

Rabkin, J. 2005. *Law Without Nations? Why Constitutional Government requires Sovereign States*. Princeton University Press.

Rawls, J. 1971. *A Theory of Justice*. Harvard University Press.

1999a. *The Law of Peoples*. Harvard University Press.

1999b. *Political Liberalism, 2nd Edition*. Columbia University Press.

1999c. "Reply to Habermas," in Rawls (1999b).

2001. *Justice as Fairness: A Restatement*. Harvard University Press.

Raz, J. 1979. *The Authority of Law: Essays on Law and Morality*. Oxford University Press.

1986. *The Morality of Freedom*. Oxford: Clarendon Press.

Raz, J. and A. Margalit. 1994. "National Self-Determination," in J. Raz (ed.), *Ethics in the Public Domain*. Oxford. Clarendon Press.

Razavi, S. 2012. "World Development Report 2012: Gender, Equality and Development. An Opportunity Both Welcome and Missed (An Extended Commentary)," *UNRISD*:1–14.

Reiss, H. (ed.). 1977. *Kant: Political Writings*. Cambridge University Press.

Renshaw, C. 2013. "The ASEAN Human Rights Declaration 2012 *Human Rights Law Review* 13(3): 557–79.

Renton, A. 2009. "Suffering the Science: Climate Change, People, and Poverty," *Oxfam International* (July 6). http://policy-practice.oxfam.org.uk/publica tions/suffering-the-science-climate-change-people-and-poverty-114606.

Reus-Smit, C. 1999. *The Moral Purpose of the State: Culture, Social Identity, and Institutional Rationality in International Relations*. Princeton University Press.

Ricardo, D. 2007. "On the Principles of Political Economy and Taxation," in M. Lewis (ed.), *The Real Price of Everything*. New York. Sterling Press.

Rorty, R. 1989. *Contingency, Irony, and Solidarity*. Cambridge University Press.

Roy, O. 1994. *The Failure of Political Islam*. Harvard University Press.

Sahle, E. 2012. "Post-Development and Alternatives to Development," in Haslam, pp. 68–85.

Schafer, J., P. Haslam, and P. Beaudet. 2012. "Meaning, Measurement, and Morality in International Development," in P. Haslam, J. Schafer, and P. Beaudet, *Introduction to International Development*.

Schaffer, J. K. 2017. "The Point of the Practice of Human Rights: International Concern or Domestic Empowerment," in R. Maliks and J. K. Schaffer (eds.), *Moral and Political Conceptions of Human Rights: Implications for Theory and Practice*. Cambridge. Cambridge University Press, pp. 33–57.

Schmalz-Bruns, R. 2007. "An den Grenzen der Entstaatlichung. Bemerkungen zu Jürgen Habermas's Modell einer Weltinnenpolitik ohne Weltregierung,"in P. Niesen and B. Herborth (eds.), *Anarchie der kommunikativen Freiheit*. Frankfurt am Main. Suhrkamp, pp. 269–93.

Schmitt, C. 1991. *Völkerrechtliche Grossraumordung*. Berlin: Duncker & Humboldt.

  1996. *The Concept of the Political*. Cambridge, MA. MIT Press.

  2006. *The Nomos of the Earth in the International Law of Jus Publicum Europaeum*. New York. TELOSscope.

Schwartz, J. 2007. "From Domestic to Global Solidarity: The Dialectic of the Particular and Universal in the Building of Social Solidarity," *Journal of Social Philosophy* 38 (1):131–47.

Schwedler, J. 2008. *Faith in Moderation: Islamist Parties in Jordan and Yemen*. Cambridge University Press.

Schweickart, D. 2002. *After Capitalism*. Lanham, MD. Rowman and Littlefield.

  2011. *After Capitalism*. Rev. Ed. Lanham, MD. Rowman and Littlefield.

  2008. "Global Poverty: Alternative Perspectives on What We Should Do – and Why," *Journal of Social Philosophy*: 471–91.

  2009. "Is Sustainable Capitalism an Oxymoron?" *PGDT* 8: 559–80.

Sen, A. 1981. *Poverty and Famines*. Oxford. Clarendon Press.

  1982. "*Equality of What?*" in Sen, *Choice, Welfare, and Measurement*. Cambridge, MA. MIT Press.

  1999. *Development as Freedom*. Oxford University Press.

  2005. "Human Rights and Capabilities," *Journal of Human Development*. 6(2): 151–66.

Shaxson, N. 2011. *Treasure Islands: Tax Havens and the Men Who Stole the World*. London. Bodley Head.

Shue, H. 1996. *Basic Rights: Subsistence, Affluence and U.S. Foreign Policy, 2nd Edition*. Princeton University Press.

Simma, B. 2009. "Universality of Law from the Standpoint of a Practitioner," *EJIL* 20(2): 265–97.

Singer, P. 1972. "Famine Affluence and Morality," *Philosophy and Public Affairs* 1(3): 229–43.

Soroush, A. 2000. *Reason, Freedom, and Democracy in Islam: Essential Writings of Abdolkarim Soroush*. Oxford University Press.

Small, M. L., Harding, D. J., and M. Lamont, 2010. "Reconsidering the Culture of Poverty," *Annals of the American Academy of Political and Social Science* 629(1): 6–27.

Steinberg, S. 2010. "Poor Reason: Culture Still Doesn't Explain Poverty," *Boston Review* (January 11).

Stern, N. 2007. *Review on the Economics of Global Climate Change*. London. HM Treasury.

Stiglitz, J. 2002a. *Globalization and Its Discontents*. New York. Norton.

2002b. "Globalization and the Logic of International Collective Action," in Neeyar D. (ed.), *Governing Globalization*. Oxford University Press.

2009. "The Global Crisis, Social Protection, and Jobs," *International Labour Review* 148(1–2): 93–106.

Stiglitz, J. and A. Charleton. 2007. *Fair Trade for All: How Trade Can Promote Development*. Oxford University Press.

Tännsjo, T. 2007. *Global Democracy: The Case for World Government*. Edinburgh University Press.

Taylor, C. 1994. "The Politics of Recognition," in A. Gutmann (ed.), pp. 25–73.

1999. "Conditions of an Unforced Consensus on Human Rights," in J. R. Bauer and D. Bell (eds.), *The East Asian Challenge for Human Rights*. Cambridge University Press, pp. 101–91.

2011. "Why We Need a Radical Redefinition of Secularism," in E. Mendieta and J. Vanantwerpen (eds.), pp. 34–59.

Teubner, G. and P. Korth. 2010. "Two Kinds of Legal Pluralism: Collision of Transnational Regimes in the Double Fragmentation of World Society," in M. Young (ed.), *Regime Interaction in International; Law: Facing Fragmentation*. Cambridge University Press, pp. 23–54.

Tezcür, G. 2007. "Constitutionalism, Judiciary, and Democracy in Islamic Societies," *Polity* 39(4): 479–501.

2010. *Paradox of Moderation. Muslim Reformers in Iran and Turkey*. University of Texas Press.

Tomosello, M. 1999. *The Cultural Origins of Human Cognition*. Harvard University Press.

Topalova, P. 2007. "Trade Liberalization, Poverty, and Inequality: Evidence from Indian Districts," in *Globalization and Poverty*. Washington, D.C. National Bureau of Economic Research.

Tuana, N. 2012. "Climate Change and Human Rights," in Cushman, pp. 410–18.

Turner, B. 1974. "Islam, Capitalism, and the Weber Thesis," *British Journal of Sociology* 25(2): 230–43.

United Nations. 2004. *High-Level Panel on Threats, Challenge, and Change: A More Secure World: Our Shared Responsibility*. New York. United Nations Department of Public Information.

UNHCR Global Trends. 2014. *World at War: Forced Displacement*. www.Unhcr.org/pages/49c3646c4d6.html.

de Vattel, E. 1916. *The Law of Nations or the Principles of Natural Law* (1758), trans. C. Fenwick, Washington, D.C. Carnegie Institute.

Vladeck, S. 2008. "Medellín, Non-Self-Executing Treaties, and the Supremacy Clause," *Opinio Juris* (March 25) http://opiniojuris.org/2008/03/25/medellin-non-self-executing-treaties-and-the-supremacy-clause/.

Waldron, J. 1993. *Liberal Rights: Collected Papers, 1981–91*. Cambridge University Press.

Walzer, M. 1983. *Spheres of justice: A Defense of Pluralism and Equality*. New York. Basic Books.

1990. "The Communitarian Critique of Liberalism," *Political Theory*, 18(1): 6–23.

Warf, F. and B. Stutz. 2007. *The World Economy: Resources, Location, Trade, and Development*, 5th Edition. Upper Saddle River. Pearson.

Weber, M. 1958. *The Protestant Ethic and the Spirit of Capitalism*. New York. Scribner.

1965. *Sociology of Religion*. London. Methuen.

Wertheimer, A. 2014. "Poverty, Voluntariness, and Consent to Participate in Research." in Meyers, pp. 273–298.

Wickham, C. 2004. "The Path to Moderation: Strategy and Learning in the Formation of Egypt's Wasat Party," *Comparative Politics* 36(2): 205–28.

Wilde, L. 2013. *Global Solidarity*. Edinburgh University Press.

Wilson, W. J. 1987. *The Truly Disadvantaged: The Inner City, the Underclass, and Public Policy*. University of Chicago.

Winnicott, D. 1965. *The Maturational Processes and the Facilitation of the Environment: Studies in the Theory of Emotional Development*. London. Hogarth Press and the Institute of Psychoanalysis.

World Bank. 2013. *World Development Indicators*. Washington, D.C. World Bank.

2012 *World Development Report: Gender Equality and Development*. Washington, D.C. The International Bank for Reconstruction and Development and the World Bank.

2016. World Bank Data on Climate Change. http://data.worldbank.org/topic/climate-change.

Young, I. M. 1997. "Asymmetrical Reciprocity: On Moral Respect, Wonder, and Enlarged Thought," *Constellations* 3(3): 340–63.

2007. "Responsibility, Social Connection, and Global Labor Justice," in Young, *Global Challenges: War, Self-Determination and Responsibility for Justice*. London. Polity Press, 159–86.

Zurn, C. 2007. *Deliberative Democracy and the Institutions of Judicial Review*. Cambridge University Press.

2015. *Axel Honneth: A Critical Theory of the Social*. London. Polity Press.

Index

abortion, 27, 93, 337–38
absolute trade advantage, 196
accountability, 274
Africa, 116
African-Americans, 75, 77
agency, 28
  agency-depriving practices, 26
  agential pathologies, 117–18
  capacity for, 49
  exploitative domination and, 26
  extreme poverty and, 50
  feminist, 80–81
  future of, 313
  harms on, 21
  institutional organization and frustration
    of, 36–37
  material embodiment of, 43
  moral agency of citizens, 57
  normative, 249
  phenomenology and, 50
  recognition and rational, 54
  recognitive theory of, 59–60
  requirements of, 125
  volitional, 54
  of women, 72
agriculture
  absolute limit on arable land, 197
  ending price control for, 178–79
  greenhouse gas emissions and, 199
  high-tech foreign agribusiness, 75
  privatization of collective farms, 92–93
  tariffs on, 22–23
  unsustainable mono-cropping, 191

U.S. production of, 10
Ake, Claude, 323
alcoholism, 88–89
alienation
  self-alienation, 57, 88
  skepticism and, 60–61
  technologically alienated work and
    leisure, 116–17
Allen, Amy, 96
American Farm Bureau Federation, 10
amnesty law, 108
antipoverty interventions, 80
antitrust legislation, 207
Apel, K.O., 238–39
Arab Spring, 333
Arellano, Elvira, 167, 168
Arendt, Hannah, 24, 112
armed resistance, 287
Ashcroft, John, 139
Asian Infrastructure Investment Bank, 11
associationist societies, 233
asylum seekers. *See also* migration; refugees
  drug-related violence and, 168
  EU and, 162
atomized individuals, 328
Australia, 134–35
authoritarian governments, 331, 339
  efficiency of, 36
  U.S. support for, 11
autism, 64
automation, 206
autonomy, 49
  capacity for, 113

autonomy (cont.)
 cultural, 324
 Hegel on, 54–55
 Kant on, 54–55
 microcredit and autonomy-empowering
  social support networks, 82

Bangkok Declaration (1993), 242, 331
bargaining leverage, 19
Barnett, Michael, 141
Bayertz, Kurt, 316
Benhabib, Seyla, 166, 238–39
Bernstein, Jay, 56
Between Facts and Norms (Habermas), 240
Bhagwati, Jagdish, 190
BICS. *See* Brazil, India, China, and South
 Africa
bio-power, 96
Black empowerment, 74
black market, 146–47
bodily desire, 54
Bohman, James, 286–88, 303
Bolivia, 253
border checks, 132
border policy, 159–62
bounded communities, 317, 318
brain drain, 121
Brandom, Robert, 59
Brazil, India, China, and South Africa
 (BICS), 12–13
Bretton Woods Conference, 178
Bretton Woods regime, 101, 212
British Commonwealth countries, 162
British miners, 75
Buchanan, Allen, 224, 229–30, 236,
 250, 273
burqa, 336
Bush, George, 180

CAFTA-DR. *See* Dominican Republic-
 Central America-United States Free
 Trade Agreement
Cairo Declaration on Human Rights in
 Islam, 329–30
Calle 18, 135–36
CAM. *See* Central American Minors
cap and trade, 222
capability, 3, 48, 49, 114
capital mobility, 194
capitalism, 213, 339
 capitalist underdevelopment, 17

critical theory on, 36
 failure of, 32
 global spread of, 319
 global warming and, 207
 green, sustainable capitalism, 207, 208
 historical trajectory from laissez faire to
  welfare state, 38, 208–9
 impersonal functioning of, 41–42
 limits of, 203–12
 pathological logic of, 88
 patrimonial, 5
 welfare state capitalism, 210
carbon emissions, 7, 14, 200
Carens, Joseph, 133, 138–39
Caribbean Basin Initiative, 182
Cartagena Declaration on Refugees
 (1984), 137
Catholicism, 236, 333–34
Central American Minors (CAM)
 Refugee/Parole Program, 137
charitable aid, 6
Charleton, Andrew, 201
Cheston, Susy, 80
children
 Convention on the Rights of the Child,
  UN, 157
 counseling for, 158
 deaths of, 305
 as refugees, 135
China, 3, 195
 absolute trade advantage of, 196
 imports from, 195
 slow growth in, 211
China Development Bank, 11
Christian natural law tradition, 244
Christman, John, 150
Ciceronian Stoicism, 278
citizen advisory boards, 113, 214
citizens
 moral agency of, 57
 U.S., 155
citizenship, 17, 104
 migration and, 125–26
 rights of, 128
civic friendship, 68
civil debate, 334
civil unrest, 143–44
civilian suffering, 274
class conflict, 319
Coase, Ronald, 200
coercion, 27, 110, 190, 263

circumstantial, 149
by legal systems, 174
by market economies, 107, 203
Marx on, 106–7
poverty and, 171
rational choices subject to, 105
supermajoritarian act of, 276
coercive environments, 106–9
discourse ethics and, 109–14
impact of, 113
Cohen, Joshua, 234
Cold War, 7, 11, 96
collaborative projects, 28
collective consciousness, 318
collective farms, 92–93
collective responsibility, 23
colonialism, 98–99
colonial expropriation of resources, 22
heyday of European colonialism, 34
injustices of, 163
reparation for, 187
communicative action
coordinating mechanism of, 112
Habermas's theory of, 39
recognition and, 56
communitarianism, 129, 154–56
comparative advantage, 193, 198
logic of, 196
opportunity costs and, 193
compensatory tax, 15
competitive advantage, 194
"The Concept of Human Dignity and the
Realistic Utopia of Human Rights"
(Habermas), 244
Conference of the Parties (COP), 13
consciousness-raising campaigns, 77
accompanied by economic changes,
82–83
by UN, 82
consent, 101
to distributive justice, 110
Habermas on, 110
libertarians on, 102
poverty expertise and, 103
rational, 102
voluntary, 279, 284
Wertheimer and, 108
conservative ideology, 95
constitutional law, 259
constitutional legitimacy, 277–82
constitutional provisions, 310

constitutional reform, 312
constitutional rights, 242
constitutionalization
elements of, 279
of human rights, 242
international law and, 277
state-centered model of, 280
unprecedented era of, 279
consumers, 192
consumption, 97
economic growth driven by, 103
expenditure, 5
free trade and, 196–97
stagnating, 196
contraception, 27
Convention on the Rights of the Child,
UN, 157
Convention on Transnational Organized
Crime, UN, 149
COP. *See* Conference of the Parties
corruption, 117–18, 255
cosmopolitanism, 127. *See also* libertarian
cosmopolitanism; utilitarian
cosmopolitanism; welfare-liberal
cosmopolitanism
case for open borders and, 150–53
cosmopolitan dystopia, 156
cosmopolitan solidarity and solidarity
networks, 341–43
counter-cosmopolitanism, 156
human rights and, 290, 322
quasi-cosmopolitan, 186
Council of Europe Convention on Action
against Trafficking in Human Beings,
150
Country Policy Institutional Assessment
(CPIA), 179
courtroom procedure, 167
CPIA. *See* Country Policy Institutional
Assessment
criminalization, 131
Cristiano, Thomas, 288
critical reconstructions, 38
critical theory
on capitalism, 36
Marx on, 29–30
on social development, 35
on technocracy, 115
cross-cultural dialog, 28
Cruz, Alba, 169–70
Cudd, Ann, 50, 83–84, 118

cultural determinism, 100
cultural identities, 328
cultural misrecognition, 74
culture of poverty, 86, 90–93
currency depreciation, 175
currency speculation, 210

DAC. *See* Development Assistance
     Committee
DACA. *See* Deferred Action for Childhood
     Arrivals
Daly, Herman, 195, 198–99
DAPA. *See* Parents of Lawful Permanent
     Residents
DDA. *See* Doha Developmental Agenda
death toll of poverty, 2
debt, 8–9, 11, 209–10
Declaration of 1970, UN, 325
Declaration on the Right to Development
     (1986), 20, 95–96, 114
deconstruction, 262
Deferred Action for Childhood Arrivals
     (DACA), 168–69
deforestation, 13
deliberative democracy, 326–29, 334
democracy, 241, 297. *See also* liberal
     democracy
  Bohman on, 286
  discourse theory and, 258–61
  economic, 212–18
  global constitutional, 301
  meaning of legitimate, 266
  political democracy, 260
  religious democracy, 337
  secular, 338, 339
  social democracy, 38, 218
  workplace, 173
democratic accountability, 263, 273, 312
democratic ethical life, 321
democratic international order, 298–304
democratic socialism, 76, 214–17
democratic structuration, 280
democratization, 190, 333
  of trade agreements, 201
deportation, 26–27, 130, 155, 157
developing world, 176
  industrialized countries and, 182
  women in, 78, 94
Development Assistance Committee
     (DAC), 6–7
Development Finance Institutions (DFIs), 11

development policy, 114–20
  anti-poverty, 125
  practical failure of, 96
  structural obstacles to implementing,
     120–22
developmental aid, 118
developmental theory, 32–33
  as ideology, 95–101
  white supremacism and, 90–91
DFIs. *See* Development Finance Institutions
Diamond, Jared, 99
dictatorships
  installed by U.S., 174
  overthrowing, 140
dignity, 32, 63, 243, 249–50
  cumulative experiences of violated, 244
  definitional problem of, 250
  formal concept of, 251
  Habermas on, 244–45, 247
  moral dignity, 69
  recognition of, 71
  substantive meaning of, 245
  UDHR on, 230–31
discourse ethics, 40,
     58–59, 341
  border policy and, 159–62
  coercive environments and, 109–14
  expertise informed by, 86
  global development policy and, 114–20
  immigration courts and, 167–70
  immigration policy and, 130, 162–66
  migration and, 127–28
  practical framework from, 113–14
  stakeholder business ethics and, 217–18
discourse theory, 40, 111, 258–61
discursive proceduralism, 42
disempowerment, 106, 114
displaced persons, 142
displaced workers, 153
distributive justice, 110, 321
Doha Development Agenda (DDA), 202
Doha Ministerial Declaration, 202
domestic violence, 137–38, 169–70
Dominican Republic-Central America-
     United States Free Trade Agreement
     (CAFTA-DR), 136, 146–47, 182
  Investor-State Dispute Settlement
     Resolution provision of, 182
drug wars, 146
drug-related violence, 168
Durkheim, Émile, 91, 314, 318, 340

East Asian financial crisis, 176
Eastern religions, 330–31
ECJ. *See* European Court of Justice
Economic and Social Council, UN
    (ECOSOC), 300–1
economic distress, 143–44
economic growth, 2, 103
economic inequality, 25, 102
economic opportunities, 77
economic oppression, 74–75
economic reconstruction, 32
economic refugees, 127, 144–47
economies of scale, 207
ECOSOC. *See* Economic and Social
    Council, UN
EITI. *See* Extractive Industries
    Transparency Initiative
eligibility requirements, 109
eliminating poverty, 16
elitism, 231
Ellerman, David, 117
Ellul, Jacques, 43
emancipation
    emancipatory empowerment, 111
    Marx on, 114
emotional bonding, 113
emotional support, 64
empathy, 112, 113
empiricist tradition, 32, 54
employment, 193
endangerment, 137
environmental economics, 197
environmental protection, 173
equality, 244, 246–47
Escobar, Arturo, 100
ethical identity, 60, 320
ethnocentric paternalism, 96–97
ethnocentrism, 250, 260
EU. *See* European Union
European Convention of Human Rights,
    249–50
European Court of Human Rights, 310
European Court of Justice (ECJ), 269,
    304, 306
European Enlightenment, 20
European Union (EU), 287–88
    asylum seekers and, 162
    crisis in, 343
    Habermas on, 301–2
    member states, 133
    Parliament, 133

expertise, 86
exploitation, 26, 76
exports, 22–23
expressive behavior, 336
Extractive Industries Transparency
    Initiative (EITI), 121
extreme poverty, 1–2
    agency and, 50
    migrants fleeing, 131
extreme socio-economic inequality, 26

face-to-face deliberation, 159
fair trade, 40
    differential fair trade responsibilities,
        12–13
    free trade versus, 188–96
Familia Latina Unida, 167
family planning assistance, 27
family reunification, 158
Fassbender, Bardo, 288, 289
Federal Reserve, U.S., 175
federal structure, 280
federal welfare payments, 90
Ferrara, Alessandro, 330
Fichte, Johann Gottlieb, 55
Food and Agriculture Organization, 3–4
Food For Peace Program, 9
food relief, 18
forced development, 98
foreign policy, 180
Forst, Rainer, 238–39
fossil fuels, 14
Foucault, Michel, 35, 94
Frankfurt School, 29–30, 37, 204, 205
Fraser, Nancy, 47–48, 74–78
free trade. *See also* Dominican Republic-
    Central America-United States Free
    Trade Agreement; North American
    Free Trade Agreement
    Charleton and Stiglitz on, 201
    fair trade versus, 188–96
    national consumption increased by,
        196–97
freedom, 32, 225
    collective and individual, 324, 328
    Hegel on, 52–53
    labor-saving technologies and, 37
    legal and moral, 37–38
    negative and positive, 67
    progressive interpretation of, 225–26
    recognitive freedom, 57

freedom (cont.)
  reflexive, 67
  as state of mind and objective capability,
    48
freedom of speech, 237
fundamentalism, 334

G-7 powers, 11
gasoline, 208
GATT negotiations, 11–12
GBD. *See* global burden of disease
GDI. *See* Gender Development Index
GDP. *See* gross domestic product
GEMs. *See* global economic multilaterals
Gender Development Index (GDI), 3
Gender Inequality Index (GII), 114
gender roles, 15
Geneva Convention on Refugees, 132, 139
genocidal wars, 145
German Idealists, 43
Germany
  guest worker policy in, 165
  Nazi Germany, 138–39
  refugees received, 141
Gheaus, Anca, 158
GII. *See* Gender Inequality Index
global burden of disease (GBD), 12
global climate control, 173
global constitutional order, 282–92
global constitutional review, 306–11
global economic multilaterals (GEMs), 23,
    222, 226
  rights-infringing policies of, 256
global financial institutions, 177
global friendship, 252
global governance, 210
  potential for abuse in, 304
  tri-level model for understanding, 298–99
  UN role in, 299, 301
global market, 173
global poor, 187
  lives altered by U.S. policies, 187
  local poor and, 17–18
Global Recession of 2008–2012, 7,
    175–76, 209
Global Resources Dividend tax, 190
global value pluralism, 238
global warming, 7, 13–16
  capitalism and, 207
  environmental degradation from, 196–99
  fighting, 318

HICs, 14
  impact on individual human lives of, 229
  poverty from, 152
global wealthy, 4–5
globalization, 81–82, 83
Goldin, I., 9, 191
Gomberg, Paul, 6
Gould, Carol, 315, 341
governance, 266, 314. *See also* global
    governance
  hegemonic, 83
  institutions of international, 280–81
government regulation, 199–203
government spending, 209
Great Society program, 102
Greece, 11, 133–34, 141
greenhouse gas emissions, 199
Griffin, James, 247, 248, 325
gross domestic product (GDP), 3
Grotius, Hugo, 278
group loyalty, 68
group rights, 326
growth. *See also* economic growth
  China slow, 211
  government spending and, 209
  necessary, 209
  rates of, 191
  Stiglitz on growth in Latin America, 194
  in sub-Saharan Africa, 195
  uneven, 194
Grundlage des Naturrechts (Fichte), 55
gun regulation, 146–47

Habermas, Jürgen, 39, 58, 246, 302–3, 317
  "The Concept of Human Dignity
    and the Realistic Utopia of Human
    Rights," 244
  on consent, 110
  on dignity, 244–45, 247
  discourse theory of law, 40, 111
  on EU, 301–2
  Between Facts and Norms, 240
  on human rights, 238–43
  on immigration quotas, 163–64
  on social cooperation, 112
  on solidarity, 317, 327
  on sovereignty, 298
  on welfare state, 109
Haiti, 177
harmony, 52
harms, 144–45

on agency of persons, 21
types of, 146
by WTO, 256
Hart, H.L.A., 293, 296–97
hate speech, 74
HDI. *See* Human Development Index
heavily indebted poor countries (HIPCs),
8–9
Hegel, G.W.F., 60, 320
on autonomy, 54–55
on freedom, 52–53
Phenomenology of Spirit, 55
Philosophy of Right, 57, 65
on self-certainty, 51–52
substantive conception of practical
reason of, 57
hegemonic powers, 28
of U.S., 265
Heidegger, Martin, 43
high-income countries (HICs), 6–7
global warming and, 14
High-Level Panel on Threats, Challenge,
and Change, UN, 263
hijab, 336
HIPCs. *See* heavily indebted poor countries
Hippocratic Oath, 58
Honduras, 136
Honneth, Axel, 6, 70, 320–21
Fraser debate with, 74–78
on identification, 53–54
on market institutions, 204–5
on recognition as ethical category, 63–65
theory of recognition, 65–69, 73
Horn of Africa, 145
hostile workplace environments, 147–48,
158
Human Development Index (HDI), 3, 114
Human Development Reports, 3
human flourishing, 48
human rights, 15–16, 223–24, 276, 297–98.
See also European Convention of
Human Rights; European Court of
Human Rights; Inter-American
Commission on Human Rights;
International Council on Human
Rights; Universal Declaration of
Human Rights
capabilities approach to, 248–49
collectivist morality and, 224
complex moral and legal genealogy of, 25
constitutional entrenchment of, 260

constitutionalization of, 242
cosmopolitanism and, 312
creation of universal, 281
deontological understanding of, 42
disputes, 310
ecological understanding of, 267
of economic refugees, 127
elitism and, 231
ethnocentric "justifications" of, 34
to family reunification, 158
food relief as, 18
group rights and, 326
Habermas on, 238–43
hierarchy of, 145
human rights courts, 230–31
individually ascribed, 323
institutional and interactional types of,
251–58
international human rights regime, 330
juridical construction of, 258
justifying international regime of, 270–77
Kyoto Protocol and, 28–29
legal practice of, 229
libertarian conception of, 252–54
Mirroring View of, 224, 232, 243, 326
monistic derivation of, 239, 240
moral and legal interpretations of, 227
as moral aspirations, 25, 251
morality and, 223, 226, 251
Pogge on, 23
primary functions of, 231
Rawls on, 232–38
robust sense of, 21
scope of, 221–22
secure access to goods guaranteed by, 23
shortfalls, 189
social justice and, 17, 21
treaties on, 295–96
utilitarianism conception of, 254–55
welfare and, 246
Human Rights Watch, 36
human trafficking, 26
decriminalizing, 148–50
humanism, 69, 338
humanitarian crimes, 269
humanitarian disasters, 280
humanitarian law, 230, 259–60
incoherence in, 322
paradox of, 27
violations of, 149
human-made famine, 10

humiliation, 50
hunger, 3–4
Huntington, Samuel, 333
Hussein, Saddam, 141

ICC. *See* International Criminal Court
ICESCR. *See* International Covenant on
    Economic, Social, and Cultural Rights
ICISS. *See* International Commission on
    Intervention and State Sovereignty;
    Intervention and State Sovereignty
ICJ. *See* International Court of Justice
ICTs. *See* information and communication
    technologies
IDA. *See* International Development
    Association
ideal speech situation, 59
ideal theory, 30
identification, 53–54
identity crisis, 58–59
identity politics
    multicultural, 64, 73
    white supremacist, 155
ideological extremism, 339
ideological fetishizing, 116
ideological superstructures, 35
IDPs. *See* internally displaced populations
ILC. *See* International Law Commission
ILO. *See* International Labor Organization
IMF. *See* International Monetary Fund
immanent critique, 32
Immigration and Nationality Act, U.S., 163
immigration courts, 167–70
immigration policy, 130, 162–66
immigration quotas, 163–64
imperialism, 68–69
    injustices of, 163
    international relations and, 173–83
    moral duties of, 183–88
    rule of law at odds with, 295
    by U.S., 172–73
imports, 191, 195
incarceration, 95
income disparity, 5, 87–88
India, 191
individual dissent, 261
individual responsibility, 95
individualism, 63
    authentic, 71
    economic, 34
    pathologies of abstract, 61–63

Western bias toward, 230–31
individuation, 51
industrialized countries, 182
infantile aggression, 71–72
inferentialist semantics, 59
infinite substitution paradigm, 198–99
information and communication
    technologies (ICTs), 43, 116–17
injustice, 74, 76, 78
institutional authorities, 261
institutional organization, 36–37
institutional racism, 75, 89
integrity, 274
Inter-American Commission on Human
    Rights, 28–29
interest rates, 178–79
internally displaced populations (IDPs),
    143–44
international aid, 6
International Commission on Intervention
    and State Sovereignty (ICISS), 223,
    256, 263–64
International Convention on the Protection
    of the Rights of All Migrant Workers
    and Members of Their Families, UN,
    147, 228
    Optional Protocol of, 256
International Council on Human Rights,
    229, 257
International Court of Justice (ICJ), 267,
    268
International Covenant on Economic,
    Social, and Cultural Rights (ICESCR),
    226–27
International Criminal Court (ICC), 268,
    309
    convictions by, 275
    legitimacy of, 275
International Development Association
    (IDA), 178
International Fund for Agricultural
    Development, 3–4
International Labor Organization (ILO), 3,
    280–81
international law, 140, 228, 259, 267, 312
    constitutionalization and, 277
    R2P and, 284
    states in system of, 271
    supremacy of, 292
    UN as supreme organ of, 269
    after World War II, 291–92

International Law Commission (ILC), 275
international loans, 120–21
International Monetary Fund (IMF), 177–78, 193
International Poverty Line (IPL), 1–2
international public goods (IPGs), 7
international relations, 173
  imperialism and, 173–83
  Miller, Richard, on, 187
international trade agreements, 258
intersubjectively recognized framework, 57
Intervention and State Sovereignty (ICISS), 138
intimate relationships, 72
intra-industry trade, 193
IPGs. *See* international public goods
IPL. *See* International Poverty Line
Islam, 91–92, 330–34
  Majority-Muslim governments, 332
  Sunni, 330
Islamic political movements, 28
Israel, 177
Israeli-Palestinian conflict, 130
  meta-political questions and, 161
  Palestine Wall, 308

Jackson, Robert, 284
Jaggar, Alison, 82–83
Johnson, Lyndon, 102
Jongh, Lourdes de, 170
judicial procedures, 167, 309
judicial review, 306–7
jus cogens prohibitions, 291

Kabeer, Naila, 79
Kadi, Yassin Abdullah, 305–6
Kant, I., 54, 145, 343
  on autonomy, 54–55
  moral theory of, 58, 244–45
Kelsen, Hans, 268, 293, 296–97, 298
  monism of, 293–94
Khader, Serene, 79–80
Khala, Hamida, 81
Kiir, Salva, 10
Kim, Jim Yong, 2, 13
King, Martin Luther, 337
Koskenniemi, Martti, 308, 309
Krugman, Paul, 5
Kuhn, Lisa, 80
Kuznets, Simon, 6
Kyoto Protocol, 14, 28–29

labor contracting, 23
labor costs, 195
labor force, 82
labor mobility, 194
labor-saving technologies, 37
landlords, 107
Latin America, 2, 194
Lauterpacht, Elihu, 290
Law of Peoples (Rawls), 233
LDCs. *See* least developed countries
League of Nations, 262
least developed countries (LDCs), 202
legal fragmentation, 308, 310
legal scholars, 285
legitimacy, 38, 109, 259, 266, 267, 269
  constitutional legitimacy, 277–82
  crisis of, 210, 211–12
  democratic, 273
  ecological model of, 273
  general criteria of, 272
  of ICC, 275
  of majority, 276–77
  modular account of, 273–74
  normative, 335
liberal democracy, 68, 261, 312, 322
  evolution of, 278
  sustaining, 327–28
liberal states, 57
liberalism, 62, 104, 335. *See also* neo-liberalism
  philosophically neutral, 104
  poverty research and, 94
  welfare liberals, 106
libertarian cosmopolitanism, 129, 172
libertarians, 38
  on consent, 102
  human rights conception from, 252–54
  on poverty, 106
liberty, 20, 50
  Rawls's liberty principle, 152
LICs. *See* lower-income countries
life-saving drugs, 22
Locke, John, 189
love, 71
  parental, 71–72
  solidarity and, 68
lower-income countries (LICs), 5–6, 9, 177

Machar, Reik, 10
mail-order brides, 149
Majority-Muslim governments, 332

malnutrition, 50
managerial elites, 36–37
manufacturing jobs, 195, 206
March, Andrew, 339
market deregulation, 179, 181
market economy, 62, 213
  coercion by, 203
market institutions, 204–5
market strategies, 199–203
Marx, Karl, 32
  on coercion, 106–7
  on critical theory, 29–30
  on emancipation, 114
  Frankfurt School and, 205
  neo-Marxian systems theory, 32
  Orthodox Marxists, 35
master-servant relationship, 55
M'Baye, Keba, 95
McCarthy, Thomas, 91
McCormick, John, 287–88
McNay, Lois, 72–73
MDG1. *See* Millennium Development Goal
Mead, George Herbert, 112
Medellín Conference of Latin American
    Bishops, 184
media, 341–42
meritocratic relationships, 72
Mexico, 146–47, 168
Meyers, Diana, 107–8
MFIs. *See* micro-finance institutions
microcredit, 79, 82
micro-economic developmental policy, 120
micro-finance, 78–84
micro-finance institutions (MFIs), 79
middle-income countries (MICs), 5–6
  carbon emissions by, 7
  climate refugees in, 152
Migrant Rights International, 147
migration. *See also* refugees
  anti-immigrant xenophobia, 127
  citizenship and, 125–26
  discourse ethics and, 127–28
  from extreme poverty, 131
  to Greece, 133–34
  illegal, so-called, 155
  migrant protection, 138
  Obama administration on, 136–37
  open border, 151
  by parents, 130, 156–59
  rates of, 125
  skilled workers, 121

social contribution of, 155
  undocumented migrants, 126
  U.S. and, 126
Milanović, Branko, 5
military expenditures, 10
military intervention, 234–35
  by U.S., 174
Mill, John Stuart, 17
Millennium Development Goals (MDG1), 4
Miller, David, 160
Miller, Richard, 6, 15, 118, 152–53, 184–85
  on international relations, 187
  on sweatshops, 119
minimum wage laws, 178–79
minorities, 161, 335
modernity, 60
modernization, 32
morality
  agency of citizens, moral, 57
  collectivist, 224
  dignity, moral, 69
  evolution, moral, 334
  human rights and, 223, 226, 251
  idea of equality from non-moral principle
    of discourse, 244
  of identity, 319
  imperialism and, 183–88
  Kant on, 58, 244–45
  legal and moral interpretations of human
    rights, 227
  meta-political questions and, 159–60
  pathology, moral, 62
  psychology, moral, 251
  universal, 60–61
  universalization, moral, 240
*A More Secure World: Our Shared
    Responsibility* (UN High-Level Panel
    on Threats, Challenge, and Change),
    263
mortality, poverty-related, 20
Moynihan, Daniel, 88–89
MS-13, 135–36
multicultural democracies, 154
*Multiculturalism and the Politics of
    Recognition* (Taylor), 51
multiculturalism challenge, 314, 329–30
multilateralism, 180
multiple personality disorder, 49–50
Murray, Charles, 88–89
  neo-racist variants of cultural
    determinism from, 100

mutual aid, 321
mutual dependency, 314
Myrdal, Gunnar, 89

NAFTA. *See* North American Free Trade
    Agreement
Nancy Fraser, 73
Narayan, Deepa, 50
national defense, 8, 321
National Network for Immigrant and
    Refugee Rights, 147
national security, 141
nationalism, 319, 327
    anti-immigrant, 134
nationality, 68
natural catastrophes, 147
natural law theory of rights, 19,
    20, 30
NDB. *See* New Development Bank
negative externalities
    efficient and just reduction of, 199–203
    markets and, 196–99
neo-conservative strategies, 97–98
neo-Keynesian policies, 12–13
neo-liberalism, 33, 172, 189–90, 285–86,
    342–43
    reigning orthodoxy of, 38
    strategies of, 97–98
neo-Malthusian concerns, 197
neo-Marxian systems theory, 32
New Deal, 178
New Development Bank (NDB), 11, 183
New Left, 211
New York Declaration for Refugees and
    Migrants (2016), 127
newly industrialized countries (NICS), 97
Niam, Nourain, 139–40
Nicaragua, 182
Nickel, James, 227
NICS. *See* newly industrialized countries
non-domination, 269, 278, 286
non-government agencies, 25
non-refoulement, 140
non-renewable resources, 198
normative standards, 63
North American Free Trade Agreement
    (NAFTA), 146
Nozick, Robert, 101, 104, 105
nuclear family, 35
Nussbaum, Martha, 48, 70, 114–15, 232
    on Khala, 81

Obama, Barack, 9–10
    administration response to migration,
        136–37
    foreign policy of, 180
object-relations theories, 71–72
O'Connor, Alice, 88, 100
ODA. *See* Official Development Assistance
OECD. *See* Organization for Economic
    Cooperation and Development
Official Development Assistance (ODA),
    6–7, 177
    effectiveness of, 7
opportunity costs, 193
Organization for Economic Cooperation
    and Development (OECD), 6–7
Orientalism, 37, 91–92
Orthodox Marxists, 35
outsourcing, 75
Oxfam America, 9–10

Palestinians, 161
Panama Papers, 8
parent-child bonding, 71–72, 113
parents, 64
    deportation of, 155, 157
    love of, 71–72
    migration of, 130, 156–59
Parents of Lawful Permanent Residents
    (DAPA), 168–69
Parfit, Derek, 49–50
Paris Agreement, 29
Parsons, Talcott, 41, 97
participatory parity, 77
paternalism
    benevolent, 143
    coercive forms of, 27
    ethnocentric paternalism, 96–97
    welfare paternalism, 102–3
patriarchy, 79, 243
    overthrowing, 81, 85–86
    right to self-determination as
        resistance to, 80
peace, 234
Peace of Westphalia, 278
personal identity, 47
pharmaceutical businesses, 181
phenomenology, 50
Phenomenology of Spirit (Hegel), 55
Philosophy of Right (Hegel), 57, 65
Pippin, Robert, 53
pluralism, 249, 284, 334

Pogge, Thomas, 2, 5, 252, 258
  on aid, 21–22
  on compensatory tax, 15–16
  on human rights, 23
  Rawls criticized by, 235–36
police violence, 90
Political Liberalism (Rawls), 102, 233
political oppression, 143–44, 317
political power-leveraging, 19
political refugees, 131–37, 145
political theologies, 340
positive social rights, 241
post-industrial nations, 6
post-modernists, 37
post-structuralists, 37
poverty, 182, 190. *See also* extreme poverty;
    severe poverty
  anti-poverty development policy, 125
  coercion and, 171
  from global warming, 152
  hostile workplace environments and,
    147–48
  libertarians on, 106
  mortality, poverty-related, 20
  threat of, 157
  U.S. discussions of, 88
  war on poverty, 94–95
  women and, 108
poverty expertise, 93–95, 100
  consent and, 103
  conservative, 104–5
  lay public and, 113
  technologies of, 113
*Poverty Knowledge: Social Science, Social
    Policy, and the Poor in Twentieth
    Century U.S. History* (O'Connor), 88
Poverty Reduction Strategy Paper (PRSP),
    179
poverty research, 94, 111
PPPs. *See* purchasing power parities
practical reason, 54, 57
PricewaterhouseCoopers, 13
primary caretakers, 51, 65
primary goods, 248–49
primary resources, 198
principle of discourse, 240
prisoner's dilemma, 207
private investment incentives, 77
private prisons, 126
private-public partnerships, 213
privatization, 210, 255

  of collective farms, 92–93
  of religion, 335–36
producers, 192
Progressive Era, 88–89, 93
property rights, 104, 105
Protestantism, 91–92
PRSP. *See* Poverty Reduction Strategy Paper
psychoanalytic self-reflection, 112
psychological dissonance, 49–50
psychological experience, 48–49
psychological health, 53
psychopathology, 88
public law, 285–86
public policy, 88
public reason, 334–35, 339
purchasing power parities (PPPs), 1–2

R2P. *See* responsibility to protect
racial discrimination, 77
racial segregation, 24
randomized control trials (RCTs), 116–17
rates of return, 193
rational choice, 101–5
rationality, 92
Rawls, John, 20, 101–104,
    184–85, 233, 321
  Difference principle from, 152, 184–85
  on human rights, 232–38
  liberty principle from, 152
  Pogge criticism of, 235–36
  primary goods approach of, 248–49
  on UDHR, 234
Razavi, Shahra, 82–83
RCTs. *See* randomized control trials
reciprocal responsibility, 47
reciprocity, 119
recognition. *See also* social recognition
  adult stages of, 71–72
  ascription and perception of, 69–74
  cultural misrecognition, 74
  of dignity, 71
  emotional and antecedent, 64
  as freedom and identity, 52–53
  global struggles for, 42
  Honneth on recognition as ethical
    category, 63–65
  Honneth's theory of, 65–69, 73
  identity-building, 85–86
  individuation from, 51
  mutual, 53–54, 153
  as ontological category, 51

rational agency and, 54
recognitive freedom, 57
recognitive theory of agency, 59–60
re-emergence of, 51
refusal to extend to some identity
groups, 74
on register of communicative action, 56
of states, 293
recognitive politics, 53
refugee camps, 142
refugees. *See also* economic refugees;
political refugees; UN High
Commissioner for Refugees
children, 135
climate refugees in, 152
evolving definition of refugee status,
137–39
in Germany, 141
human rights of economic refugees, 127
outdated legal definition of, 128
political refugees, 131–37
resettling, 133
resistance to, 135
returning to homelands, 142
states rights and rights of, 139–41
United Nations Summit on Addressing
Large Movements of Refugees and
Migrants (2016), 127
religion, 315, 329–30
cosmopolitan solidarity and, 339–41
democracy, religious, 337
Eastern religions, 330–31
ethical legacy of, 34
privatization of, 335–36
rationality and, 92
religious solidarity and civic solidarity,
334–39
schism, religious, 319
Report of the World Commission on the
Environment and Development: Our
Common Future, UN, 198
reproductive labor, 90
residential segregation, 75
resource extraction, 196
responsibility to protect (R2P), 223
extension of, 224
First Pillar of, 264
ICISS draft of, 256
international law and, 284
limited, 226
restricted trade, 194

Reus-Smit, Christian, 277–78
Ricardo, David, 192–93
right-wing death squads, 177
Rohingyans, 143
rule of law, 279, 295
Rwanda crisis, 141

Said, Edward, 37
Saudi Arabia, 329
Schaffer, Johan Karlsson, 251
Schweickart, David, 208, 214–16
SDT. *See* special and differential treatment
search and rescue programs, 134
self-certainty, 51–52, 55, 59–60
self-determination, 68
collective, 259
communitarian right to, 127
large-scale, 68
loss of, 257
as resistance to patriarchy, 80
self-esteem, 81
self-realization, 69
self-reflection
critical, 37
dialectic of socially mediated, 49
psychoanalytic self-reflection, 112
self-reification, 61, 62
Self-Subordination Social Recognition
Paradox, 80
Sen, Amartya, 2–3, 20, 48, 114–15
severe poverty, 1–2
stubborn fact of, 16
worldwide increase in, 3
sex trafficking, 108, 149
sexist norms, 80–81
shari'a, 339–40
Shue, Henry, 20–21, 252
Singer, Peter, 6
skeptical realism, 284
skepticism, 60–61
skilled workers, 121
slaves, 39, 48, 126
small tribal societies, 318
smuggling vessels, 132
social brainwashing, 50
social concerns, 341
social conformism, 71
social connectedness, 189
social contract theory, 30
limits of rational choice and, 101–5
pathology of, 110

social cooperation, 112
social crisis, 58–59
social development, 32
  critical theory on, 35
  processes of, 47
social domination, 32
social inequality, 19
social justice, 18
  duties of, 27
  human rights and, 17, 21
social media, 116, 342
social pathology, 38
social recognition, 26, 41, 55–56
social roles, 52
social safety net, 104
socialism, 33, 203–4, 217. *See also*
  democratic socialism
  market socialism, 173
society, 337
socio-economic environments, 88
soldiers, 309
solidarity, 154, 313
  civic, 68, 314, 320, 326
  cosmopolitan solidarity, 316
  cosmopolitan solidarity and solidarity
    networks, 341–43
  descriptive uses of, 317–18
  destabilization of group, 326–29
  Habermas on, 317, 327
  love and, 68
  mechanical and organic, 318–20
  multiculturalism challenge to, 329–30
  network solidarity, 315
  prescriptive uses of, 316–17
  religion and cosmopolitan solidarity,
    339–41
  religious solidarity and civic solidarity,
    334–39
  supranational, 68–69
Soroush, Abdolkarim, 337
South Africa, 24
South Asia, 2
South Sudan, 10
sovereignty, 78, 271, 279, 298
speaker, 58
special and differential treatment (SDT),
  202
Special United Nations Fund for Economic
  Development, 178
specialization, 194
speech acts, 58

stakeholder business ethics, 217–18
starvation, 145, 222
"The State of Food Insecurity in the World"
  (UN), 3–4
state of nature, 294
states, 271, 293
states rights, 139–41
state-sanctioned predations, 226
status egalitarianism, 230
Stiglitz, Joseph, 178, 180, 201
  on free trade, 201
  on growth in Latin America, 194
stigma, 63–64
strategic self-interest, 118
structural adjustment loans, 179
sub-Saharan Africa
  growth in, 195
  poverty in, 1
  structural adjustment loans in, 179
subsistence, 251, 252
suffrage, 235
supranational law, 307
sweatshops, 15, 19, 76
  Miller, Richard, on, 119
  profits generated by, 118–19
  workers in, 23
symbiotic division of labor, 259
systems theory, 284–85

tax codes, 8
tax evasion, 121, 184
tax havens, 121
Taylor, Charles, 51, 54, 232, 327
technocracy, 38, 109–10, 115
technological cooperation, 117
technological determinism, 35
technological elites, 116
technological redundancy, 75
technology, 43, 116–17
Temporary Protected Status (TPS), 138
terrorists, 305
theocracies, 329
A Theory of Justice (Rawls), 102, 103
Third Estate, 96–97
tied aid, 10
TNCs. *See* transnational corporations
toleration, 234
totalitarianism, 320
TPS. *See* Temporary Protected Status
trade agreements, 121, 201
trade justice, 190–91

Trade Related Aspects of Intellectual
Property Rights Agreement (TRIPS),
12, 181–82
Trade Related Investment Measures
Agreement (TRIMS), 195
trade relationships, 27
traditional societies, 72
transcendentalist tradition, 54
transitional societies, 72
transnational corporations (TNCs), 23
transnational economic and legal systems, 283
transnational governance, 301
treaties, 222, 259–60, 275, 321–22
human rights treaties, 295–96
self-executing treaties, 295
superseded by UN Charter, 290
TRIMS. *See* Trade Related Investment
Measures Agreement
TRIPS. *See* Trade Related Aspects of
Intellectual Property Rights Agreement
Truman, Harry, 96–97
Trump, Donald, 134
Turkey, 133–34, 141
Turner, Bryan, 92
tyrannical bureaucracy, 265

UDHR. *See* Universal Declaration of
Human Rights
UN. *See* United Nations
UN Charter, 265, 267, 274–75, 280, 284
as constitution of single legal order,
292–98
as supreme constitution of the
international order, 289
treaties superseded by, 290
UN General Assembly (UNGA), 267
powers of, 267–68
veto rights of, 304
UN High Commissioner for Refugees
(UNHCR), 128–29, 132, 137
evolving role of, 141–44
financial and organizational interests
of, 143
UN Human Rights Council (UNHRC), 276
UN Security Council (UNSC), 263, 304–6
accountability of, 274
harsh sanctions from, 305
unemployment, 206, 215
UNGA. *See* UN General Assembly
UNHCR. *See* UN High Commissioner for
Refugees

UNHRC. *See* UN Human Rights Council
unions, 178–79, 194, 211
United Nations (UN), 312
consciousness-raising campaigns by, 82
Convention on the Rights of the Child, 157
creation of, 262
Declaration of 1970, 325
Economic and Social Council, 300–1
Framework Convention on Climate
Change, 13, 28–29
General Assembly, 95
global constitutional order and, 282–92
global governance role of, 299, 301
High-Level Panel on Threats, Challenge,
and Change, 263
International Convention on the
Protection of the Rights of All Migrant
Workers and Members of Their
Families, 147, 228, 256
Report of the World Commission on the
Environment and Development: Our
Common Future, 198
Special United Nations Fund for
Economic Development, 178
"The State of Food Insecurity in the
World," 3–4
as supreme organ of international law, 269
United Nations Summit on Addressing
Large Movements of Refugees and
Migrants (2016), 127
United States (U.S.), 126, 175, 186, 195
agricultural production in, 10
authoritarian governments support
from, 11
borrowing prerogative of, 175
carbon emissions by, 14
dictatorships installed by, 174
economic influence of, 174
embedded racial and ethnic restrictions in
immigration policies of, 154
global poor lives altered by policies of, 187
hegemonic powers of, 265
IMF and WB funding from, 177–78
Immigration and Nationality Act, 163
imperial aggression by, 172–73
labor violence in, 342
military intervention by, 174
poverty in, 88
professed desire for peace by, 180
threat potential of, 176–77
xenophobia in, 135

United States v. Texas, 169
Universal Declaration of Human Rights
    (UDHR), 19, 227, 228
    article 14 of, 139
    Article 21 of, 235
    on dignity, 230–31
    Preamble to, 225
    Rawls on, 234
UNSC. *See* UN Security Council
U.S. *See* United States
U.S. Citizenship and Immigration Services
    (USCIS), 138
utilitarian cosmopolitanism, 129, 151–52,
    172
utilitarianism, 17, 30–32, 254–55

Vattel, Emer de, 278
veil of ignorance, 188
Victims of Trafficking and Violence
    Protection Act (2000), 136
Victorian sexual mores, 35
Vienna Declaration (1993), 246

wage labor, 214
Wahhabism, 330
Wallerstein, Immanuel, 33
Walzer, Michael, 154, 155
war on drugs, 136
war on poverty, 101
Washington Consensus, 178, 182–83
water scarcity, 14
WB. *See* World Bank
wealthy retailers, 19
Weber, Max, 34, 91–92
welfare, 94
    federal welfare payments, 90
    human rights and, 246
    right to, 228
    welfare liberals, 106
    welfare paternalism, 102–3
welfare reform, 94–95
welfare state, 38, 208–9
    assault on, 104
    deepening skepticism toward, 211–12
    Habermas on, 109
    legitimation crisis of welfare state
        capitalism, 210
welfare-liberal cosmopolitanism, 129, 153
Wertheimer, Alan, 108
Western values, 42
Wet, Erika de, 310

white privilege, 74
white supremacism, 74
    developmental theory and, 90–91
    identity politics of, 155
Wilde, Lawrence, 319
Winnicott, Donald, 51
women
    agency of, 72
    in developing world, 78, 94
    domestic caregivers, 83
    education of, 15
    empowerment of, 27
    participation in labor force, 82
    patriarchal domination of, 79
    poverty and, 108
    responsibility of, 156–57
    self-employed, 79
    unremunerated reproductive and
        childrearing activity of, 76
working-class vices, 88–89
World Bank (WB)
    during Cold War, 11
    Poverty Data for 2015 from, 1
    U.S. funding for, 177–78
    *World Development Report: Gender
        Equality and Development*, 82
World Conference on Human Rights
    (1993), 21
*World Development Report: Gender Equality
    and Development* (World Bank), 82
World Federation of Public Health
    Associations, 121
World Food Program, 3–4
World Food Summit (1996), 4
World Social Forum (WSF), 101
World Trade Organization (WTO), 11–12,
    180–81
    harms by, 256
    Mode 4 of, 147
    rights threatened by, 292
World War II, 139, 291–92
WSF. *See* World Social Forum
WTO. *See* World Trade Organization

xenophobia, 127, 342–43
    in U.S., 135

Young, Iris, 188–89

Zelaya, Manuel, 136
Zurn, Christopher, 78, 310